Garfield
FAT CAT 3-PACK
VOLUME 21

Garfield

FAT CAT 3-PACK

VOLUME 21

BY
JIM DAVIS

BALLANTINE BOOKS · NEW YORK

2019 Ballantine Books Trade Paperback Edition

Published in the United States by Ballantine Books, an imprint of Random House, a division of Penguin Random House LLC, New York.

GARFIELD CHICKENS OUT and GARFIELD LISTENS TO HIS GUT were each published separately by Ballantine Books, an imprint of Random House, a division of Penguin Random House LLC, New York, in 2016. GARFIELD COOKS UP TROUBLE was published separately by Ballantine Books, an imprint of Random House, a division of Penguin Random House LLC, New York, in 2017.

ISBN 978-1-9848-1775-4

Printed in China on acid-free paper

randomhousebooks.com

9 8 7 6 5

Garfield chickens out

BY JIM DAVIS

Ballantine Books • New York

The TRUTH about cats

Cats aren't finicky...

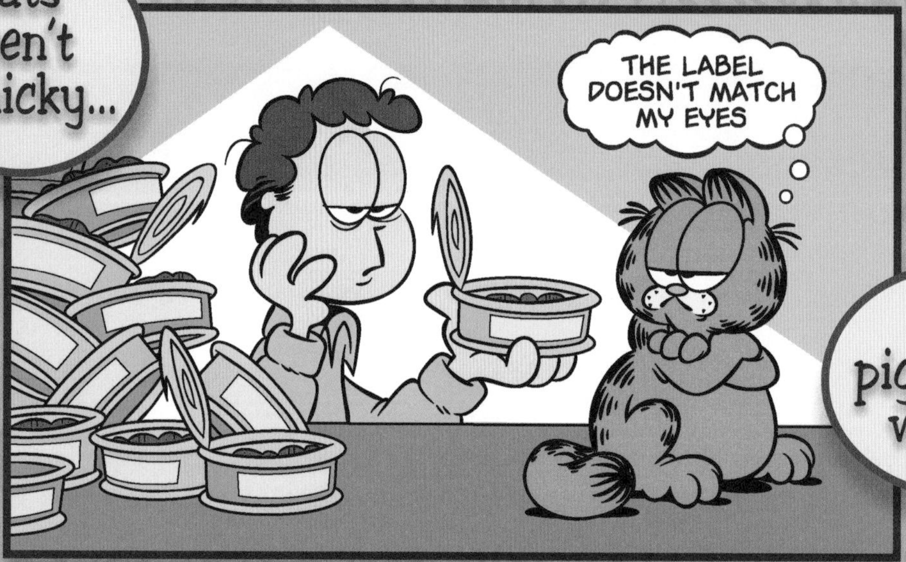
THE LABEL DOESN'T MATCH MY EYES

and pigs have wings.

Cats know better...

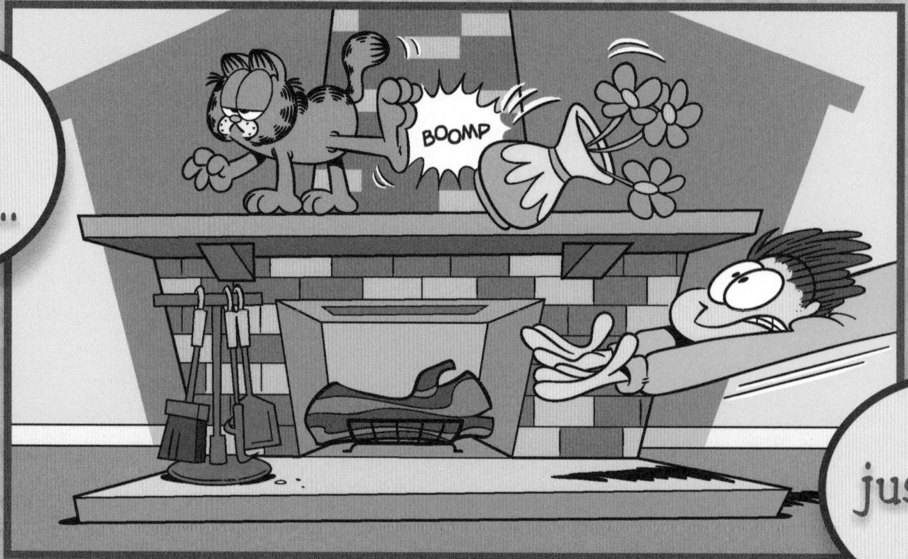
BOOMP

they just don't care.

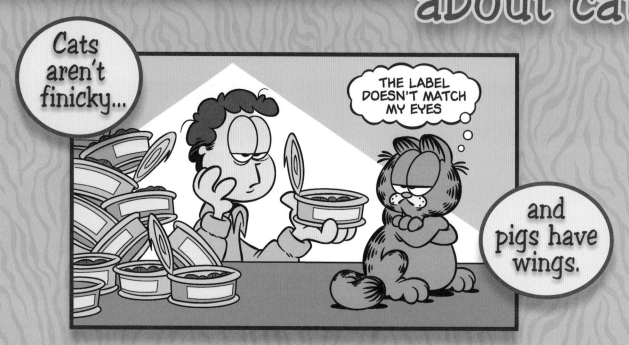

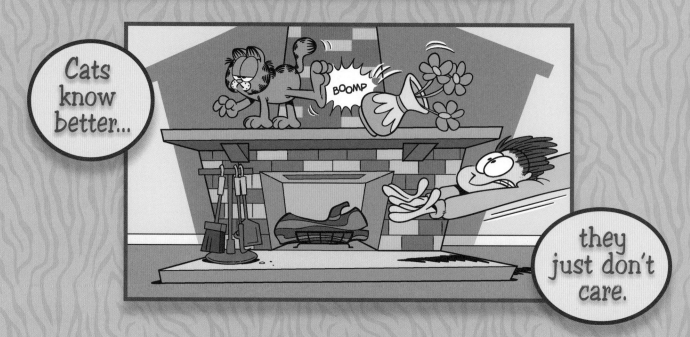

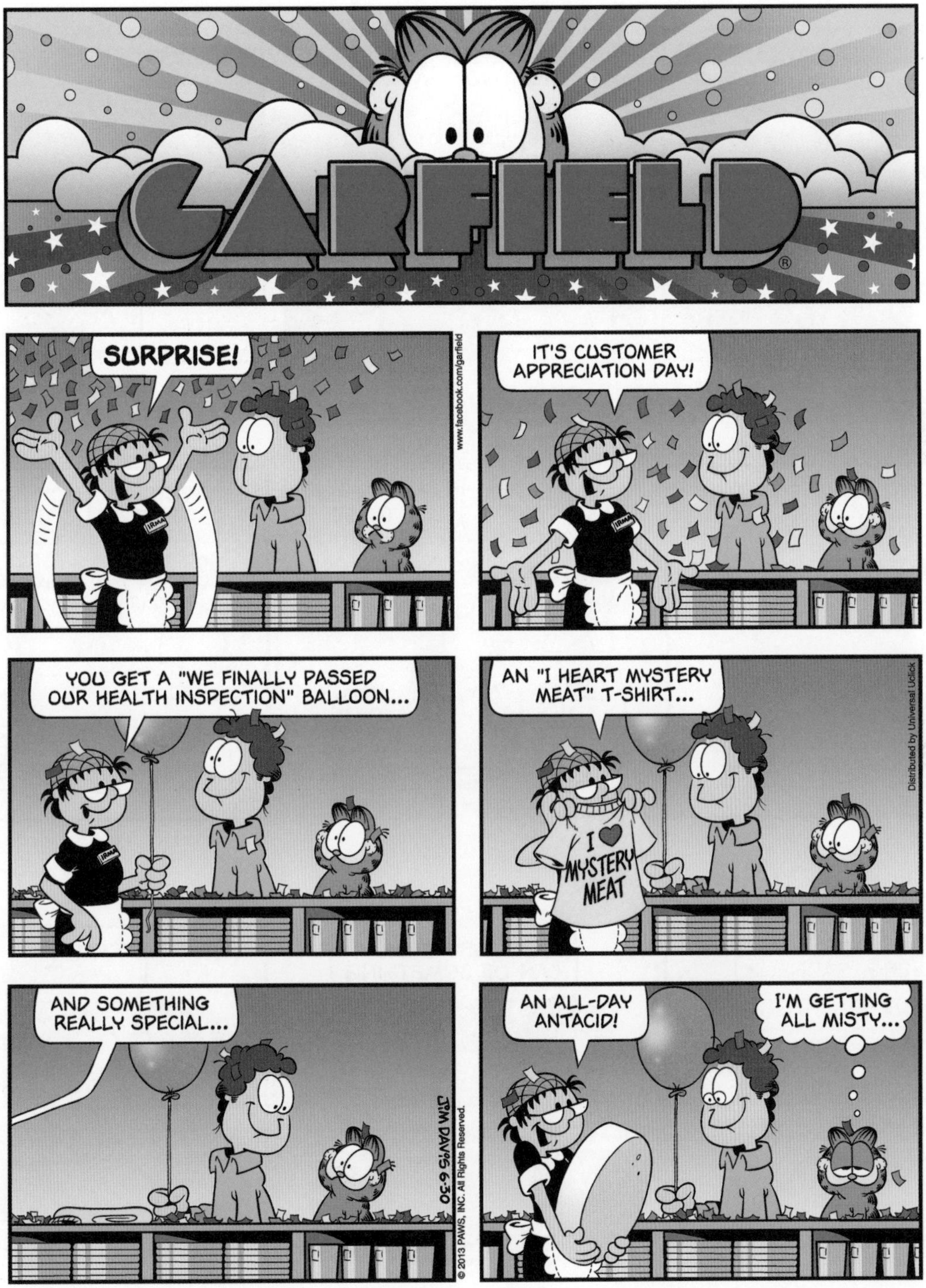
GARFIELD®
SURPRISE!
IT'S CUSTOMER APPRECIATION DAY!
YOU GET A "WE FINALLY PASSED OUR HEALTH INSPECTION" BALLOON...
AN "I HEART MYSTERY MEAT" T-SHIRT...
I ♥ MYSTERY MEAT
AND SOMETHING REALLY SPECIAL...
AN ALL-DAY ANTACID!
I'M GETTING ALL MISTY...
JIM DAVIS 6-30
www.facebook.com/garfield
Distributed by Universal Uclick
© 2013 PAWS, INC. All Rights Reserved.

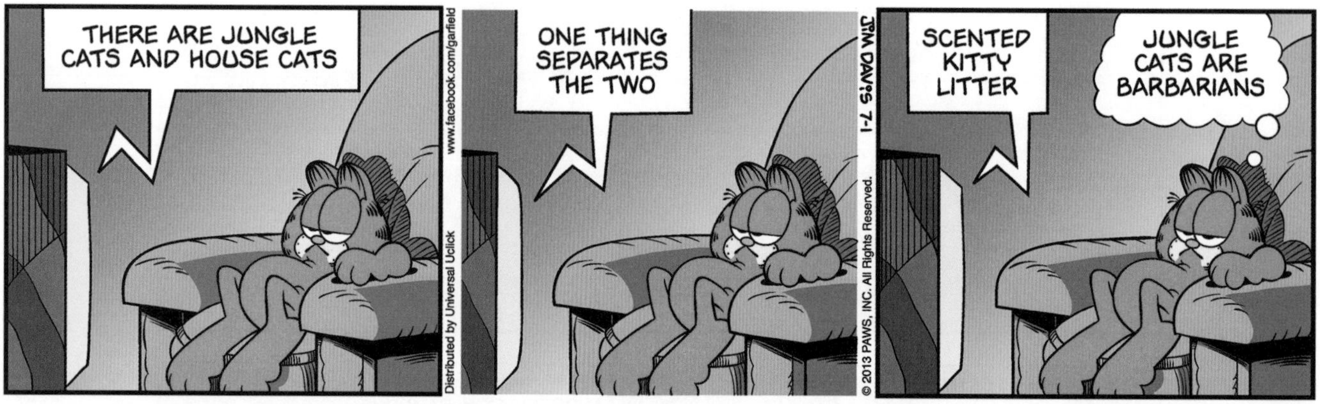
THERE ARE JUNGLE CATS AND HOUSE CATS
ONE THING SEPARATES THE TWO
SCENTED KITTY LITTER
JUNGLE CATS ARE BARBARIANS
JIM DAVIS 7-1
Distributed by Universal Uclick www.facebook.com/garfield
© 2013 PAWS, INC. All Rights Reserved.

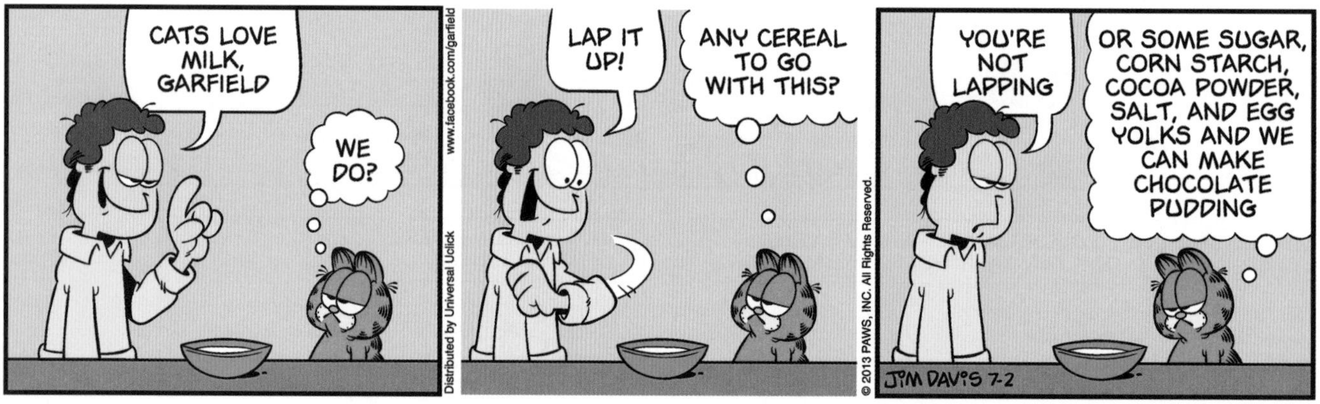
CATS LOVE MILK, GARFIELD
WE DO?
LAP IT UP!
ANY CEREAL TO GO WITH THIS?
YOU'RE NOT LAPPING
OR SOME SUGAR, CORN STARCH, COCOA POWDER, SALT, AND EGG YOLKS AND WE CAN MAKE CHOCOLATE PUDDING
JIM DAVIS 7-2
Distributed by Universal Uclick www.facebook.com/garfield
© 2013 PAWS, INC. All Rights Reserved.

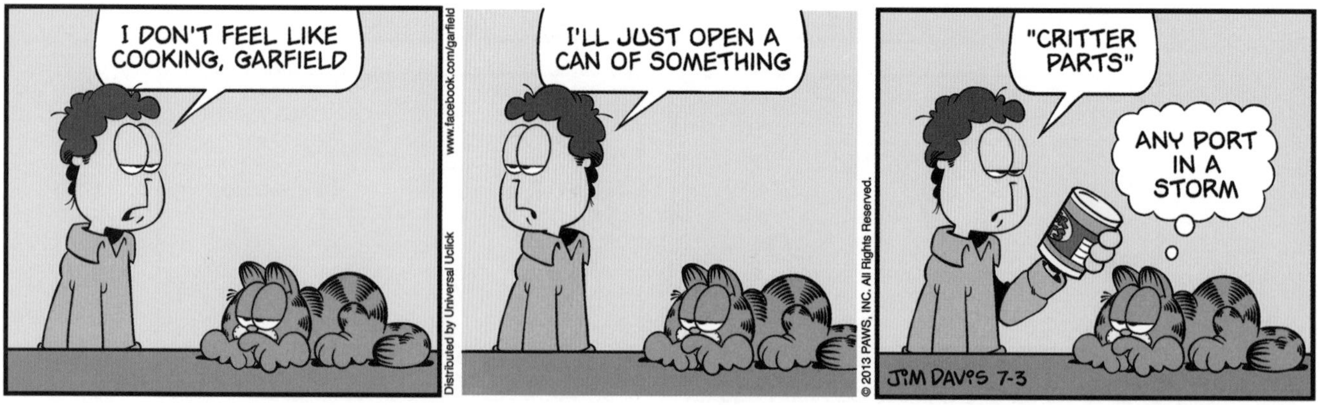
I DON'T FEEL LIKE COOKING, GARFIELD
I'LL JUST OPEN A CAN OF SOMETHING
"CRITTER PARTS"
ANY PORT IN A STORM
JIM DAVIS 7-3
Distributed by Universal Uclick www.facebook.com/garfield
© 2013 PAWS, INC. All Rights Reserved.

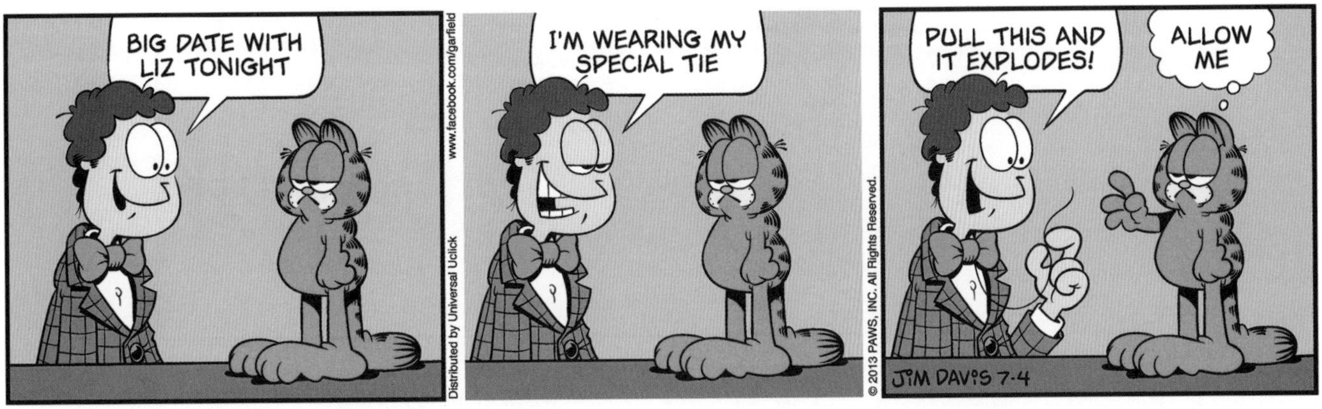
BIG DATE WITH LIZ TONIGHT
Distributed by Universal Uclick
www.facebook.com/garfield
I'M WEARING MY SPECIAL TIE
PULL THIS AND IT EXPLODES!
ALLOW ME
© 2013 PAWS, INC. All Rights Reserved.
JIM DAVIS 7-4

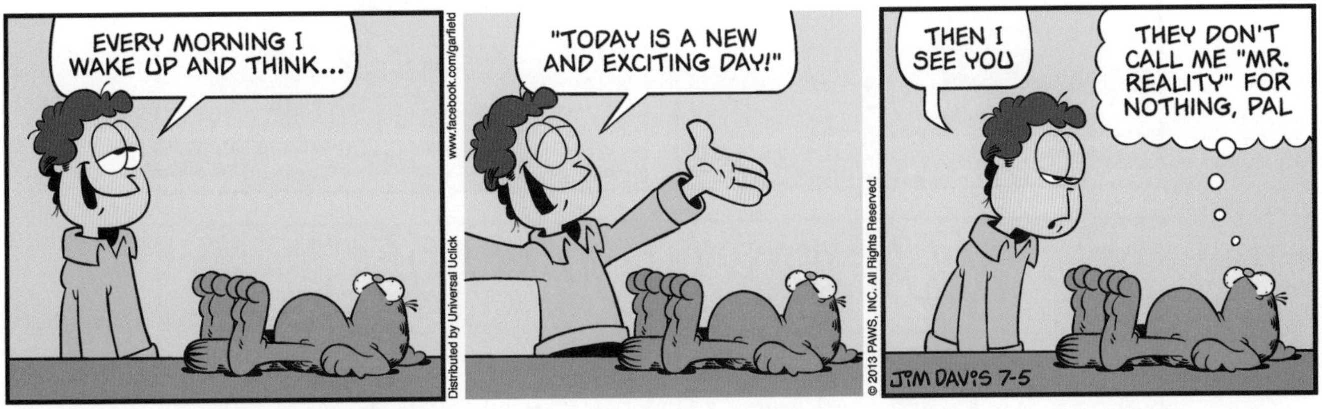
EVERY MORNING I WAKE UP AND THINK...
Distributed by Universal Uclick
www.facebook.com/garfield
"TODAY IS A NEW AND EXCITING DAY!"
THEN I SEE YOU
THEY DON'T CALL ME "MR. REALITY" FOR NOTHING, PAL
© 2013 PAWS, INC. All Rights Reserved.
JIM DAVIS 7-5

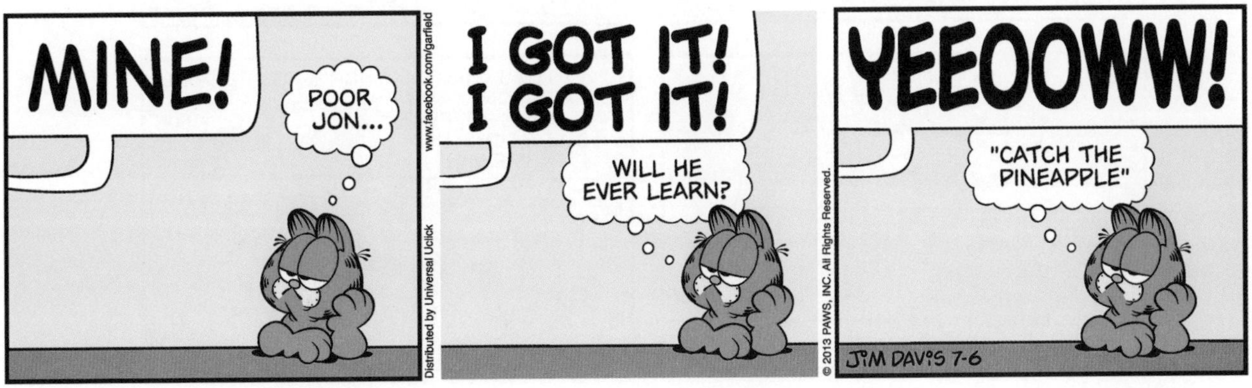
MINE!
POOR JON...
Distributed by Universal Uclick
www.facebook.com/garfield
I GOT IT! I GOT IT!
WILL HE EVER LEARN?
YEEOOWW!
"CATCH THE PINEAPPLE"
© 2013 PAWS, INC. All Rights Reserved.
JIM DAVIS 7-6

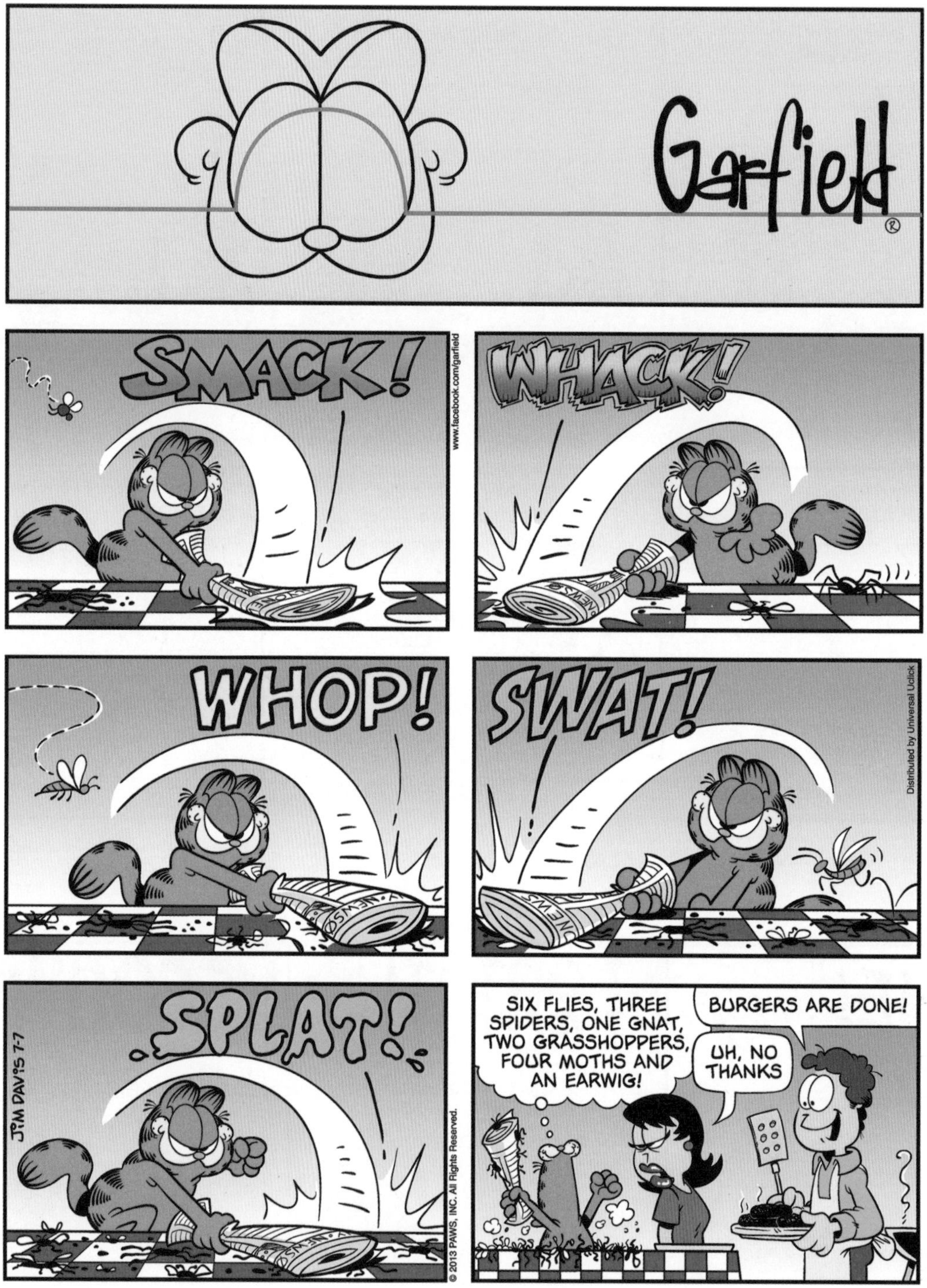
Garfield®
SMACK!
www.facebook.com/garfield
WHACK!
WHOP!
SWAT!
Distributed by Universal Uclick
SPLAT!
JIM DAVIS 7-7
© 2013 PAWS, INC. All Rights Reserved.
SIX FLIES, THREE SPIDERS, ONE GNAT, TWO GRASSHOPPERS, FOUR MOTHS AND AN EARWIG!
BURGERS ARE DONE!
UH, NO THANKS

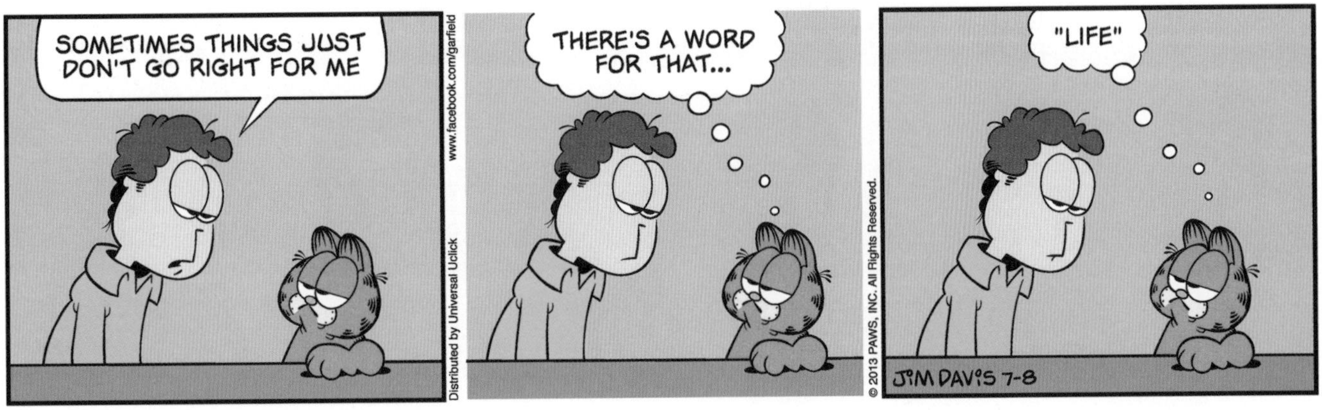
SOMETIMES THINGS JUST DON'T GO RIGHT FOR ME
THERE'S A WORD FOR THAT...
"LIFE"
Distributed by Universal Uclick www.facebook.com/garfield
© 2013 PAWS, INC. All Rights Reserved.
JIM DAVIS 7-8

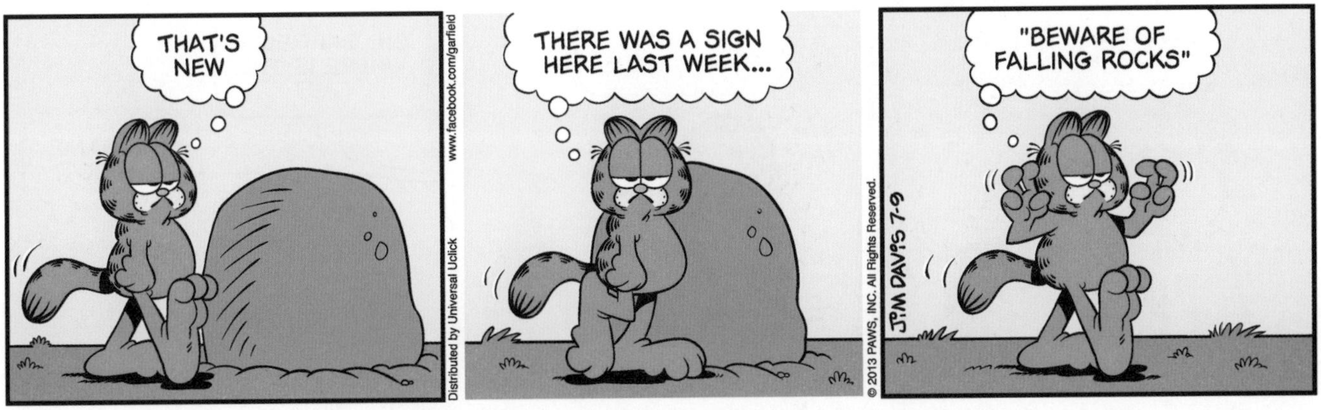
THAT'S NEW
THERE WAS A SIGN HERE LAST WEEK...
"BEWARE OF FALLING ROCKS"
Distributed by Universal Uclick www.facebook.com/garfield
© 2013 PAWS, INC. All Rights Reserved.
JIM DAVIS 7-9

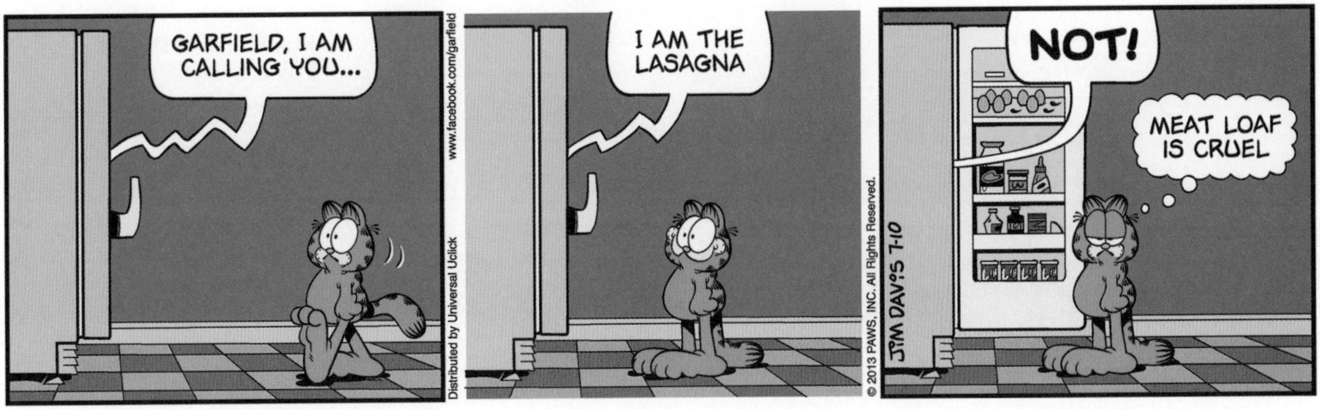
GARFIELD, I AM CALLING YOU...
I AM THE LASAGNA
NOT!
MEAT LOAF IS CRUEL
Distributed by Universal Uclick www.facebook.com/garfield
© 2013 PAWS, INC. All Rights Reserved.
JIM DAVIS 7-10

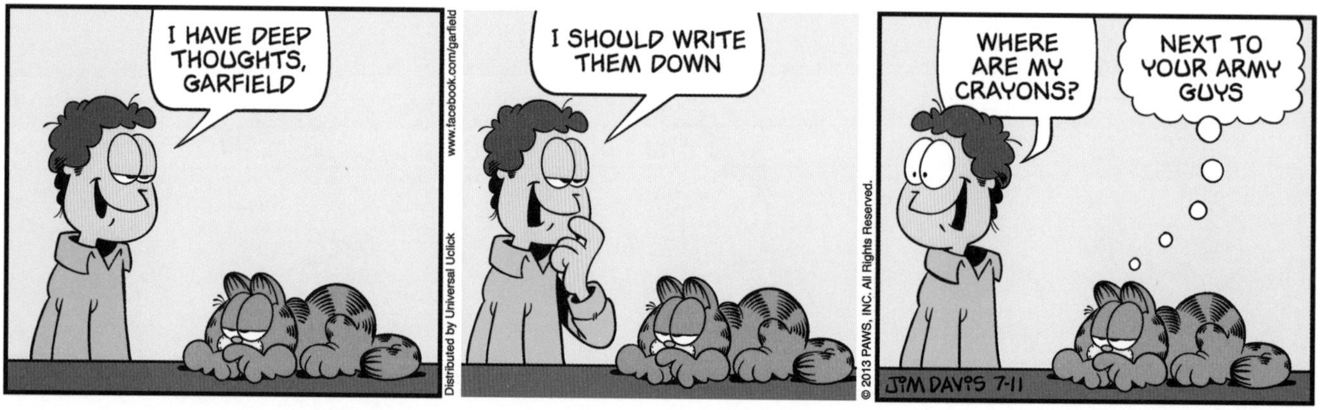
I HAVE DEEP THOUGHTS, GARFIELD
I SHOULD WRITE THEM DOWN
WHERE ARE MY CRAYONS?
NEXT TO YOUR ARMY GUYS
Distributed by Universal Uclick www.facebook.com/garfield
© 2013 PAWS, INC. All Rights Reserved.
JIM DAVIS 7-11

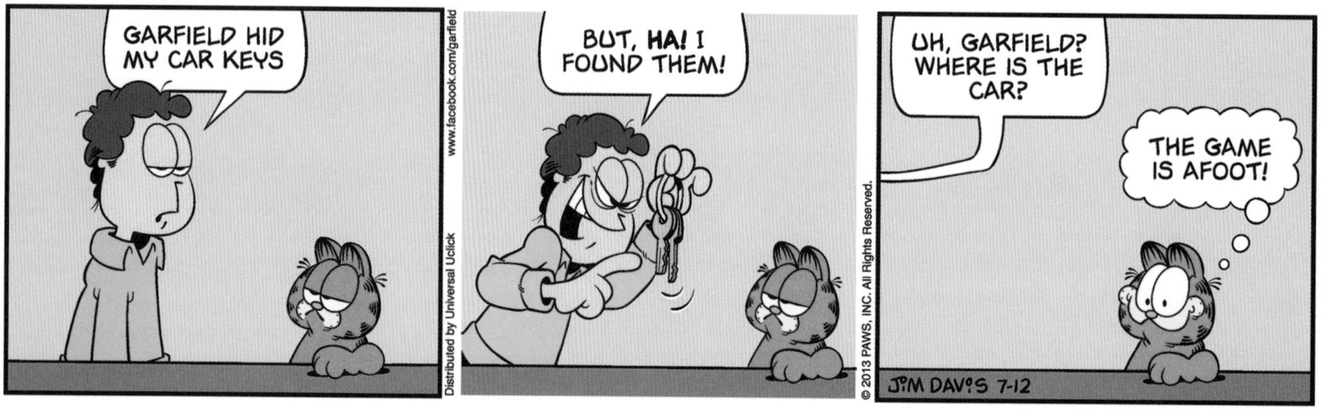
GARFIELD HID MY CAR KEYS
BUT, **HA!** I FOUND THEM!
UH, GARFIELD? WHERE IS THE CAR?
THE GAME IS AFOOT!
Distributed by Universal Uclick www.facebook.com/garfield
© 2013 PAWS, INC. All Rights Reserved.
JIM DAVIS 7-12

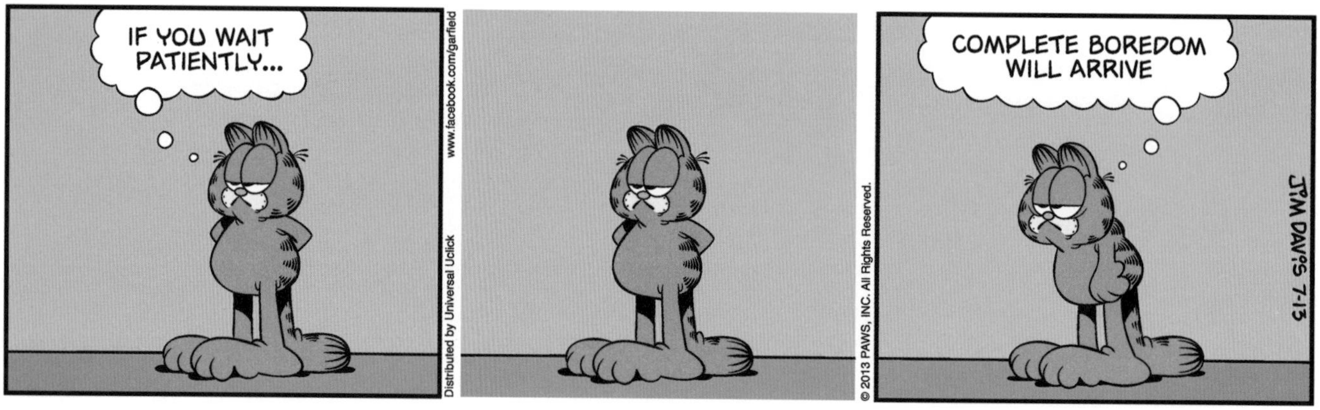
IF YOU WAIT PATIENTLY...
COMPLETE BOREDOM WILL ARRIVE
Distributed by Universal Uclick www.facebook.com/garfield
© 2013 PAWS, INC. All Rights Reserved.
JIM DAVIS 7-13

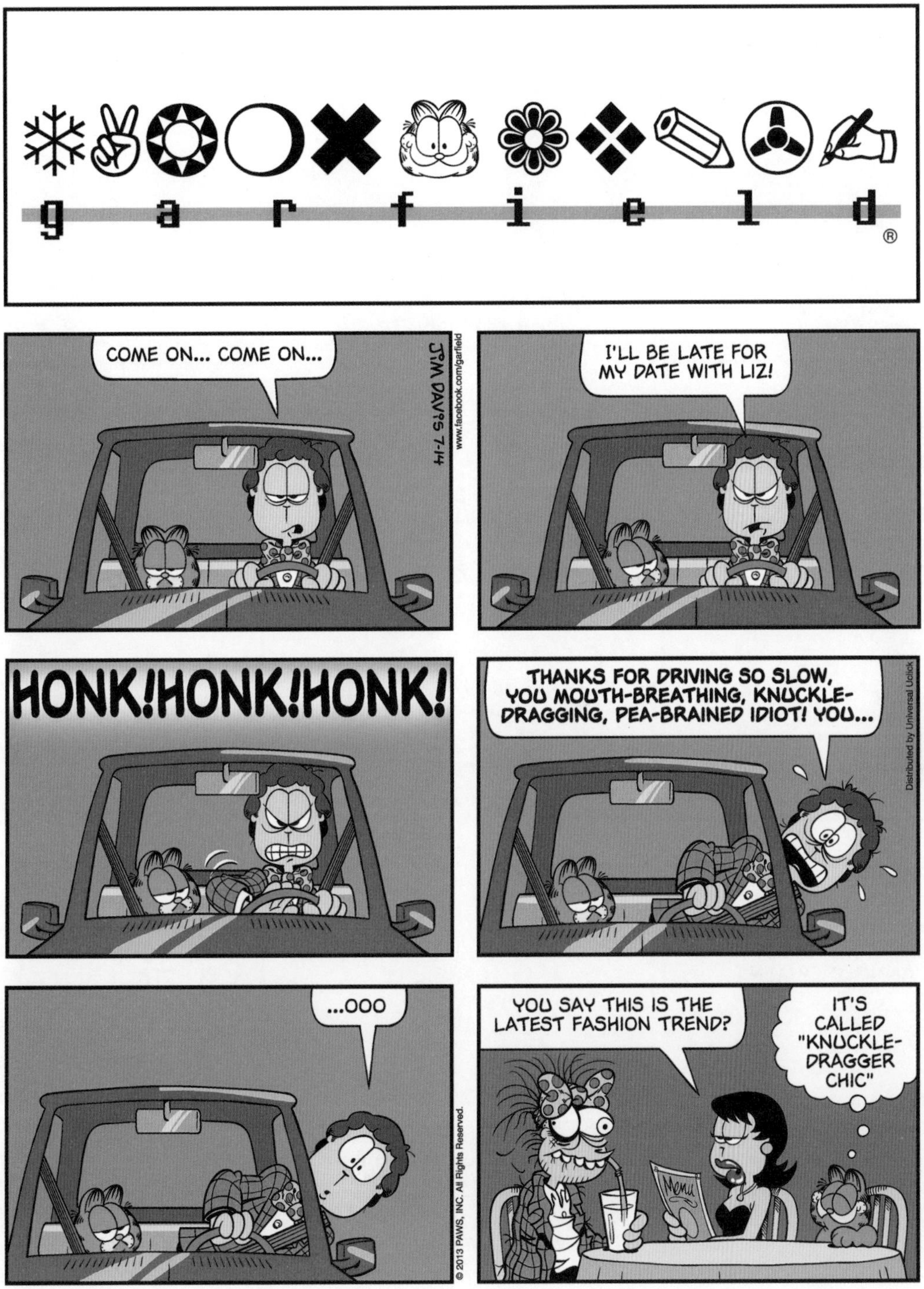
garfield®
COME ON... COME ON...
JIM DAVIS 7-14
www.facebook.com/garfield
I'LL BE LATE FOR MY DATE WITH LIZ!
HONK!HONK!HONK!
THANKS FOR DRIVING SO SLOW, YOU MOUTH-BREATHING, KNUCKLE-DRAGGING, PEA-BRAINED IDIOT! YOU...
Distributed by Universal Uclick
...OOO
© 2013 PAWS, INC. All Rights Reserved.
YOU SAY THIS IS THE LATEST FASHION TREND?
IT'S CALLED "KNUCKLE-DRAGGER CHIC"
Menu

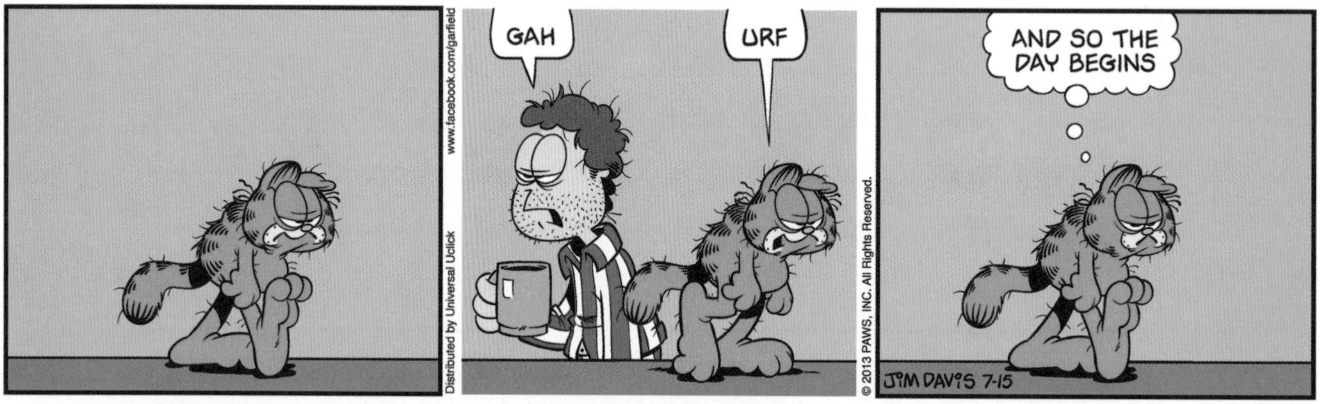
Distributed by Universal Uclick www.facebook.com/garfield
GAH
URF
© 2013 PAWS, INC. All Rights Reserved.
AND SO THE DAY BEGINS
JIM DAVIS 7-15

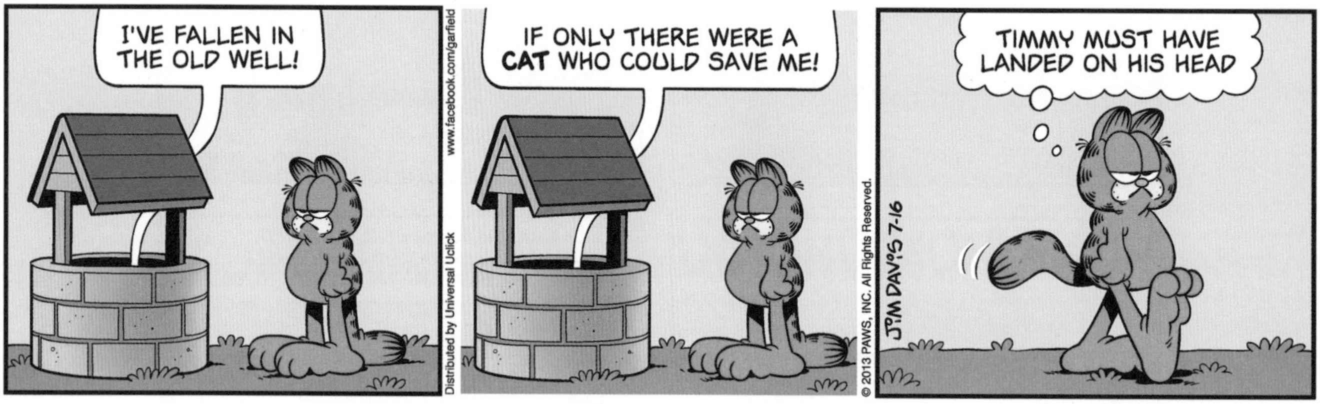
I'VE FALLEN IN THE OLD WELL!
Distributed by Universal Uclick www.facebook.com/garfield
IF ONLY THERE WERE A **CAT** WHO COULD SAVE ME!
© 2013 PAWS, INC. All Rights Reserved.
JIM DAVIS 7-16
TIMMY MUST HAVE LANDED ON HIS HEAD

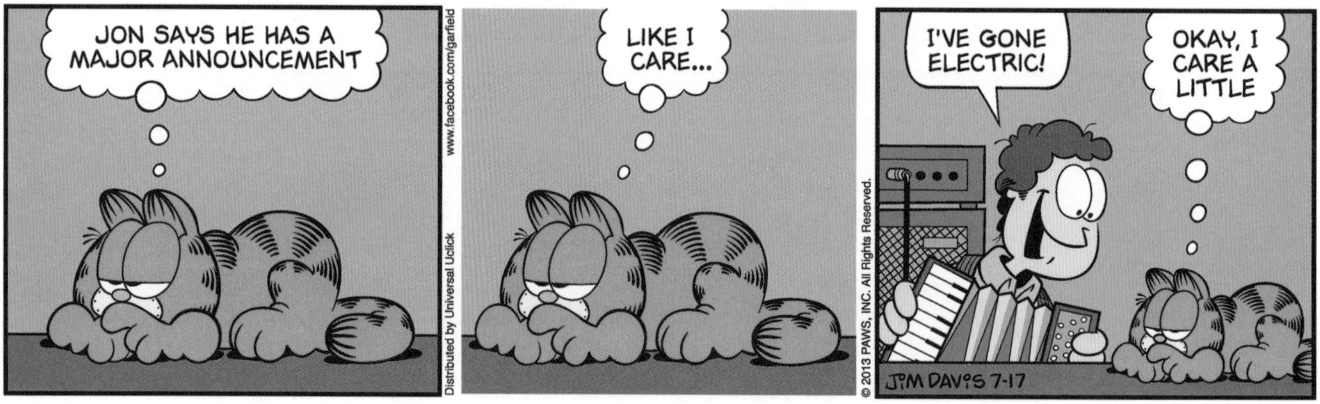
JON SAYS HE HAS A MAJOR ANNOUNCEMENT
Distributed by Universal Uclick www.facebook.com/garfield
LIKE I CARE...
© 2013 PAWS, INC. All Rights Reserved.
I'VE GONE ELECTRIC!
OKAY, I CARE A LITTLE
JIM DAVIS 7-17

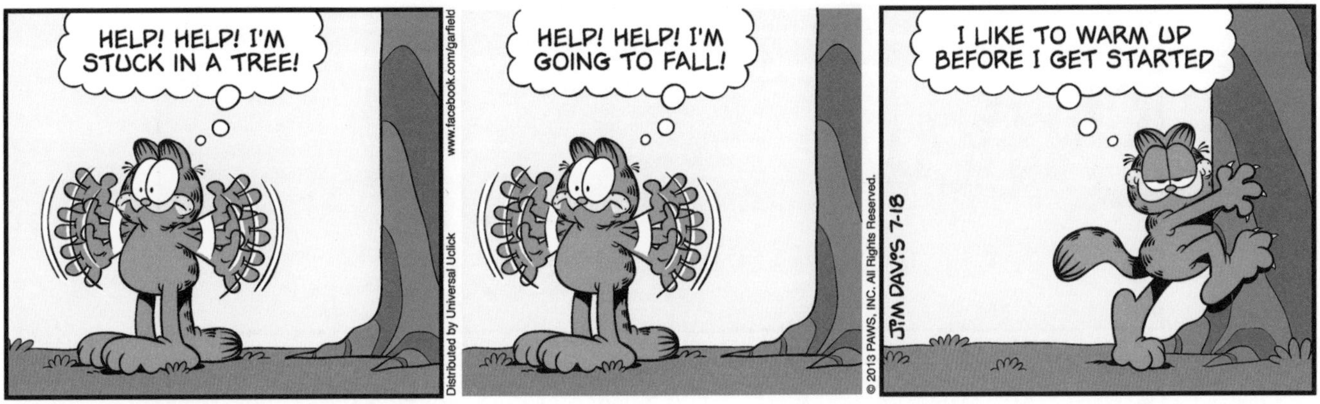
HELP! HELP! I'M STUCK IN A TREE!
HELP! HELP! I'M GOING TO FALL!
I LIKE TO WARM UP BEFORE I GET STARTED
Distributed by Universal Uclick
www.facebook.com/garfield
© 2013 PAWS, INC. All Rights Reserved.
JIM DAVIS 7-18

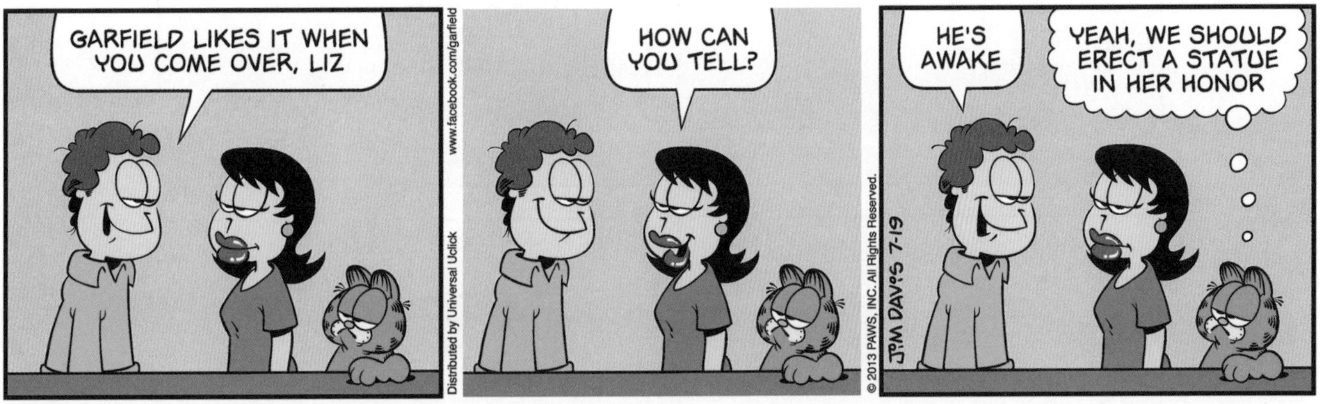
GARFIELD LIKES IT WHEN YOU COME OVER, LIZ
HOW CAN YOU TELL?
HE'S AWAKE
YEAH, WE SHOULD ERECT A STATUE IN HER HONOR
Distributed by Universal Uclick
www.facebook.com/garfield
© 2013 PAWS, INC. All Rights Reserved.
JIM DAVIS 7-19

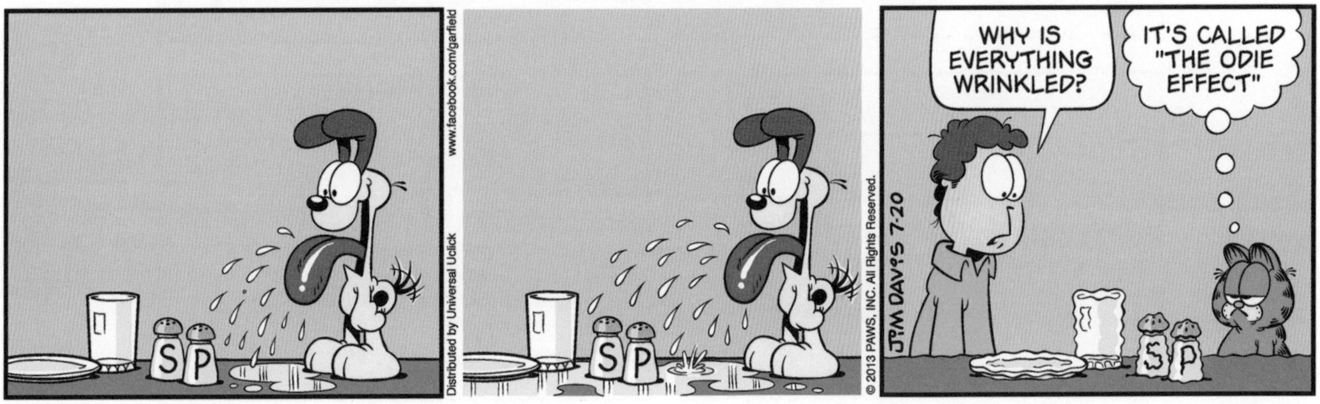
S P
WHY IS EVERYTHING WRINKLED?
IT'S CALLED "THE ODIE EFFECT"
Distributed by Universal Uclick
www.facebook.com/garfield
© 2013 PAWS, INC. All Rights Reserved.
JIM DAVIS 7-20

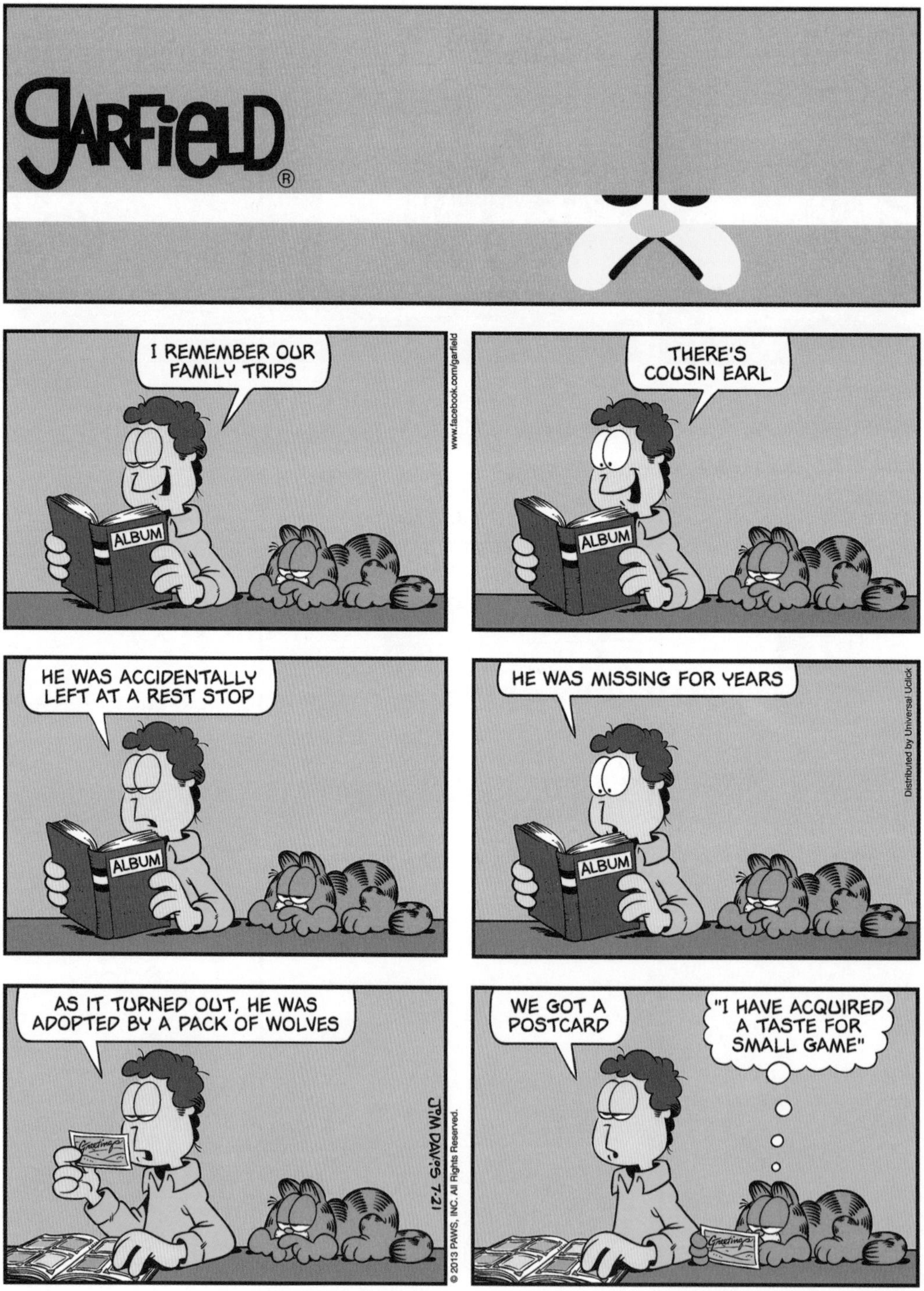
GARFIELD®
I REMEMBER OUR FAMILY TRIPS
www.facebook.com/garfield
THERE'S COUSIN EARL
ALBUM
HE WAS ACCIDENTALLY LEFT AT A REST STOP
HE WAS MISSING FOR YEARS
Distributed by Universal Uclick
AS IT TURNED OUT, HE WAS ADOPTED BY A PACK OF WOLVES
JIM DAVIS 7-21
© 2013 PAWS, INC. All Rights Reserved.
Greetings
WE GOT A POSTCARD
"I HAVE ACQUIRED A TASTE FOR SMALL GAME"

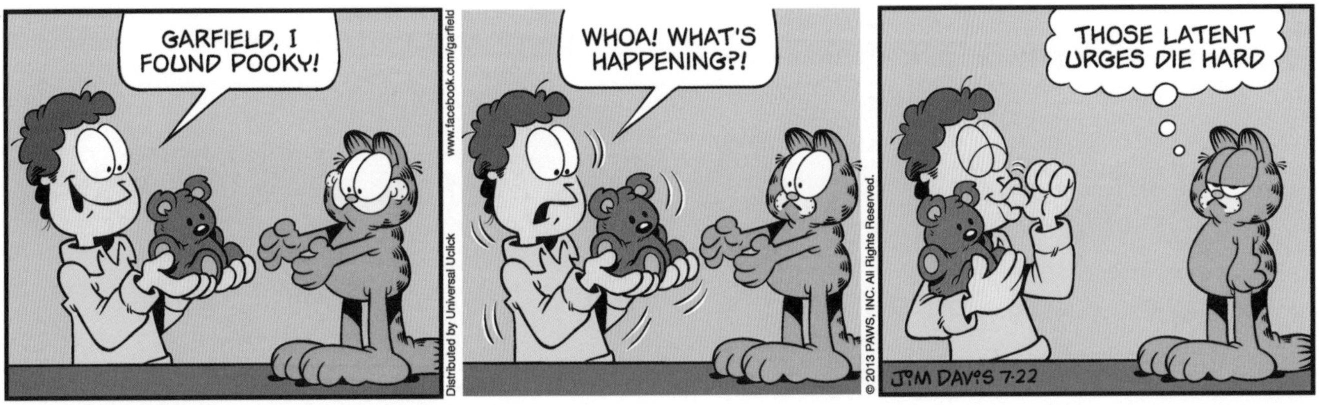
GARFIELD, I FOUND POOKY!
Distributed by Universal Uclick
www.facebook.com/garfield
WHOA! WHAT'S HAPPENING?!
© 2013 PAWS, INC. All Rights Reserved.
THOSE LATENT URGES DIE HARD
JIM DAVIS 7-22

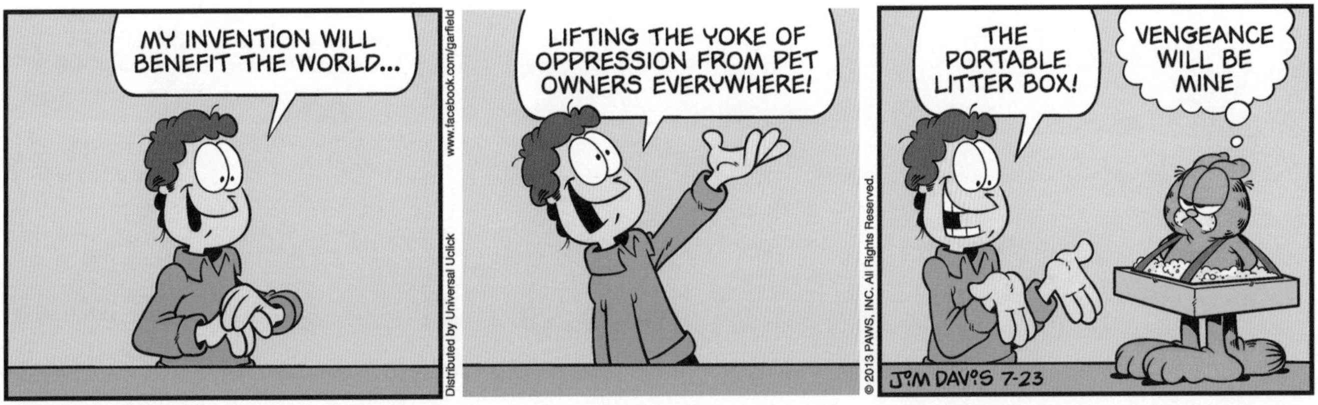
MY INVENTION WILL BENEFIT THE WORLD...
Distributed by Universal Uclick
www.facebook.com/garfield
LIFTING THE YOKE OF OPPRESSION FROM PET OWNERS EVERYWHERE!
© 2013 PAWS, INC. All Rights Reserved.
THE PORTABLE LITTER BOX!
VENGEANCE WILL BE MINE
JIM DAVIS 7-23

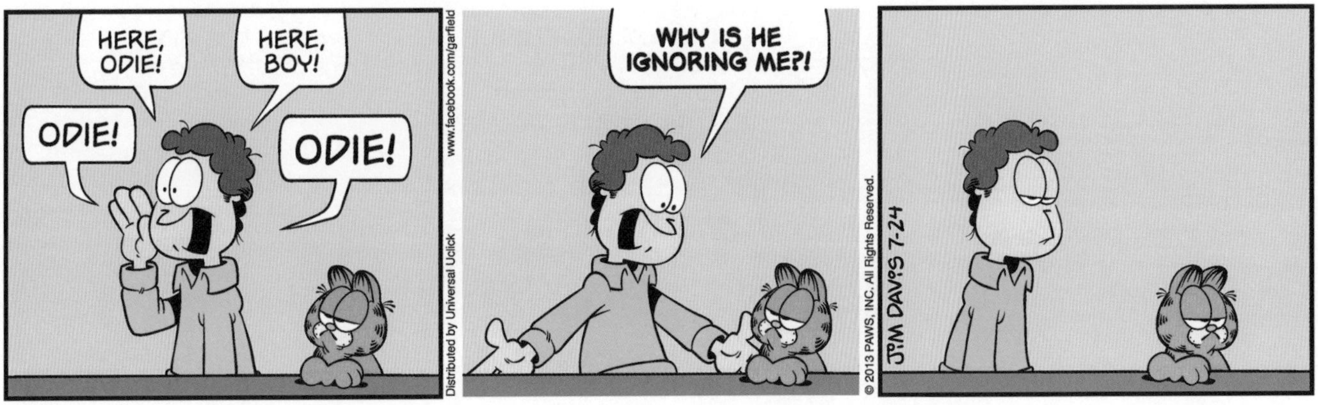
ODIE!
HERE, ODIE!
HERE, BOY!
ODIE!
Distributed by Universal Uclick
www.facebook.com/garfield
WHY IS HE IGNORING ME?!
© 2013 PAWS, INC. All Rights Reserved.
JIM DAVIS 7-24

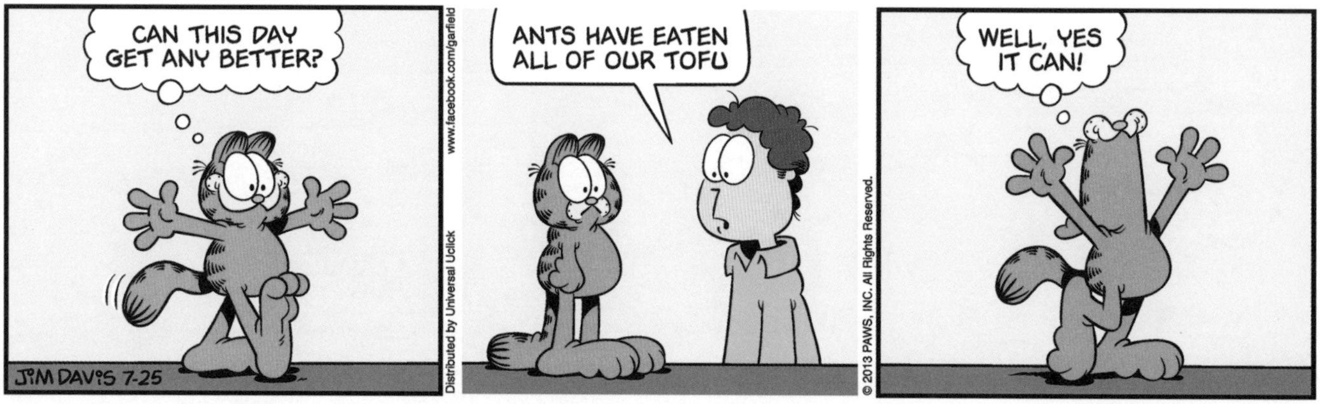
CAN THIS DAY GET ANY BETTER?
JIM DAVIS 7-25
Distributed by Universal Uclick www.facebook.com/garfield
ANTS HAVE EATEN ALL OF OUR TOFU
© 2013 PAWS, INC. All Rights Reserved.
WELL, YES IT CAN!

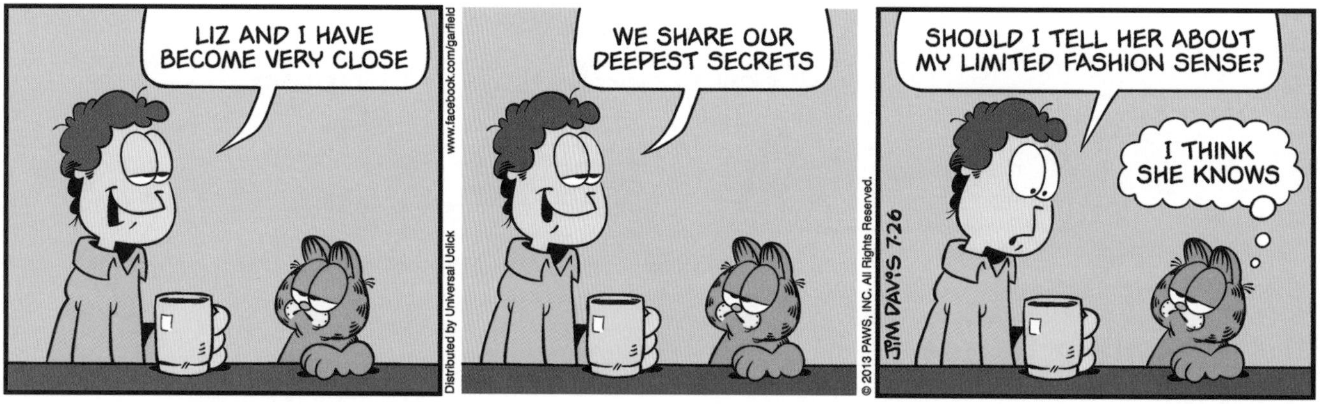
LIZ AND I HAVE BECOME VERY CLOSE
Distributed by Universal Uclick www.facebook.com/garfield
WE SHARE OUR DEEPEST SECRETS
© 2013 PAWS, INC. All Rights Reserved.
JIM DAVIS 7-26
SHOULD I TELL HER ABOUT MY LIMITED FASHION SENSE?
I THINK SHE KNOWS

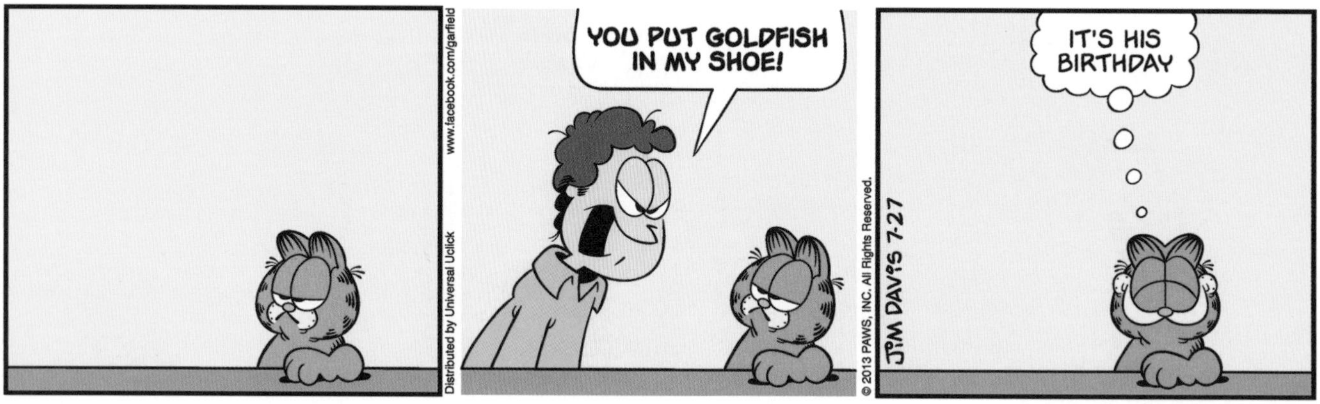
Distributed by Universal Uclick www.facebook.com/garfield
YOU PUT GOLDFISH IN MY SHOE!
© 2013 PAWS, INC. All Rights Reserved.
JIM DAVIS 7-27
IT'S HIS BIRTHDAY

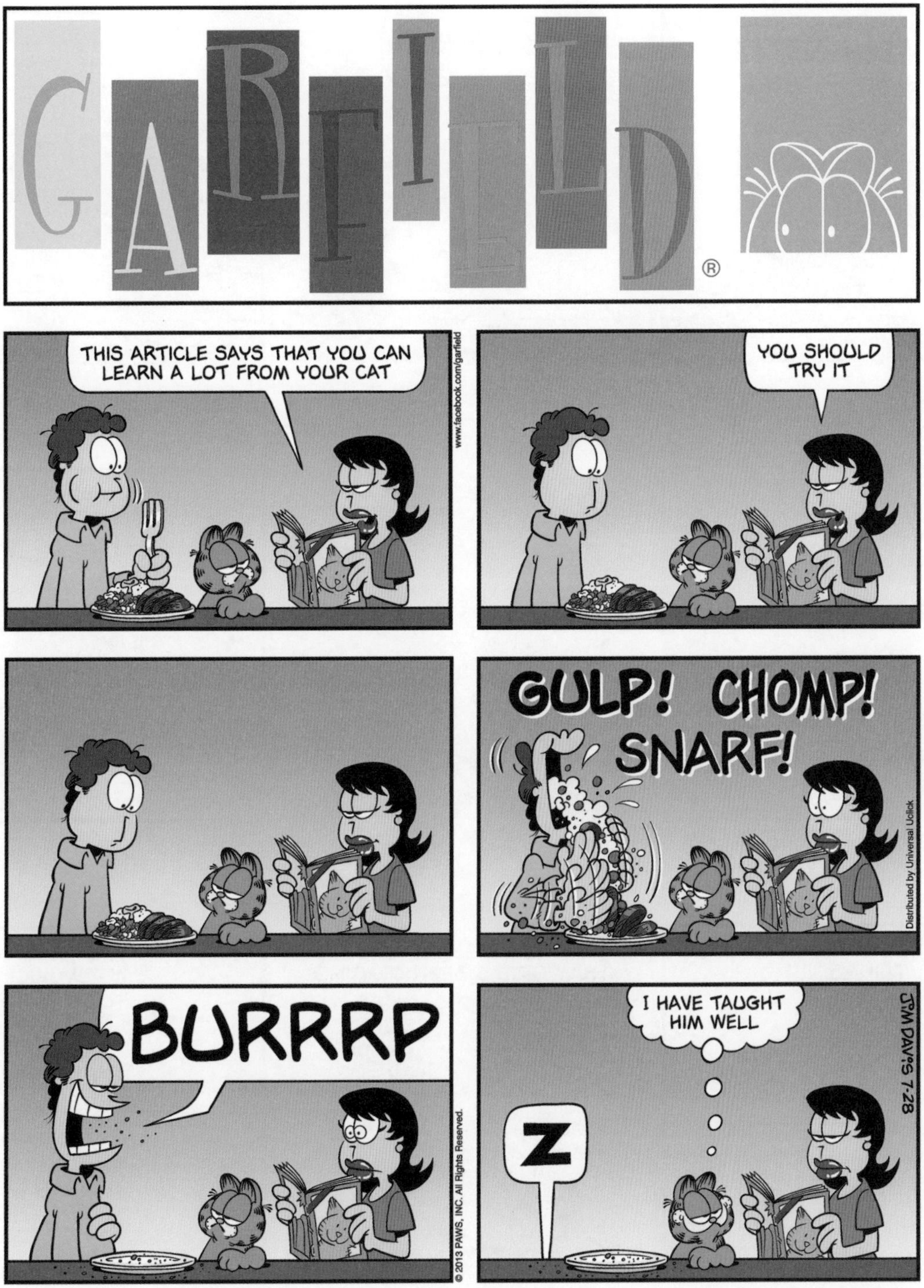
GARFIELD®
THIS ARTICLE SAYS THAT YOU CAN LEARN A LOT FROM YOUR CAT
www.facebook.com/garfield
YOU SHOULD TRY IT
GULP! CHOMP!
SNARF!
Distributed by Universal Uclick
BURRRP
© 2013 PAWS, INC. All Rights Reserved.
Z
I HAVE TAUGHT HIM WELL
JIM DAVIS 7-28

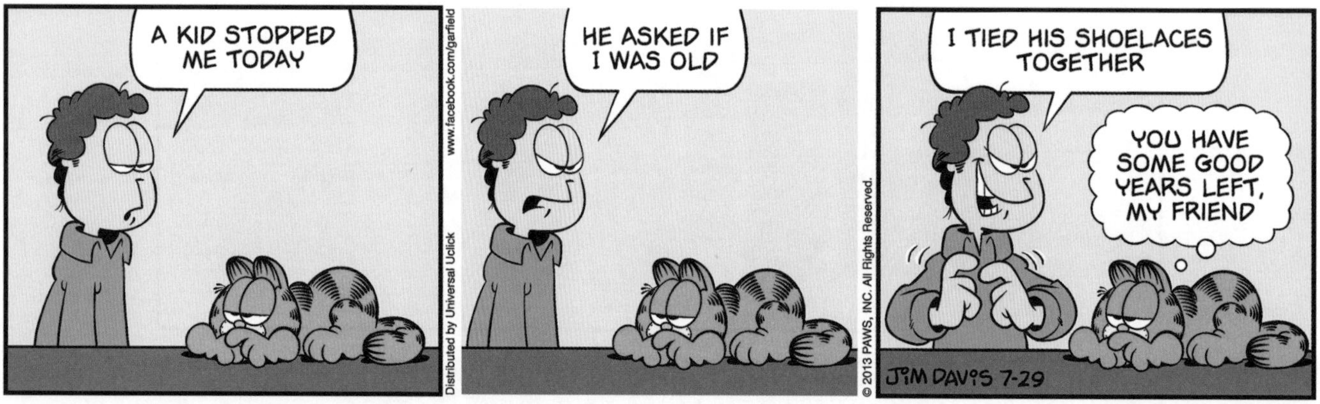
A KID STOPPED ME TODAY
www.facebook.com/garfield
Distributed by Universal Uclick
HE ASKED IF I WAS OLD
© 2013 PAWS, INC. All Rights Reserved.
I TIED HIS SHOELACES TOGETHER
YOU HAVE SOME GOOD YEARS LEFT, MY FRIEND
JIM DAVIS 7-29

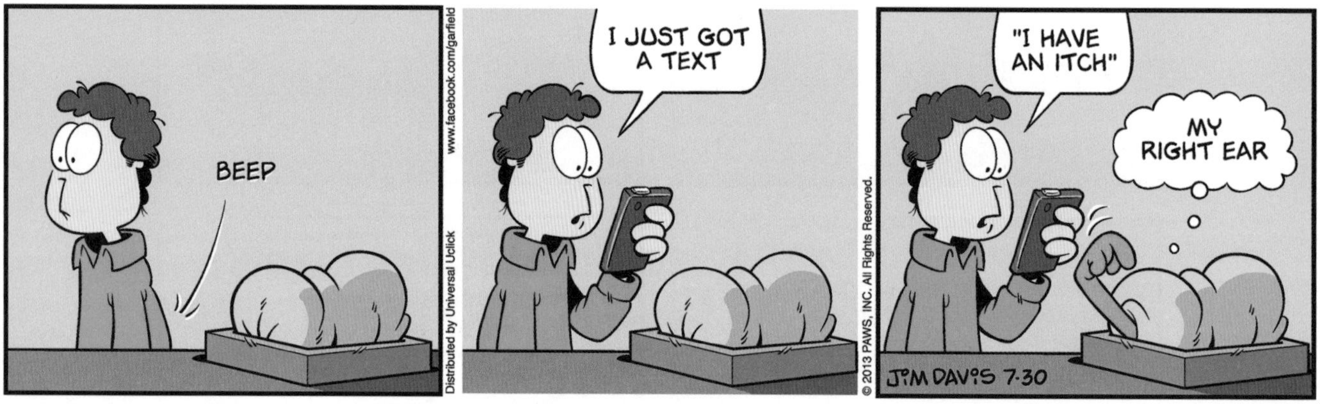
BEEP
www.facebook.com/garfield
Distributed by Universal Uclick
I JUST GOT A TEXT
© 2013 PAWS, INC. All Rights Reserved.
"I HAVE AN ITCH"
MY RIGHT EAR
JIM DAVIS 7-30

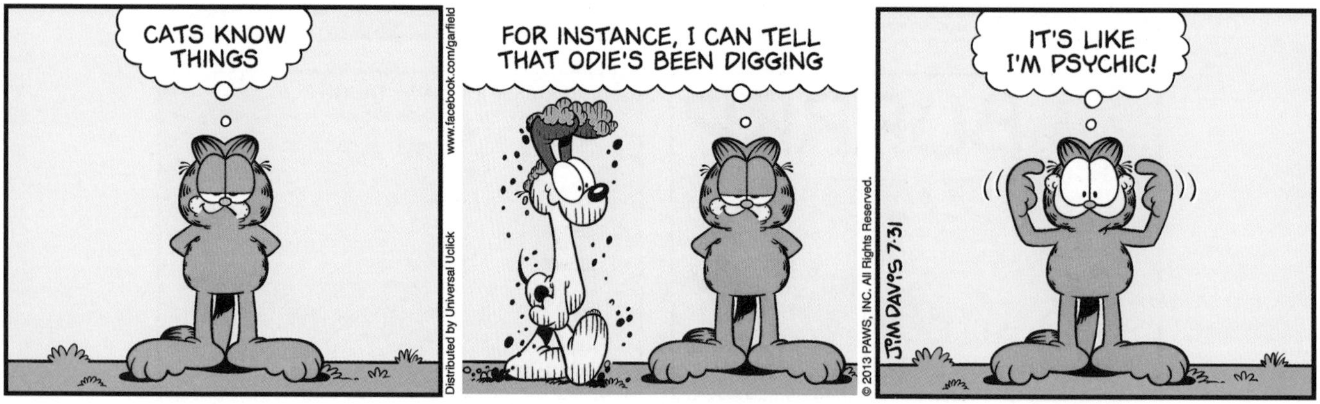
CATS KNOW THINGS
www.facebook.com/garfield
Distributed by Universal Uclick
FOR INSTANCE, I CAN TELL THAT ODIE'S BEEN DIGGING
© 2013 PAWS, INC. All Rights Reserved.
JIM DAVIS 7-31
IT'S LIKE I'M PSYCHIC!

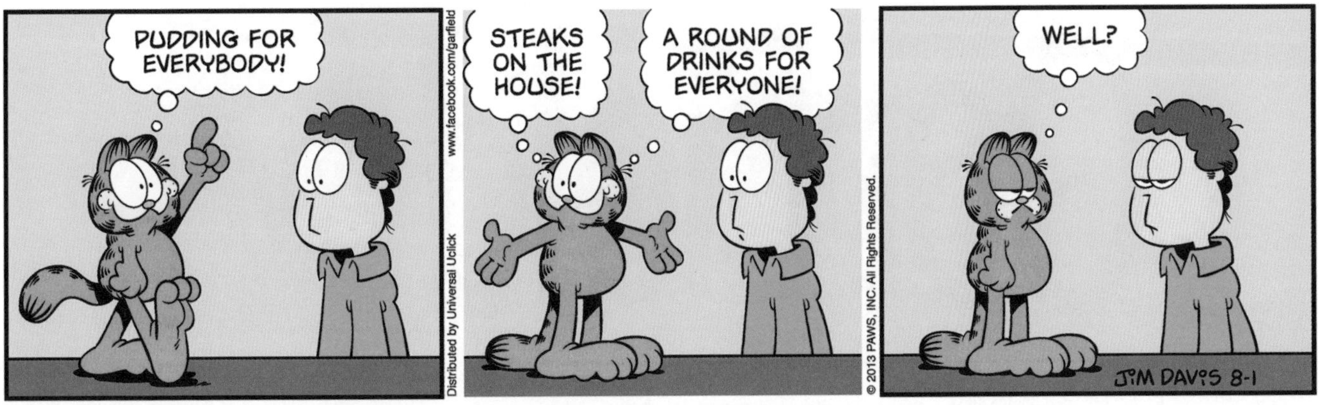
PUDDING FOR EVERYBODY!
STEAKS ON THE HOUSE!
A ROUND OF DRINKS FOR EVERYONE!
WELL?
JIM DAVIS 8-1
Distributed by Universal Uclick
www.facebook.com/garfield
© 2013 PAWS, INC. All Rights Reserved.

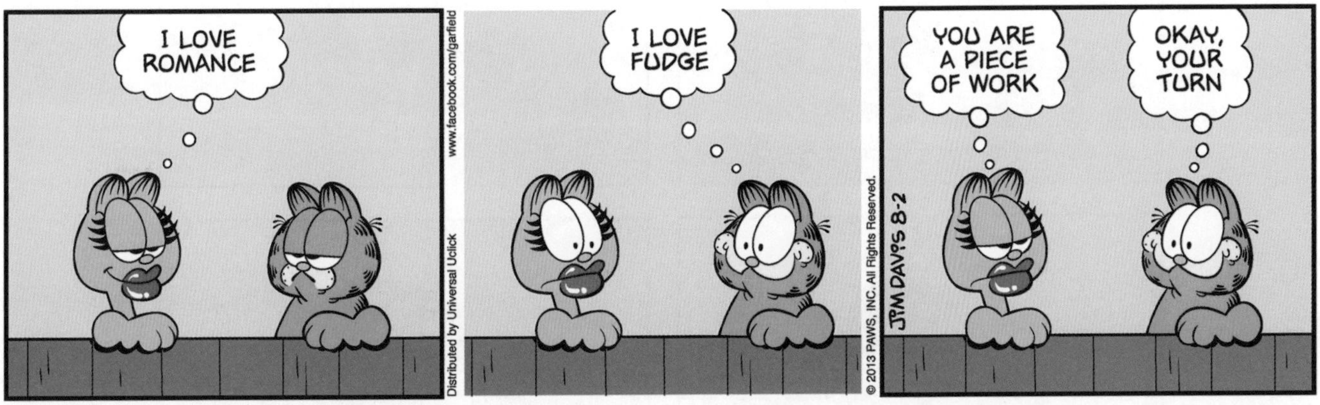
I LOVE ROMANCE
I LOVE FUDGE
YOU ARE A PIECE OF WORK
OKAY, YOUR TURN
JIM DAVIS 8-2
Distributed by Universal Uclick
www.facebook.com/garfield
© 2013 PAWS, INC. All Rights Reserved.

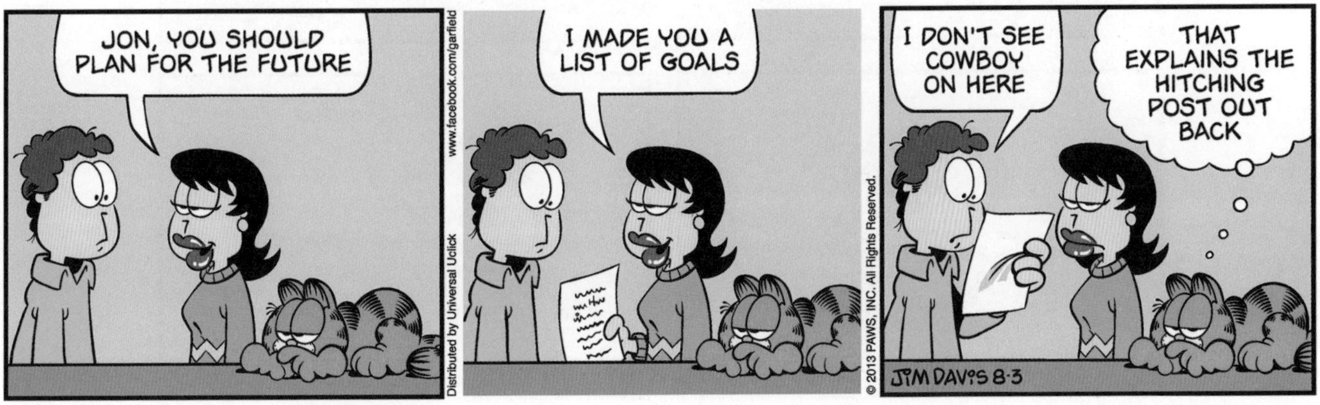
JON, YOU SHOULD PLAN FOR THE FUTURE
I MADE YOU A LIST OF GOALS
I DON'T SEE COWBOY ON HERE
THAT EXPLAINS THE HITCHING POST OUT BACK
JIM DAVIS 8-3
Distributed by Universal Uclick
www.facebook.com/garfield
© 2013 PAWS, INC. All Rights Reserved.

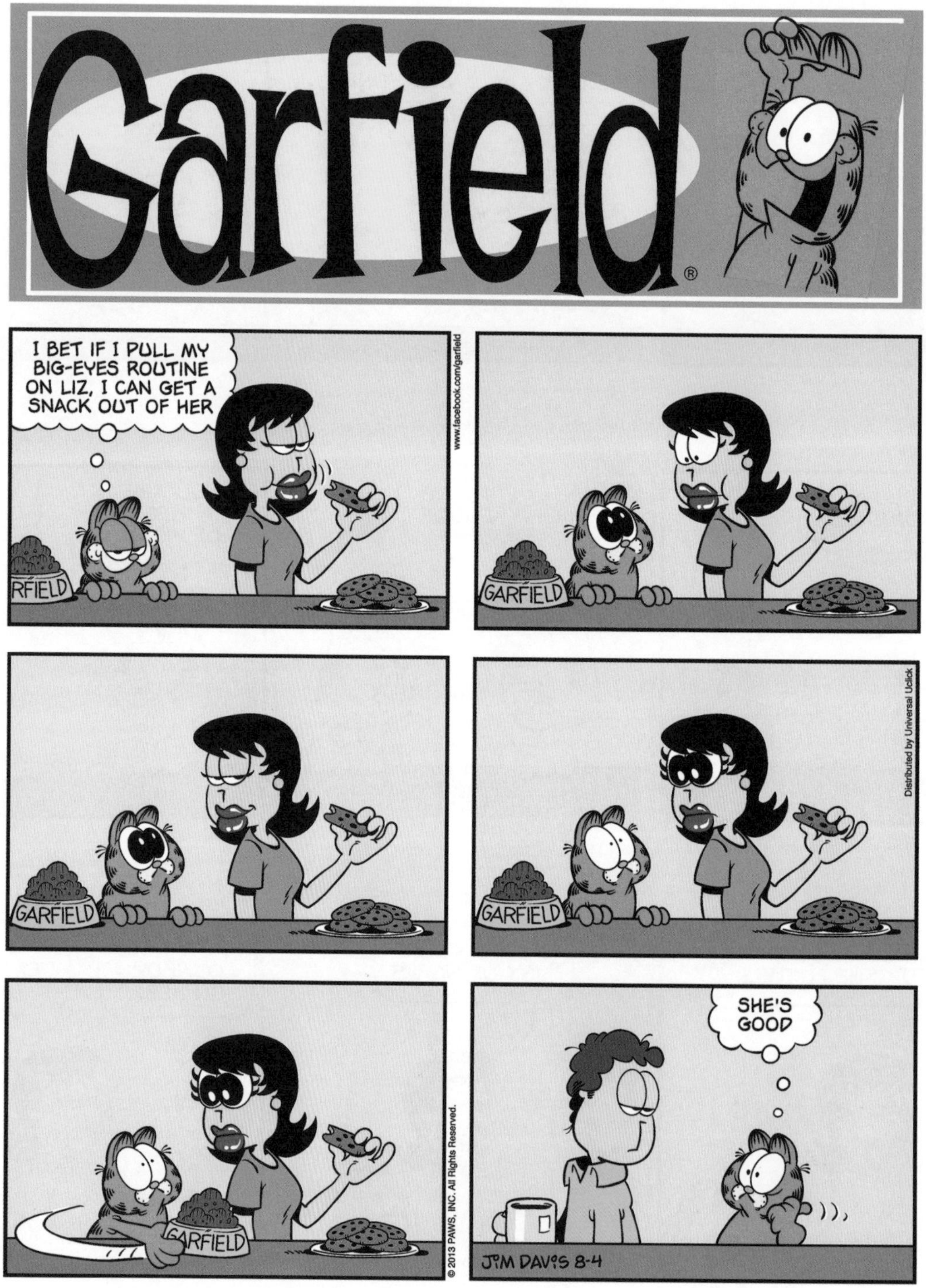
Garfield
I BET IF I PULL MY BIG-EYES ROUTINE ON LIZ, I CAN GET A SNACK OUT OF HER
www.facebook.com/garfield
GARFIELD
Distributed by Universal Uclick
SHE'S GOOD
© 2013 PAWS, INC. All Rights Reserved.
JIM DAVIS 8-4

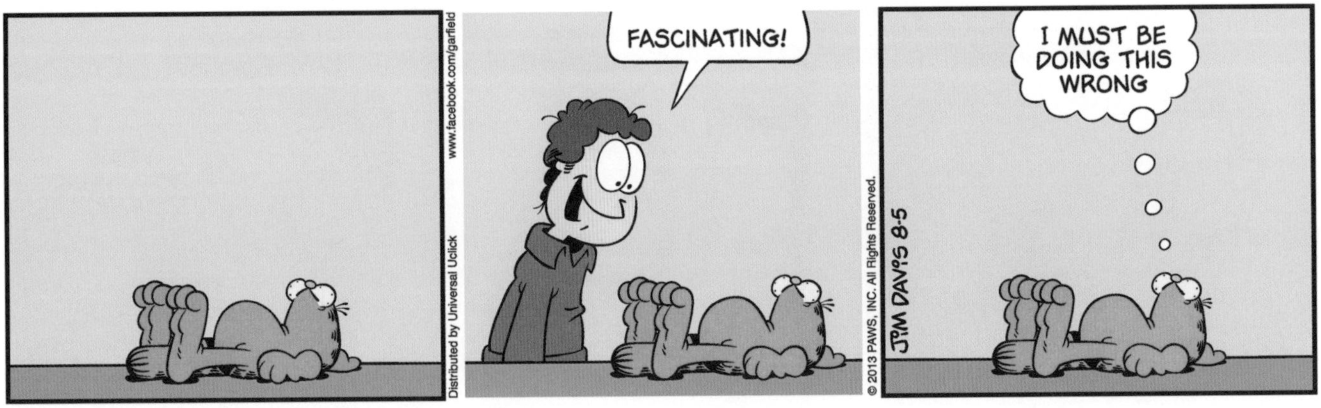
Distributed by Universal Uclick
www.facebook.com/garfield
FASCINATING!
© 2013 PAWS, INC. All Rights Reserved.
JIM DAVIS 8-5
I MUST BE DOING THIS WRONG

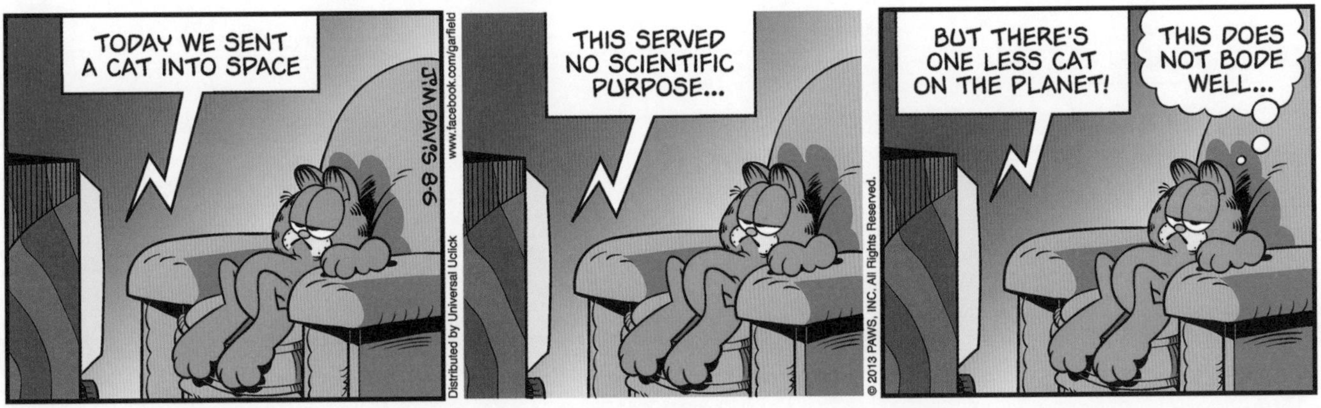
TODAY WE SENT A CAT INTO SPACE
JIM DAVIS 8-6
Distributed by Universal Uclick
www.facebook.com/garfield
THIS SERVED NO SCIENTIFIC PURPOSE...
© 2013 PAWS, INC. All Rights Reserved.
BUT THERE'S ONE LESS CAT ON THE PLANET!
THIS DOES NOT BODE WELL...

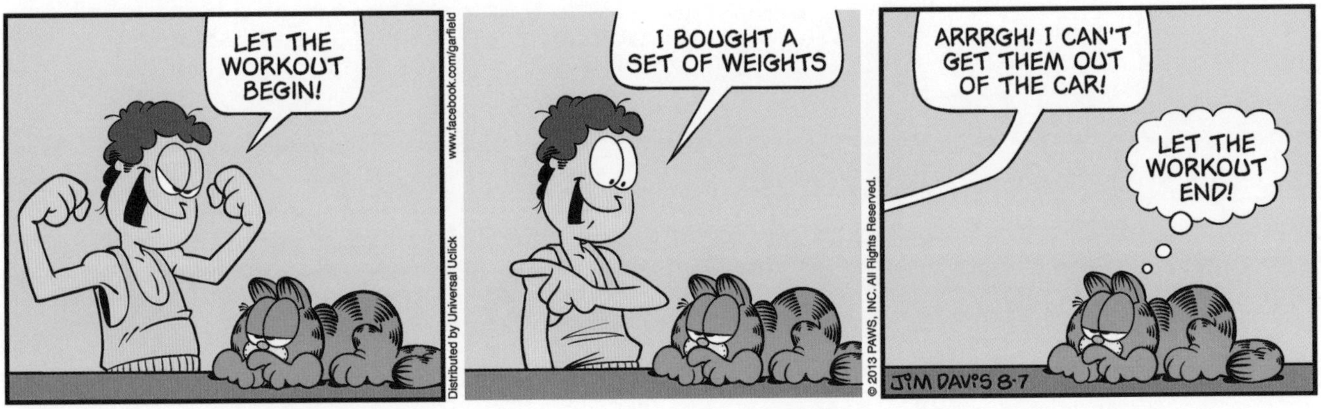
LET THE WORKOUT BEGIN!
Distributed by Universal Uclick
www.facebook.com/garfield
I BOUGHT A SET OF WEIGHTS
© 2013 PAWS, INC. All Rights Reserved.
ARRRGH! I CAN'T GET THEM OUT OF THE CAR!
LET THE WORKOUT END!
JIM DAVIS 8-7

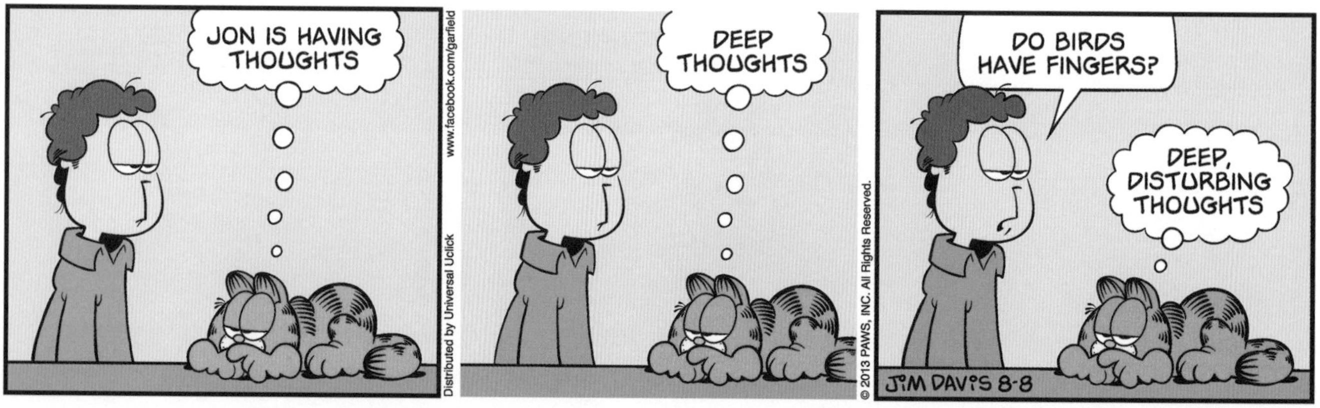
JON IS HAVING THOUGHTS
Distributed by Universal Uclick www.facebook.com/garfield
DEEP THOUGHTS
© 2013 PAWS, INC. All Rights Reserved.
DO BIRDS HAVE FINGERS?
DEEP, DISTURBING THOUGHTS
JIM DAVIS 8-8

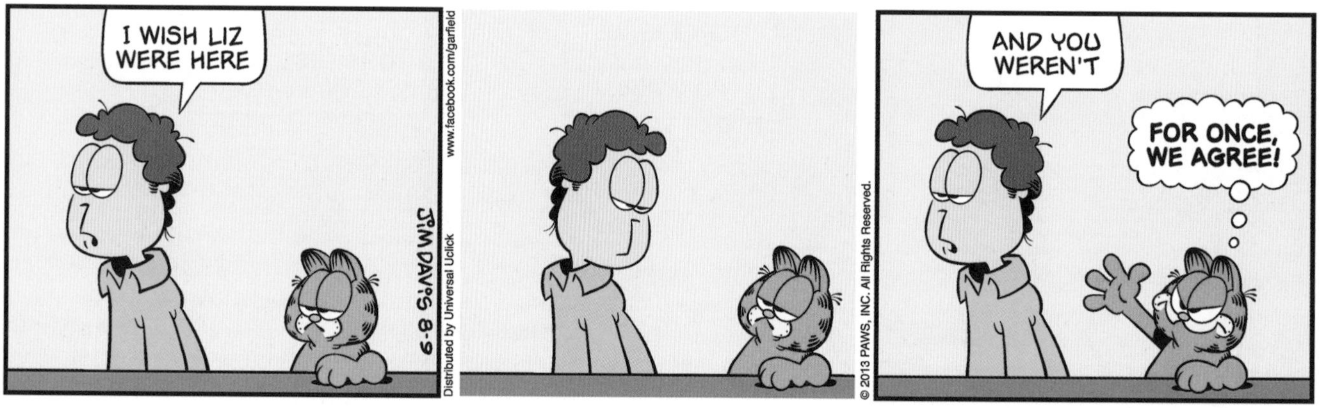
I WISH LIZ WERE HERE
JIM DAVIS 8-9
Distributed by Universal Uclick www.facebook.com/garfield
© 2013 PAWS, INC. All Rights Reserved.
AND YOU WEREN'T
FOR ONCE, WE AGREE!

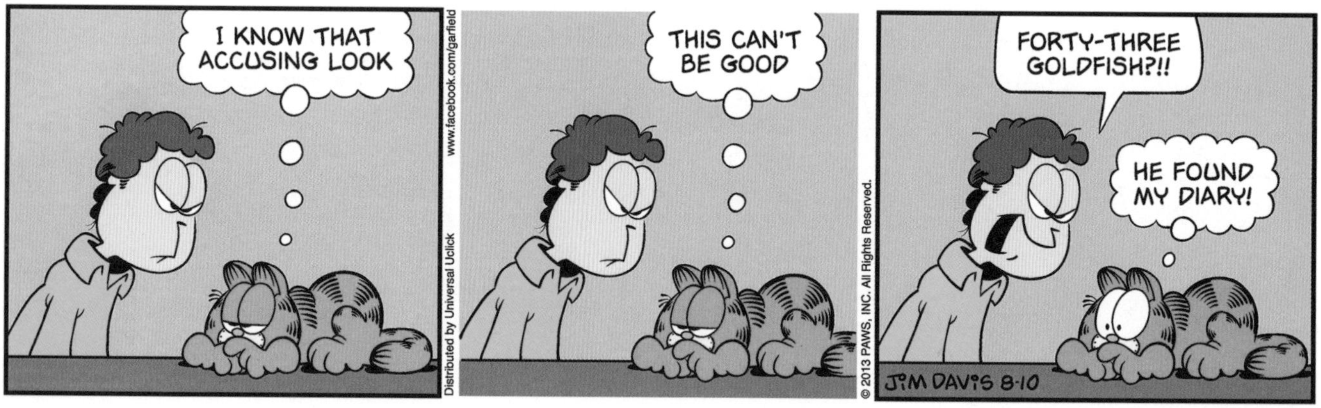
I KNOW THAT ACCUSING LOOK
Distributed by Universal Uclick www.facebook.com/garfield
THIS CAN'T BE GOOD
© 2013 PAWS, INC. All Rights Reserved.
FORTY-THREE GOLDFISH?!!
HE FOUND MY DIARY!
JIM DAVIS 8-10

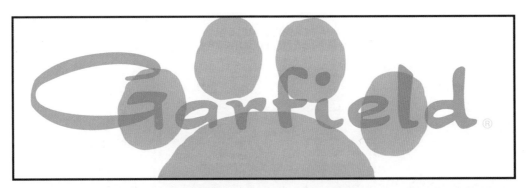

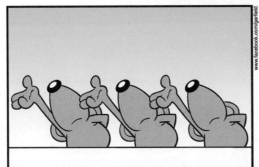

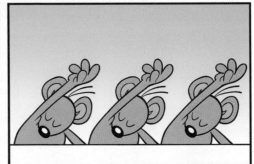

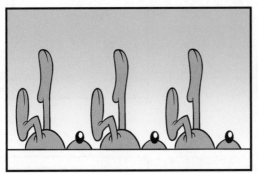

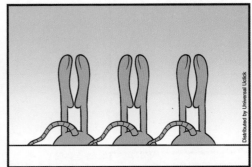

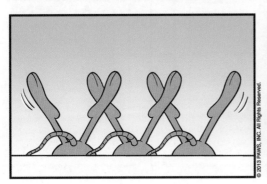

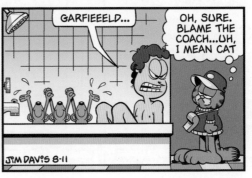

Garfield®
www.facebook.com/garfield
Distributed by Universal Uclick
© 2013 PAWS, INC. All Rights Reserved.
GARFIEEELD...
OH, SURE. BLAME THE COACH...UH, I MEAN CAT
JIM DAVIS 8-11

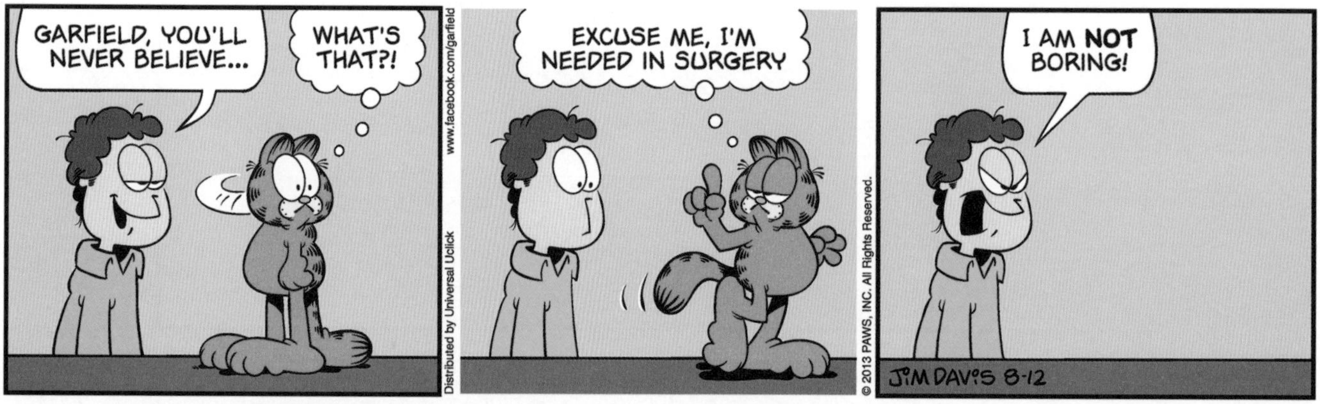
GARFIELD, YOU'LL NEVER BELIEVE...
WHAT'S THAT?!
EXCUSE ME, I'M NEEDED IN SURGERY
I AM **NOT** BORING!
Distributed by Universal Uclick www.facebook.com/garfield
© 2013 PAWS, INC. All Rights Reserved.
JIM DAVIS 8-12

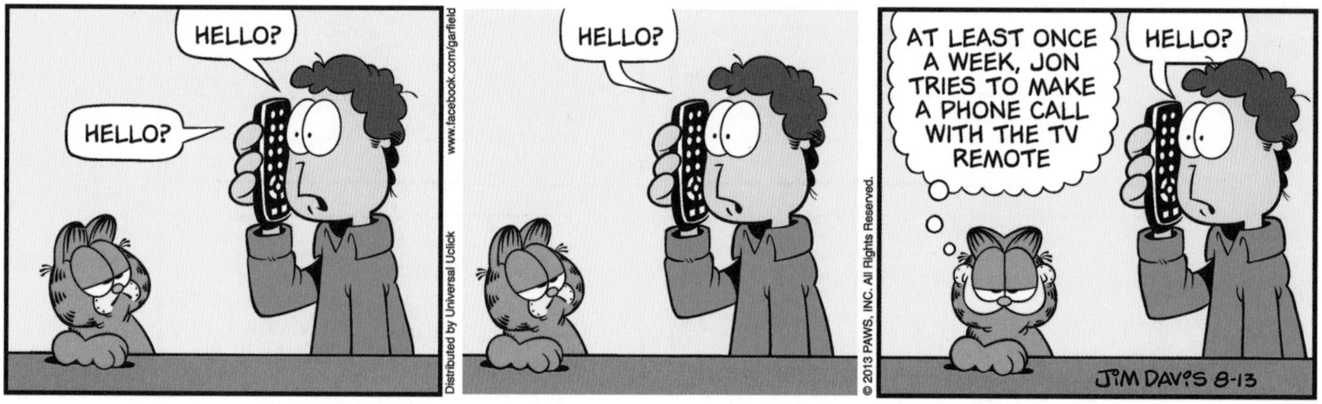
HELLO?
HELLO?
HELLO?
AT LEAST ONCE A WEEK, JON TRIES TO MAKE A PHONE CALL WITH THE TV REMOTE
HELLO?
Distributed by Universal Uclick www.facebook.com/garfield
© 2013 PAWS, INC. All Rights Reserved.
JIM DAVIS 8-13

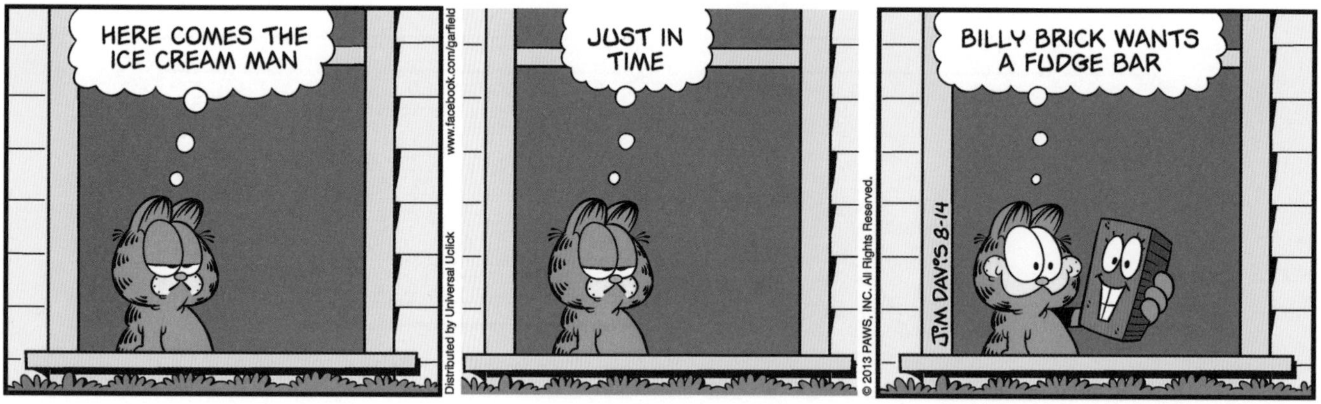
HERE COMES THE ICE CREAM MAN
JUST IN TIME
BILLY BRICK WANTS A FUDGE BAR
Distributed by Universal Uclick www.facebook.com/garfield
© 2013 PAWS, INC. All Rights Reserved.
JIM DAVIS 8-14

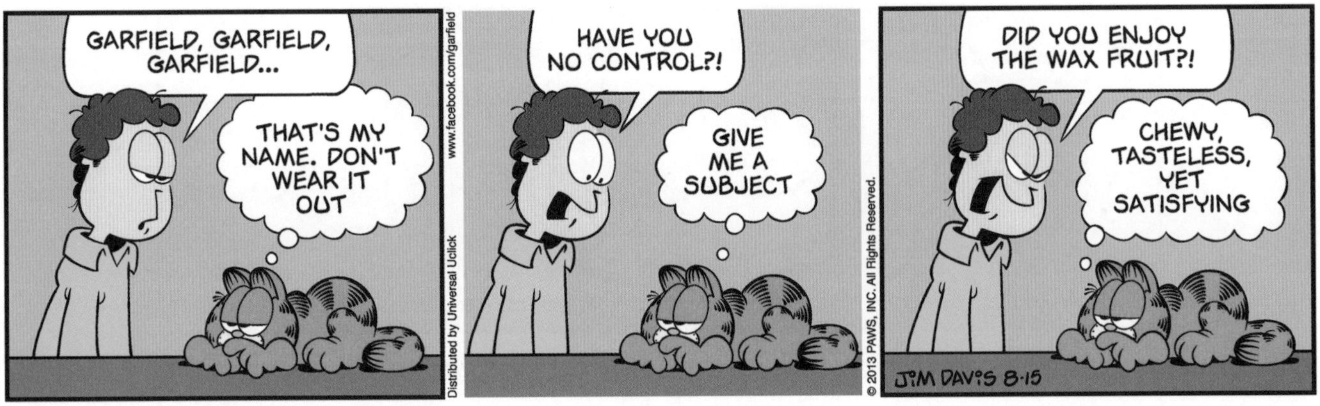
GARFIELD, GARFIELD, GARFIELD...
THAT'S MY NAME. DON'T WEAR IT OUT
Distributed by Universal Uclick
www.facebook.com/garfield
HAVE YOU NO CONTROL?!
GIVE ME A SUBJECT
© 2013 PAWS, INC. All Rights Reserved.
DID YOU ENJOY THE WAX FRUIT?!
CHEWY, TASTELESS, YET SATISFYING
JIM DAVIS 8-15

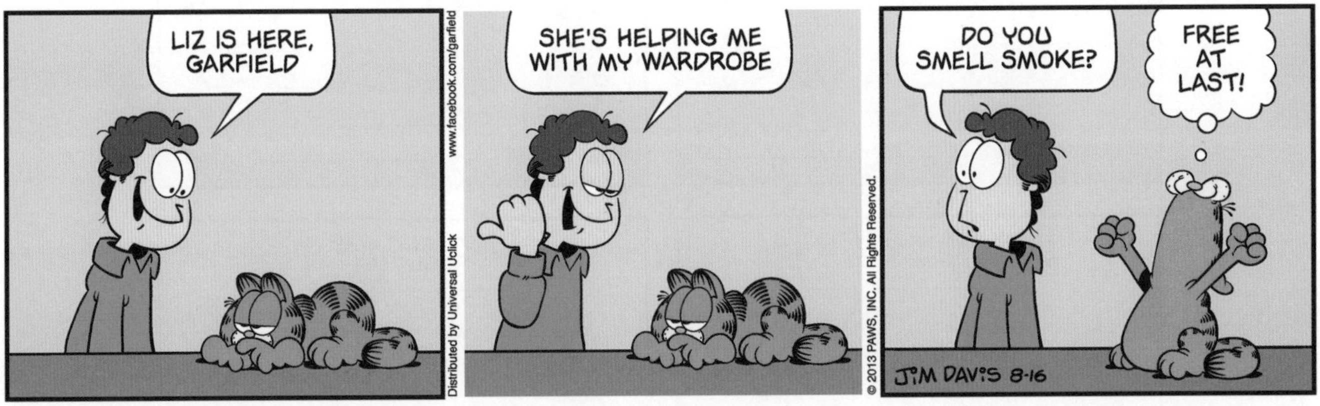
LIZ IS HERE, GARFIELD
Distributed by Universal Uclick
www.facebook.com/garfield
SHE'S HELPING ME WITH MY WARDROBE
© 2013 PAWS, INC. All Rights Reserved.
DO YOU SMELL SMOKE?
FREE AT LAST!
JIM DAVIS 8-16

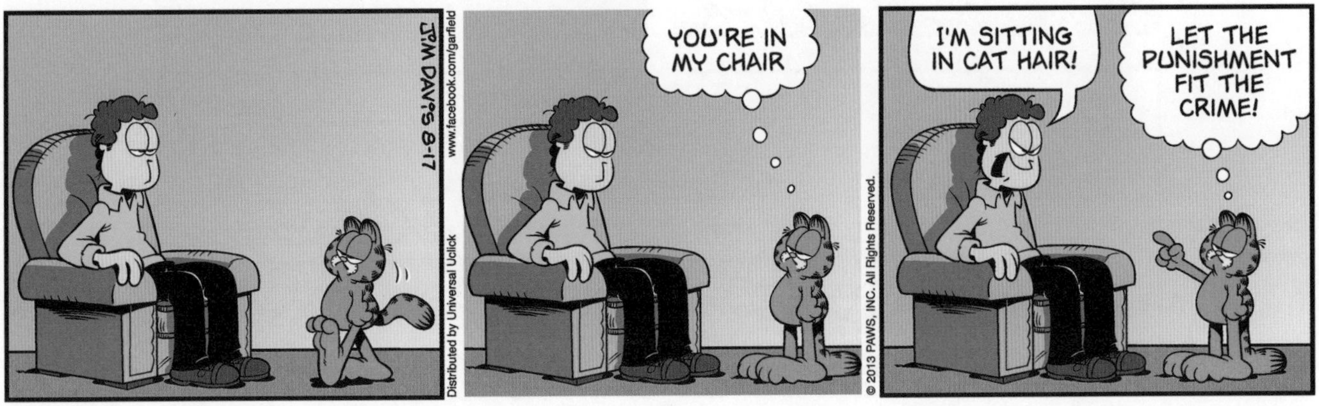
JIM DAVIS 8-17
Distributed by Universal Uclick
www.facebook.com/garfield
YOU'RE IN MY CHAIR
© 2013 PAWS, INC. All Rights Reserved.
I'M SITTING IN CAT HAIR!
LET THE PUNISHMENT FIT THE CRIME!

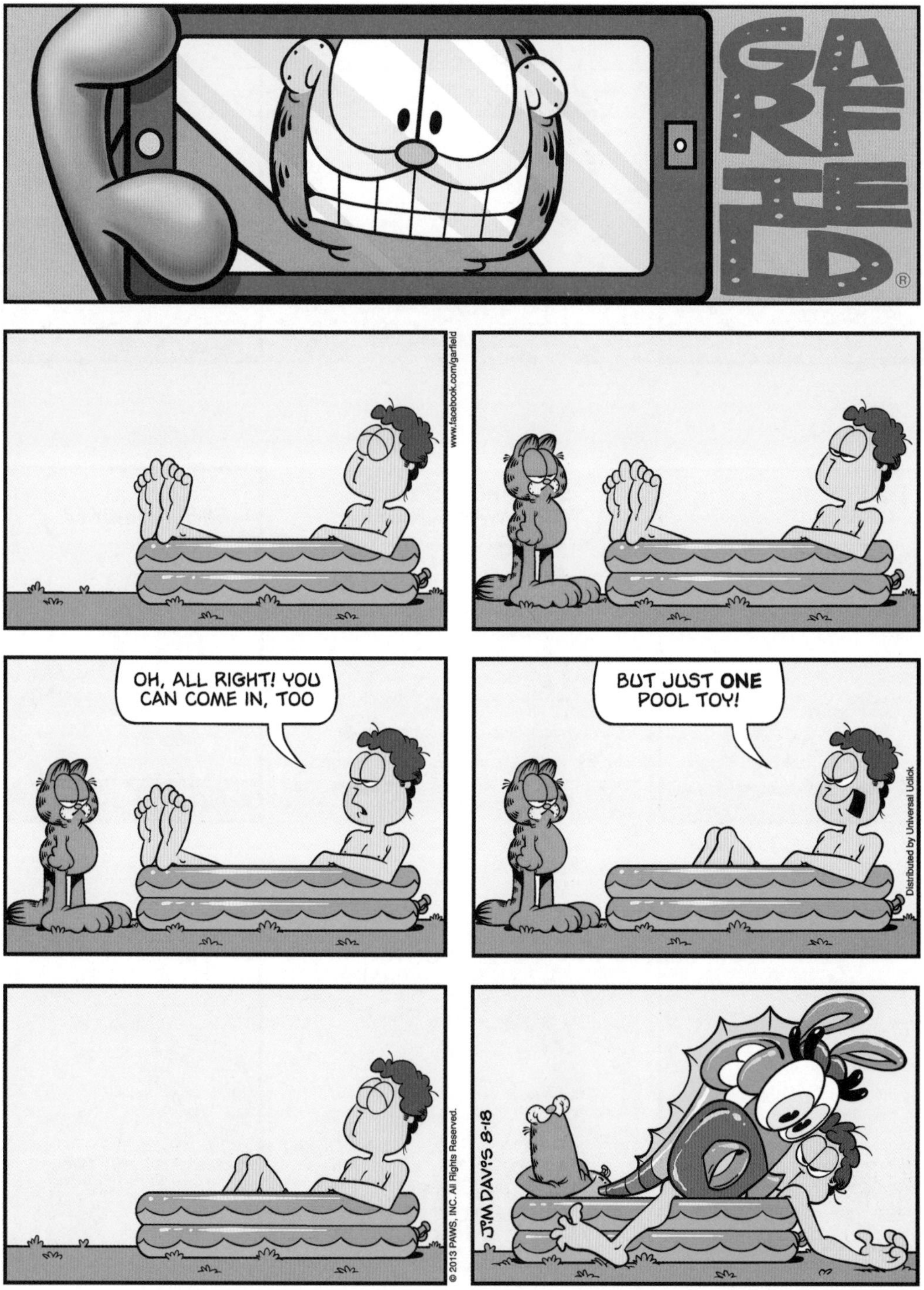
GARFIELD®
www.facebook.com/garfield
OH, ALL RIGHT! YOU CAN COME IN, TOO
BUT JUST **ONE** POOL TOY!
Distributed by Universal Uclick
© 2013 PAWS, INC. All Rights Reserved.
JIM DAVIS 8-18

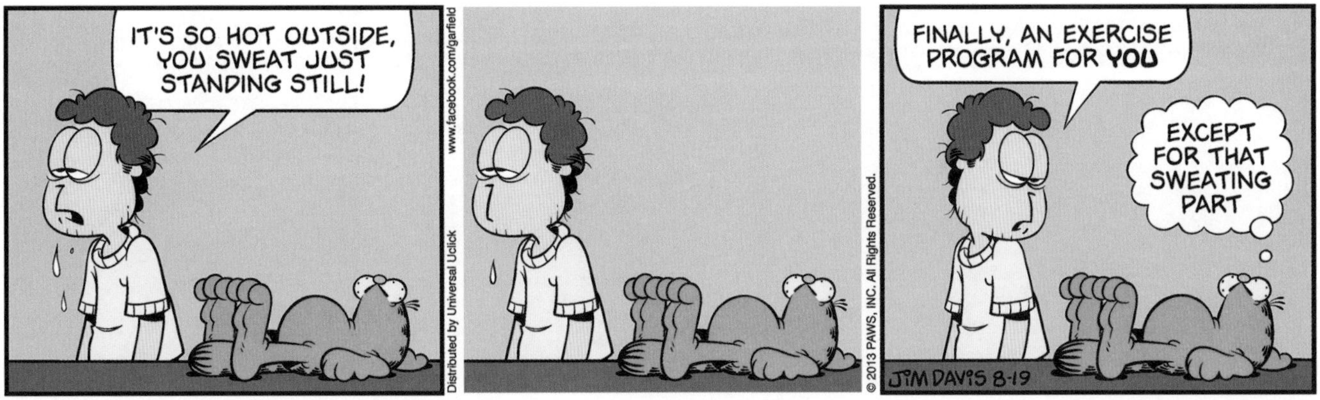
IT'S SO HOT OUTSIDE, YOU SWEAT JUST STANDING STILL!
FINALLY, AN EXERCISE PROGRAM FOR **YOU**
EXCEPT FOR THAT SWEATING PART
JIM DAVIS 8-19
Distributed by Universal Uclick www.facebook.com/garfield
© 2013 PAWS, INC. All Rights Reserved.

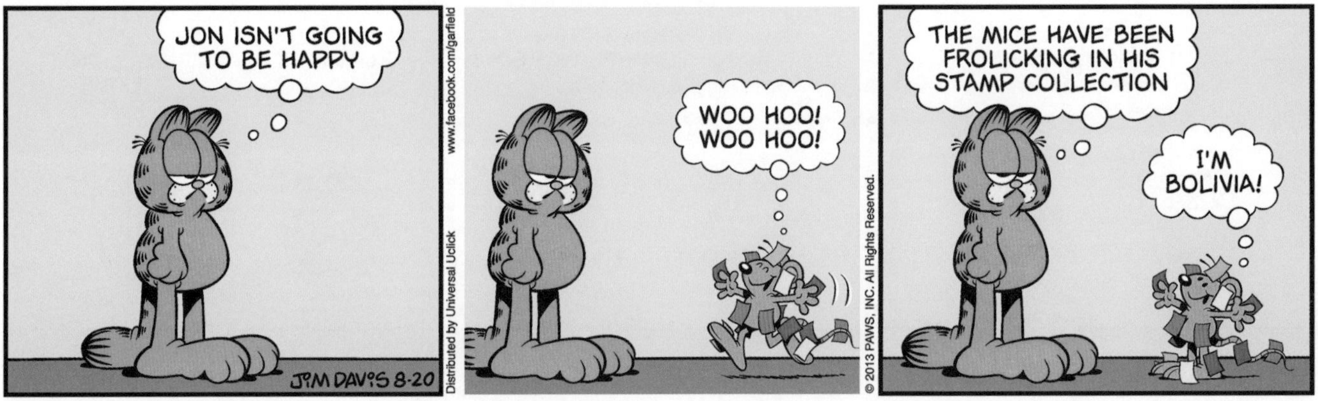
JON ISN'T GOING TO BE HAPPY
JIM DAVIS 8-20
WOO HOO! WOO HOO!
THE MICE HAVE BEEN FROLICKING IN HIS STAMP COLLECTION
I'M BOLIVIA!
Distributed by Universal Uclick www.facebook.com/garfield
© 2013 PAWS, INC. All Rights Reserved.

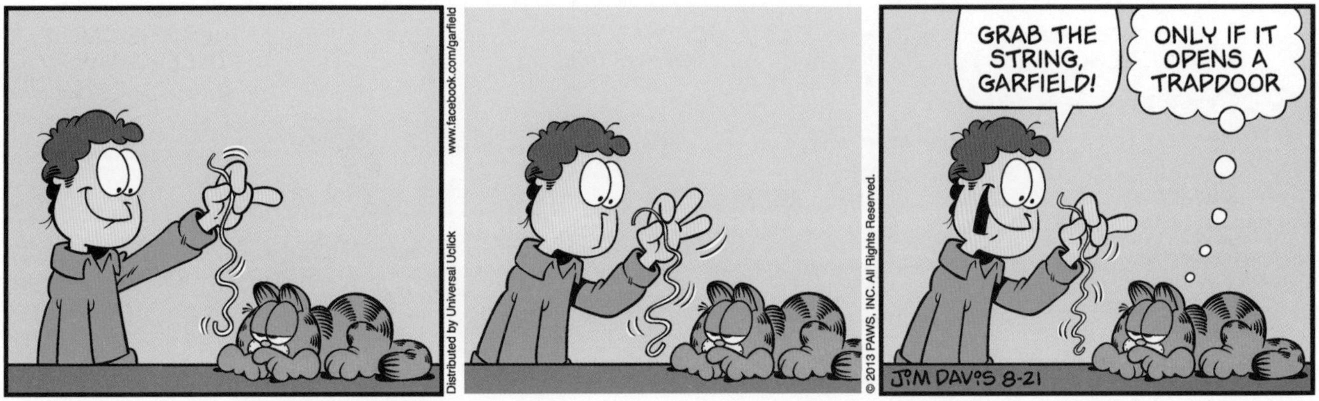
GRAB THE STRING, GARFIELD!
ONLY IF IT OPENS A TRAPDOOR
JIM DAVIS 8-21
Distributed by Universal Uclick www.facebook.com/garfield
© 2013 PAWS, INC. All Rights Reserved.

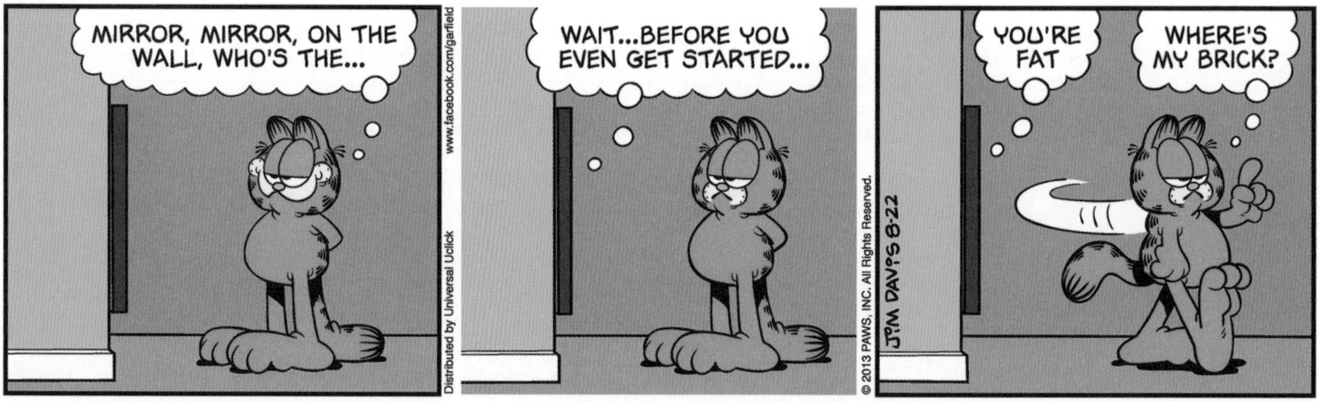
MIRROR, MIRROR, ON THE WALL, WHO'S THE...
www.facebook.com/garfield
Distributed by Universal Uclick
WAIT...BEFORE YOU EVEN GET STARTED...
© 2013 PAWS, INC. All Rights Reserved.
JIM DAVIS 8-22
YOU'RE FAT
WHERE'S MY BRICK?

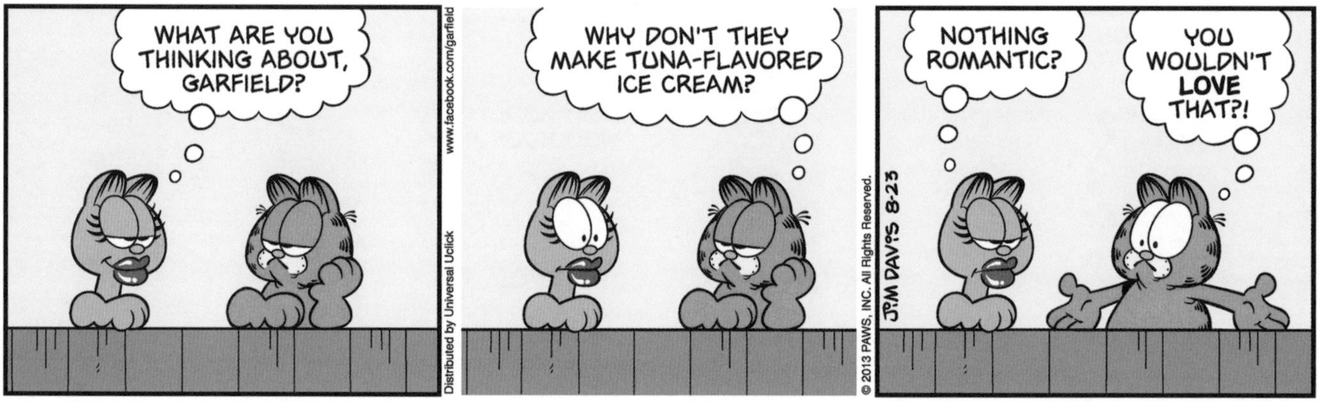
WHAT ARE YOU THINKING ABOUT, GARFIELD?
www.facebook.com/garfield
Distributed by Universal Uclick
WHY DON'T THEY MAKE TUNA-FLAVORED ICE CREAM?
© 2013 PAWS, INC. All Rights Reserved.
JIM DAVIS 8-23
NOTHING ROMANTIC?
YOU WOULDN'T **LOVE** THAT?!

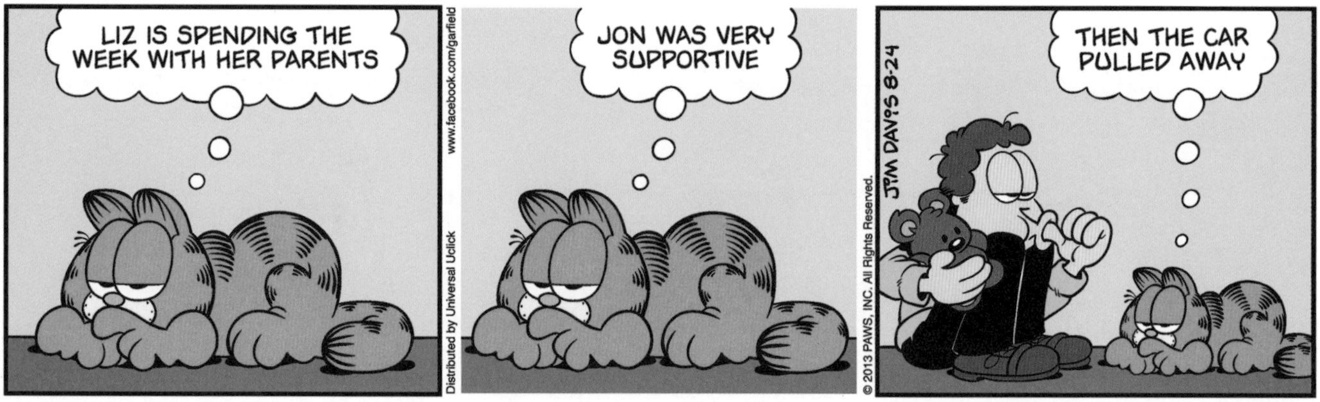
LIZ IS SPENDING THE WEEK WITH HER PARENTS
www.facebook.com/garfield
Distributed by Universal Uclick
JON WAS VERY SUPPORTIVE
© 2013 PAWS, INC. All Rights Reserved.
JIM DAVIS 8-24
THEN THE CAR PULLED AWAY

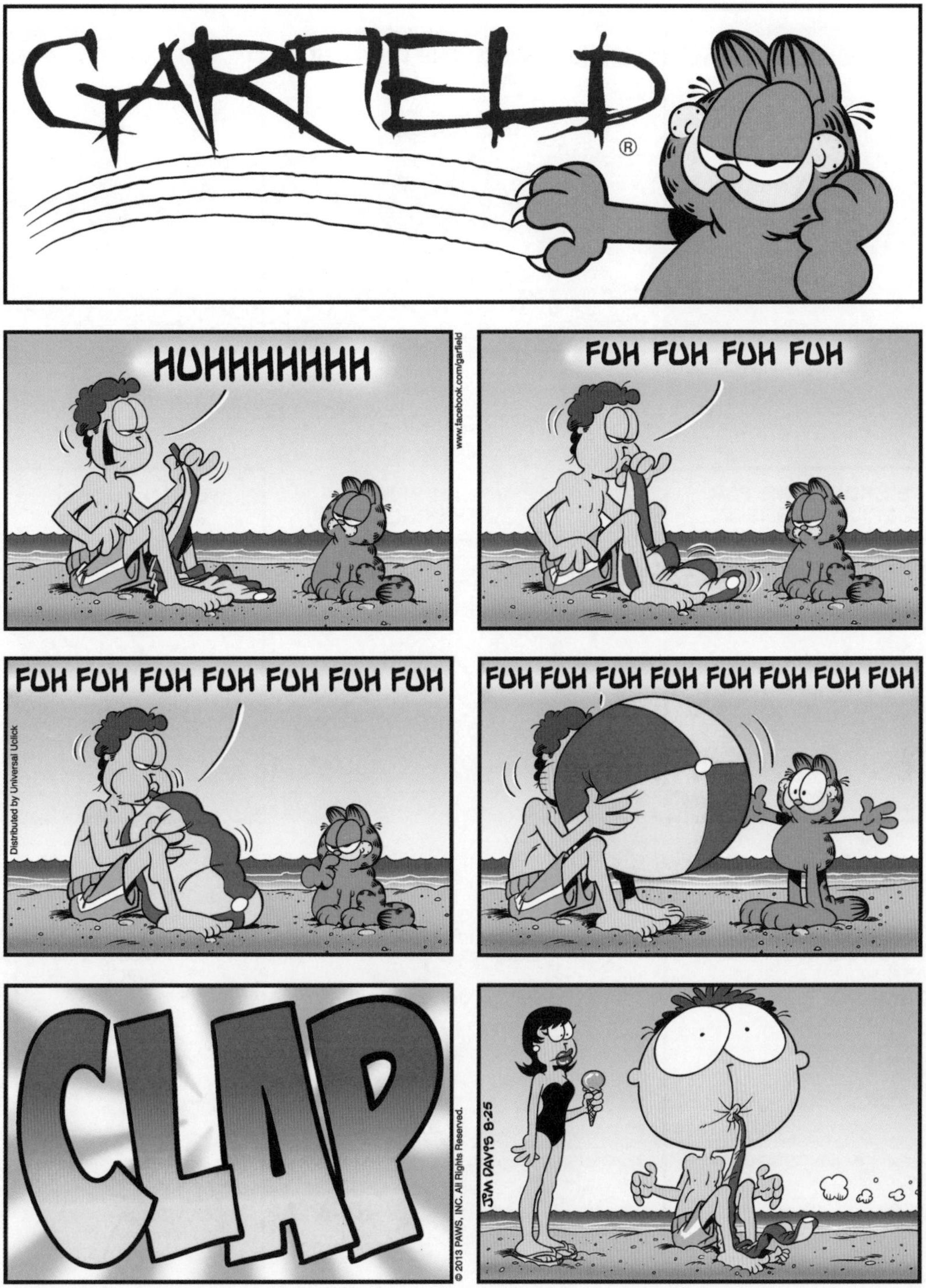

GARFIELD®
HUHHHHHHH
www.facebook.com/garfield
FUH FUH FUH FUH
FUH FUH FUH FUH FUH FUH FUH
Distributed by Universal Uclick
FUH FUH FUH FUH FUH FUH FUH FUH
CLAP
© 2013 PAWS, INC. All Rights Reserved.
JIM DAVIS 8-25

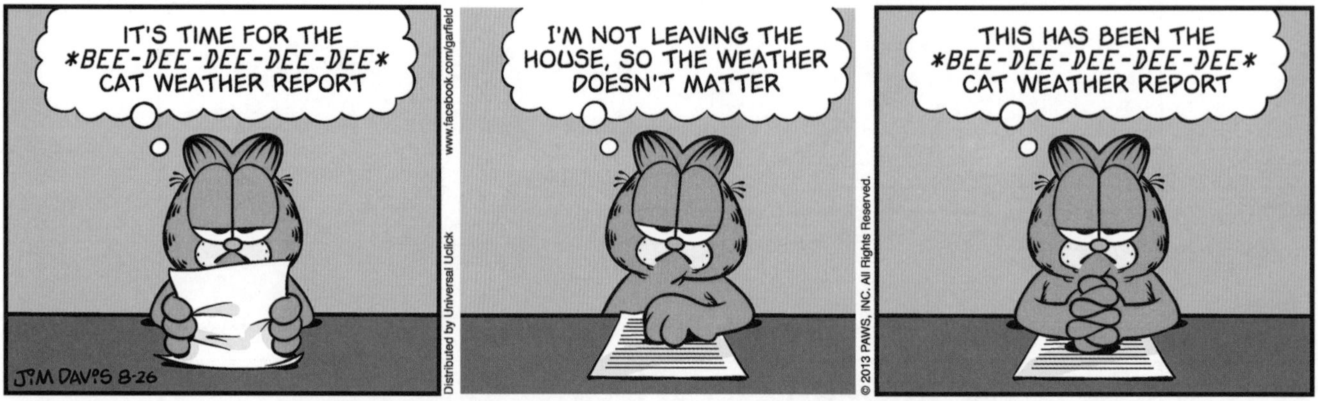
IT'S TIME FOR THE *BEE-DEE-DEE-DEE-DEE* CAT WEATHER REPORT
JIM DAVIS 8-26
I'M NOT LEAVING THE HOUSE, SO THE WEATHER DOESN'T MATTER
THIS HAS BEEN THE *BEE-DEE-DEE-DEE-DEE* CAT WEATHER REPORT
Distributed by Universal Uclick www.facebook.com/garfield
© 2013 PAWS, INC. All Rights Reserved.

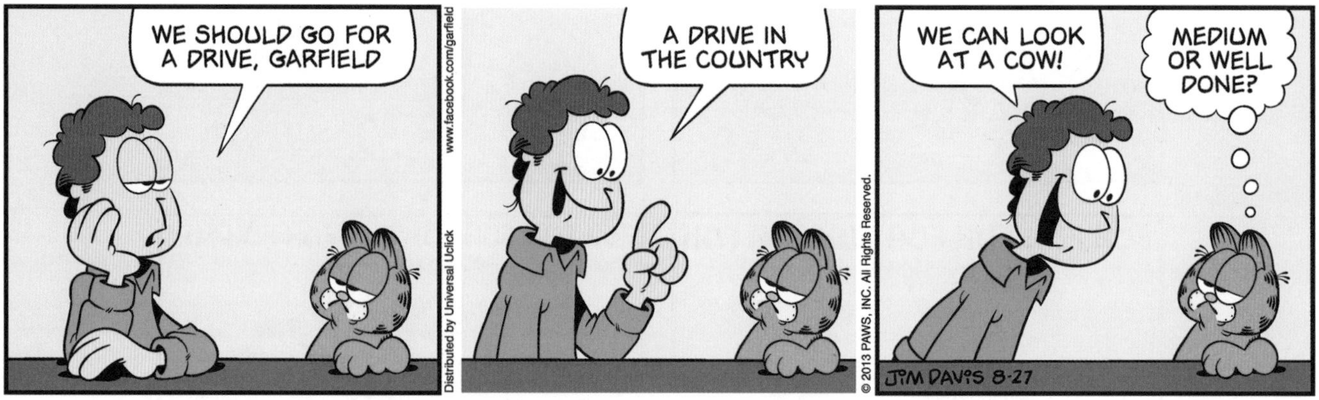
WE SHOULD GO FOR A DRIVE, GARFIELD
A DRIVE IN THE COUNTRY
WE CAN LOOK AT A COW!
MEDIUM OR WELL DONE?
JIM DAVIS 8-27
Distributed by Universal Uclick www.facebook.com/garfield
© 2013 PAWS, INC. All Rights Reserved.

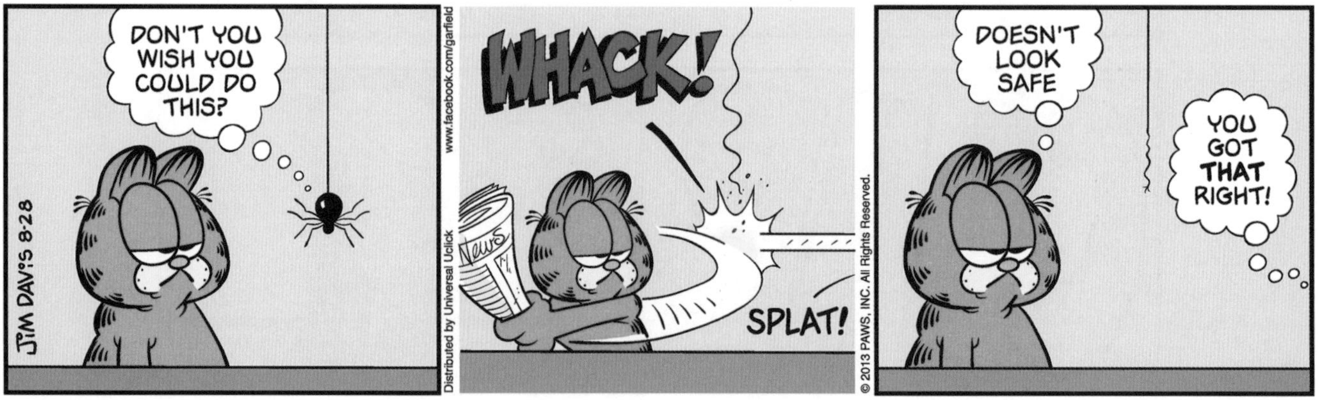
DON'T YOU WISH YOU COULD DO THIS?
JIM DAVIS 8-28
WHACK!
SPLAT!
DOESN'T LOOK SAFE
YOU GOT THAT RIGHT!
Distributed by Universal Uclick www.facebook.com/garfield
© 2013 PAWS, INC. All Rights Reserved.

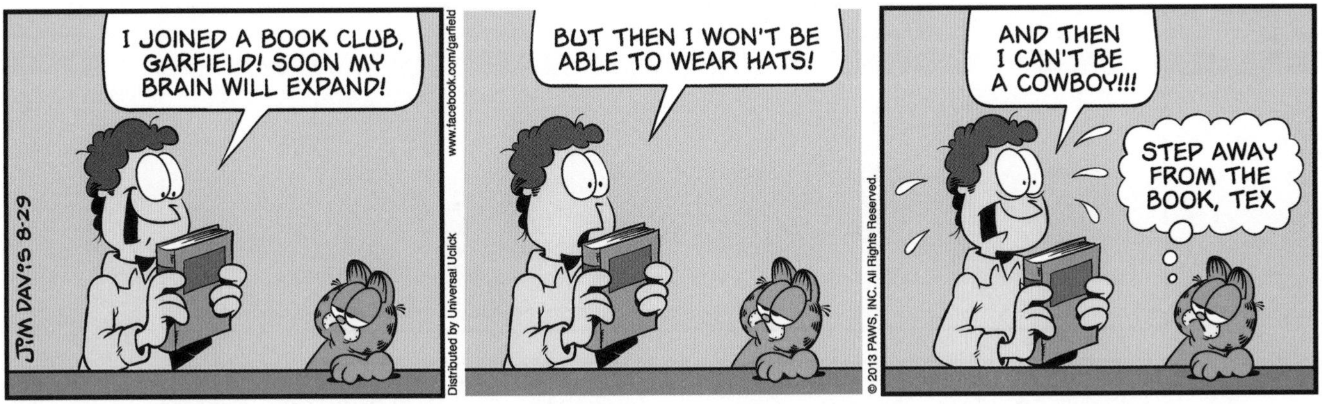
JIM DAVIS 8-29
I JOINED A BOOK CLUB, GARFIELD! SOON MY BRAIN WILL EXPAND!
Distributed by Universal Uclick
www.facebook.com/garfield
BUT THEN I WON'T BE ABLE TO WEAR HATS!
© 2013 PAWS, INC. All Rights Reserved.
AND THEN I CAN'T BE A COWBOY!!!
STEP AWAY FROM THE BOOK, TEX

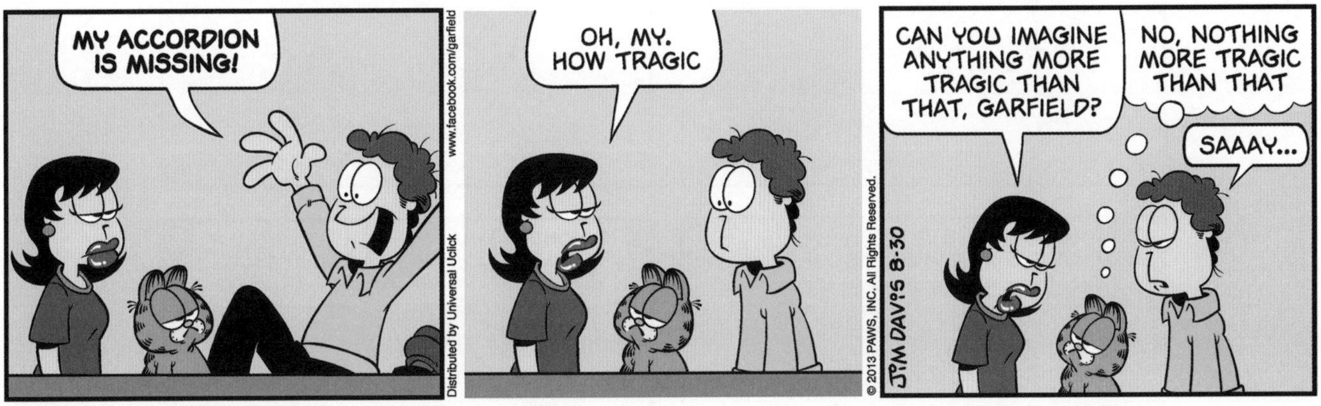
MY ACCORDION IS MISSING!
Distributed by Universal Uclick
www.facebook.com/garfield
OH, MY. HOW TRAGIC
© 2013 PAWS, INC. All Rights Reserved.
JIM DAVIS 8-30
CAN YOU IMAGINE ANYTHING MORE TRAGIC THAN THAT, GARFIELD?
NO, NOTHING MORE TRAGIC THAN THAT
SAAAY...

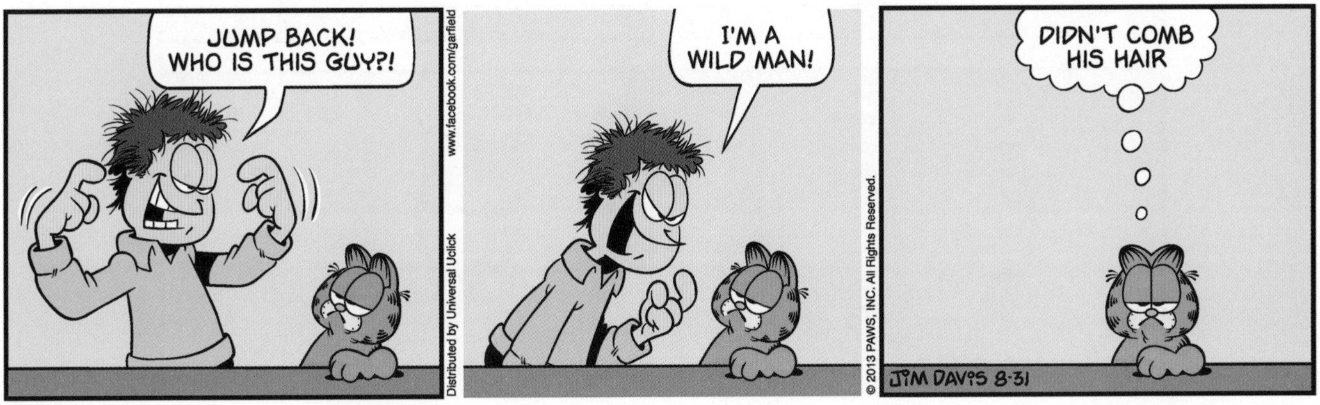
JUMP BACK! WHO IS THIS GUY?!
Distributed by Universal Uclick
www.facebook.com/garfield
I'M A WILD MAN!
© 2013 PAWS, INC. All Rights Reserved.
DIDN'T COMB HIS HAIR
JIM DAVIS 8-31

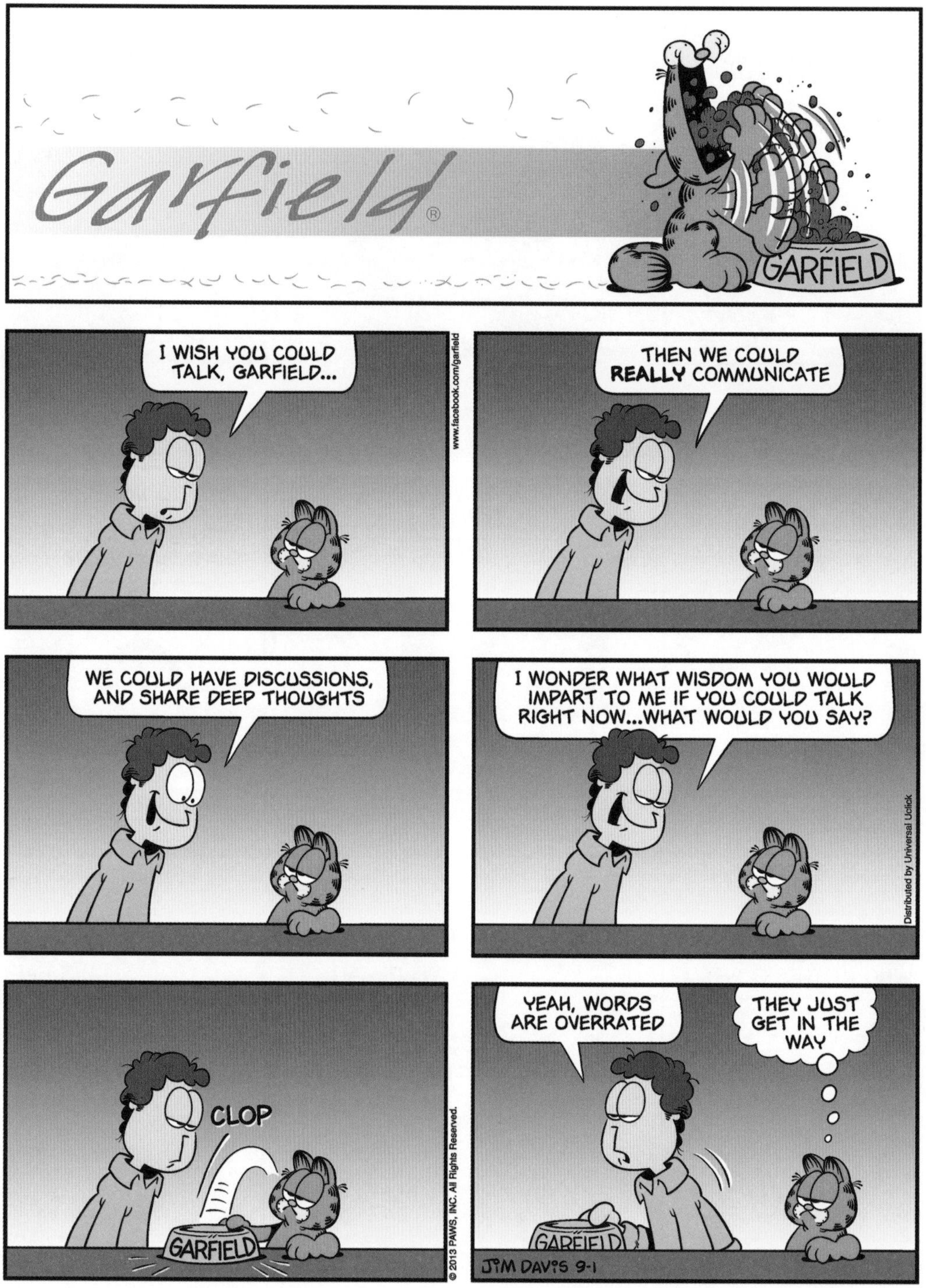
Garfield®
GARFIELD
I WISH YOU COULD TALK, GARFIELD...
www.facebook.com/garfield
THEN WE COULD REALLY COMMUNICATE
WE COULD HAVE DISCUSSIONS, AND SHARE DEEP THOUGHTS
I WONDER WHAT WISDOM YOU WOULD IMPART TO ME IF YOU COULD TALK RIGHT NOW...WHAT WOULD YOU SAY?
Distributed by Universal Uclick
CLOP
GARFIELD
© 2013 PAWS, INC. All Rights Reserved.
YEAH, WORDS ARE OVERRATED
THEY JUST GET IN THE WAY
GARFIELD
JIM DAVIS 9-1

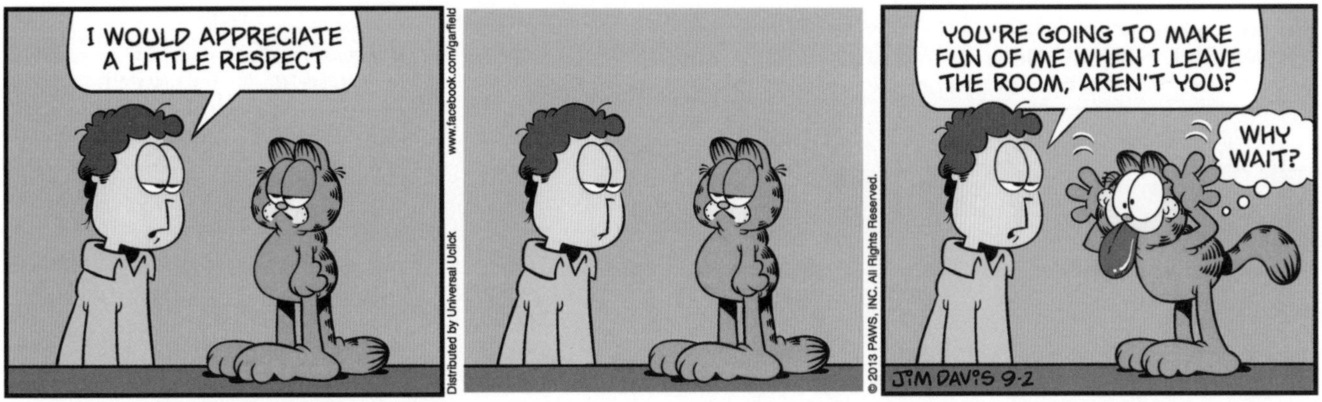
I WOULD APPRECIATE A LITTLE RESPECT
Distributed by Universal Uclick
www.facebook.com/garfield
YOU'RE GOING TO MAKE FUN OF ME WHEN I LEAVE THE ROOM, AREN'T YOU?
WHY WAIT?
© 2013 PAWS, INC. All Rights Reserved.
JIM DAVIS 9-2

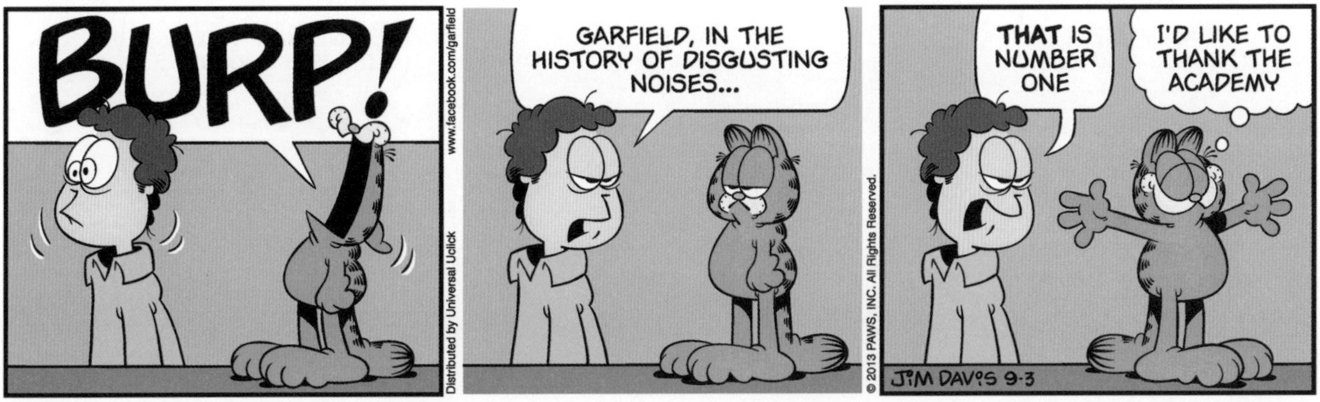
BURP!
Distributed by Universal Uclick
www.facebook.com/garfield
GARFIELD, IN THE HISTORY OF DISGUSTING NOISES...
THAT IS NUMBER ONE
I'D LIKE TO THANK THE ACADEMY
© 2013 PAWS, INC. All Rights Reserved.
JIM DAVIS 9-3

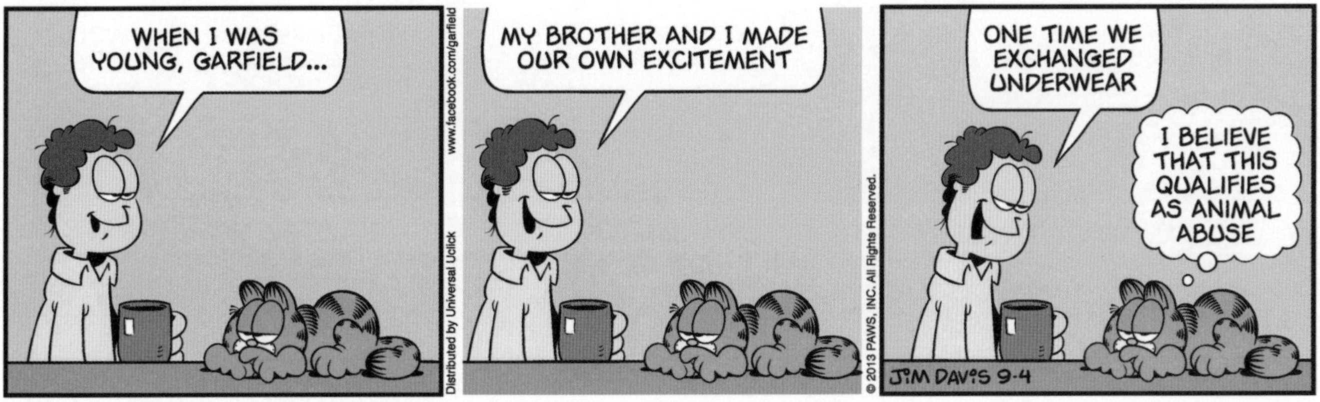
WHEN I WAS YOUNG, GARFIELD...
Distributed by Universal Uclick
www.facebook.com/garfield
MY BROTHER AND I MADE OUR OWN EXCITEMENT
ONE TIME WE EXCHANGED UNDERWEAR
I BELIEVE THAT THIS QUALIFIES AS ANIMAL ABUSE
© 2013 PAWS, INC. All Rights Reserved.
JIM DAVIS 9-4

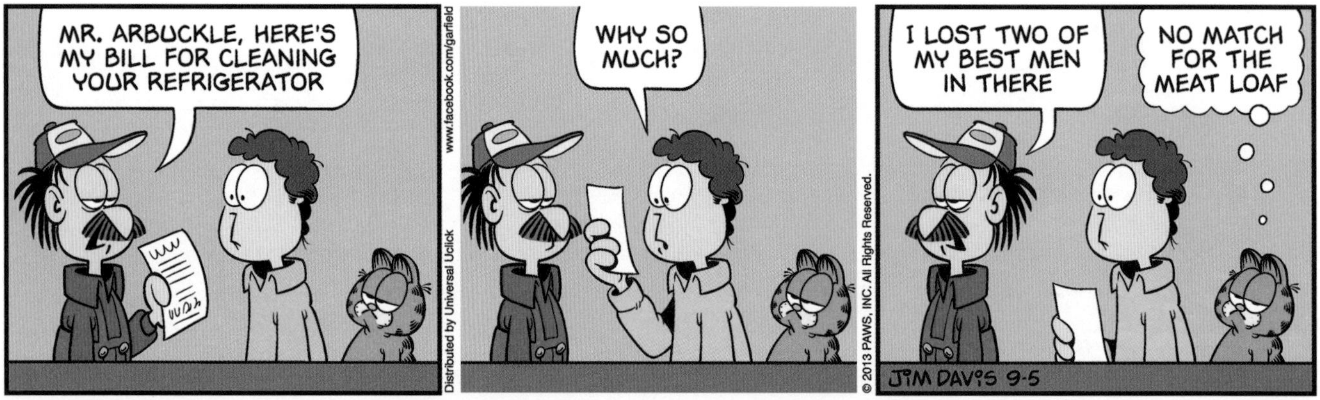
MR. ARBUCKLE, HERE'S MY BILL FOR CLEANING YOUR REFRIGERATOR
WHY SO MUCH?
I LOST TWO OF MY BEST MEN IN THERE
NO MATCH FOR THE MEAT LOAF
JIM DAVIS 9-5
Distributed by Universal Uclick www.facebook.com/garfield
© 2013 PAWS, INC. All Rights Reserved.

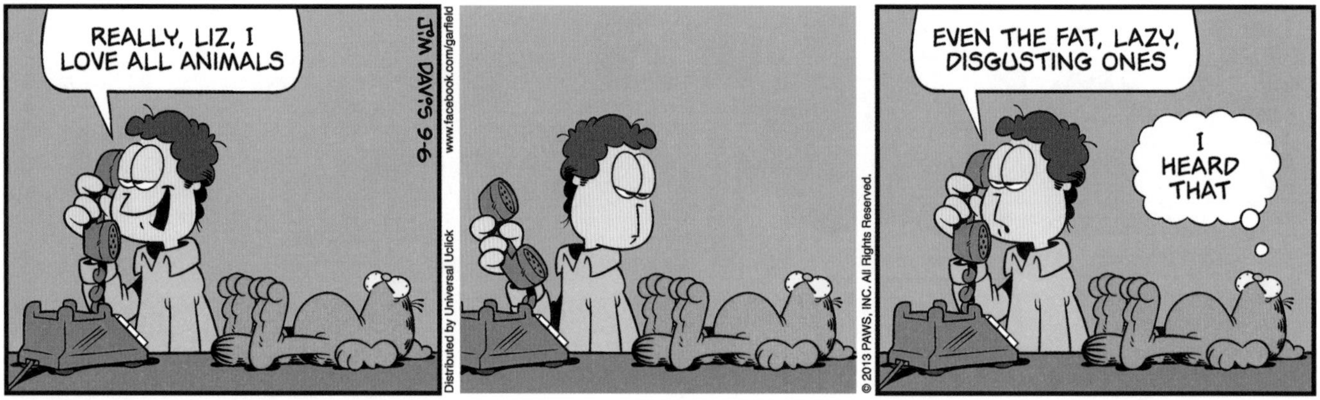
REALLY, LIZ, I LOVE ALL ANIMALS
JIM DAVIS 9-6
EVEN THE FAT, LAZY, DISGUSTING ONES
I HEARD THAT
Distributed by Universal Uclick www.facebook.com/garfield
© 2013 PAWS, INC. All Rights Reserved.

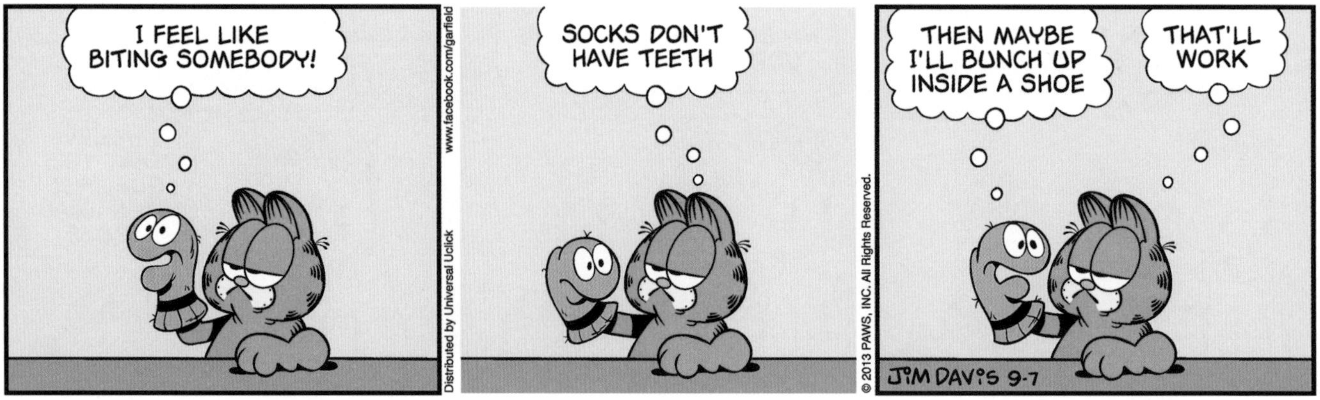
I FEEL LIKE BITING SOMEBODY!
SOCKS DON'T HAVE TEETH
THEN MAYBE I'LL BUNCH UP INSIDE A SHOE
THAT'LL WORK
JIM DAVIS 9-7
Distributed by Universal Uclick www.facebook.com/garfield
© 2013 PAWS, INC. All Rights Reserved.

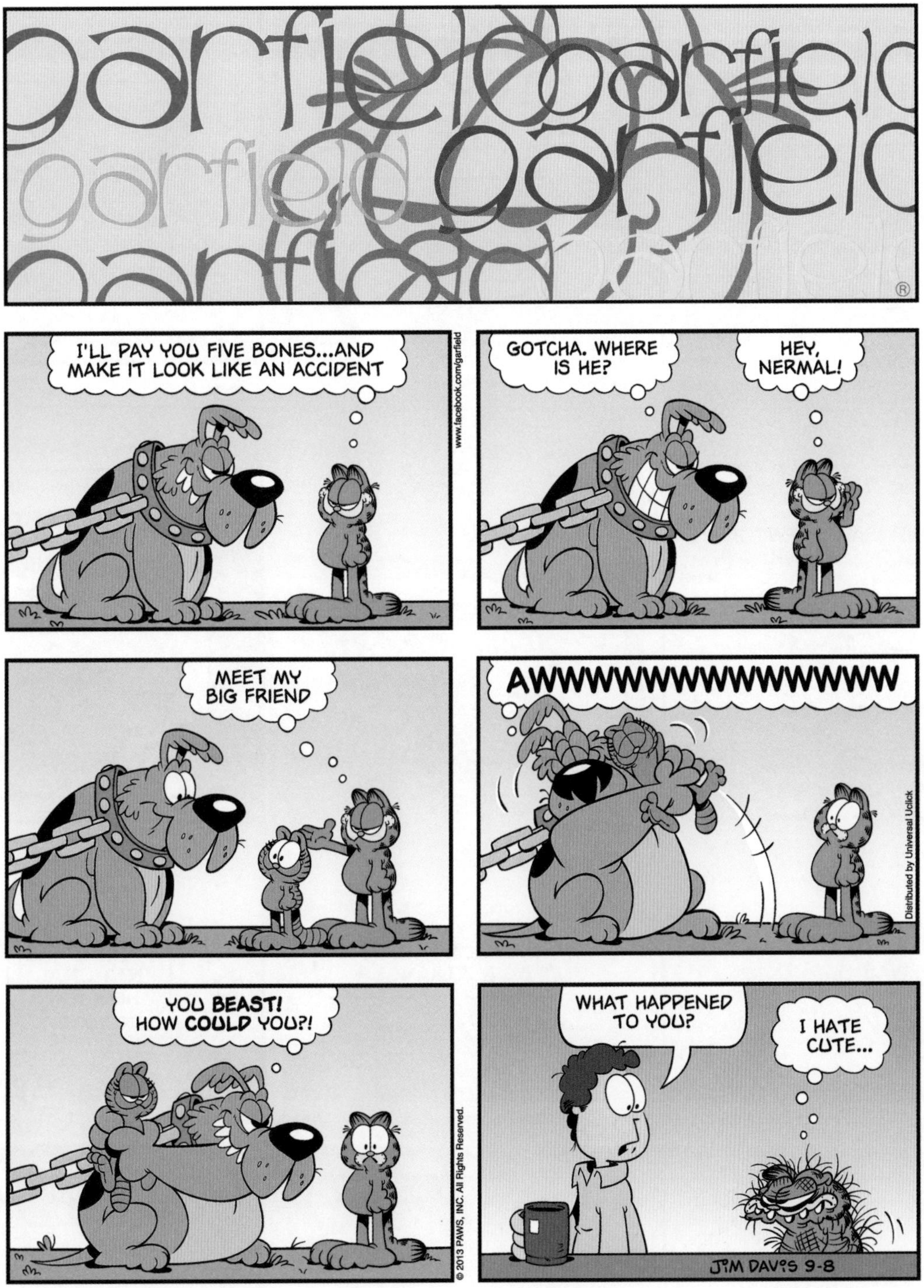
garfield
I'LL PAY YOU FIVE BONES...AND MAKE IT LOOK LIKE AN ACCIDENT
www.facebook.com/garfield
GOTCHA. WHERE IS HE?
HEY, NERMAL!
MEET MY BIG FRIEND
AWWWWWWWWWWWWW
Distributed by Universal Uclick
YOU BEAST! HOW COULD YOU?!
© 2013 PAWS, INC. All Rights Reserved.
WHAT HAPPENED TO YOU?
I HATE CUTE...
JIM DAVIS 9-8

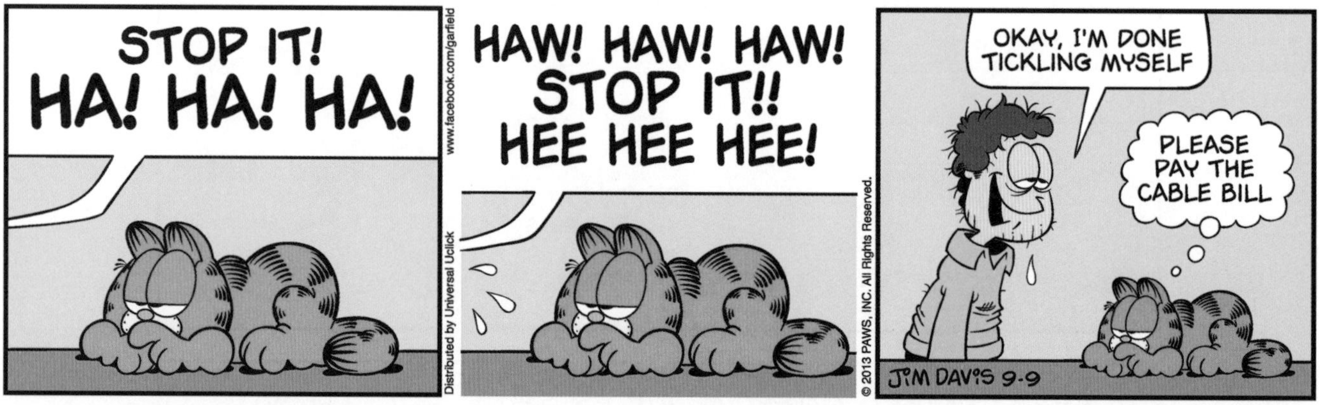
STOP IT!
HA! HA! HA!
Distributed by Universal Uclick www.facebook.com/garfield
HAW! HAW! HAW! STOP IT!! HEE HEE HEE!
© 2013 PAWS, INC. All Rights Reserved.
OKAY, I'M DONE TICKLING MYSELF
PLEASE PAY THE CABLE BILL
JIM DAVIS 9-9

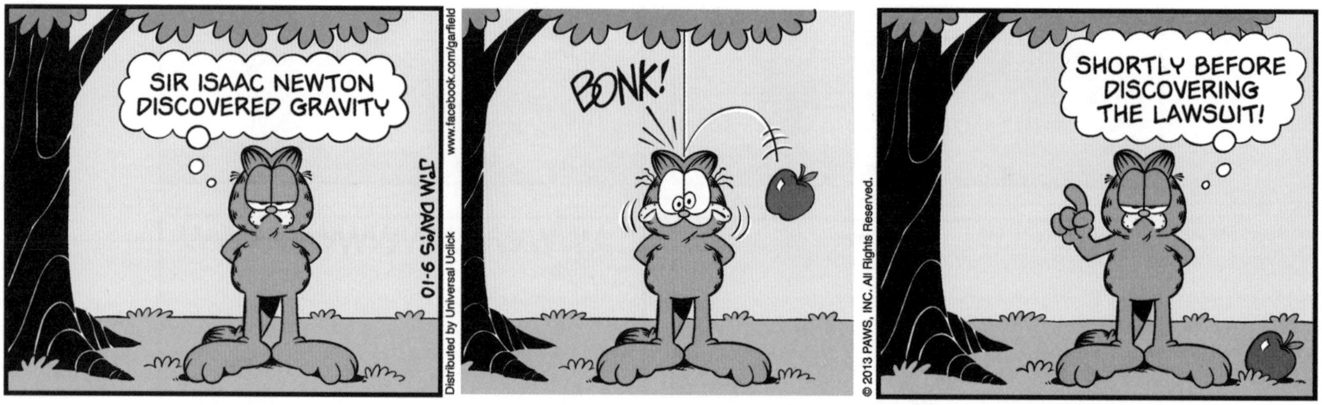
SIR ISAAC NEWTON DISCOVERED GRAVITY
JIM DAVIS 9-10
Distributed by Universal Uclick www.facebook.com/garfield
BONK!
© 2013 PAWS, INC. All Rights Reserved.
SHORTLY BEFORE DISCOVERING THE LAWSUIT!

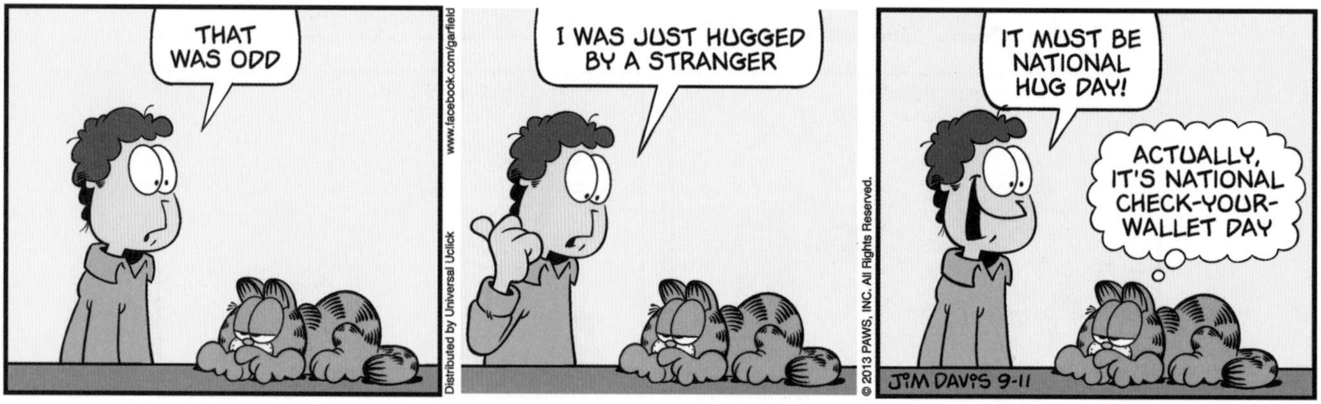
THAT WAS ODD
Distributed by Universal Uclick www.facebook.com/garfield
I WAS JUST HUGGED BY A STRANGER
© 2013 PAWS, INC. All Rights Reserved.
IT MUST BE NATIONAL HUG DAY!
ACTUALLY, IT'S NATIONAL CHECK-YOUR-WALLET DAY
JIM DAVIS 9-11

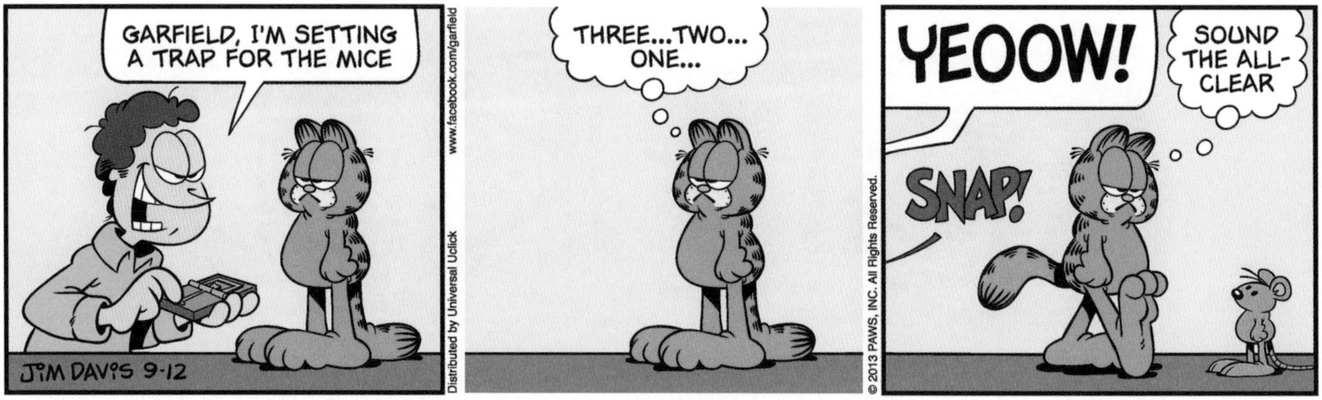
GARFIELD, I'M SETTING A TRAP FOR THE MICE
JIM DAVIS 9-12
Distributed by Universal Uclick www.facebook.com/garfield
THREE...TWO... ONE...
© 2013 PAWS, INC. All Rights Reserved.
YEOOW!
SNAP!
SOUND THE ALL-CLEAR

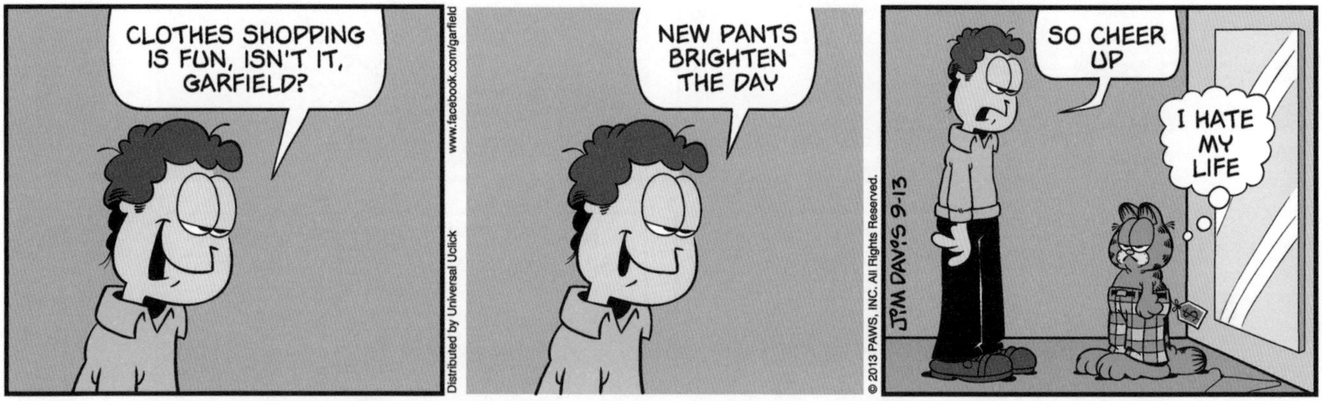
CLOTHES SHOPPING IS FUN, ISN'T IT, GARFIELD?
Distributed by Universal Uclick www.facebook.com/garfield
NEW PANTS BRIGHTEN THE DAY
© 2013 PAWS, INC. All Rights Reserved.
JIM DAVIS 9-13
SO CHEER UP
I HATE MY LIFE

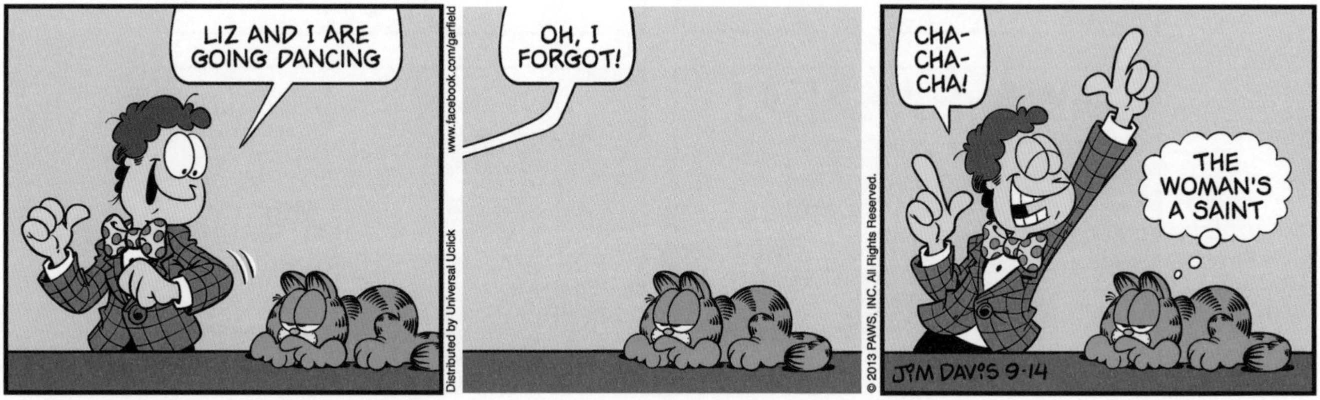
LIZ AND I ARE GOING DANCING
Distributed by Universal Uclick www.facebook.com/garfield
OH, I FORGOT!
© 2013 PAWS, INC. All Rights Reserved.
CHA-CHA-CHA!
THE WOMAN'S A SAINT
JIM DAVIS 9-14

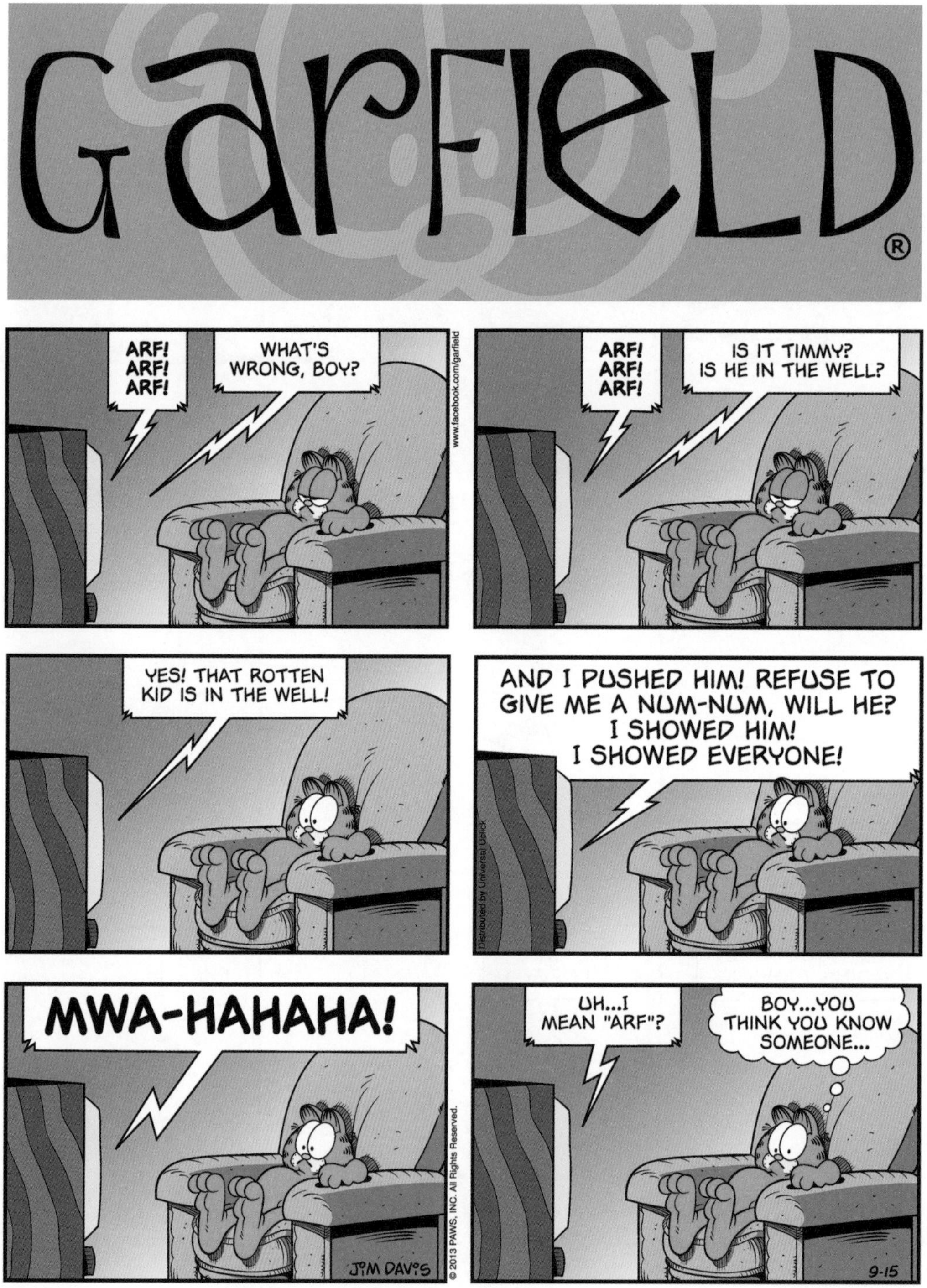
GARFIELD®
ARF! ARF! ARF!
WHAT'S WRONG, BOY?
ARF! ARF! ARF!
IS IT TIMMY? IS HE IN THE WELL?
YES! THAT ROTTEN KID IS IN THE WELL!
AND I PUSHED HIM! REFUSE TO GIVE ME A NUM-NUM, WILL HE? I SHOWED HIM! I SHOWED EVERYONE!
MWA-HAHAHA!
UH...I MEAN "ARF"?
BOY...YOU THINK YOU KNOW SOMEONE...
JIM DAVIS
9-15
www.facebook.com/garfield
Distributed by Universal Uclick
© 2013 PAWS, INC. All Rights Reserved.

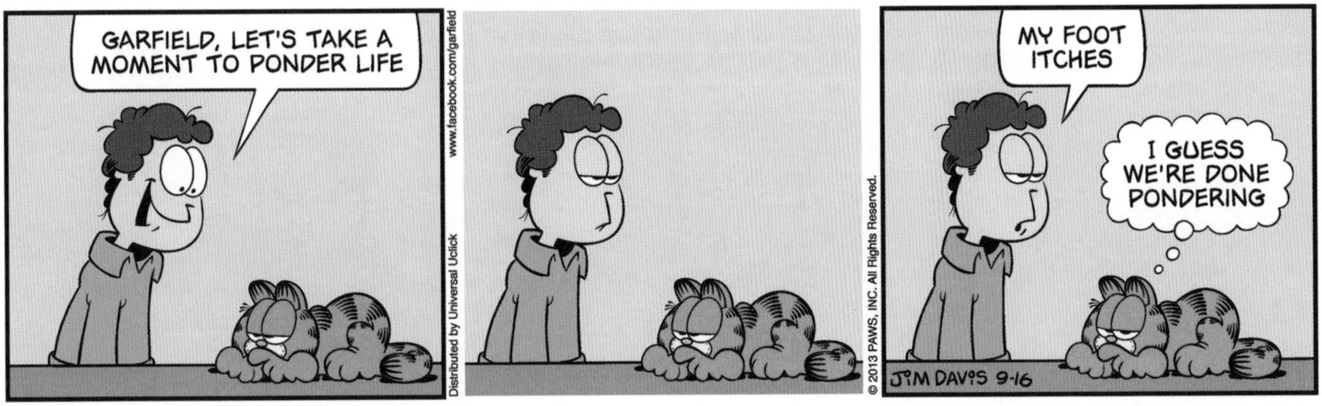
GARFIELD, LET'S TAKE A MOMENT TO PONDER LIFE
MY FOOT ITCHES
I GUESS WE'RE DONE PONDERING
JIM DAVIS 9-16
Distributed by Universal Uclick
www.facebook.com/garfield
© 2013 PAWS, INC. All Rights Reserved.

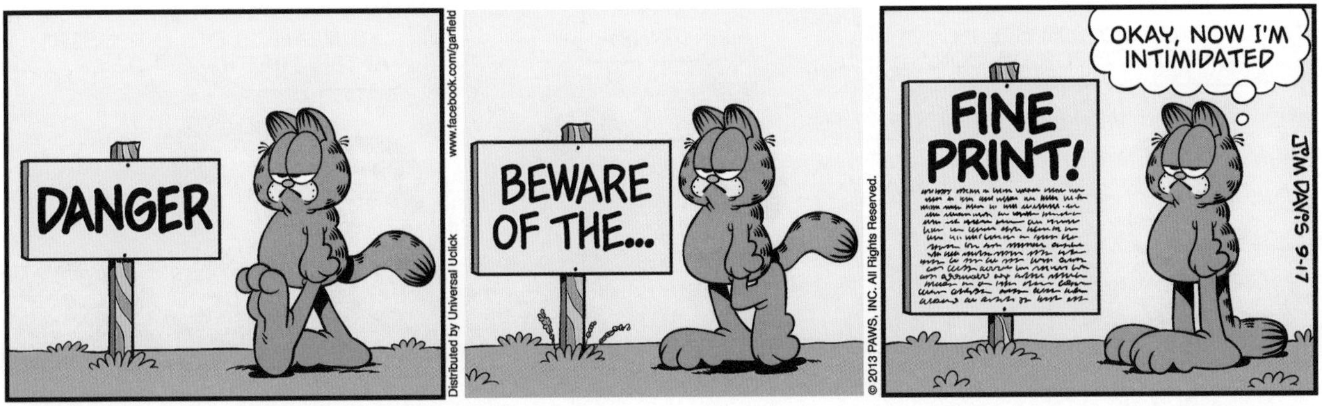
DANGER
BEWARE OF THE...
FINE PRINT!
OKAY, NOW I'M INTIMIDATED
JIM DAVIS 9-17
Distributed by Universal Uclick
www.facebook.com/garfield
© 2013 PAWS, INC. All Rights Reserved.

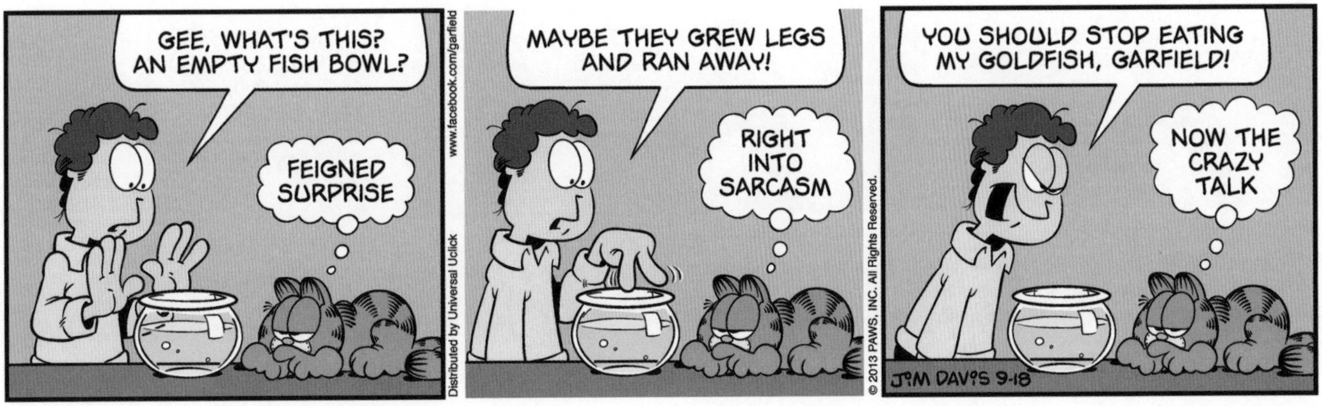
GEE, WHAT'S THIS? AN EMPTY FISH BOWL?
FEIGNED SURPRISE
MAYBE THEY GREW LEGS AND RAN AWAY!
RIGHT INTO SARCASM
YOU SHOULD STOP EATING MY GOLDFISH, GARFIELD!
NOW THE CRAZY TALK
JIM DAVIS 9-18
Distributed by Universal Uclick
www.facebook.com/garfield
© 2013 PAWS, INC. All Rights Reserved.

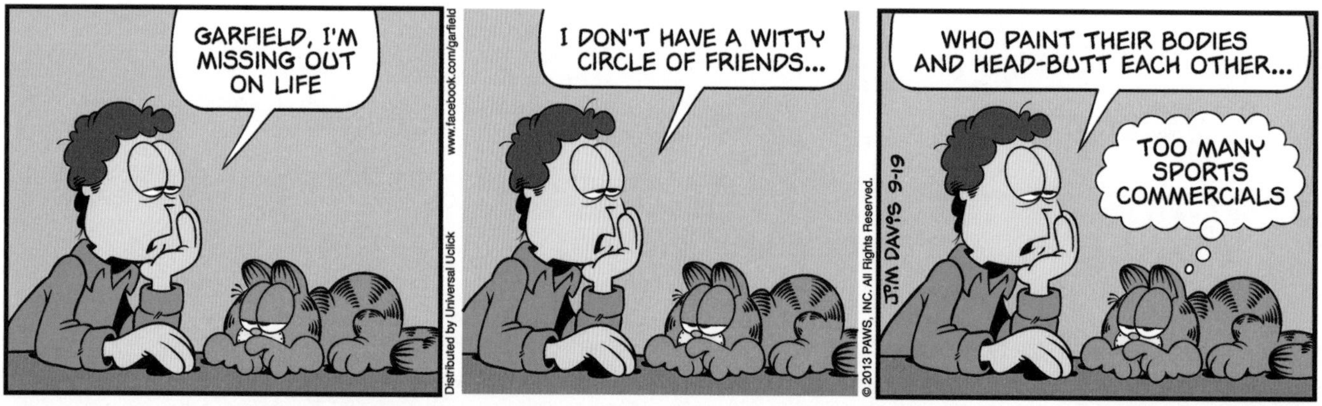
GARFIELD, I'M MISSING OUT ON LIFE
www.facebook.com/garfield
Distributed by Universal Uclick
I DON'T HAVE A WITTY CIRCLE OF FRIENDS...
© 2013 PAWS, INC. All Rights Reserved.
JIM DAVIS 9-19
WHO PAINT THEIR BODIES AND HEAD-BUTT EACH OTHER...
TOO MANY SPORTS COMMERCIALS

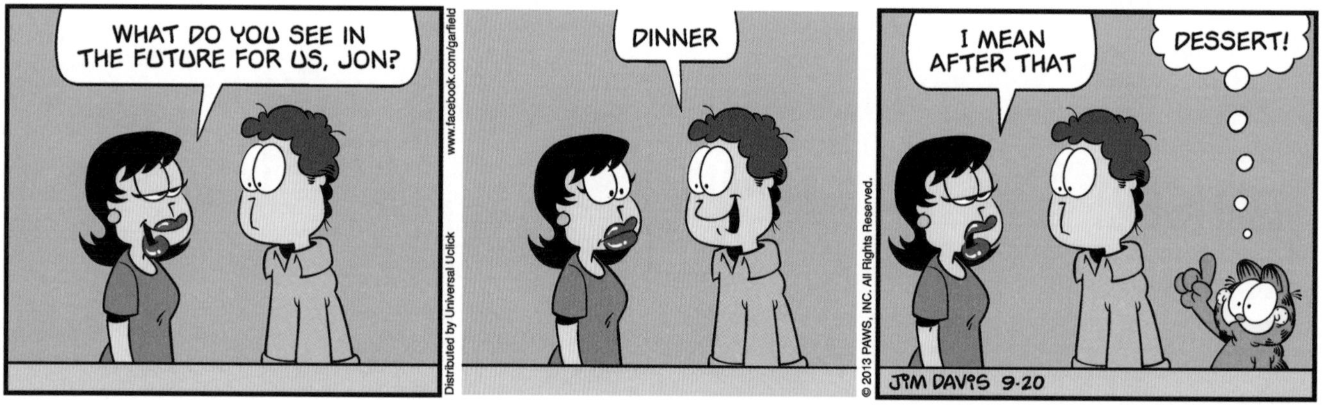
WHAT DO YOU SEE IN THE FUTURE FOR US, JON?
www.facebook.com/garfield
Distributed by Universal Uclick
DINNER
© 2013 PAWS, INC. All Rights Reserved.
I MEAN AFTER THAT
DESSERT!
JIM DAVIS 9-20

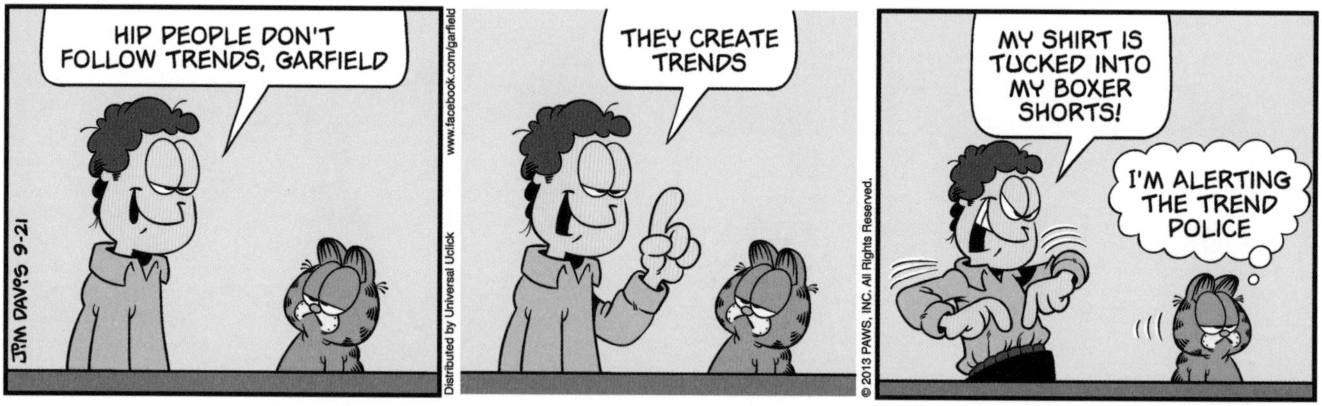
HIP PEOPLE DON'T FOLLOW TRENDS, GARFIELD
JIM DAVIS 9-21
www.facebook.com/garfield
Distributed by Universal Uclick
THEY CREATE TRENDS
© 2013 PAWS, INC. All Rights Reserved.
MY SHIRT IS TUCKED INTO MY BOXER SHORTS!
I'M ALERTING THE TREND POLICE

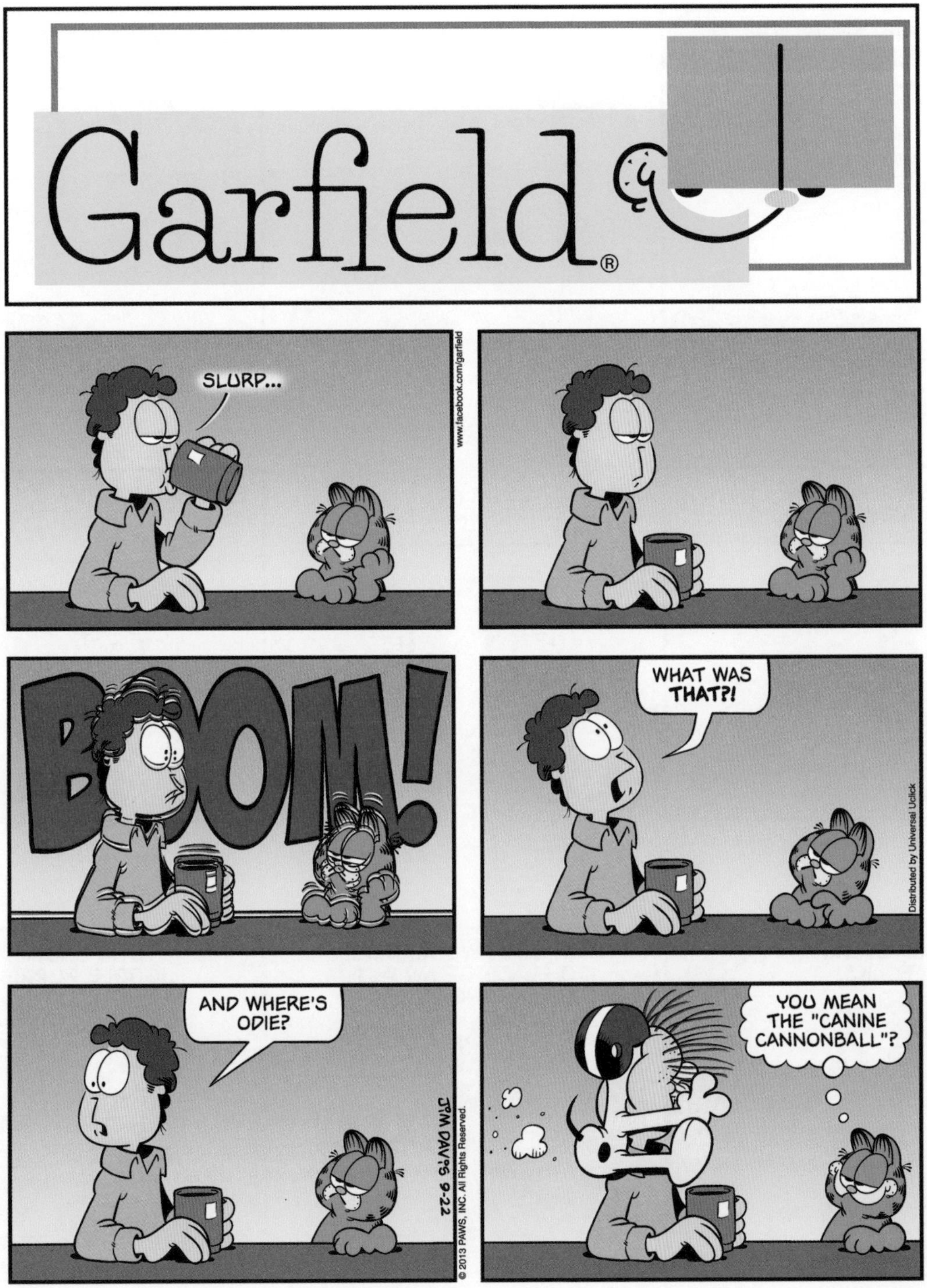
Garfield®
SLURP...
www.facebook.com/garfield
BOOM!
WHAT WAS THAT?!
Distributed by Universal Uclick
AND WHERE'S ODIE?
JIM DAVIS 9-22
© 2013 PAWS, INC. All Rights Reserved.
YOU MEAN THE "CANINE CANNONBALL"?

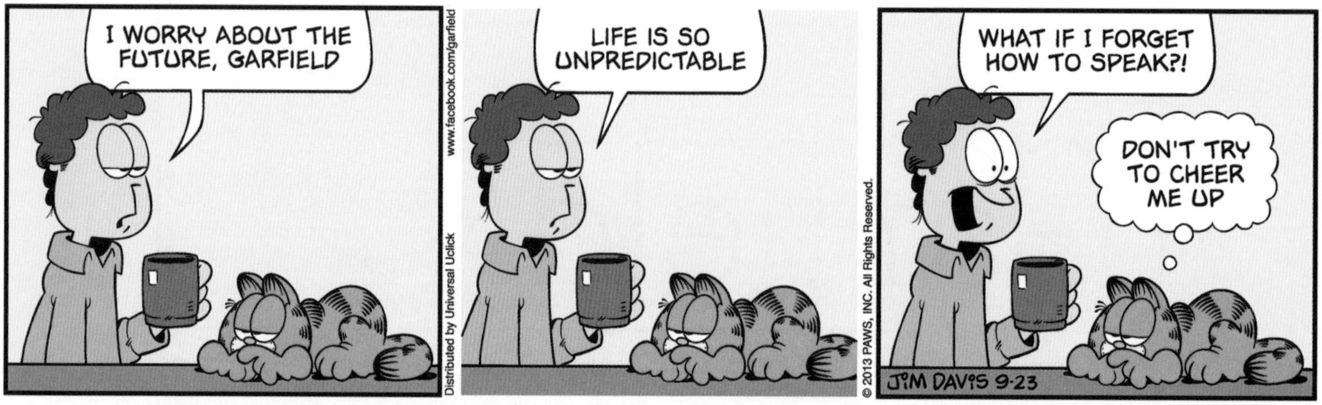
I WORRY ABOUT THE FUTURE, GARFIELD
www.facebook.com/garfield
Distributed by Universal Uclick
LIFE IS SO UNPREDICTABLE
© 2013 PAWS, INC. All Rights Reserved.
WHAT IF I FORGET HOW TO SPEAK?!
DON'T TRY TO CHEER ME UP
JIM DAVIS 9-23

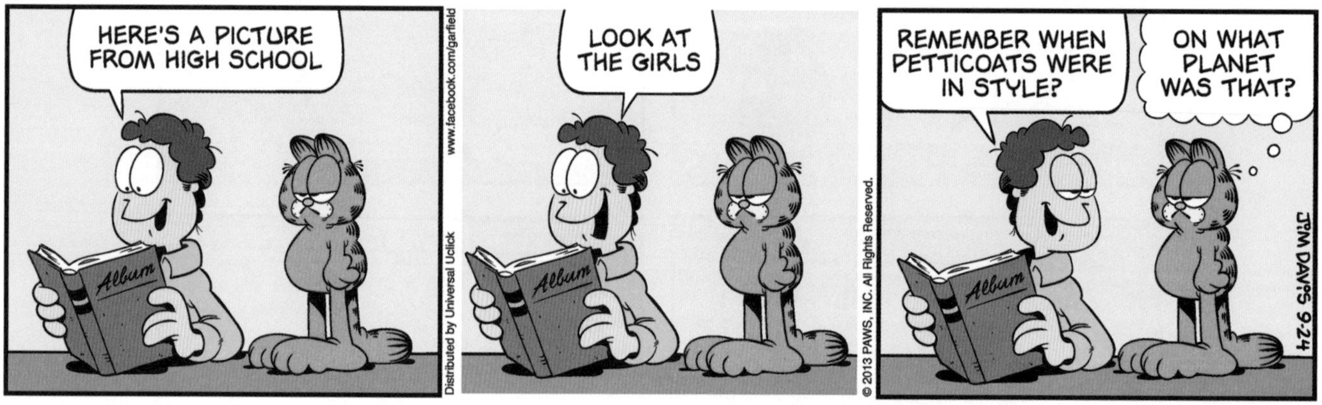
HERE'S A PICTURE FROM HIGH SCHOOL
Album
www.facebook.com/garfield
Distributed by Universal Uclick
LOOK AT THE GIRLS
Album
© 2013 PAWS, INC. All Rights Reserved.
REMEMBER WHEN PETTICOATS WERE IN STYLE?
ON WHAT PLANET WAS THAT?
Album
JIM DAVIS 9-24

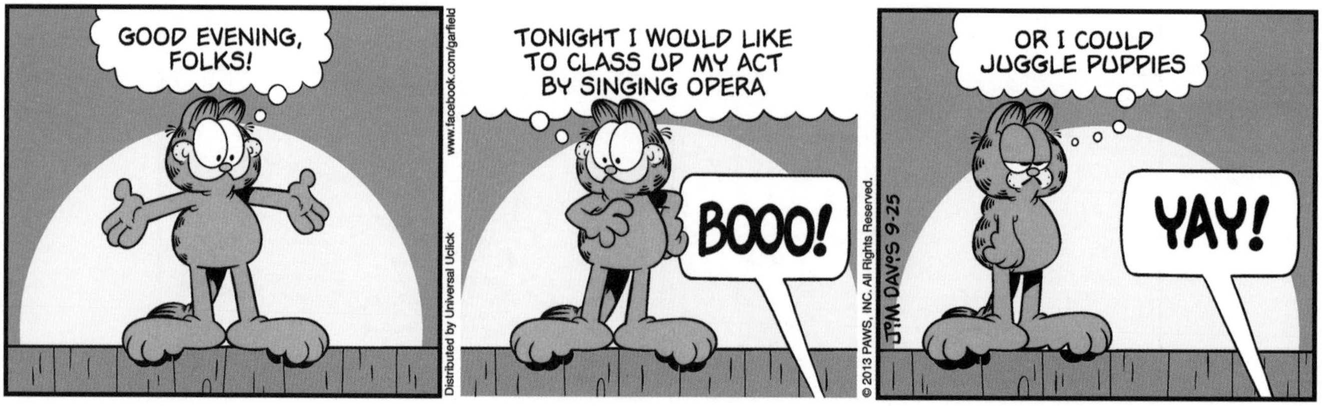
GOOD EVENING, FOLKS!
www.facebook.com/garfield
Distributed by Universal Uclick
TONIGHT I WOULD LIKE TO CLASS UP MY ACT BY SINGING OPERA
BOOO!
© 2013 PAWS, INC. All Rights Reserved.
JIM DAVIS 9-25
OR I COULD JUGGLE PUPPIES
YAY!

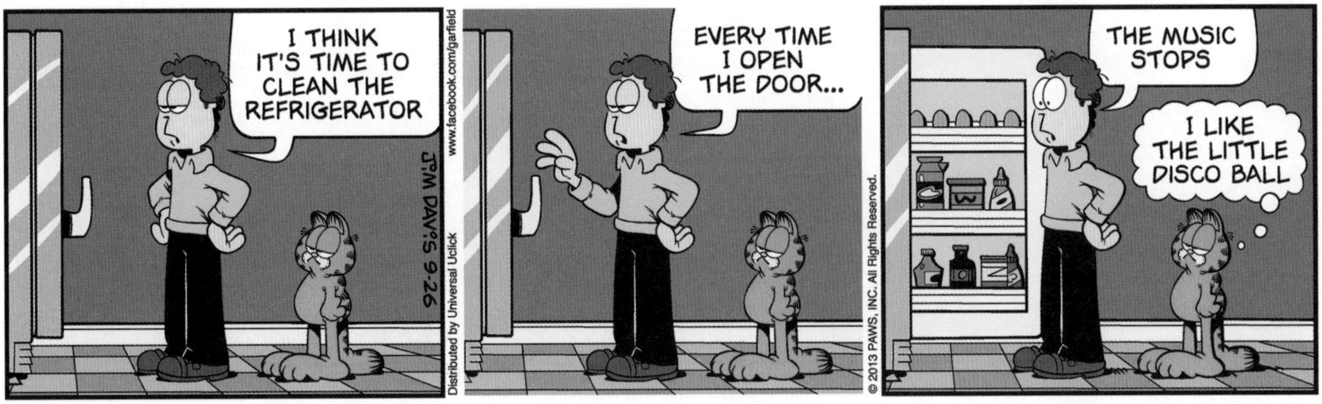
I THINK IT'S TIME TO CLEAN THE REFRIGERATOR
JIM DAVIS 9-26
www.facebook.com/garfield
Distributed by Universal Uclick
EVERY TIME I OPEN THE DOOR...
© 2013 PAWS, INC. All Rights Reserved.
THE MUSIC STOPS
I LIKE THE LITTLE DISCO BALL

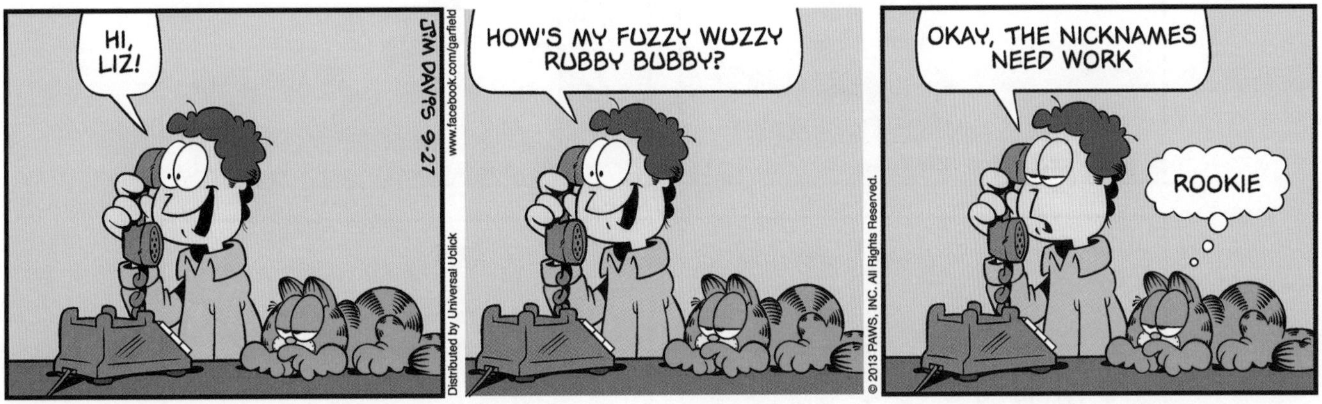
HI, LIZ!
JIM DAVIS 9-27
www.facebook.com/garfield
Distributed by Universal Uclick
HOW'S MY FUZZY WUZZY RUBBY BUBBY?
© 2013 PAWS, INC. All Rights Reserved.
OKAY, THE NICKNAMES NEED WORK
ROOKIE

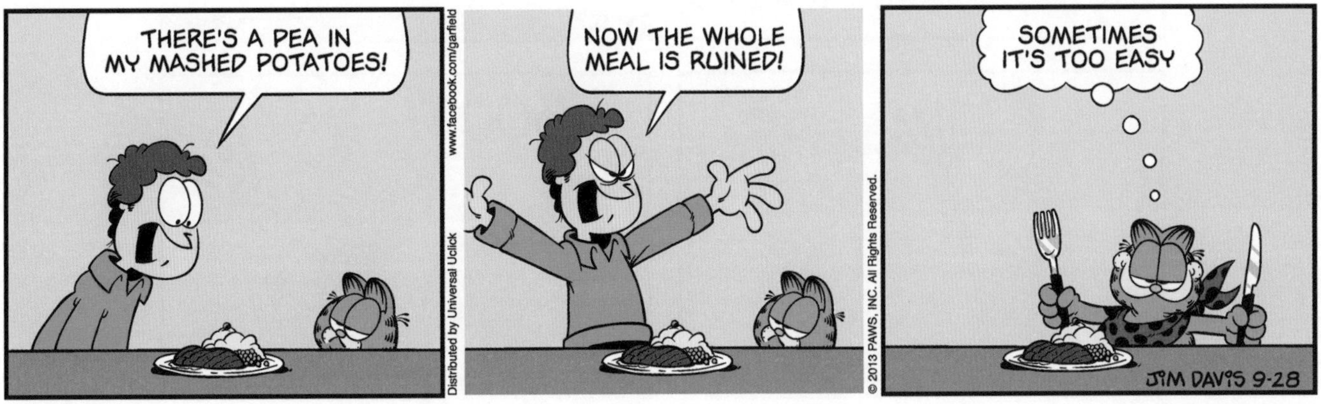
THERE'S A PEA IN MY MASHED POTATOES!
www.facebook.com/garfield
Distributed by Universal Uclick
NOW THE WHOLE MEAL IS RUINED!
© 2013 PAWS, INC. All Rights Reserved.
SOMETIMES IT'S TOO EASY
JIM DAVIS 9-28

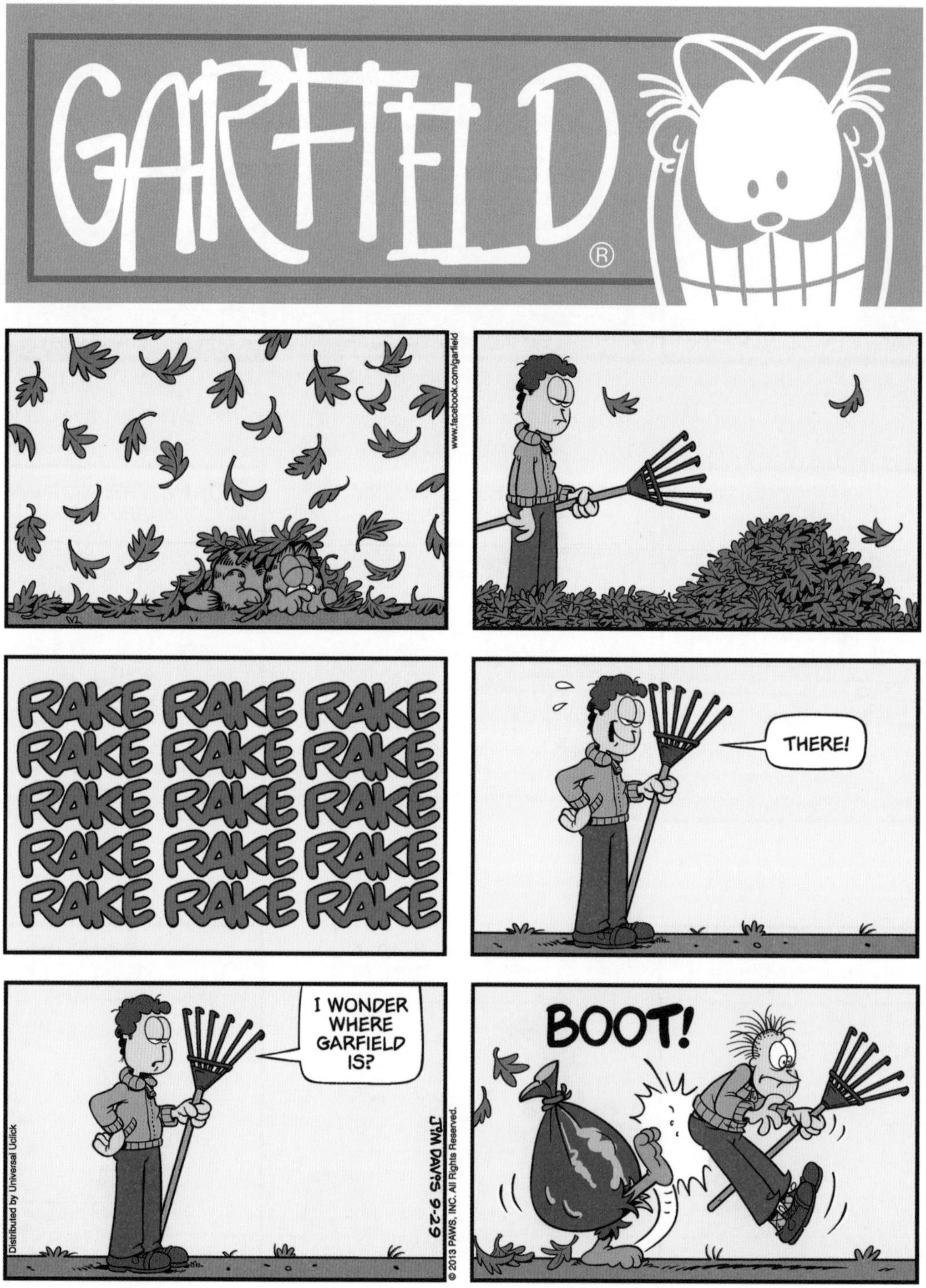
GARFIELD ®
www.facebook.com/garfield
RAKE RAKE RAKE RAKE RAKE RAKE RAKE RAKE RAKE RAKE RAKE RAKE RAKE RAKE RAKE
THERE!
I WONDER WHERE GARFIELD IS?
Distributed by Universal Uclick
JIM DAVIS 9-29
© 2013 PAWS, INC. All Rights Reserved.
BOOT!

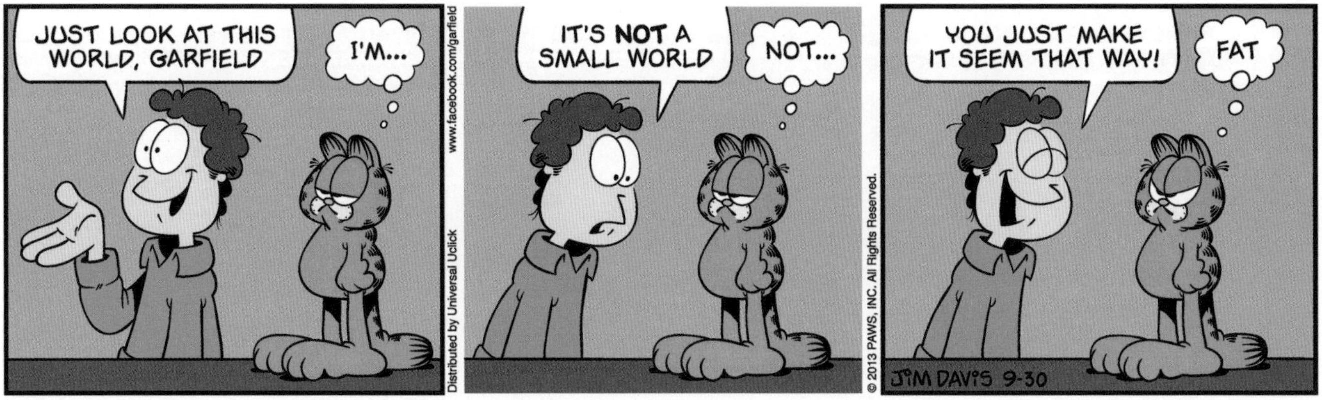
JUST LOOK AT THIS WORLD, GARFIELD
I'M...
IT'S **NOT** A SMALL WORLD
NOT...
YOU JUST MAKE IT SEEM THAT WAY!
FAT
Distributed by Universal Uclick
www.facebook.com/garfield
© 2013 PAWS, INC. All Rights Reserved.
JIM DAVIS 9-30

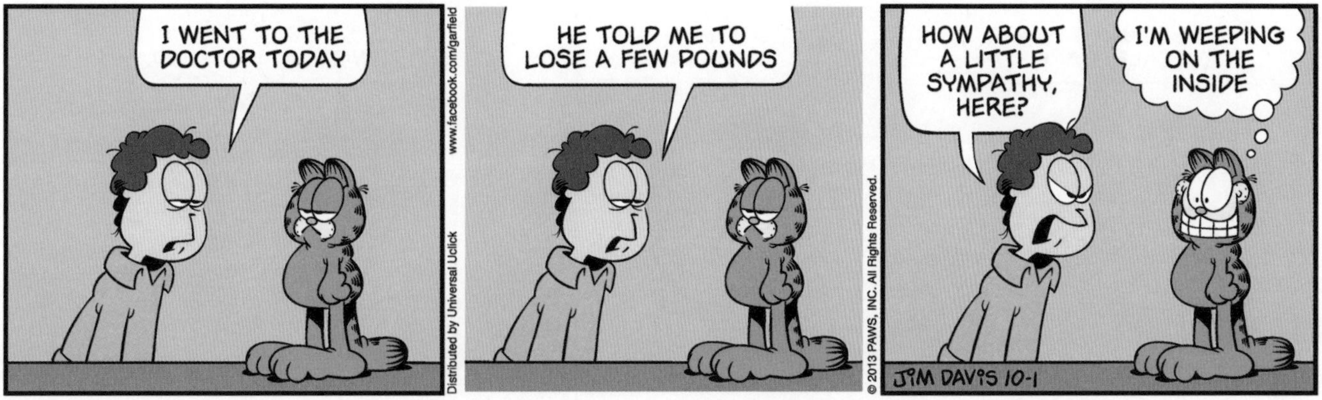
I WENT TO THE DOCTOR TODAY
HE TOLD ME TO LOSE A FEW POUNDS
HOW ABOUT A LITTLE SYMPATHY, HERE?
I'M WEEPING ON THE INSIDE
Distributed by Universal Uclick
www.facebook.com/garfield
© 2013 PAWS, INC. All Rights Reserved.
JIM DAVIS 10-1

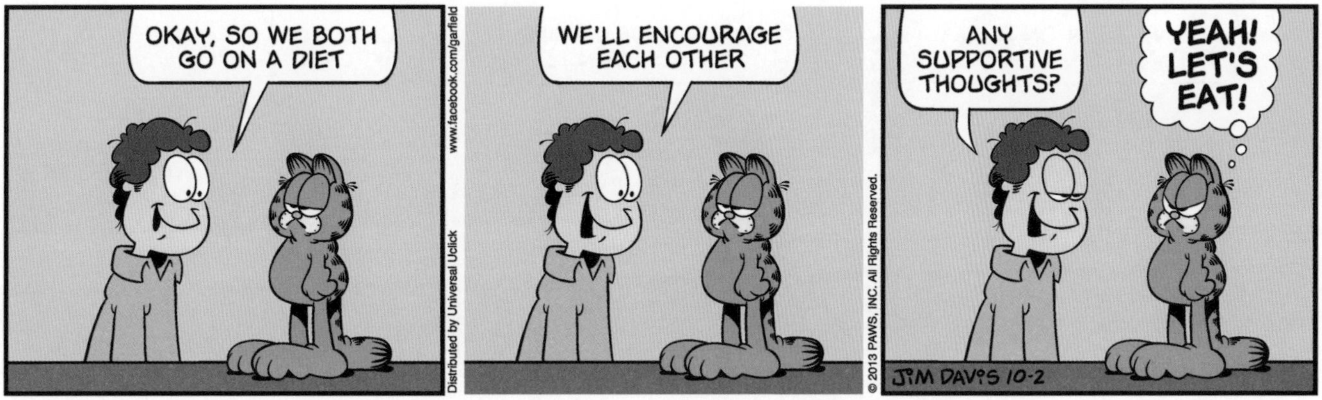
OKAY, SO WE BOTH GO ON A DIET
WE'LL ENCOURAGE EACH OTHER
ANY SUPPORTIVE THOUGHTS?
YEAH! LET'S EAT!
Distributed by Universal Uclick
www.facebook.com/garfield
© 2013 PAWS, INC. All Rights Reserved.
JIM DAVIS 10-2

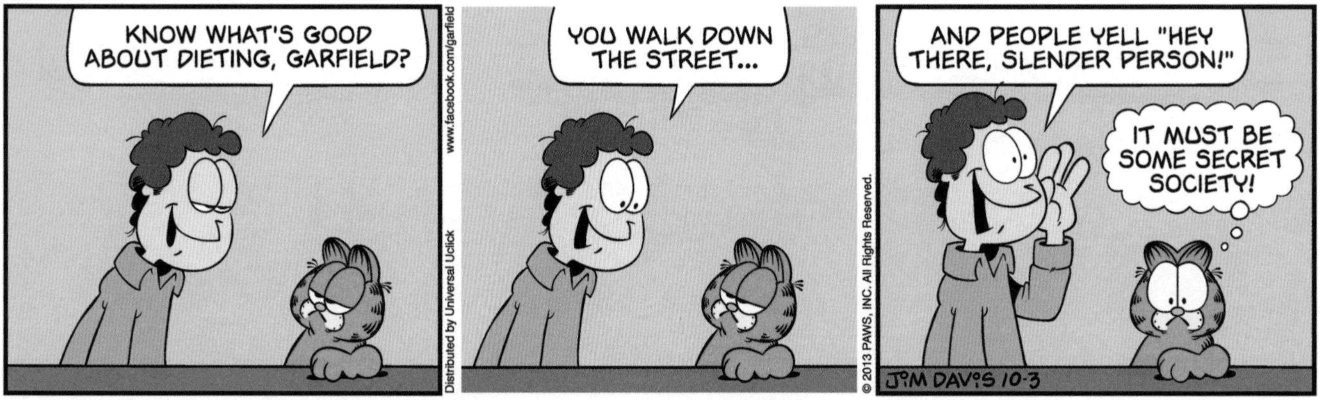
KNOW WHAT'S GOOD ABOUT DIETING, GARFIELD?
Distributed by Universal Uclick www.facebook.com/garfield
YOU WALK DOWN THE STREET...
AND PEOPLE YELL "HEY THERE, SLENDER PERSON!"
IT MUST BE SOME SECRET SOCIETY!
© 2013 PAWS, INC. All Rights Reserved.
JIM DAVIS 10-3

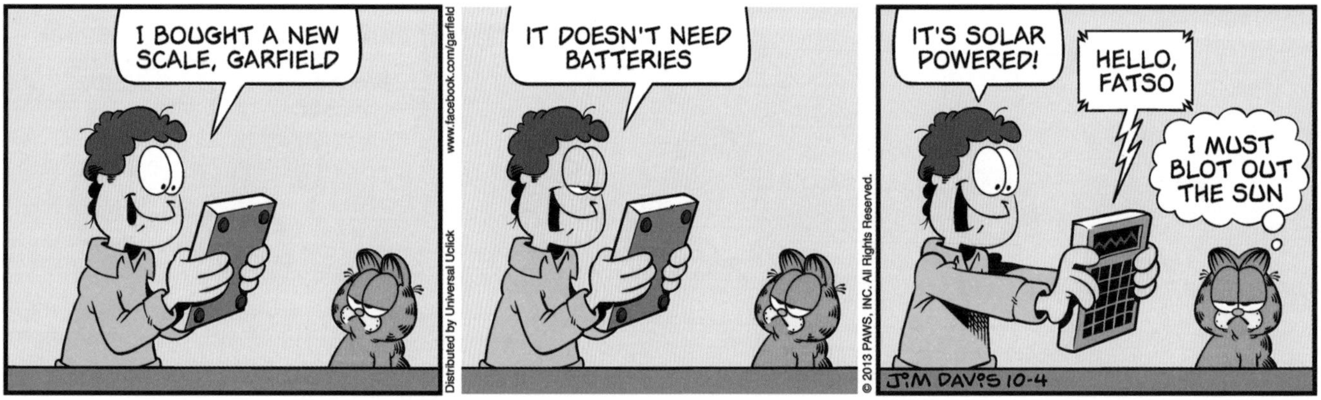
I BOUGHT A NEW SCALE, GARFIELD
Distributed by Universal Uclick www.facebook.com/garfield
IT DOESN'T NEED BATTERIES
IT'S SOLAR POWERED!
HELLO, FATSO
I MUST BLOT OUT THE SUN
© 2013 PAWS, INC. All Rights Reserved.
JIM DAVIS 10-4

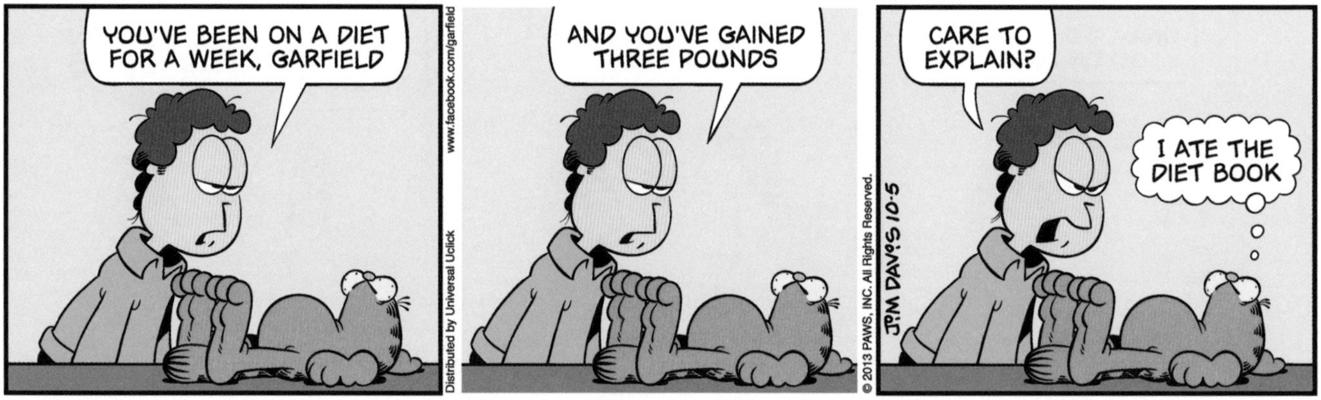
YOU'VE BEEN ON A DIET FOR A WEEK, GARFIELD
Distributed by Universal Uclick www.facebook.com/garfield
AND YOU'VE GAINED THREE POUNDS
CARE TO EXPLAIN?
I ATE THE DIET BOOK
© 2013 PAWS, INC. All Rights Reserved.
JIM DAVIS 10-5

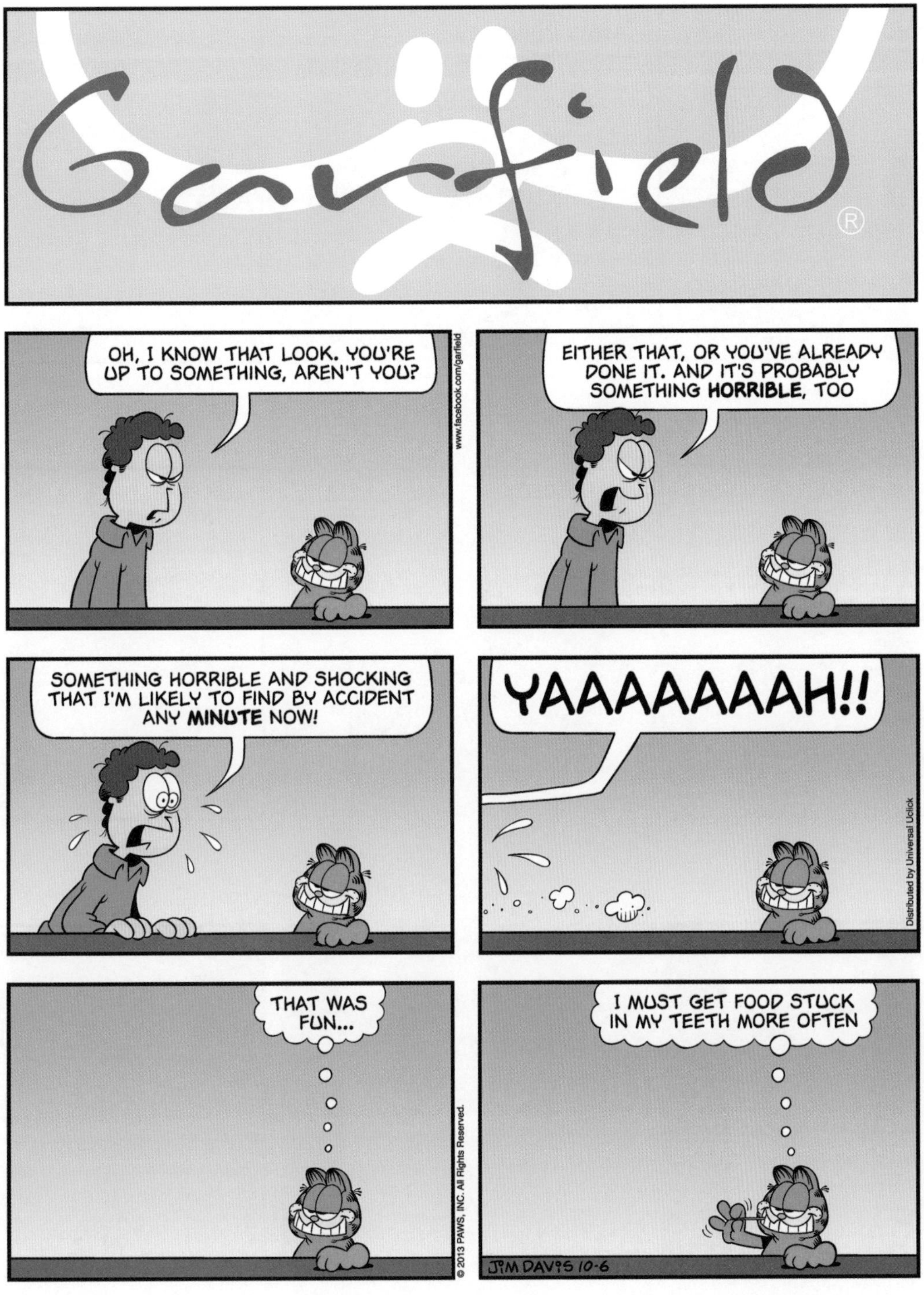
Garfield®
OH, I KNOW THAT LOOK. YOU'RE UP TO SOMETHING, AREN'T YOU?
www.facebook.com/garfield
EITHER THAT, OR YOU'VE ALREADY DONE IT. AND IT'S PROBABLY SOMETHING HORRIBLE, TOO
SOMETHING HORRIBLE AND SHOCKING THAT I'M LIKELY TO FIND BY ACCIDENT ANY MINUTE NOW!
YAAAAAAAH!!
Distributed by Universal Uclick
THAT WAS FUN...
© 2013 PAWS, INC. All Rights Reserved.
I MUST GET FOOD STUCK IN MY TEETH MORE OFTEN
JIM DAVIS 10-6

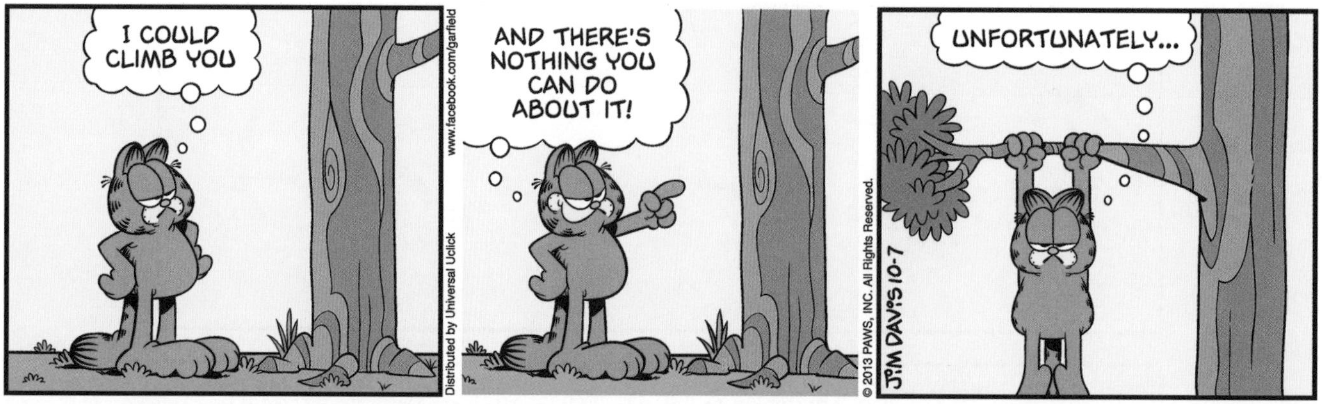
I COULD CLIMB YOU
Distributed by Universal Uclick
www.facebook.com/garfield
AND THERE'S NOTHING YOU CAN DO ABOUT IT!
© 2013 PAWS, INC. All Rights Reserved.
JIM DAVIS 10-7
UNFORTUNATELY...

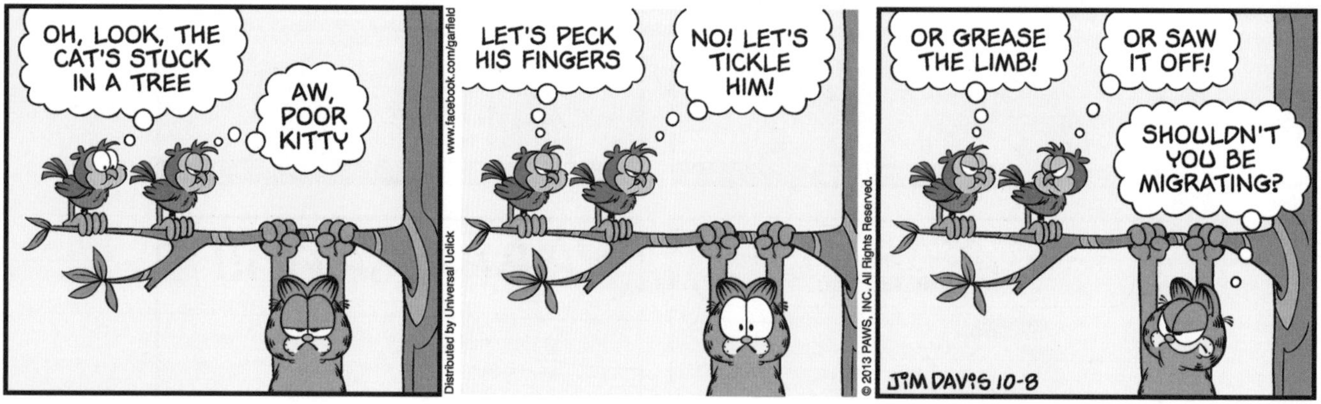
OH, LOOK, THE CAT'S STUCK IN A TREE
AW, POOR KITTY
Distributed by Universal Uclick
www.facebook.com/garfield
LET'S PECK HIS FINGERS
NO! LET'S TICKLE HIM!
© 2013 PAWS, INC. All Rights Reserved.
OR GREASE THE LIMB!
OR SAW IT OFF!
SHOULDN'T YOU BE MIGRATING?
JIM DAVIS 10-8

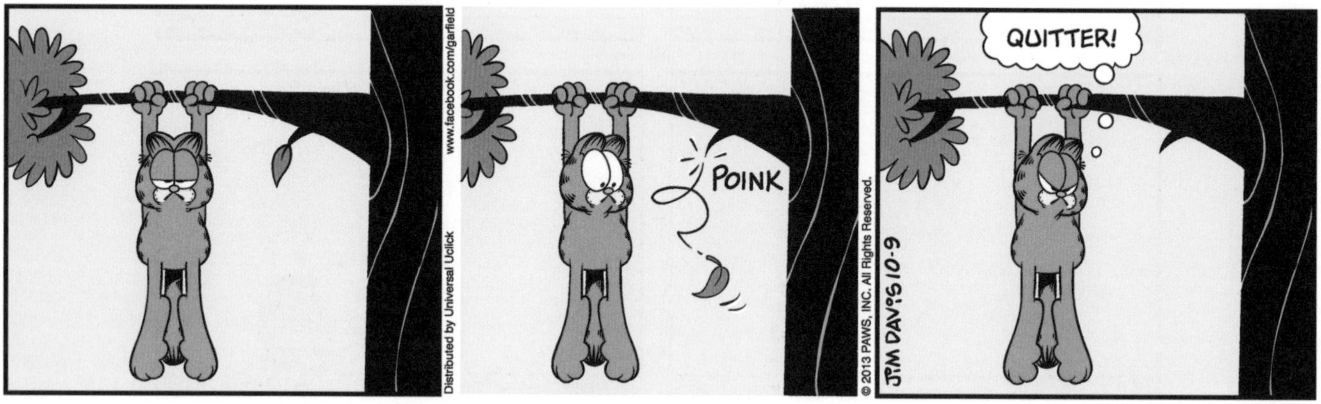
Distributed by Universal Uclick
www.facebook.com/garfield
POINK
© 2013 PAWS, INC. All Rights Reserved.
JIM DAVIS 10-9
QUITTER!

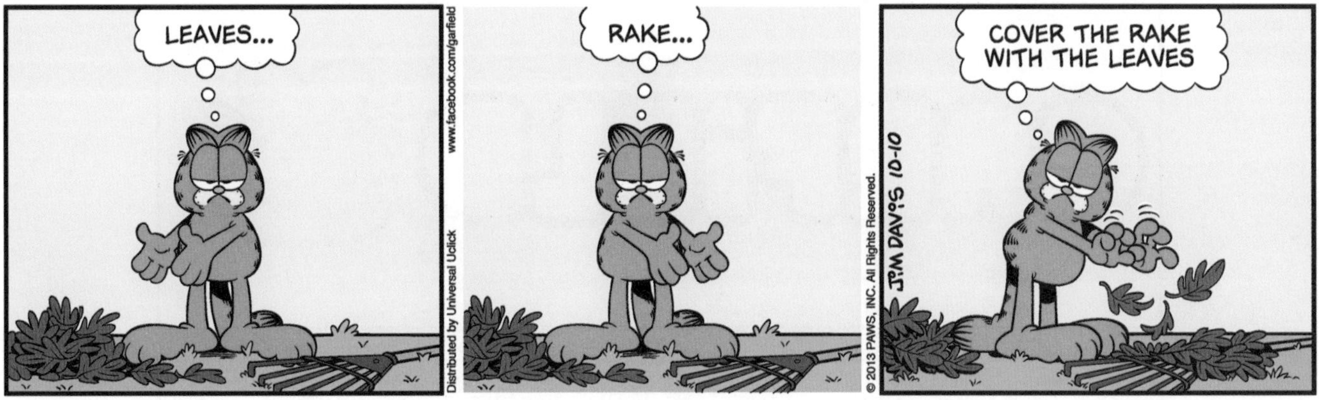
LEAVES...
RAKE...
COVER THE RAKE WITH THE LEAVES
JIM DAVIS 10-10
Distributed by Universal Uclick
www.facebook.com/garfield
© 2013 PAWS, INC. All Rights Reserved.

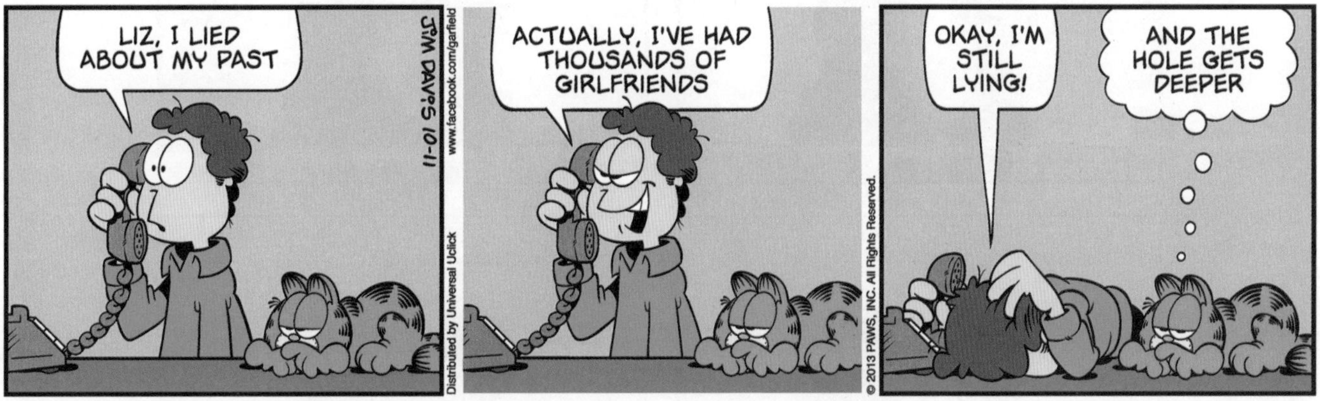
LIZ, I LIED ABOUT MY PAST
ACTUALLY, I'VE HAD THOUSANDS OF GIRLFRIENDS
OKAY, I'M STILL LYING!
AND THE HOLE GETS DEEPER
JIM DAVIS 10-11
Distributed by Universal Uclick
www.facebook.com/garfield
© 2013 PAWS, INC. All Rights Reserved.

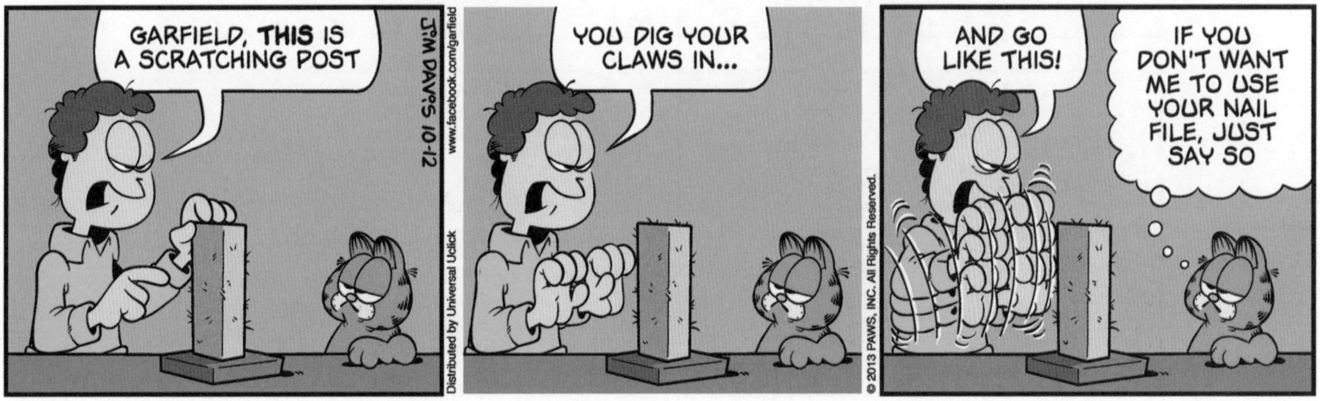
GARFIELD, **THIS** IS A SCRATCHING POST
YOU DIG YOUR CLAWS IN...
AND GO LIKE THIS!
IF YOU DON'T WANT ME TO USE YOUR NAIL FILE, JUST SAY SO
JIM DAVIS 10-12
Distributed by Universal Uclick
www.facebook.com/garfield
© 2013 PAWS, INC. All Rights Reserved.

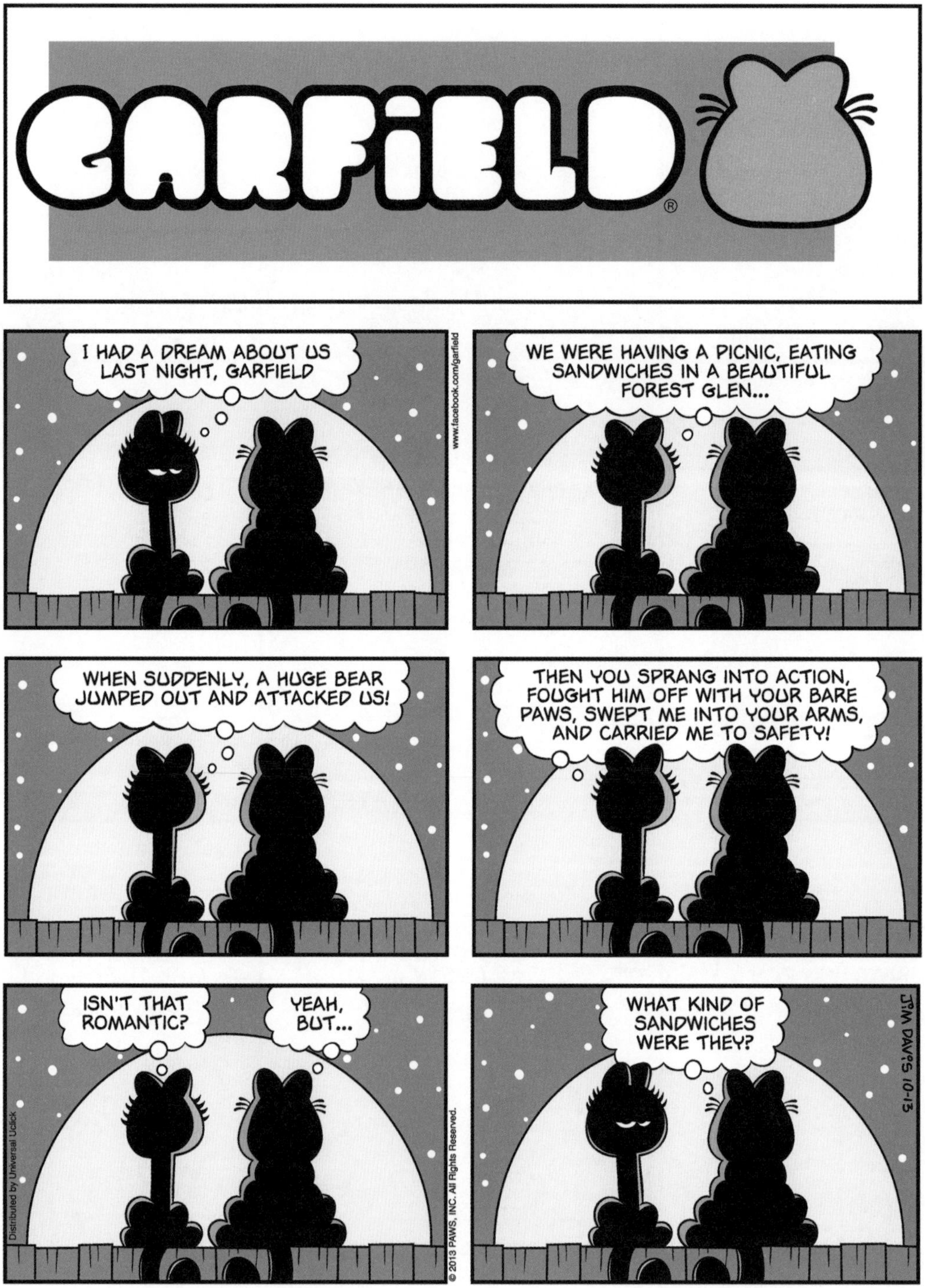
GARFIELD®
I HAD A DREAM ABOUT US LAST NIGHT, GARFIELD
www.facebook.com/garfield
WE WERE HAVING A PICNIC, EATING SANDWICHES IN A BEAUTIFUL FOREST GLEN...
WHEN SUDDENLY, A HUGE BEAR JUMPED OUT AND ATTACKED US!
THEN YOU SPRANG INTO ACTION, FOUGHT HIM OFF WITH YOUR BARE PAWS, SWEPT ME INTO YOUR ARMS, AND CARRIED ME TO SAFETY!
ISN'T THAT ROMANTIC?
YEAH, BUT...
Distributed by Universal Uclick
© 2013 PAWS, INC. All Rights Reserved.
WHAT KIND OF SANDWICHES WERE THEY?
JIM DAVIS 10-13

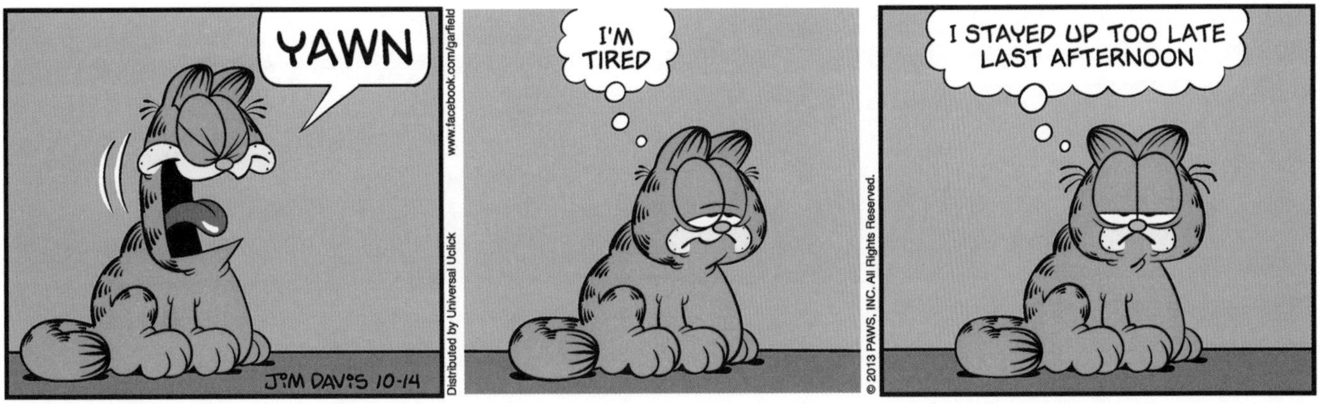
YAWN
JIM DAVIS 10-14
www.facebook.com/garfield
Distributed by Universal Uclick
I'M TIRED
© 2013 PAWS, INC. All Rights Reserved.
I STAYED UP TOO LATE LAST AFTERNOON

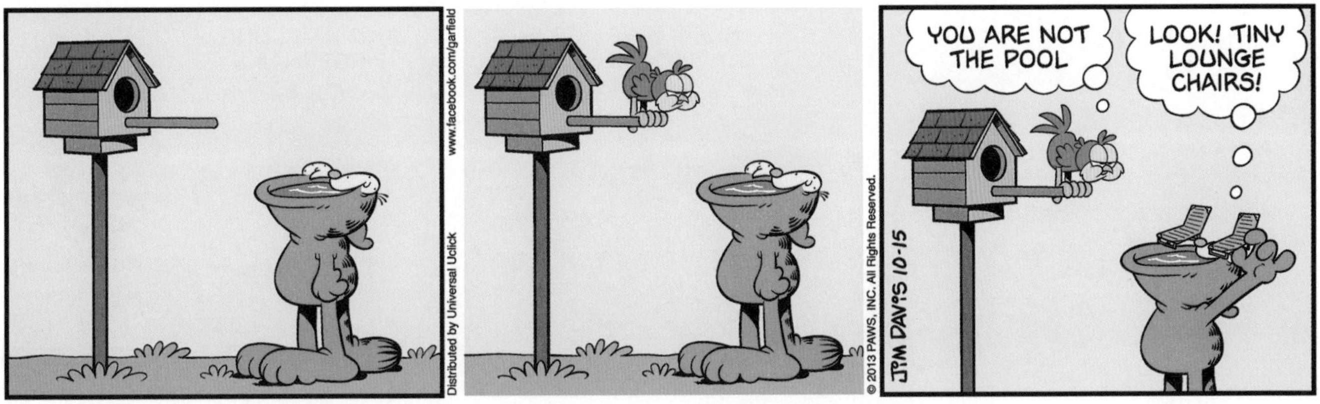
www.facebook.com/garfield
Distributed by Universal Uclick
© 2013 PAWS, INC. All Rights Reserved.
JIM DAVIS 10-15
YOU ARE NOT THE POOL
LOOK! TINY LOUNGE CHAIRS!

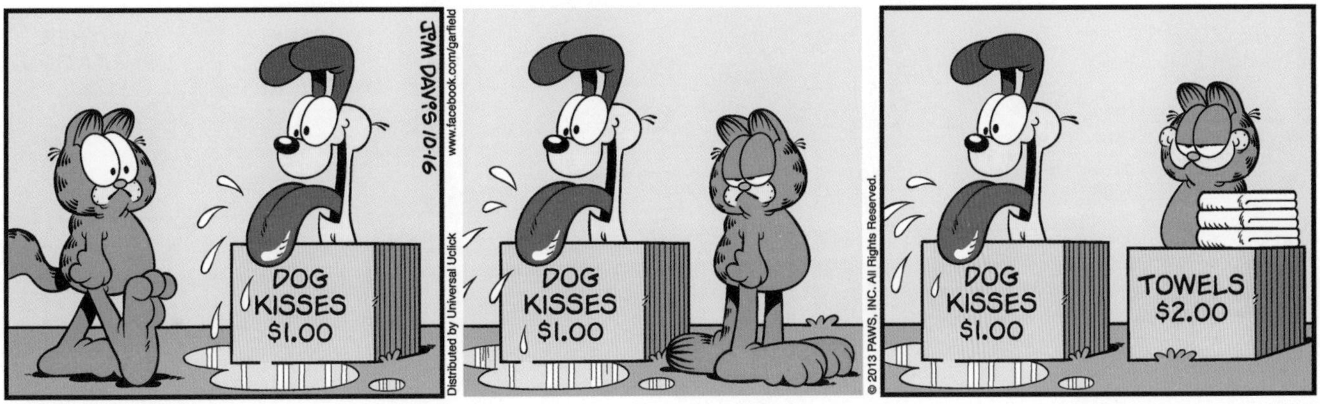
JIM DAVIS 10-16
www.facebook.com/garfield
Distributed by Universal Uclick
DOG KISSES $1.00
DOG KISSES $1.00
© 2013 PAWS, INC. All Rights Reserved.
DOG KISSES $1.00
TOWELS $2.00

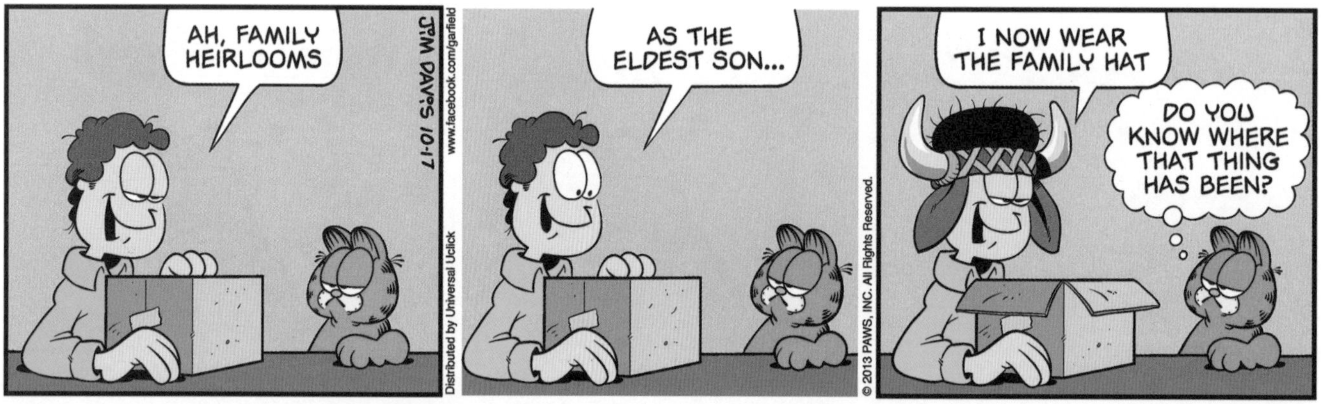
AH, FAMILY HEIRLOOMS
JIM DAVIS 10-17
www.facebook.com/garfield
Distributed by Universal Uclick
AS THE ELDEST SON...
© 2013 PAWS, INC. All Rights Reserved.
I NOW WEAR THE FAMILY HAT
DO YOU KNOW WHERE THAT THING HAS BEEN?

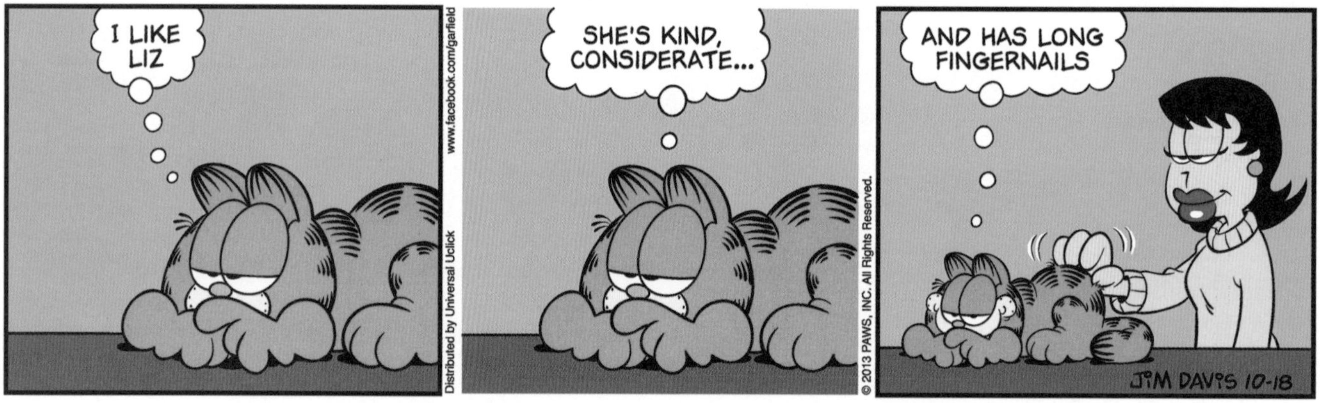
I LIKE LIZ
www.facebook.com/garfield
Distributed by Universal Uclick
SHE'S KIND, CONSIDERATE...
© 2013 PAWS, INC. All Rights Reserved.
AND HAS LONG FINGERNAILS
JIM DAVIS 10-18

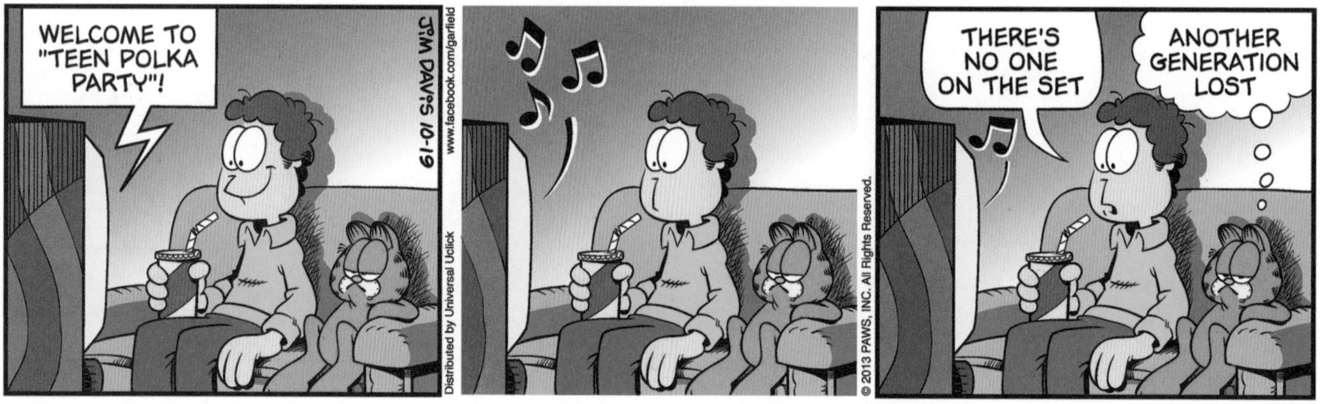
WELCOME TO "TEEN POLKA PARTY"!
JIM DAVIS 10-19
www.facebook.com/garfield
Distributed by Universal Uclick
© 2013 PAWS, INC. All Rights Reserved.
THERE'S NO ONE ON THE SET
ANOTHER GENERATION LOST

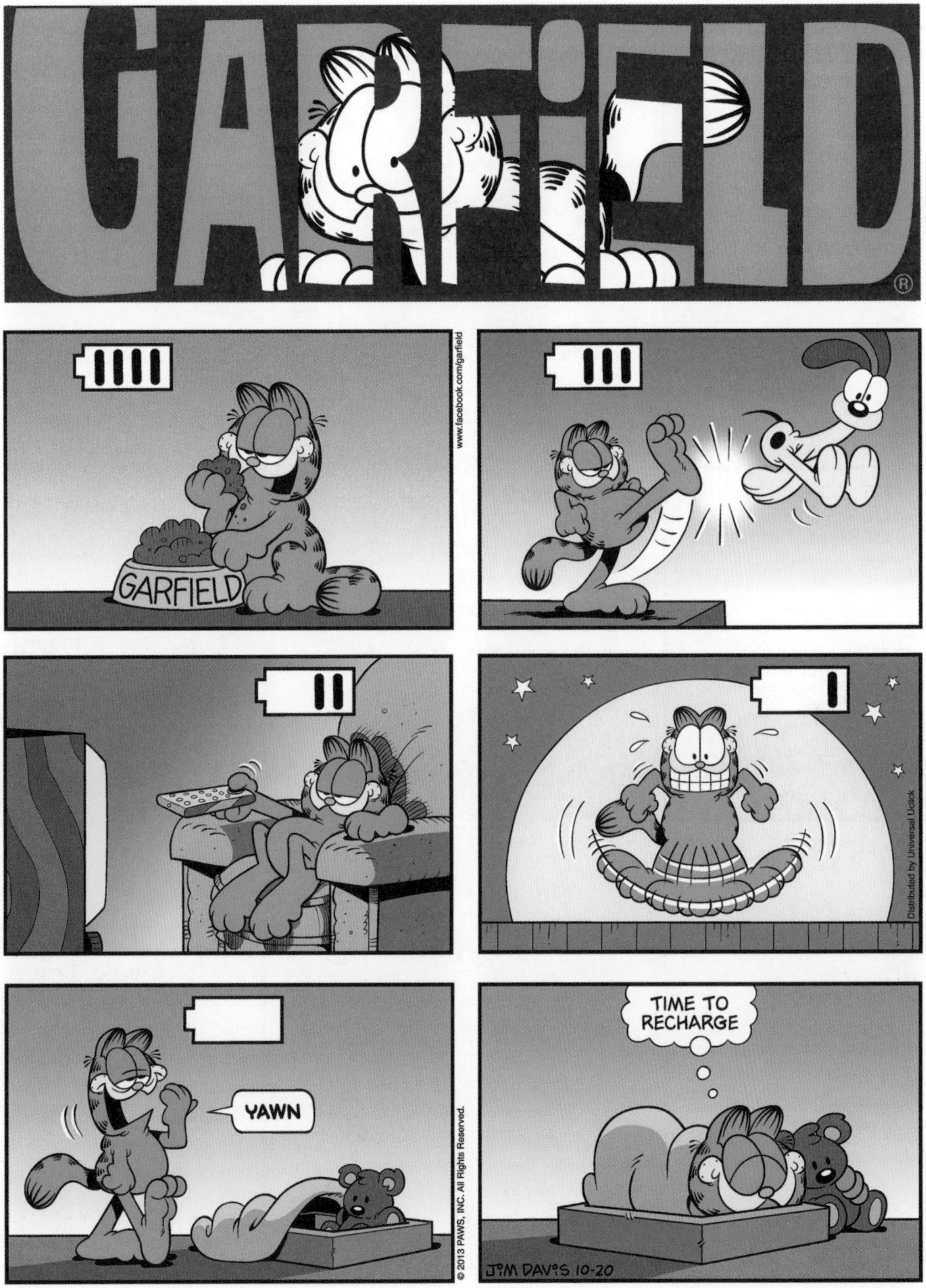
GARFIELD
www.facebook.com/garfield
GARFIELD
YAWN
TIME TO RECHARGE
© 2013 PAWS, INC. All Rights Reserved.
Distributed by Universal Uclick
JIM DAVIS 10-20

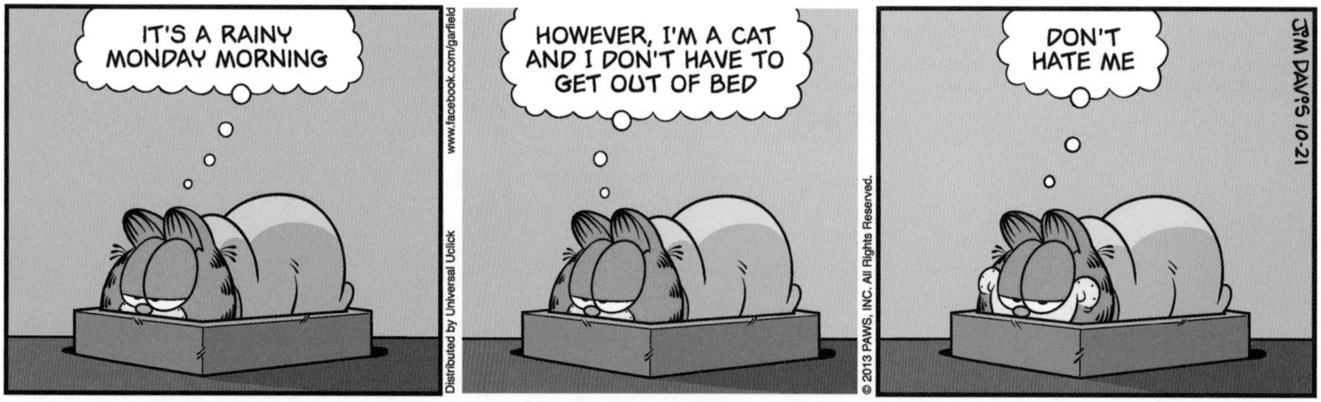
IT'S A RAINY MONDAY MORNING
HOWEVER, I'M A CAT AND I DON'T HAVE TO GET OUT OF BED
DON'T HATE ME
JIM DAVIS 10-21
Distributed by Universal Uclick www.facebook.com/garfield
© 2013 PAWS, INC. All Rights Reserved.

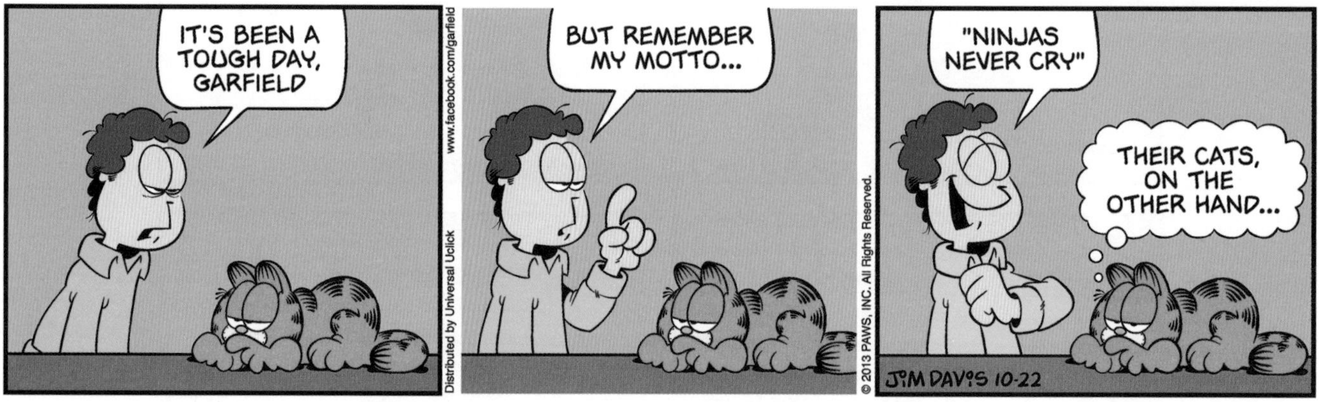
IT'S BEEN A TOUGH DAY, GARFIELD
BUT REMEMBER MY MOTTO...
"NINJAS NEVER CRY"
THEIR CATS, ON THE OTHER HAND...
JIM DAVIS 10-22
Distributed by Universal Uclick www.facebook.com/garfield
© 2013 PAWS, INC. All Rights Reserved.

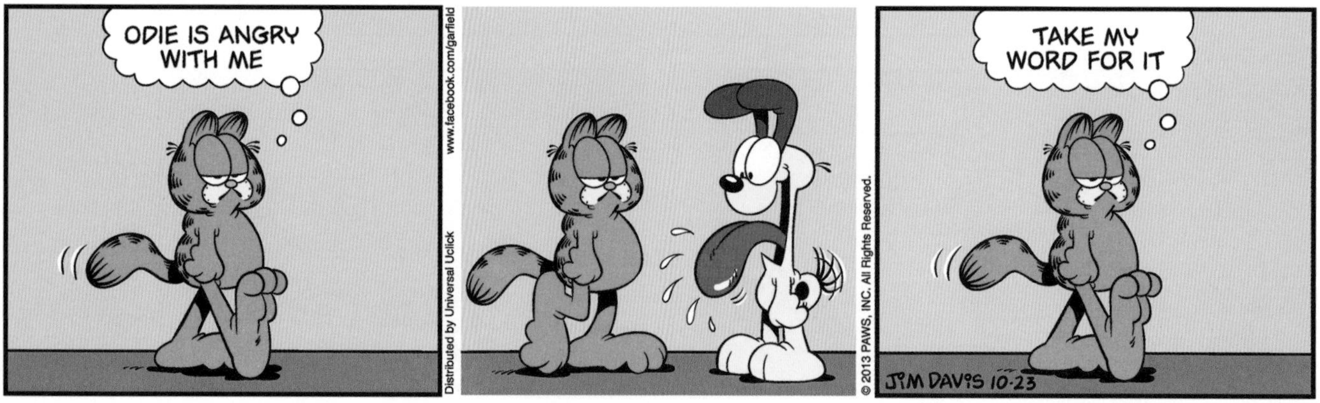
ODIE IS ANGRY WITH ME
TAKE MY WORD FOR IT
JIM DAVIS 10-23
Distributed by Universal Uclick www.facebook.com/garfield
© 2013 PAWS, INC. All Rights Reserved.

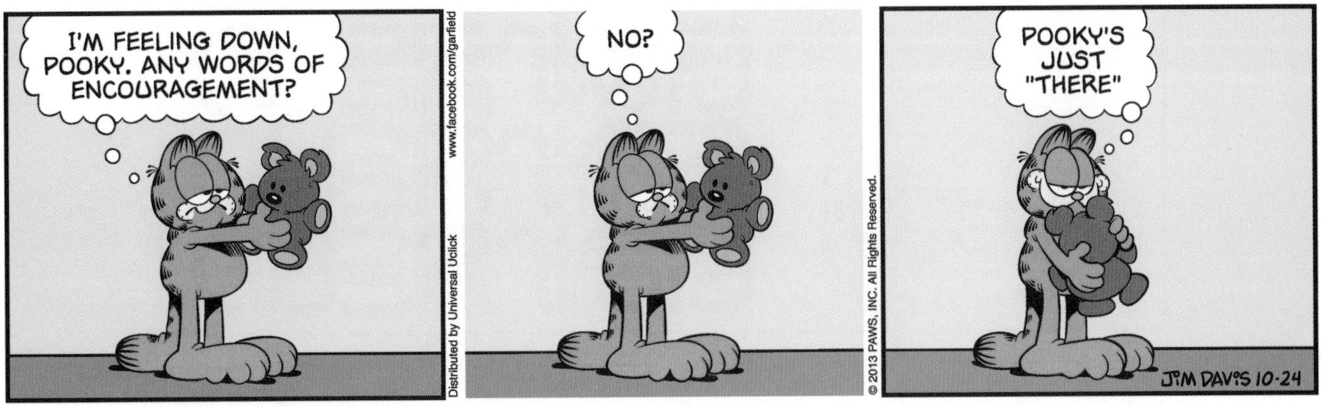
I'M FEELING DOWN, POOKY. ANY WORDS OF ENCOURAGEMENT?
NO?
POOKY'S JUST "THERE"
JIM DAVIS 10-24
Distributed by Universal Uclick
www.facebook.com/garfield
© 2013 PAWS, INC. All Rights Reserved.

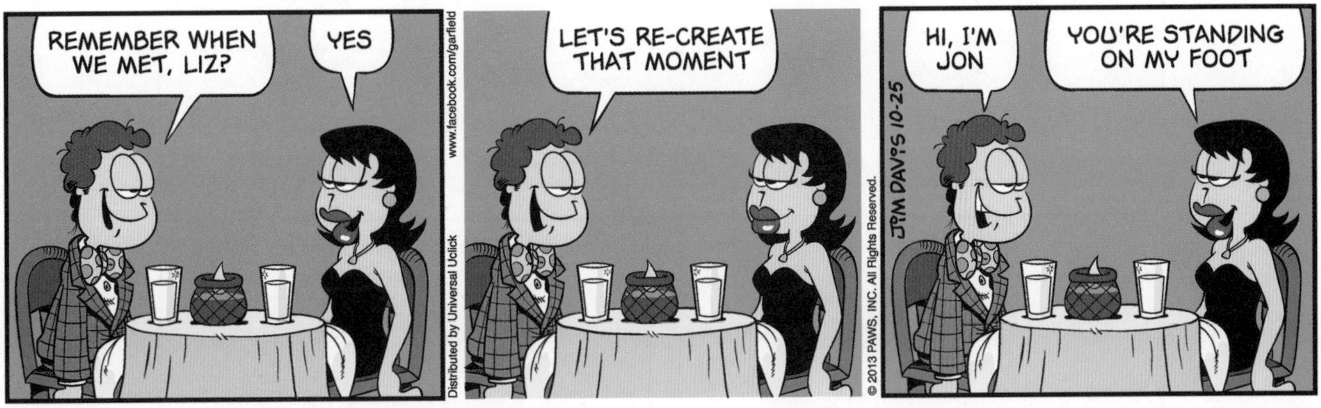
REMEMBER WHEN WE MET, LIZ?
YES
LET'S RE-CREATE THAT MOMENT
HI, I'M JON
YOU'RE STANDING ON MY FOOT
JIM DAVIS 10-25
Distributed by Universal Uclick
www.facebook.com/garfield
© 2013 PAWS, INC. All Rights Reserved.

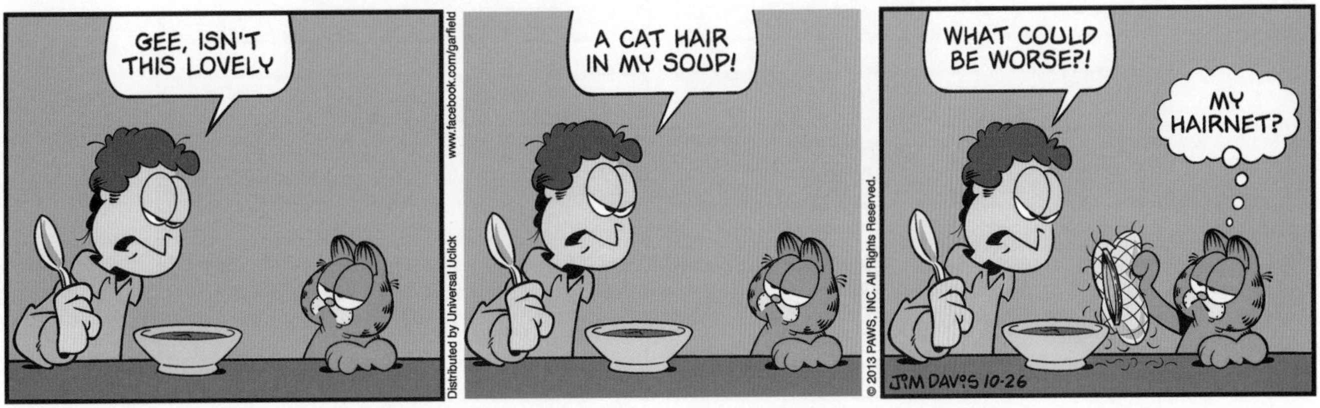
GEE, ISN'T THIS LOVELY
A CAT HAIR IN MY SOUP!
WHAT COULD BE WORSE?!
MY HAIRNET?
JIM DAVIS 10-26
Distributed by Universal Uclick
www.facebook.com/garfield
© 2013 PAWS, INC. All Rights Reserved.

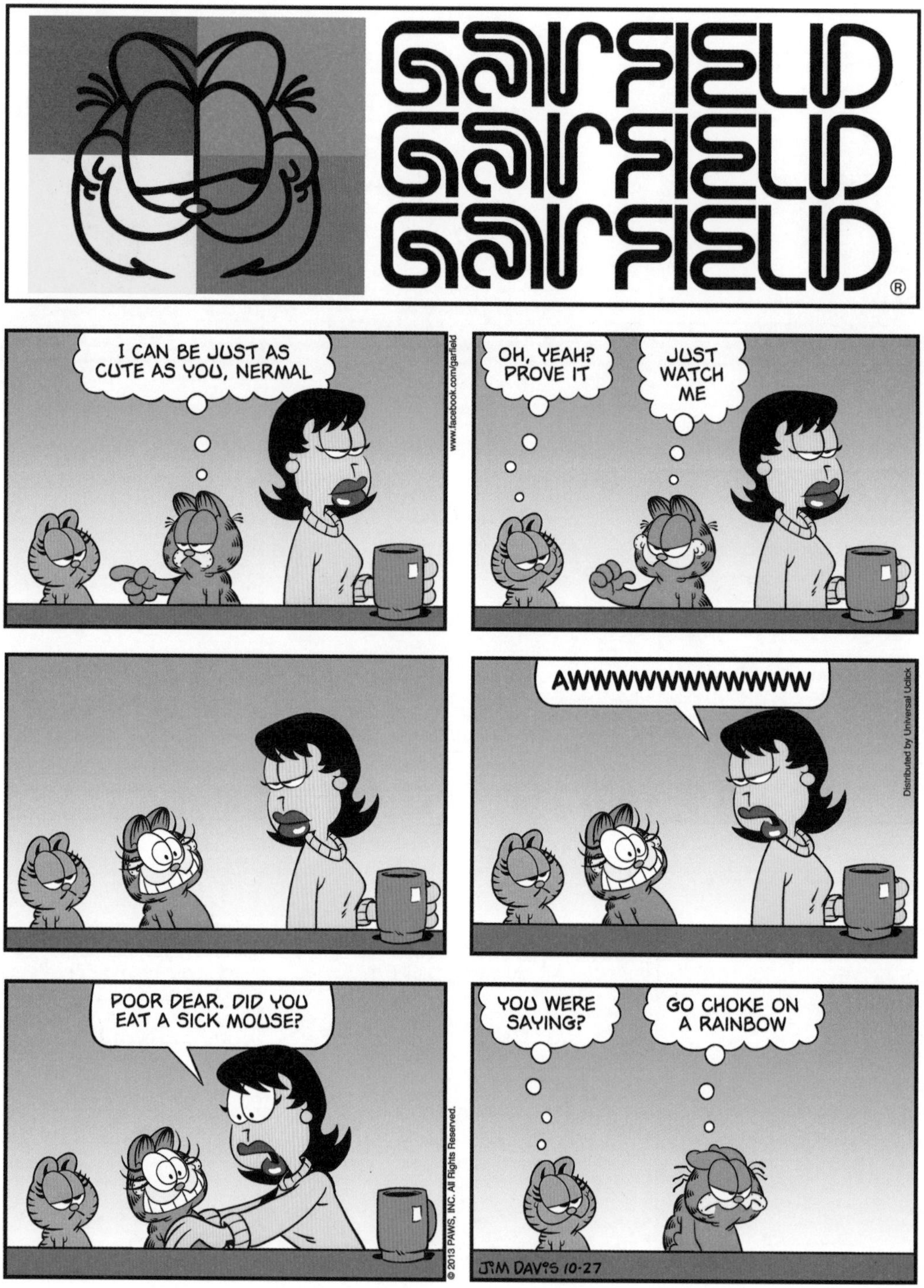
GARFIELD
GARFIELD
GARFIELD
I CAN BE JUST AS CUTE AS YOU, NERMAL
www.facebook.com/garfield
OH, YEAH? PROVE IT
JUST WATCH ME
AWWWWWWWWWWWW
Distributed by Universal Uclick
POOR DEAR. DID YOU EAT A SICK MOUSE?
© 2013 PAWS, INC. All Rights Reserved.
YOU WERE SAYING?
GO CHOKE ON A RAINBOW
JIM DAVIS 10-27

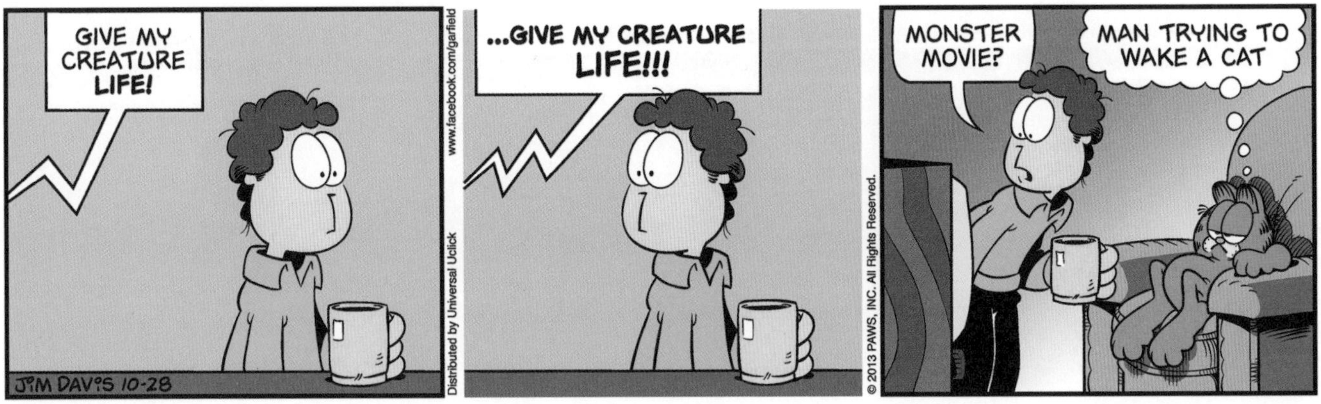
GIVE MY CREATURE LIFE!
JIM DAVIS 10-28
Distributed by Universal Uclick www.facebook.com/garfield
...GIVE MY CREATURE LIFE!!!
© 2013 PAWS, INC. All Rights Reserved.
MONSTER MOVIE?
MAN TRYING TO WAKE A CAT

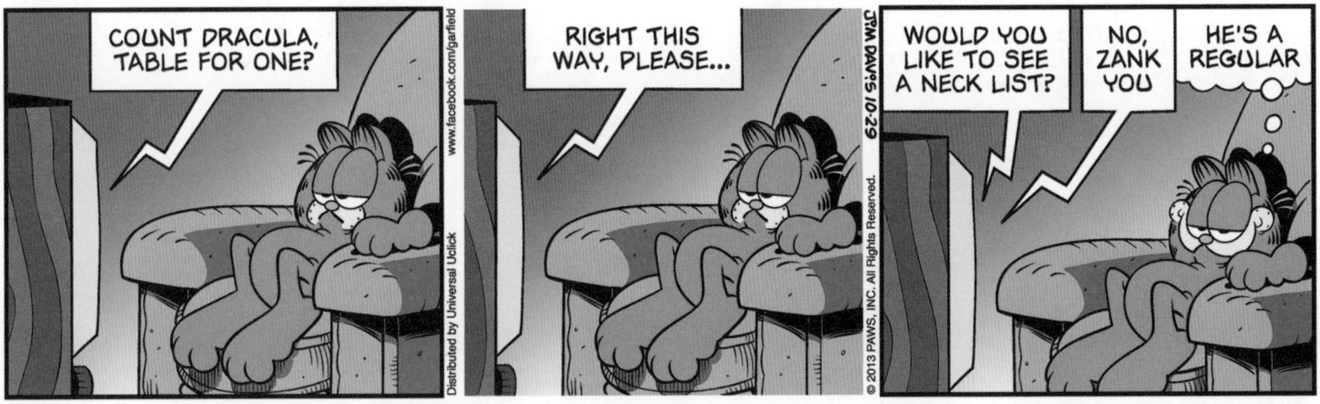
COUNT DRACULA, TABLE FOR ONE?
Distributed by Universal Uclick www.facebook.com/garfield
RIGHT THIS WAY, PLEASE...
JIM DAVIS 10-29
© 2013 PAWS, INC. All Rights Reserved.
WOULD YOU LIKE TO SEE A NECK LIST?
NO, ZANK YOU
HE'S A REGULAR

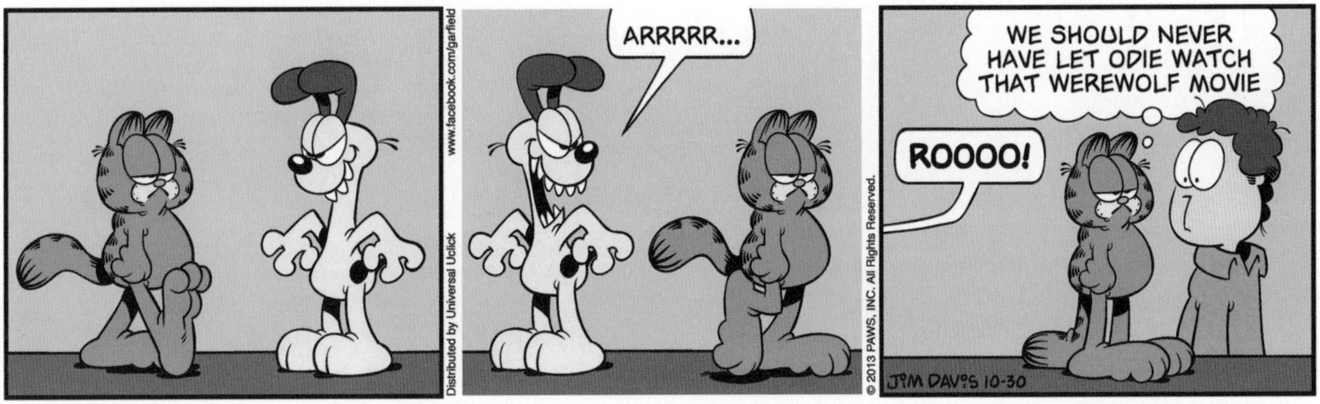
Distributed by Universal Uclick www.facebook.com/garfield
ARRRRR...
© 2013 PAWS, INC. All Rights Reserved.
WE SHOULD NEVER HAVE LET ODIE WATCH THAT WEREWOLF MOVIE
ROOOO!
JIM DAVIS 10-30

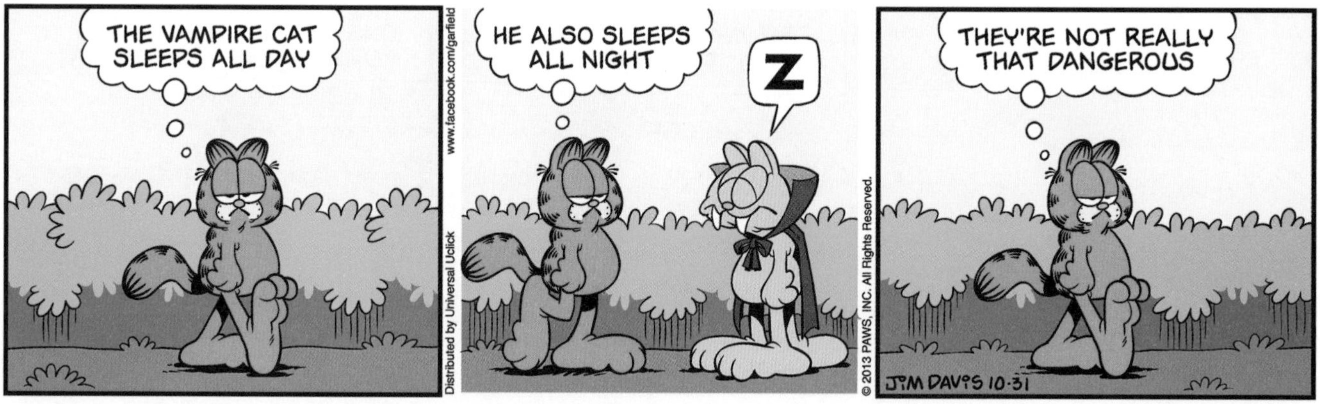
THE VAMPIRE CAT SLEEPS ALL DAY
HE ALSO SLEEPS ALL NIGHT
Z
THEY'RE NOT REALLY THAT DANGEROUS
JIM DAVIS 10-31
Distributed by Universal Uclick
www.facebook.com/garfield
© 2013 PAWS, INC. All Rights Reserved.

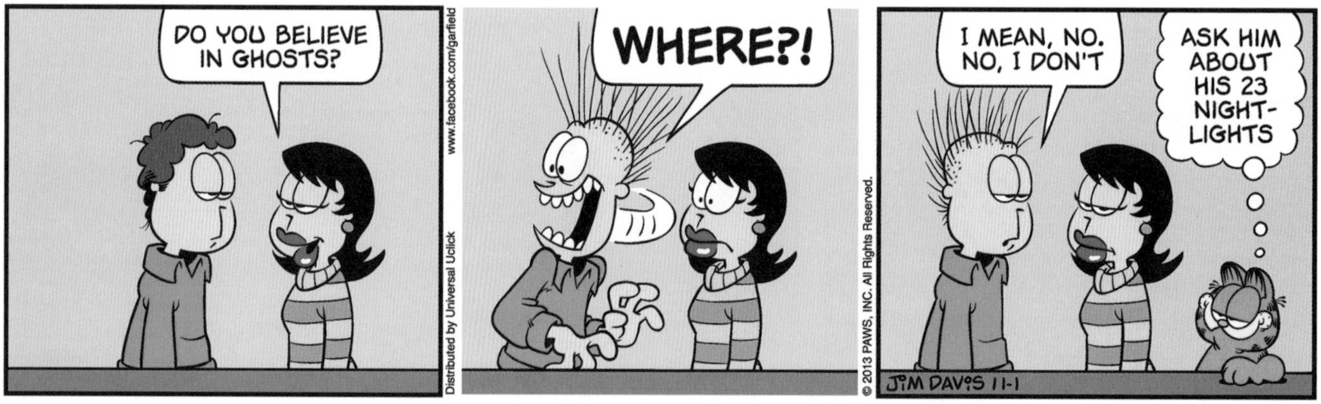
DO YOU BELIEVE IN GHOSTS?
WHERE?!
I MEAN, NO. NO, I DON'T
ASK HIM ABOUT HIS 23 NIGHT-LIGHTS
JIM DAVIS 11-1
Distributed by Universal Uclick
www.facebook.com/garfield
© 2013 PAWS, INC. All Rights Reserved.

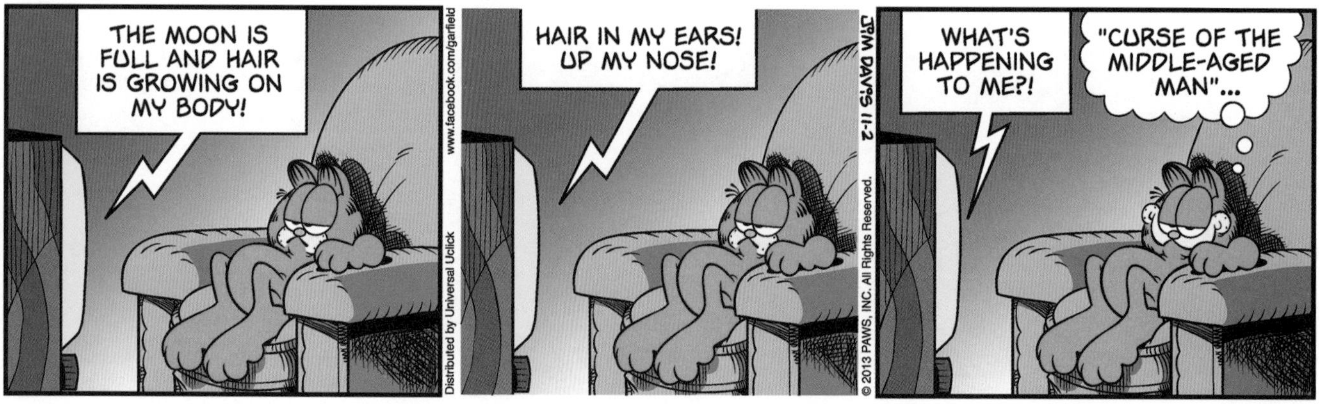
THE MOON IS FULL AND HAIR IS GROWING ON MY BODY!
HAIR IN MY EARS! UP MY NOSE!
WHAT'S HAPPENING TO ME?!
"CURSE OF THE MIDDLE-AGED MAN"...
JIM DAVIS 11-2
Distributed by Universal Uclick
www.facebook.com/garfield
© 2013 PAWS, INC. All Rights Reserved.

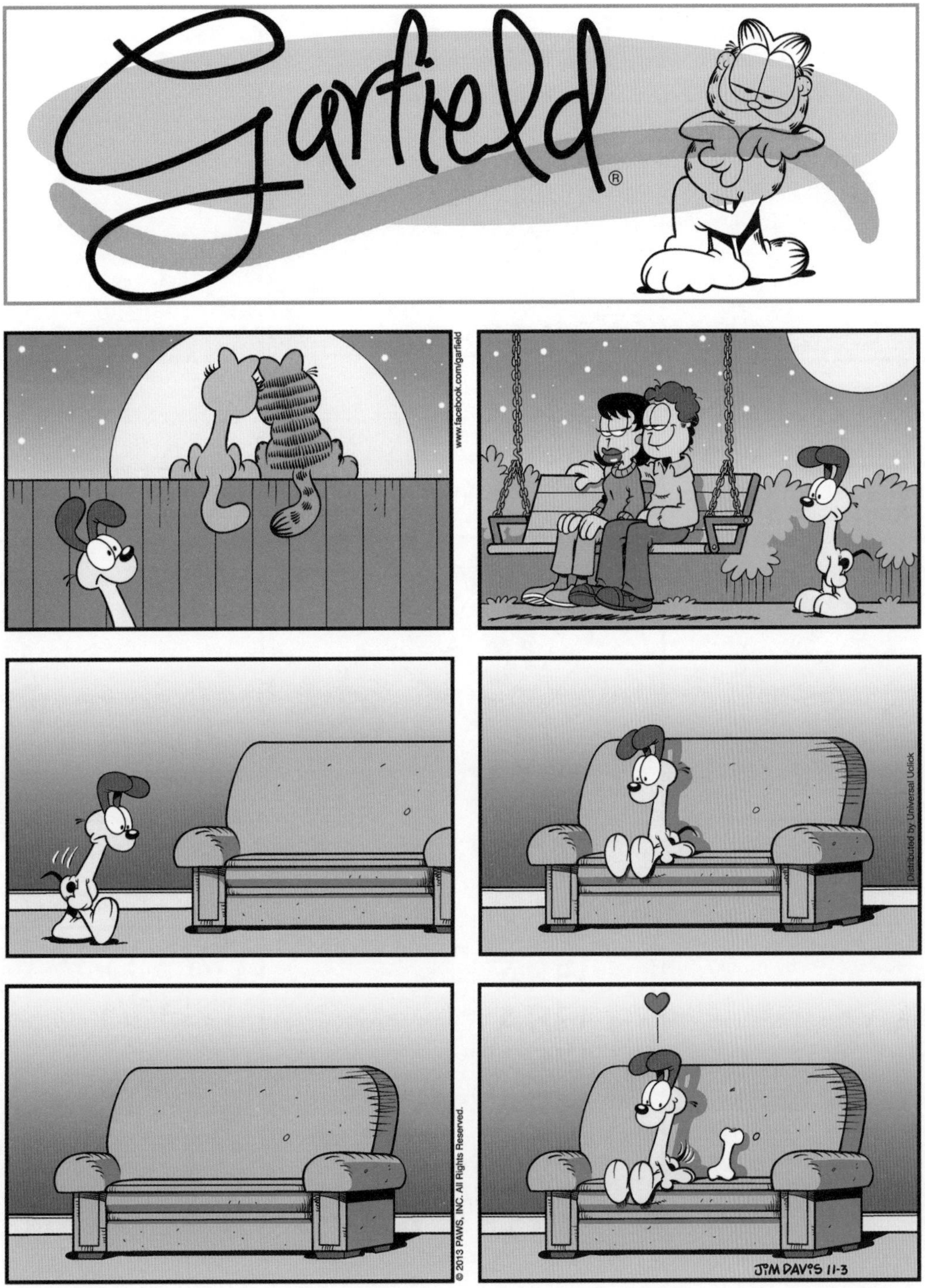
Garfield
www.facebook.com/garfield
Distributed by Universal Uclick
© 2013 PAWS, INC. All Rights Reserved.
JIM DAVIS 11-3

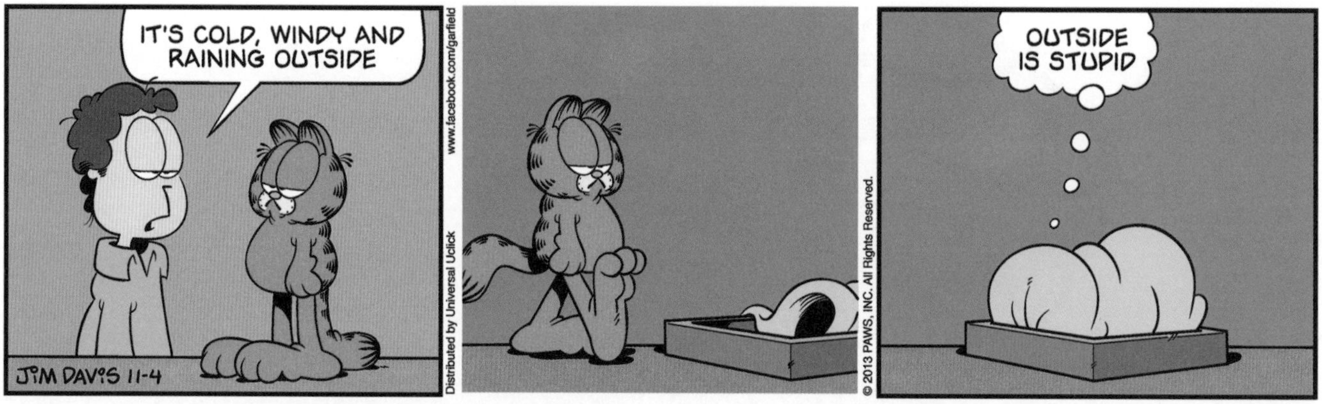
IT'S COLD, WINDY AND RAINING OUTSIDE
OUTSIDE IS STUPID
JIM DAVIS 11-4
Distributed by Universal Uclick
www.facebook.com/garfield
© 2013 PAWS, INC. All Rights Reserved.

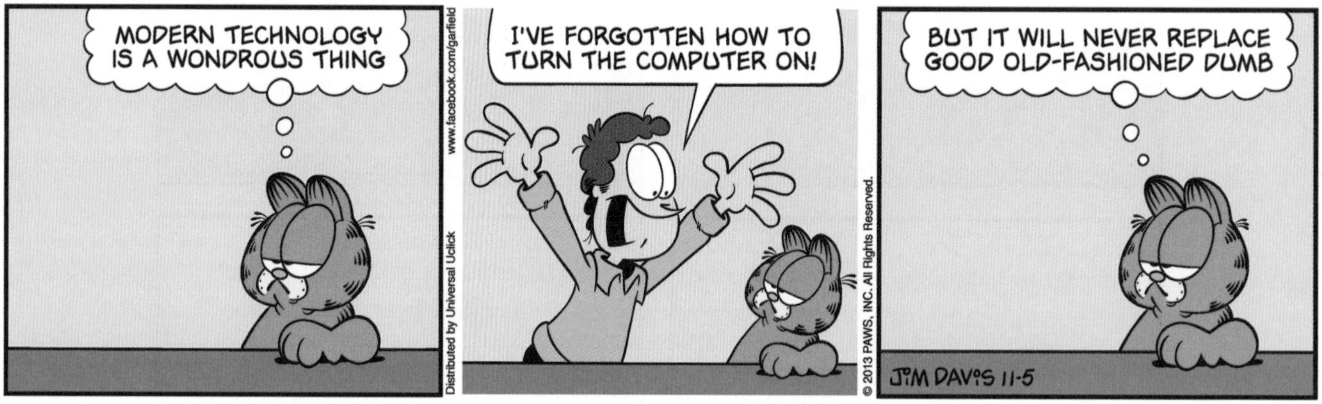
MODERN TECHNOLOGY IS A WONDROUS THING
I'VE FORGOTTEN HOW TO TURN THE COMPUTER ON!
BUT IT WILL NEVER REPLACE GOOD OLD-FASHIONED DUMB
JIM DAVIS 11-5
Distributed by Universal Uclick
www.facebook.com/garfield
© 2013 PAWS, INC. All Rights Reserved.

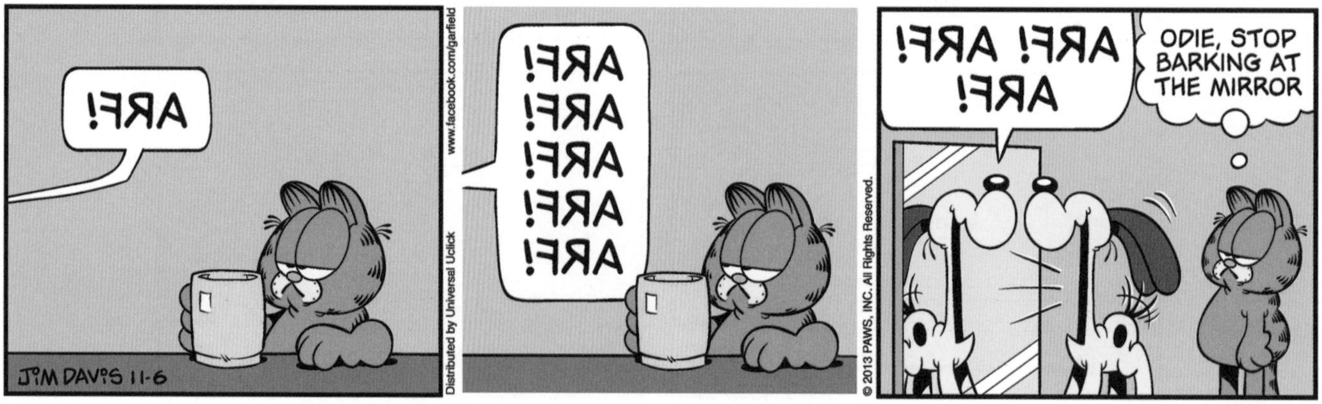
ARF!
ARF! ARF! ARF! ARF! ARF!
ARF! ARF! ARF!
ODIE, STOP BARKING AT THE MIRROR
JIM DAVIS 11-6
Distributed by Universal Uclick
www.facebook.com/garfield
© 2013 PAWS, INC. All Rights Reserved.

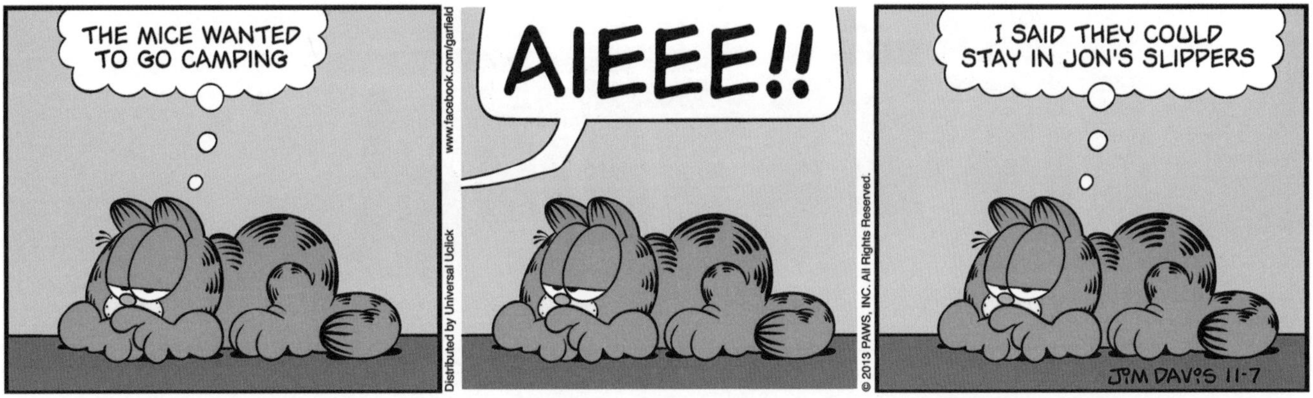
THE MICE WANTED TO GO CAMPING
AIEEE!!
I SAID THEY COULD STAY IN JON'S SLIPPERS
JIM DAVIS 11-7
Distributed by Universal Uclick www.facebook.com/garfield
© 2013 PAWS, INC. All Rights Reserved.

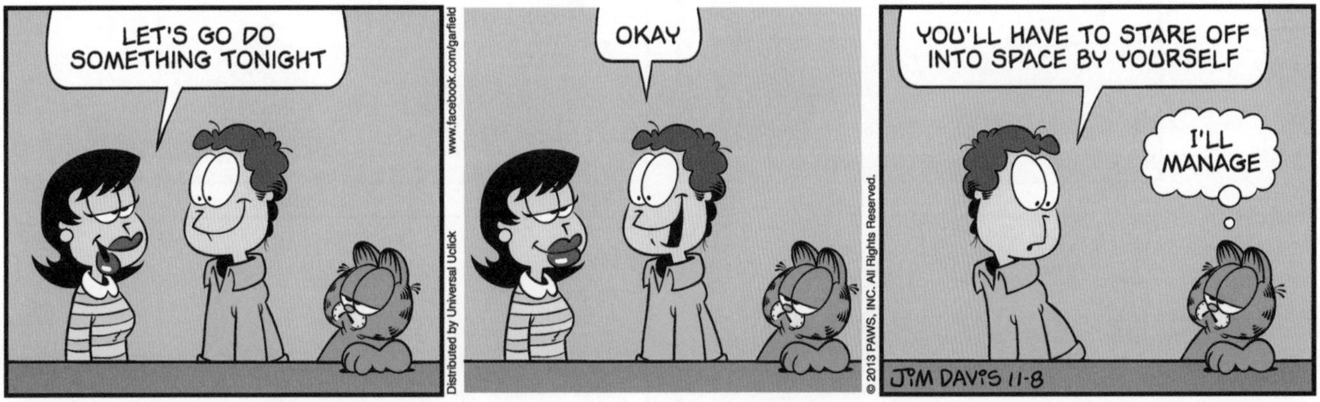
LET'S GO DO SOMETHING TONIGHT
OKAY
YOU'LL HAVE TO STARE OFF INTO SPACE BY YOURSELF
I'LL MANAGE
JIM DAVIS 11-8
Distributed by Universal Uclick www.facebook.com/garfield
© 2013 PAWS, INC. All Rights Reserved.

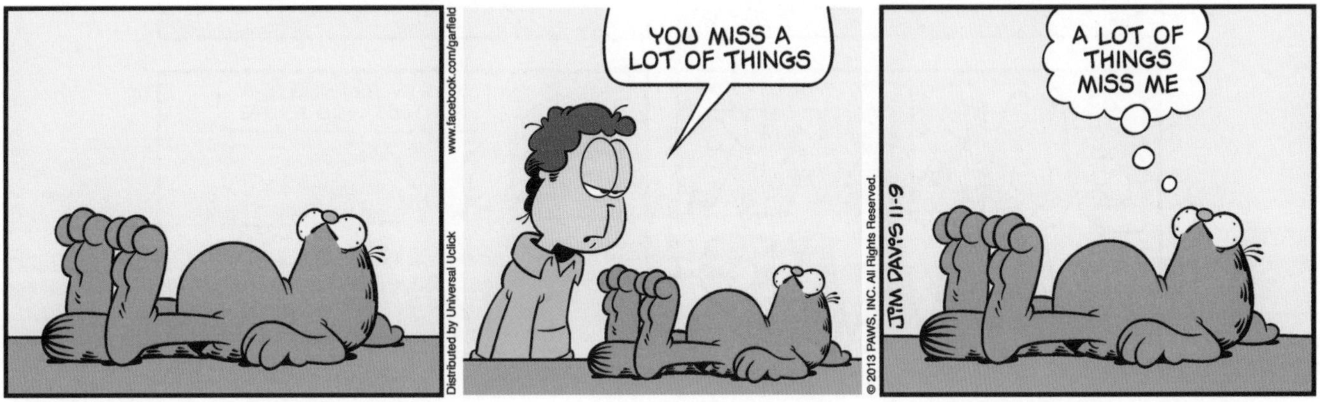
YOU MISS A LOT OF THINGS
A LOT OF THINGS MISS ME
JIM DAVIS 11-9
Distributed by Universal Uclick www.facebook.com/garfield
© 2013 PAWS, INC. All Rights Reserved.

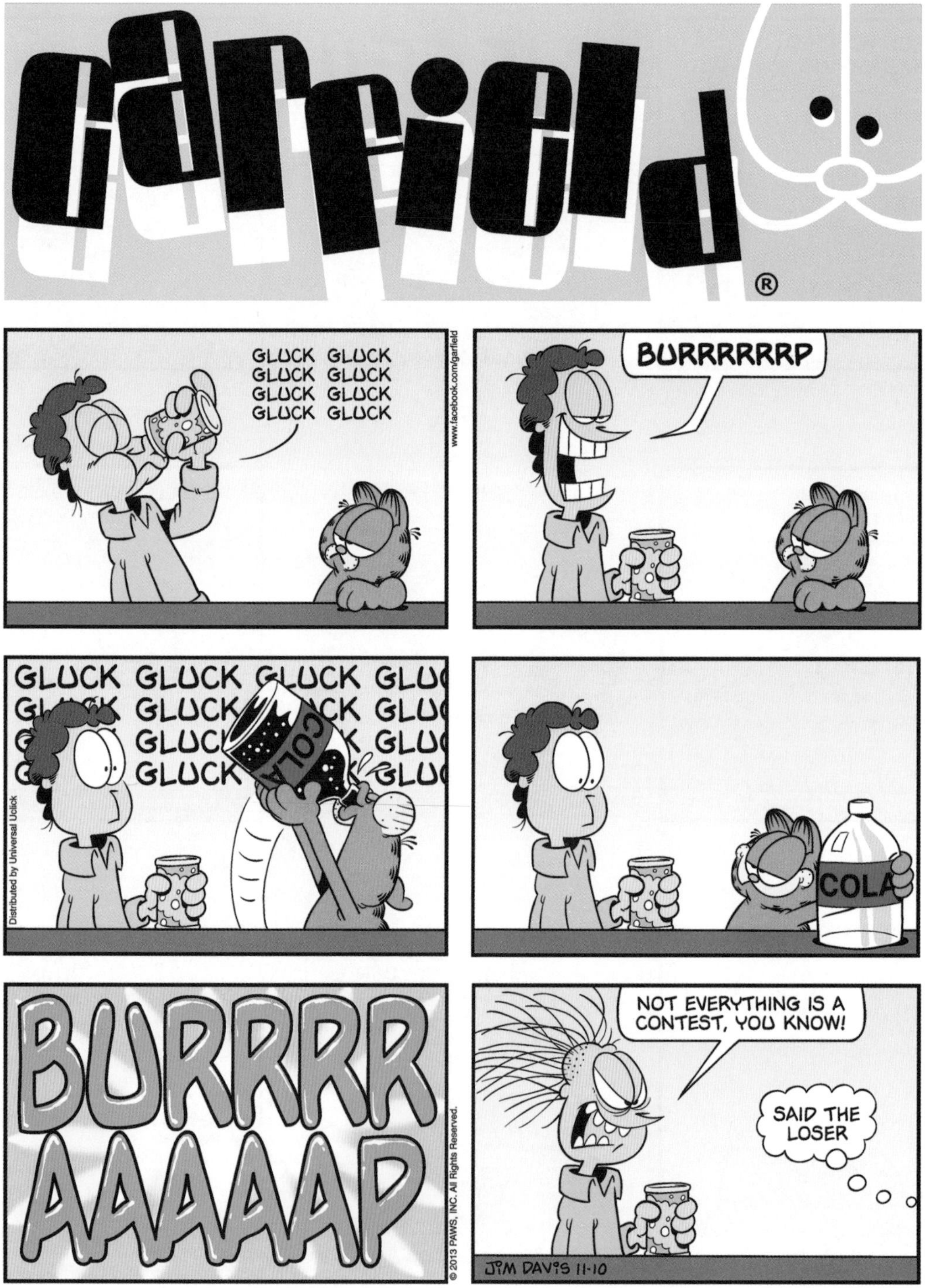
garfield®
GLUCK GLUCK GLUCK GLUCK GLUCK GLUCK GLUCK GLUCK
www.facebook.com/garfield
BURRRRRRP
GLUCK GLUCK GLUCK GLUCK
Distributed by Universal Uclick
COLA
COLA
BURRRR AAAAAP
© 2013 PAWS, INC. All Rights Reserved.
NOT EVERYTHING IS A CONTEST, YOU KNOW!
SAID THE LOSER
JIM DAVIS 11-10

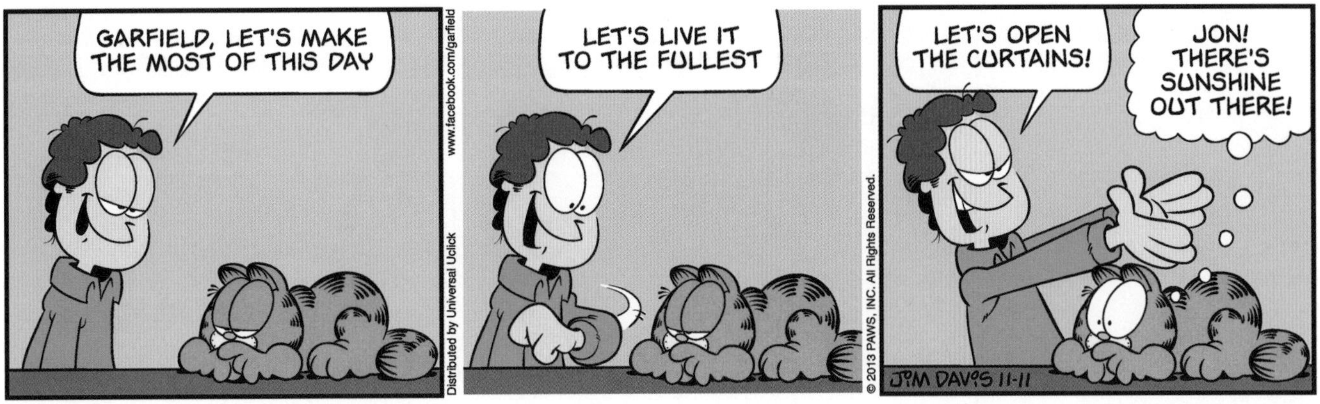
GARFIELD, LET'S MAKE THE MOST OF THIS DAY
www.facebook.com/garfield
Distributed by Universal Uclick
LET'S LIVE IT TO THE FULLEST
© 2013 PAWS, INC. All Rights Reserved.
LET'S OPEN THE CURTAINS!
JON! THERE'S SUNSHINE OUT THERE!
JIM DAVIS 11-11

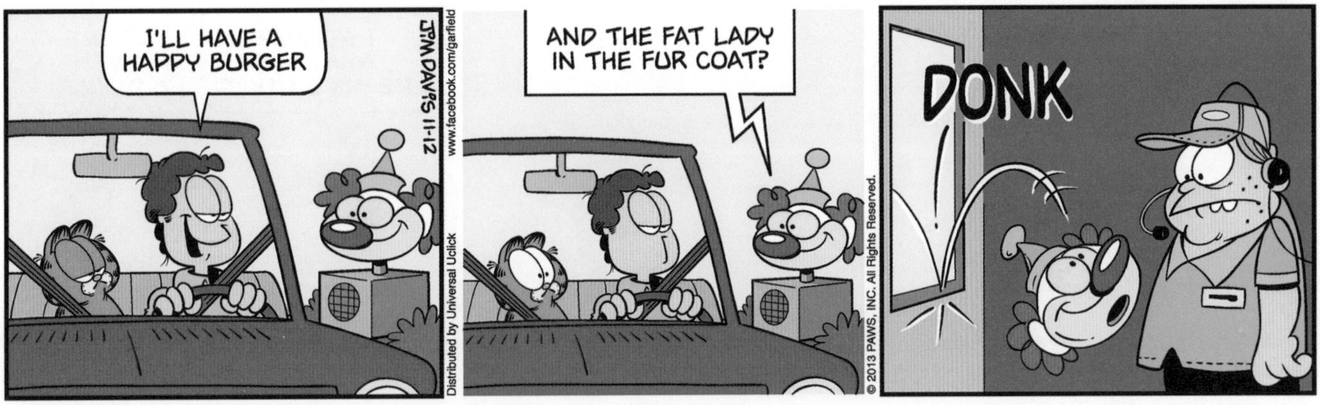
I'LL HAVE A HAPPY BURGER
JIM DAVIS 11-12
www.facebook.com/garfield
Distributed by Universal Uclick
AND THE FAT LADY IN THE FUR COAT?
© 2013 PAWS, INC. All Rights Reserved.
DONK

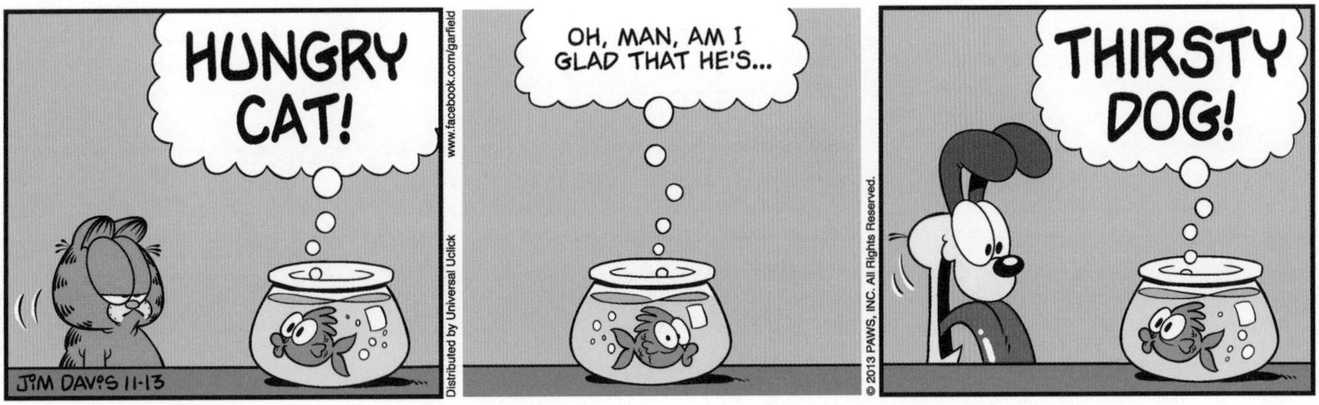
HUNGRY CAT!
JIM DAVIS 11-13
www.facebook.com/garfield
Distributed by Universal Uclick
OH, MAN, AM I GLAD THAT HE'S...
© 2013 PAWS, INC. All Rights Reserved.
THIRSTY DOG!

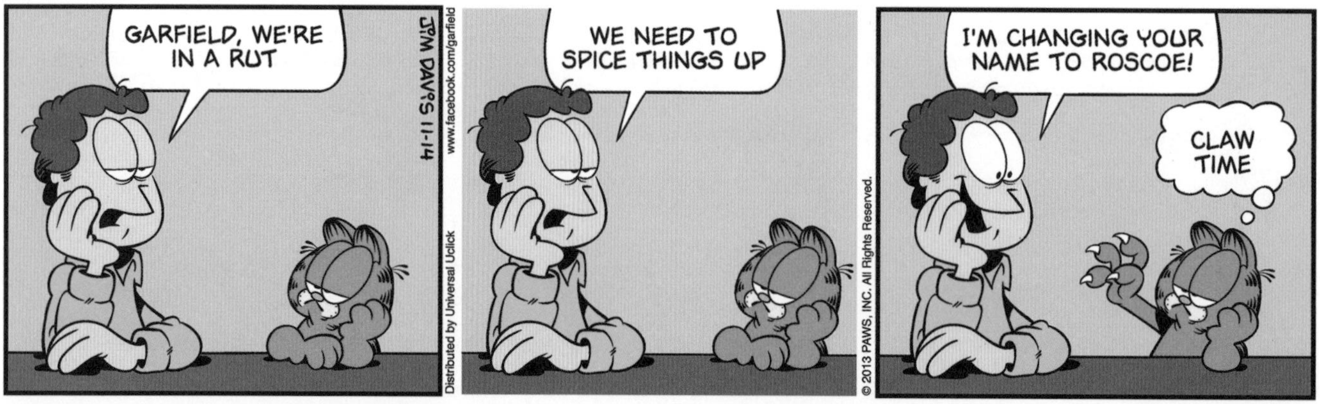
GARFIELD, WE'RE IN A RUT
JIM DAVIS 11-14
www.facebook.com/garfield
Distributed by Universal Uclick
WE NEED TO SPICE THINGS UP
© 2013 PAWS, INC. All Rights Reserved.
I'M CHANGING YOUR NAME TO ROSCOE!
CLAW TIME

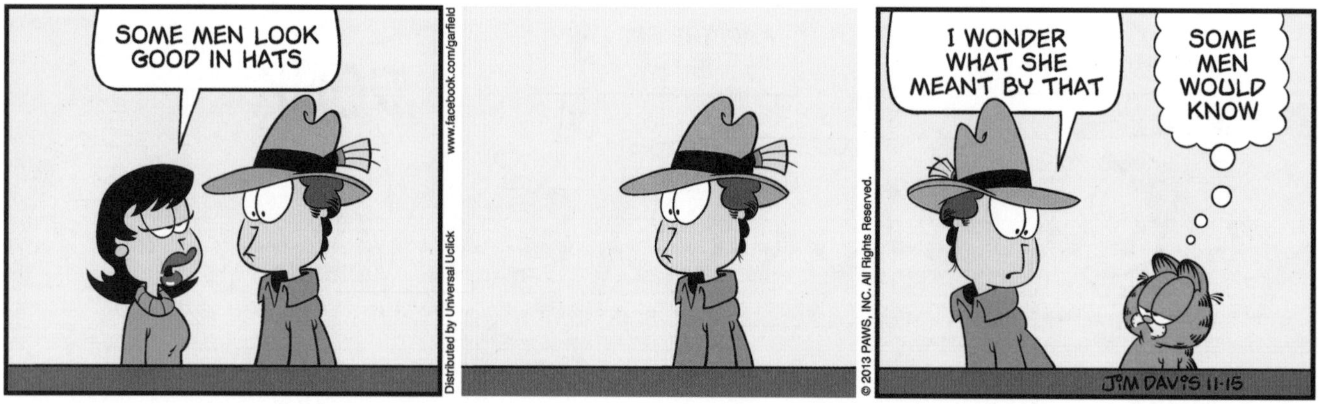
SOME MEN LOOK GOOD IN HATS
www.facebook.com/garfield
Distributed by Universal Uclick
© 2013 PAWS, INC. All Rights Reserved.
I WONDER WHAT SHE MEANT BY THAT
SOME MEN WOULD KNOW
JIM DAVIS 11-15

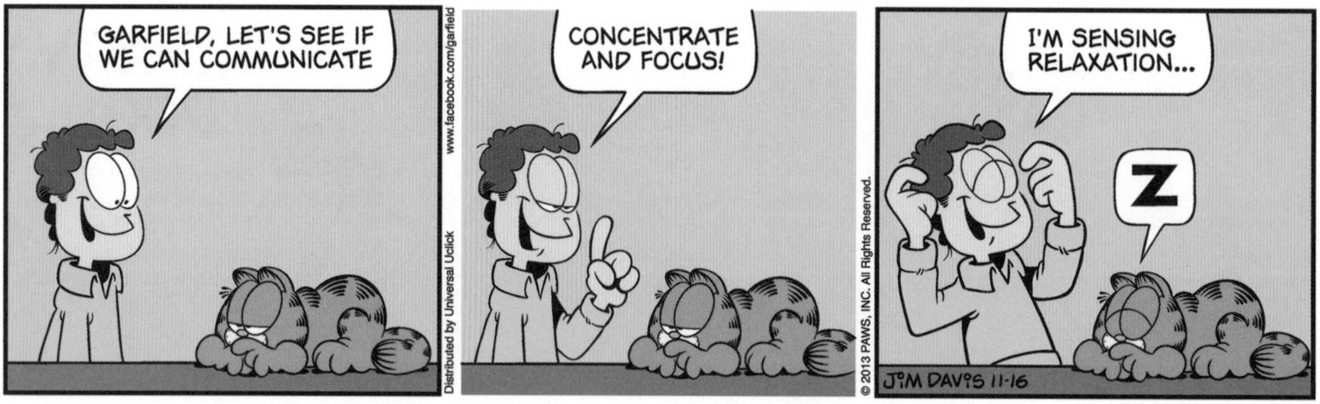
GARFIELD, LET'S SEE IF WE CAN COMMUNICATE
www.facebook.com/garfield
Distributed by Universal Uclick
CONCENTRATE AND FOCUS!
© 2013 PAWS, INC. All Rights Reserved.
I'M SENSING RELAXATION...
Z
JIM DAVIS 11-16

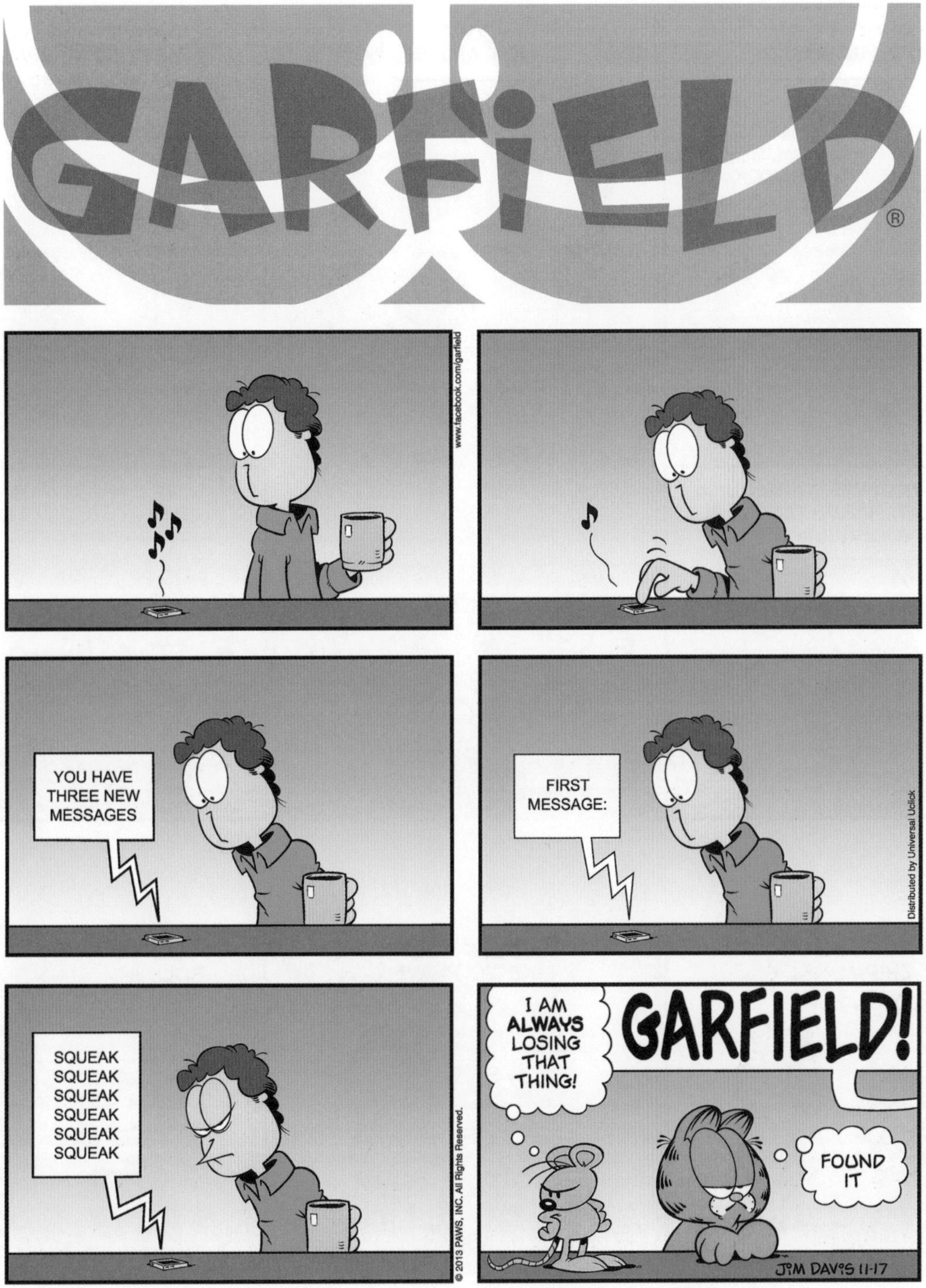
GARFIELD®
www.facebook.com/garfield
YOU HAVE THREE NEW MESSAGES
FIRST MESSAGE:
Distributed by Universal Uclick
SQUEAK SQUEAK SQUEAK SQUEAK SQUEAK SQUEAK
© 2013 PAWS, INC. All Rights Reserved.
I AM ALWAYS LOSING THAT THING!
GARFIELD!
FOUND IT
JIM DAVIS 11-17

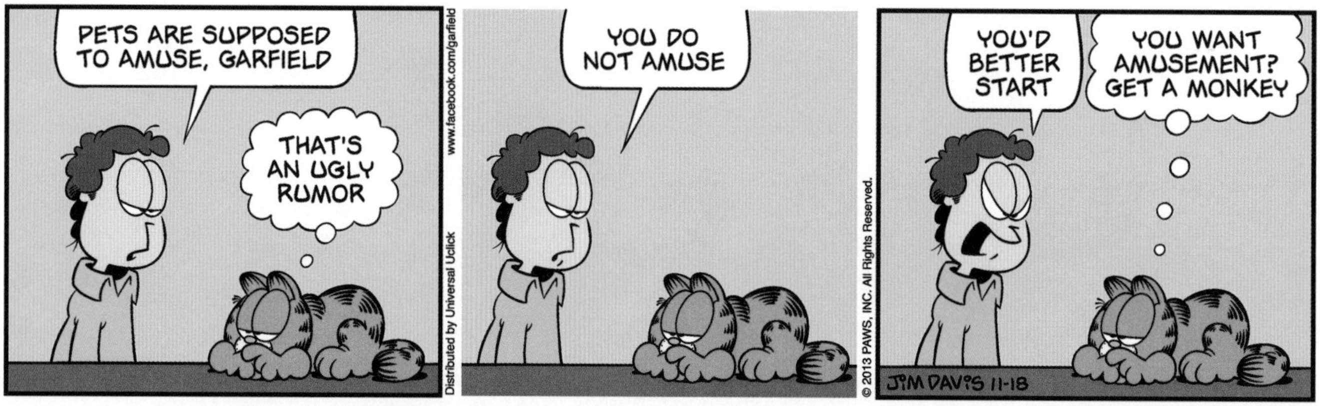
PETS ARE SUPPOSED TO AMUSE, GARFIELD
THAT'S AN UGLY RUMOR
YOU DO NOT AMUSE
YOU'D BETTER START
YOU WANT AMUSEMENT? GET A MONKEY
Distributed by Universal Uclick www.facebook.com/garfield
© 2013 PAWS, INC. All Rights Reserved.
JIM DAVIS 11-18

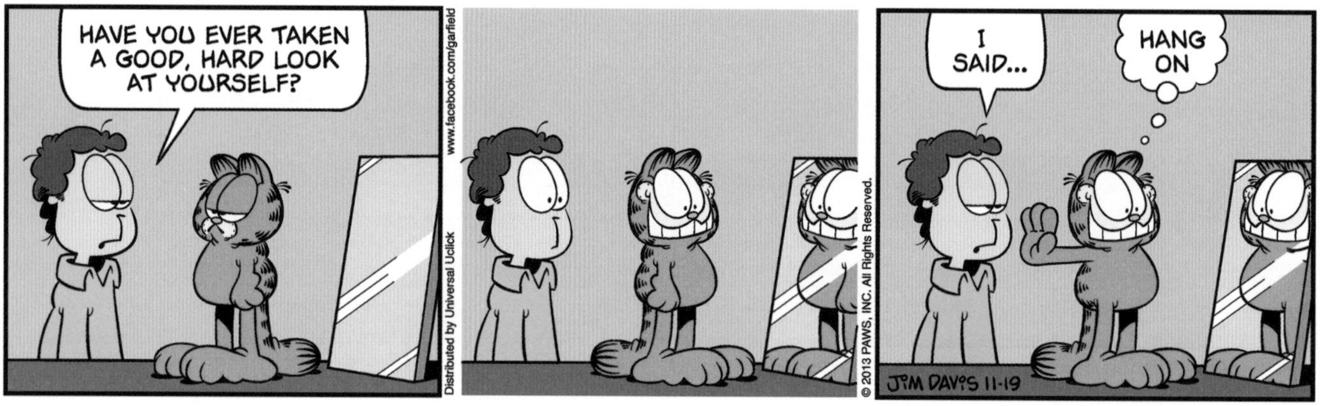
HAVE YOU EVER TAKEN A GOOD, HARD LOOK AT YOURSELF?
I SAID...
HANG ON
Distributed by Universal Uclick www.facebook.com/garfield
© 2013 PAWS, INC. All Rights Reserved.
JIM DAVIS 11-19

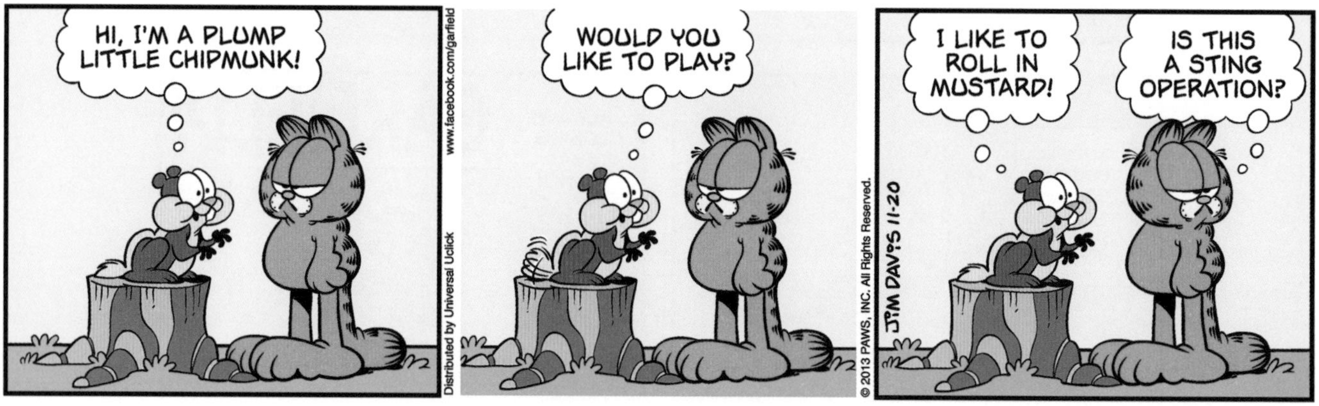
HI, I'M A PLUMP LITTLE CHIPMUNK!
WOULD YOU LIKE TO PLAY?
I LIKE TO ROLL IN MUSTARD!
IS THIS A STING OPERATION?
Distributed by Universal Uclick www.facebook.com/garfield
© 2013 PAWS, INC. All Rights Reserved.
JIM DAVIS 11-20

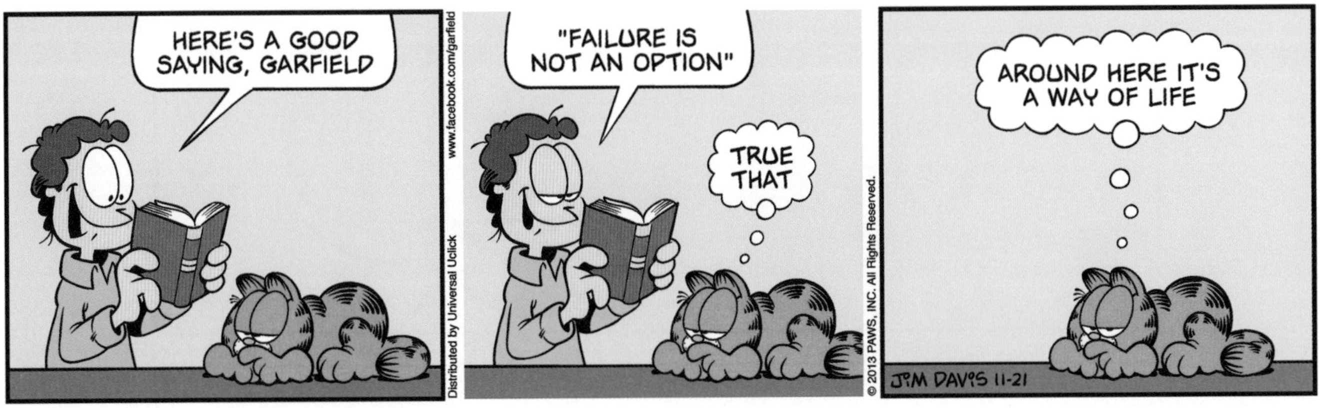
HERE'S A GOOD SAYING, GARFIELD
"FAILURE IS NOT AN OPTION"
TRUE THAT
AROUND HERE IT'S A WAY OF LIFE
JIM DAVIS 11-21
Distributed by Universal Uclick www.facebook.com/garfield
© 2013 PAWS, INC. All Rights Reserved.

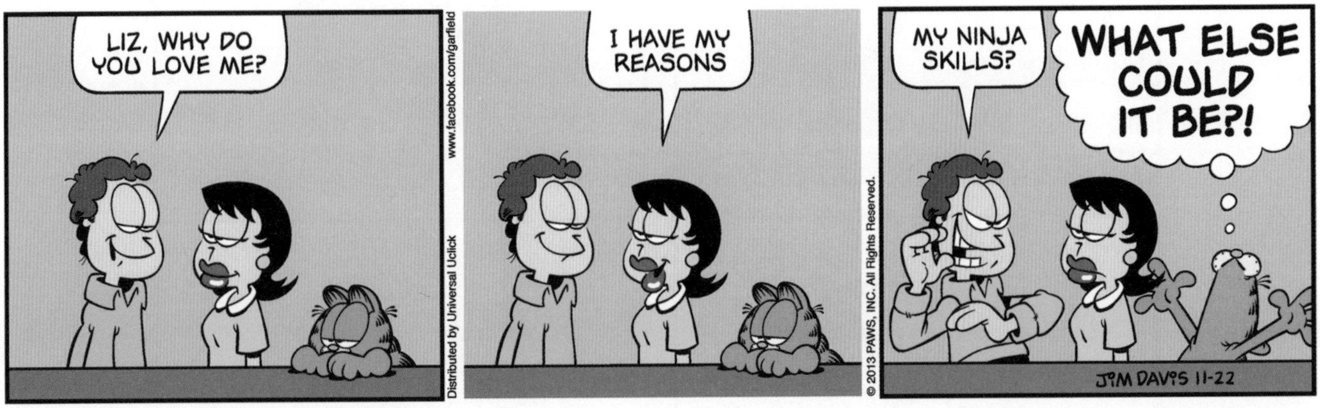
LIZ, WHY DO YOU LOVE ME?
I HAVE MY REASONS
MY NINJA SKILLS?
WHAT ELSE COULD IT BE?!
JIM DAVIS 11-22
Distributed by Universal Uclick www.facebook.com/garfield
© 2013 PAWS, INC. All Rights Reserved.

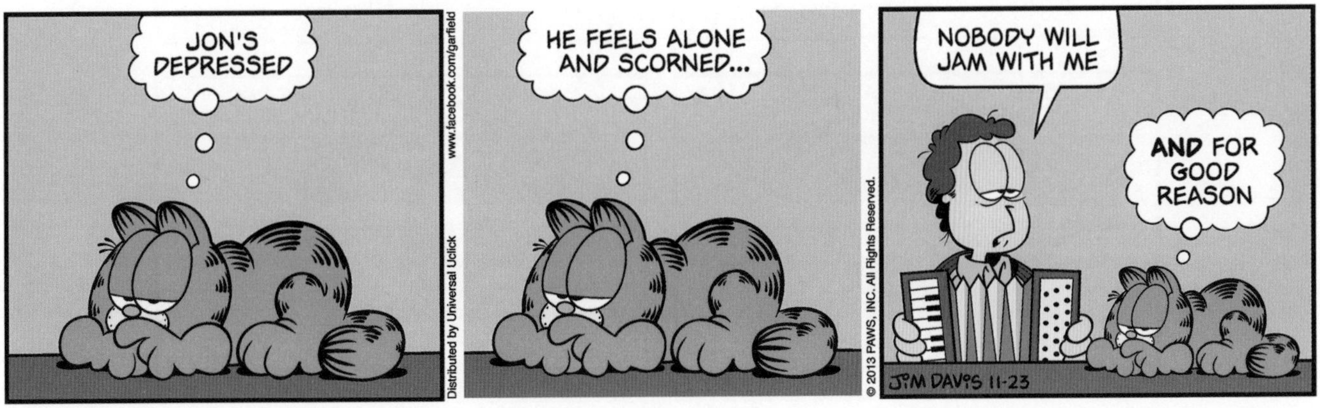
JON'S DEPRESSED
HE FEELS ALONE AND SCORNED...
NOBODY WILL JAM WITH ME
AND FOR GOOD REASON
JIM DAVIS 11-23
Distributed by Universal Uclick www.facebook.com/garfield
© 2013 PAWS, INC. All Rights Reserved.

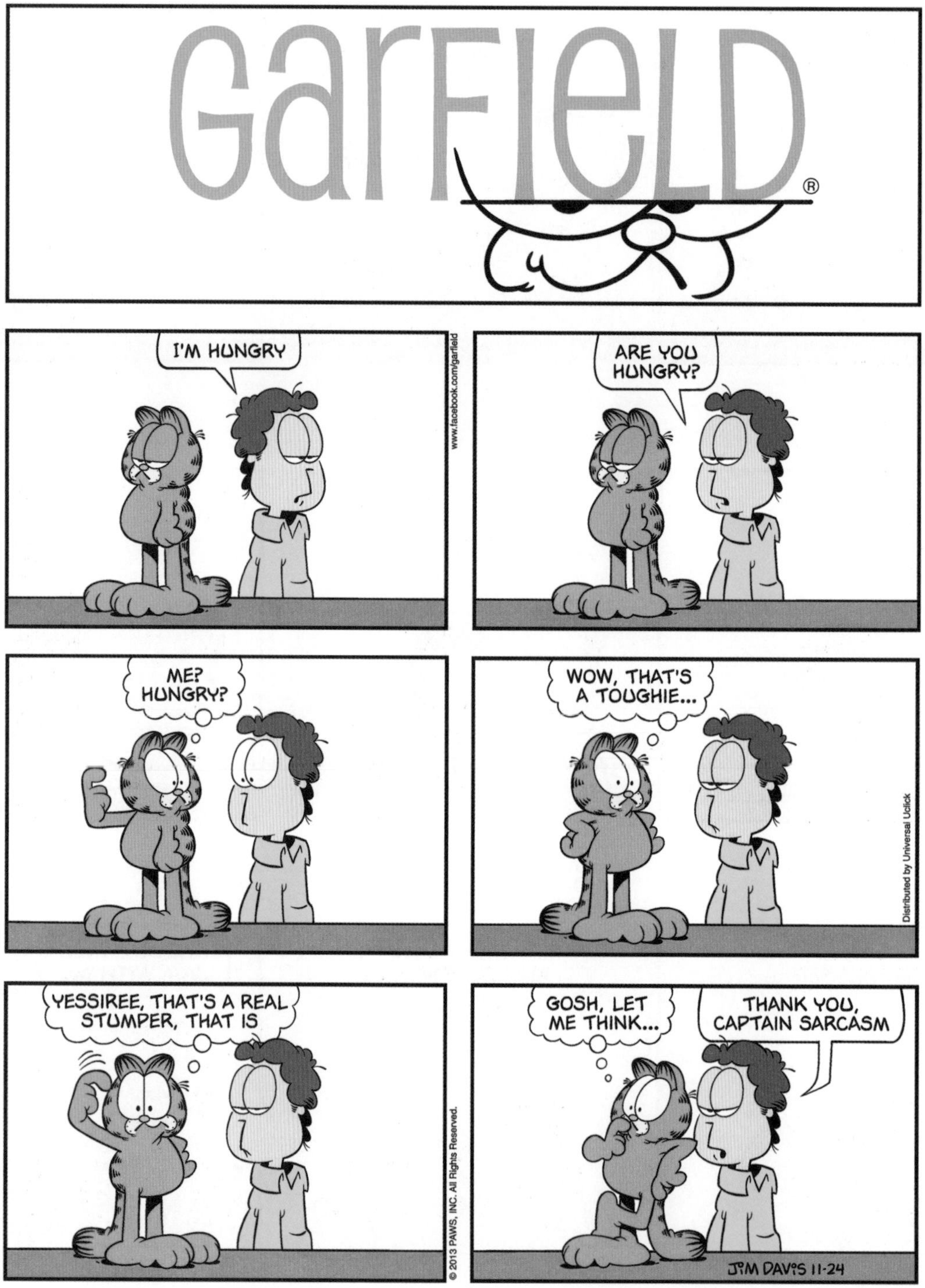
GARFIELD
I'M HUNGRY
www.facebook.com/garfield
ARE YOU HUNGRY?
ME? HUNGRY?
WOW, THAT'S A TOUGHIE...
Distributed by Universal Uclick
YESSIREE, THAT'S A REAL STUMPER, THAT IS
© 2013 PAWS, INC. All Rights Reserved.
GOSH, LET ME THINK...
THANK YOU, CAPTAIN SARCASM
JIM DAVIS 11-24

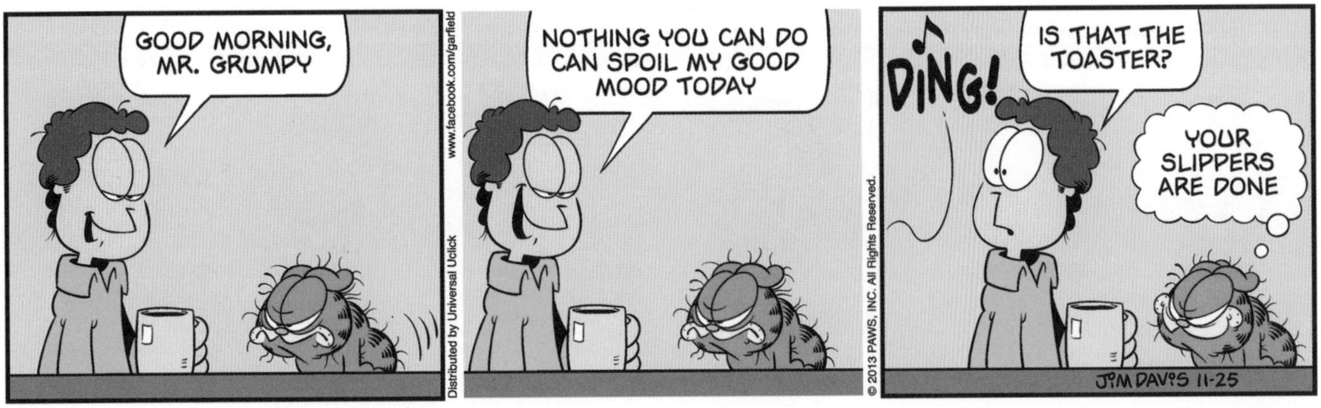
GOOD MORNING, MR. GRUMPY
www.facebook.com/garfield
Distributed by Universal Uclick
NOTHING YOU CAN DO CAN SPOIL MY GOOD MOOD TODAY
DING!
IS THAT THE TOASTER?
YOUR SLIPPERS ARE DONE
© 2013 PAWS, INC. All Rights Reserved.
JIM DAVIS 11-25

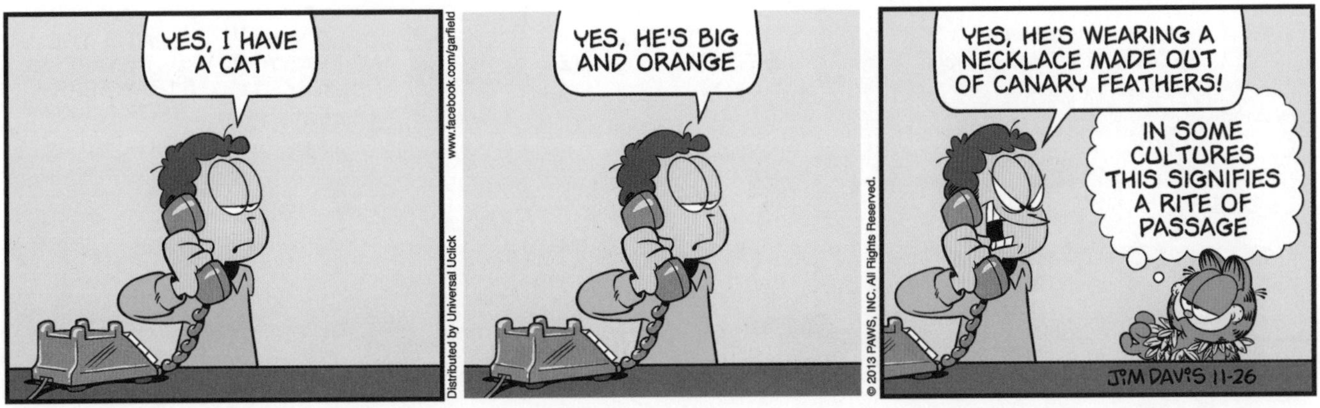
YES, I HAVE A CAT
www.facebook.com/garfield
Distributed by Universal Uclick
YES, HE'S BIG AND ORANGE
YES, HE'S WEARING A NECKLACE MADE OUT OF CANARY FEATHERS!
IN SOME CULTURES THIS SIGNIFIES A RITE OF PASSAGE
© 2013 PAWS, INC. All Rights Reserved.
JIM DAVIS 11-26

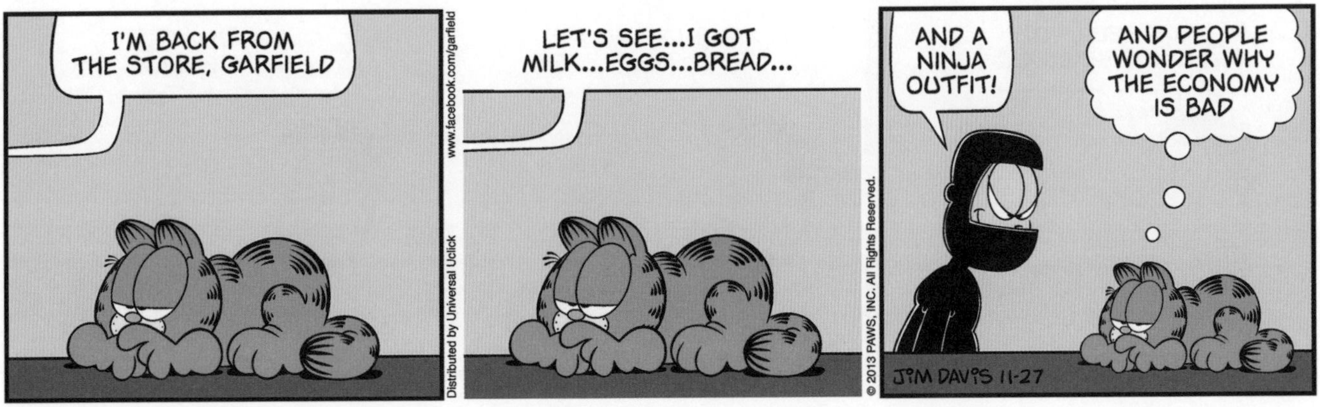
I'M BACK FROM THE STORE, GARFIELD
www.facebook.com/garfield
Distributed by Universal Uclick
LET'S SEE...I GOT MILK...EGGS...BREAD...
AND A NINJA OUTFIT!
AND PEOPLE WONDER WHY THE ECONOMY IS BAD
© 2013 PAWS, INC. All Rights Reserved.
JIM DAVIS 11-27

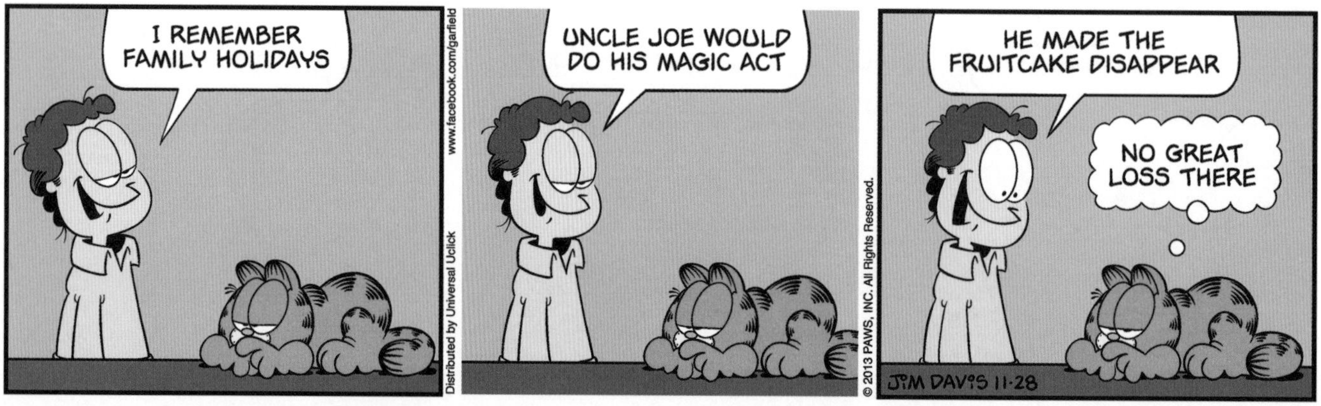
I REMEMBER FAMILY HOLIDAYS
UNCLE JOE WOULD DO HIS MAGIC ACT
HE MADE THE FRUITCAKE DISAPPEAR
NO GREAT LOSS THERE
JIM DAVIS 11-28
Distributed by Universal Uclick www.facebook.com/garfield
© 2013 PAWS, INC. All Rights Reserved.

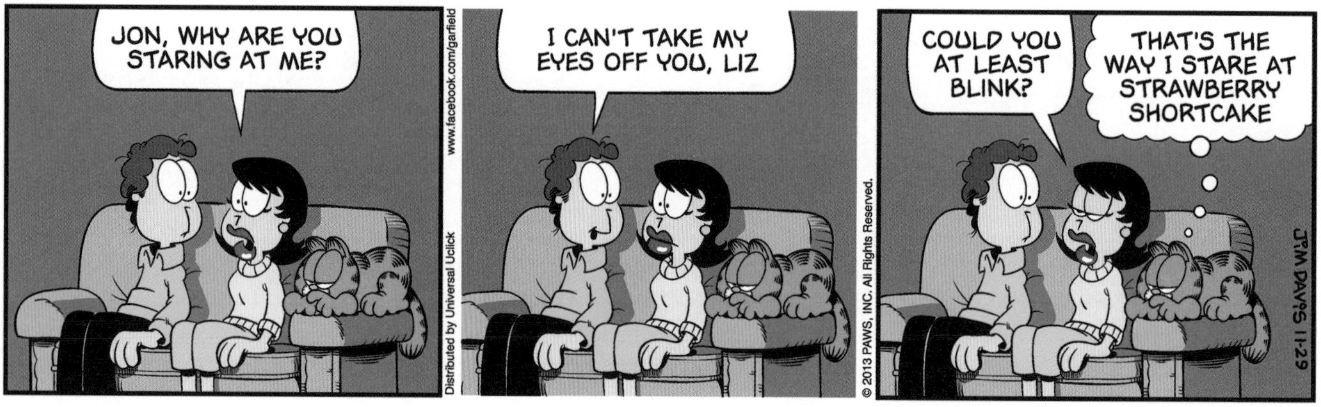
JON, WHY ARE YOU STARING AT ME?
I CAN'T TAKE MY EYES OFF YOU, LIZ
COULD YOU AT LEAST BLINK?
THAT'S THE WAY I STARE AT STRAWBERRY SHORTCAKE
JIM DAVIS 11-29
Distributed by Universal Uclick www.facebook.com/garfield
© 2013 PAWS, INC. All Rights Reserved.

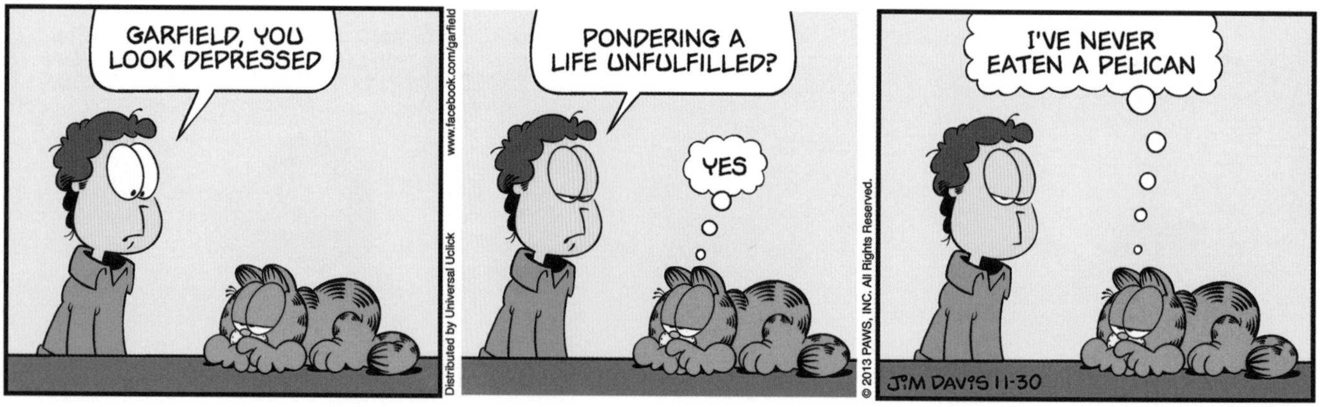
GARFIELD, YOU LOOK DEPRESSED
PONDERING A LIFE UNFULFILLED?
YES
I'VE NEVER EATEN A PELICAN
JIM DAVIS 11-30
Distributed by Universal Uclick www.facebook.com/garfield
© 2013 PAWS, INC. All Rights Reserved.

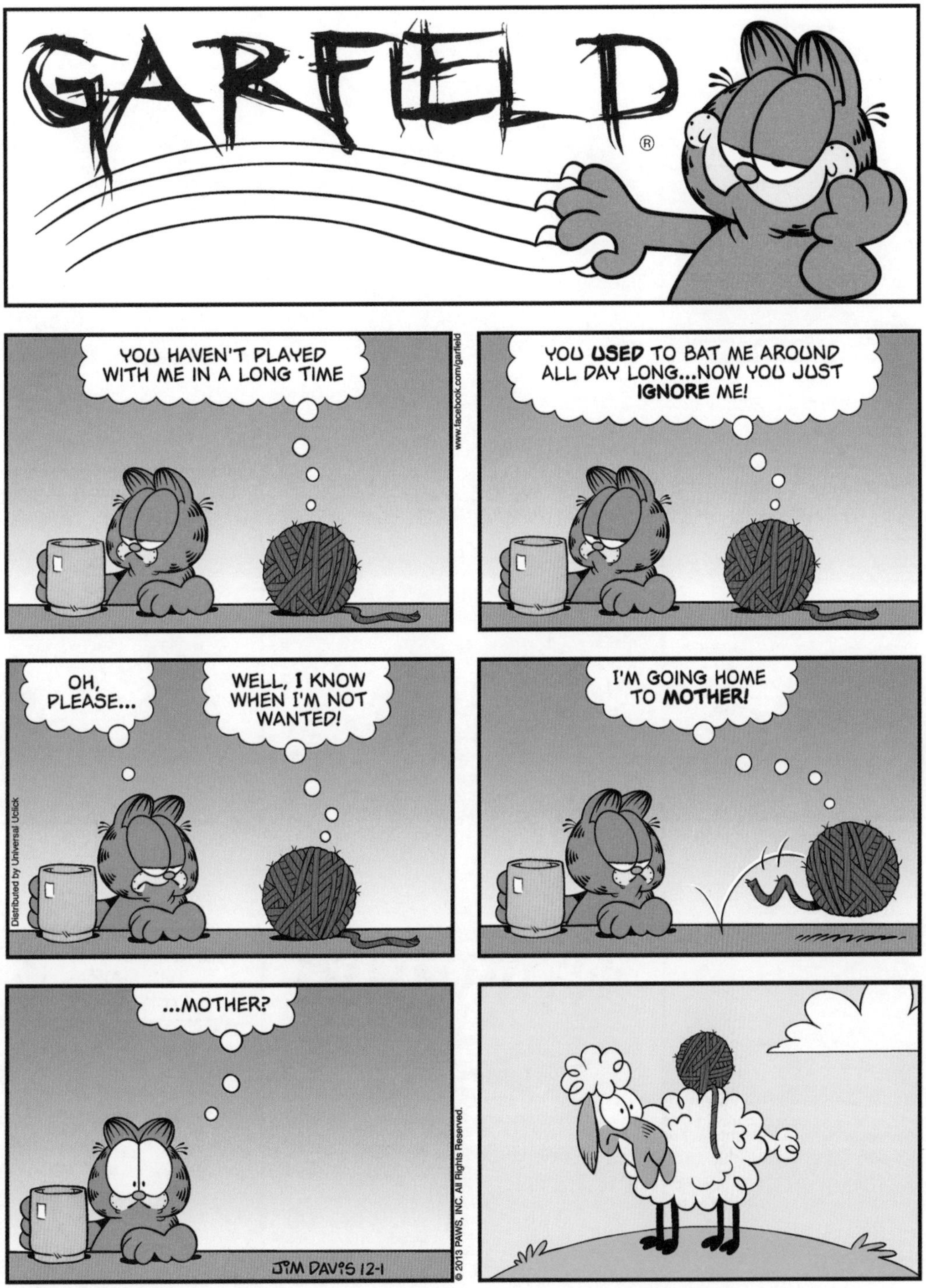
GARFIELD®
YOU HAVEN'T PLAYED WITH ME IN A LONG TIME
YOU USED TO BAT ME AROUND ALL DAY LONG...NOW YOU JUST IGNORE ME!
OH, PLEASE...
WELL, I KNOW WHEN I'M NOT WANTED!
I'M GOING HOME TO MOTHER!
...MOTHER?
JIM DAVIS 12-1
www.facebook.com/garfield
Distributed by Universal Uclick
© 2013 PAWS, INC. All Rights Reserved.

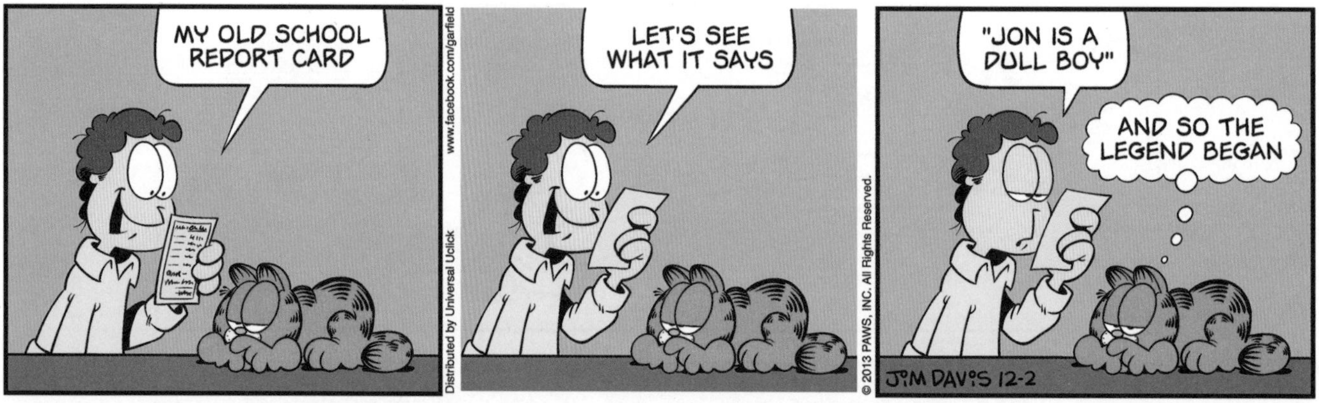
MY OLD SCHOOL REPORT CARD
LET'S SEE WHAT IT SAYS
"JON IS A DULL BOY"
AND SO THE LEGEND BEGAN
JIM DAVIS 12-2
www.facebook.com/garfield
Distributed by Universal Uclick
© 2013 PAWS, INC. All Rights Reserved.

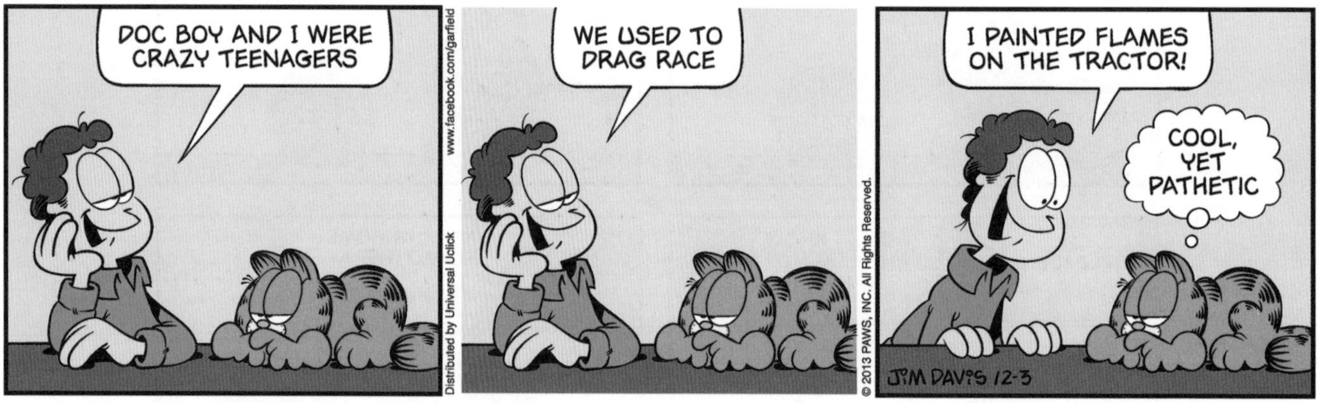
DOC BOY AND I WERE CRAZY TEENAGERS
WE USED TO DRAG RACE
I PAINTED FLAMES ON THE TRACTOR!
COOL, YET PATHETIC
JIM DAVIS 12-3
www.facebook.com/garfield
Distributed by Universal Uclick
© 2013 PAWS, INC. All Rights Reserved.

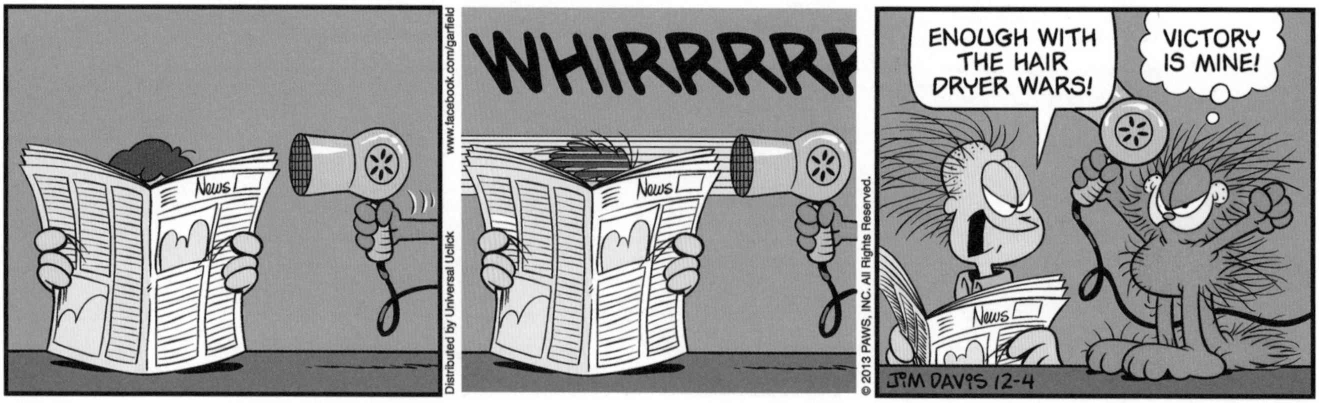
News
WHIRRRRR
News
ENOUGH WITH THE HAIR DRYER WARS!
VICTORY IS MINE!
News
JIM DAVIS 12-4
www.facebook.com/garfield
Distributed by Universal Uclick
© 2013 PAWS, INC. All Rights Reserved.

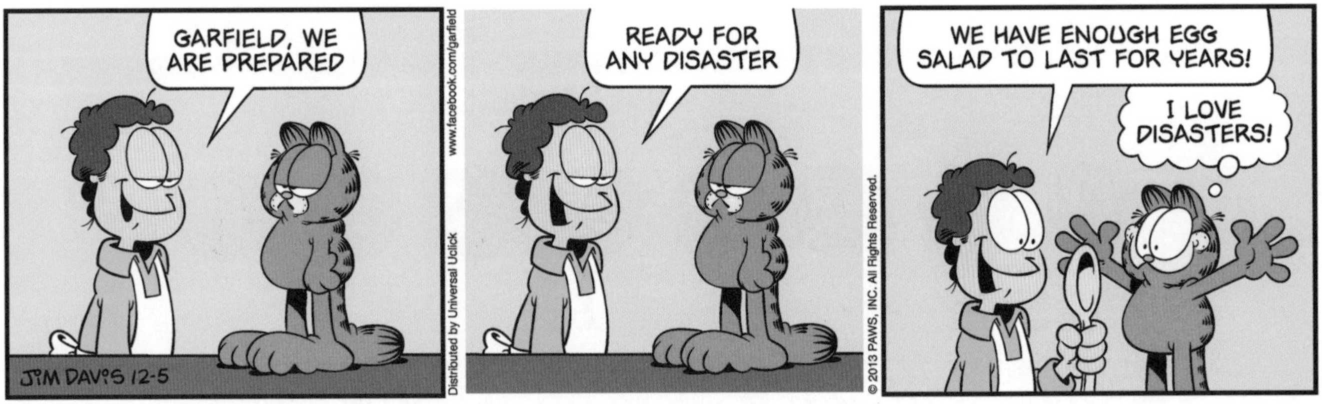
GARFIELD, WE ARE PREPARED
JIM DAVIS 12-5
Distributed by Universal Uclick
www.facebook.com/garfield
READY FOR ANY DISASTER
© 2013 PAWS, INC. All Rights Reserved.
WE HAVE ENOUGH EGG SALAD TO LAST FOR YEARS!
I LOVE DISASTERS!

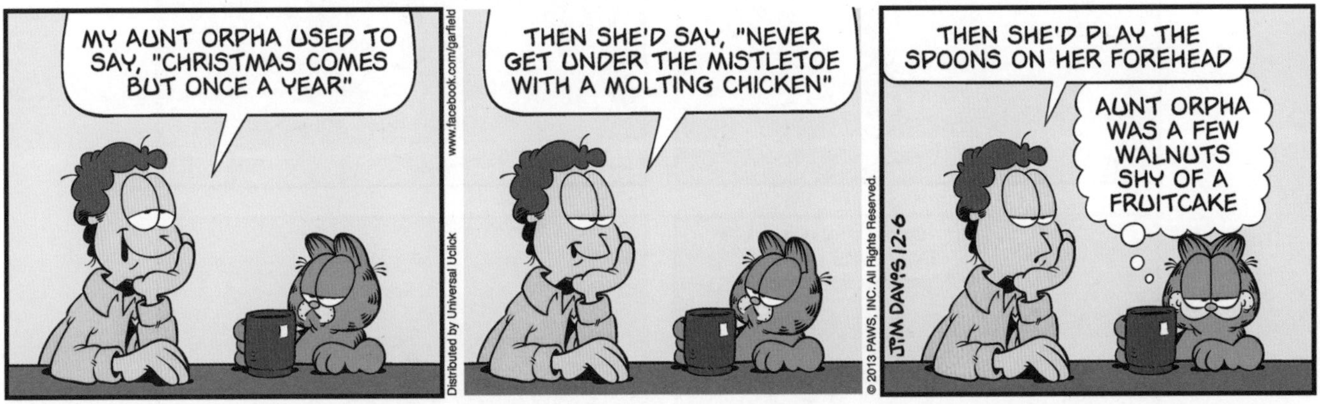
MY AUNT ORPHA USED TO SAY, "CHRISTMAS COMES BUT ONCE A YEAR"
Distributed by Universal Uclick
www.facebook.com/garfield
THEN SHE'D SAY, "NEVER GET UNDER THE MISTLETOE WITH A MOLTING CHICKEN"
© 2013 PAWS, INC. All Rights Reserved.
JIM DAVIS 12-6
THEN SHE'D PLAY THE SPOONS ON HER FOREHEAD
AUNT ORPHA WAS A FEW WALNUTS SHY OF A FRUITCAKE

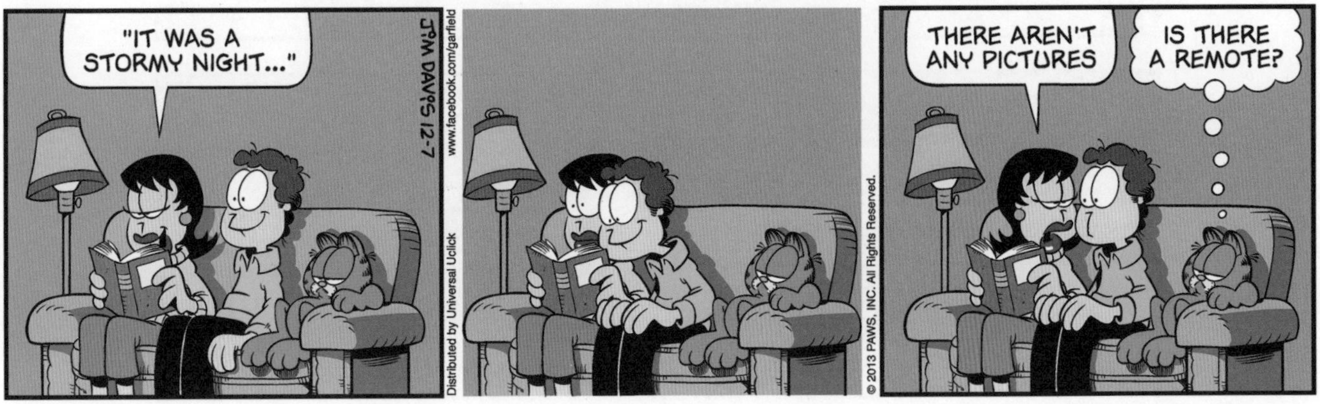
"IT WAS A STORMY NIGHT..."
JIM DAVIS 12-7
Distributed by Universal Uclick
www.facebook.com/garfield
© 2013 PAWS, INC. All Rights Reserved.
THERE AREN'T ANY PICTURES
IS THERE A REMOTE?

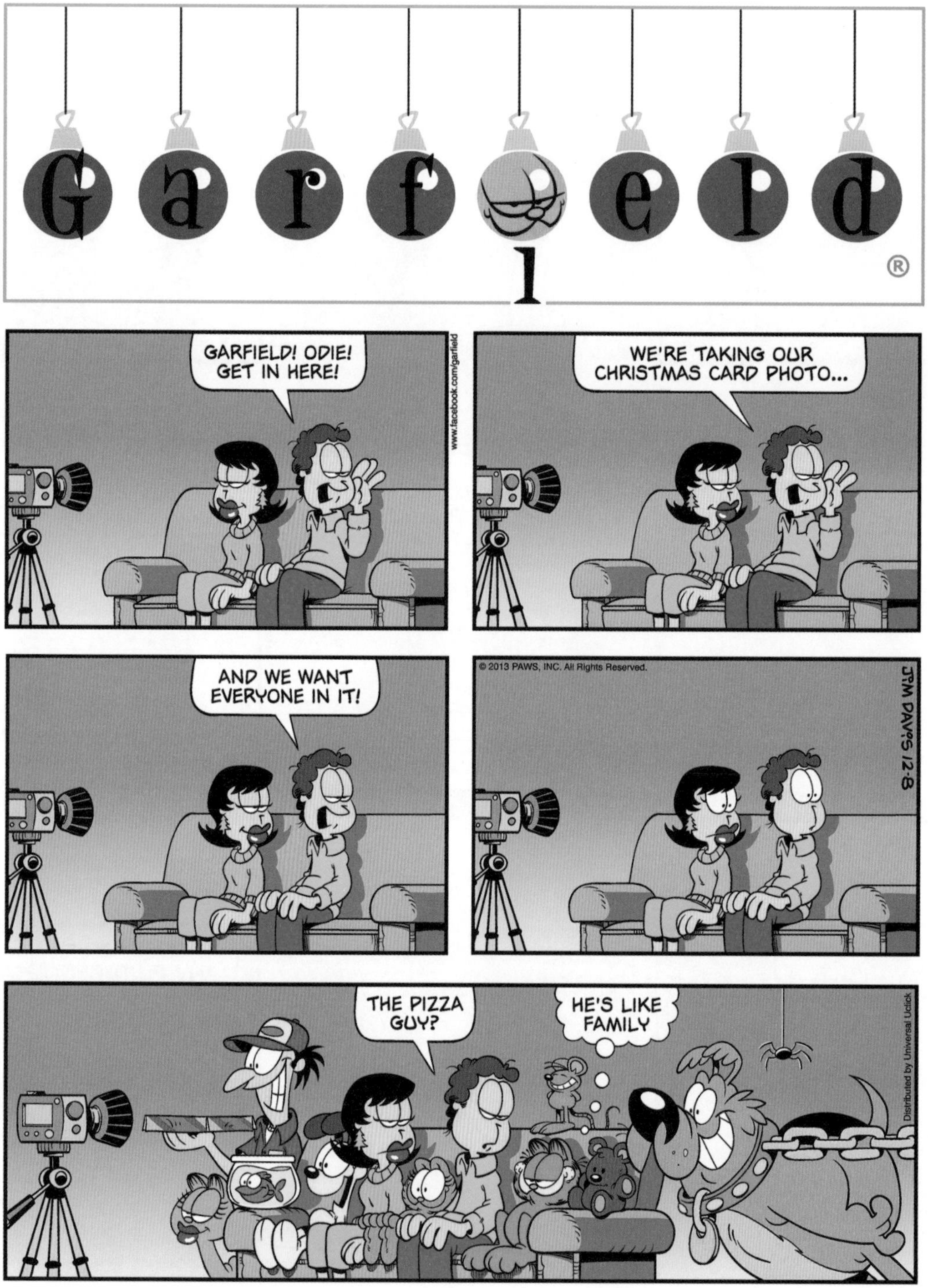
Garfield®
www.facebook.com/garfield
GARFIELD! ODIE! GET IN HERE!
WE'RE TAKING OUR CHRISTMAS CARD PHOTO...
AND WE WANT EVERYONE IN IT!
© 2013 PAWS, INC. All Rights Reserved.
JIM DAVIS 12-8
THE PIZZA GUY?
HE'S LIKE FAMILY
Distributed by Universal Uclick

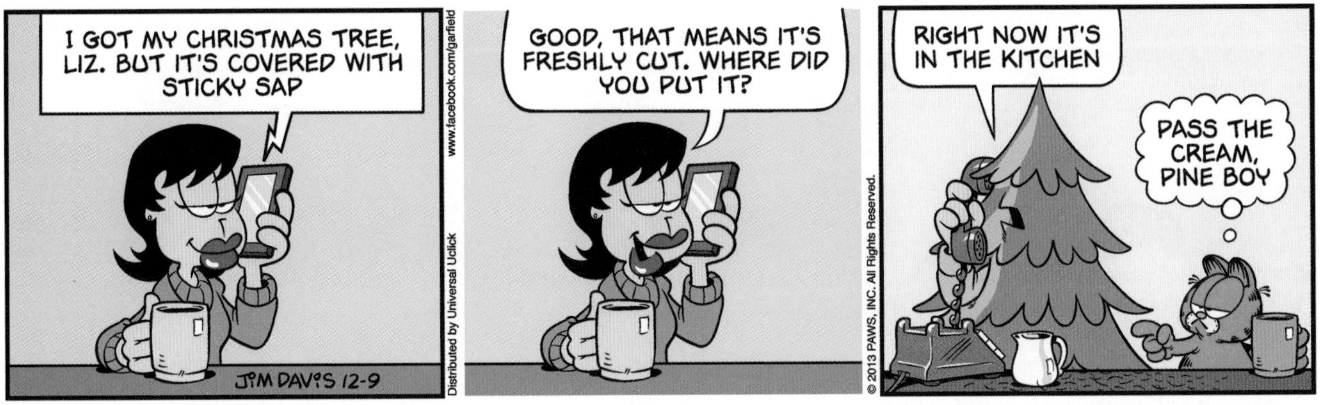
I GOT MY CHRISTMAS TREE, LIZ. BUT IT'S COVERED WITH STICKY SAP
JIM DAVIS 12-9
Distributed by Universal Uclick www.facebook.com/garfield
GOOD, THAT MEANS IT'S FRESHLY CUT. WHERE DID YOU PUT IT?
© 2013 PAWS, INC. All Rights Reserved.
RIGHT NOW IT'S IN THE KITCHEN
PASS THE CREAM, PINE BOY

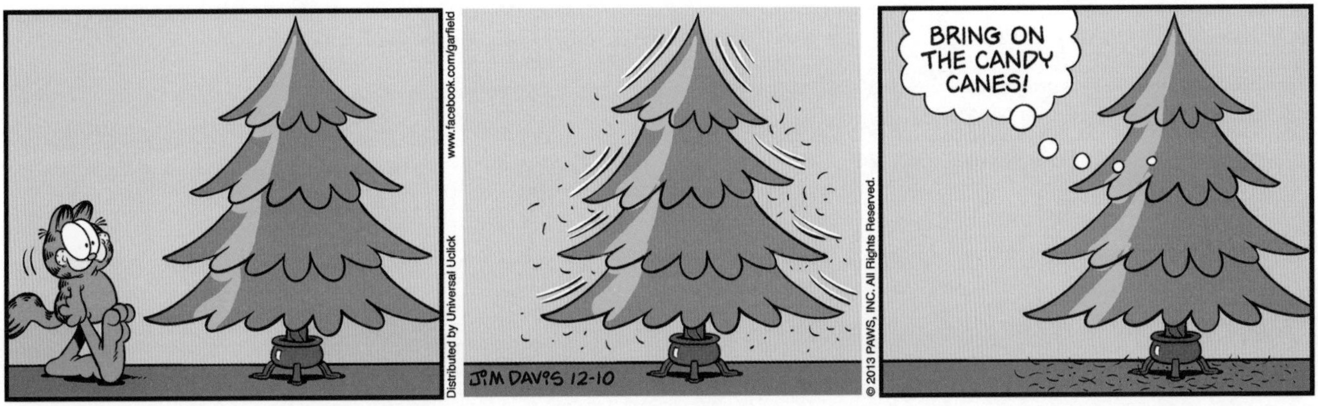
Distributed by Universal Uclick www.facebook.com/garfield
JIM DAVIS 12-10
© 2013 PAWS, INC. All Rights Reserved.
BRING ON THE CANDY CANES!

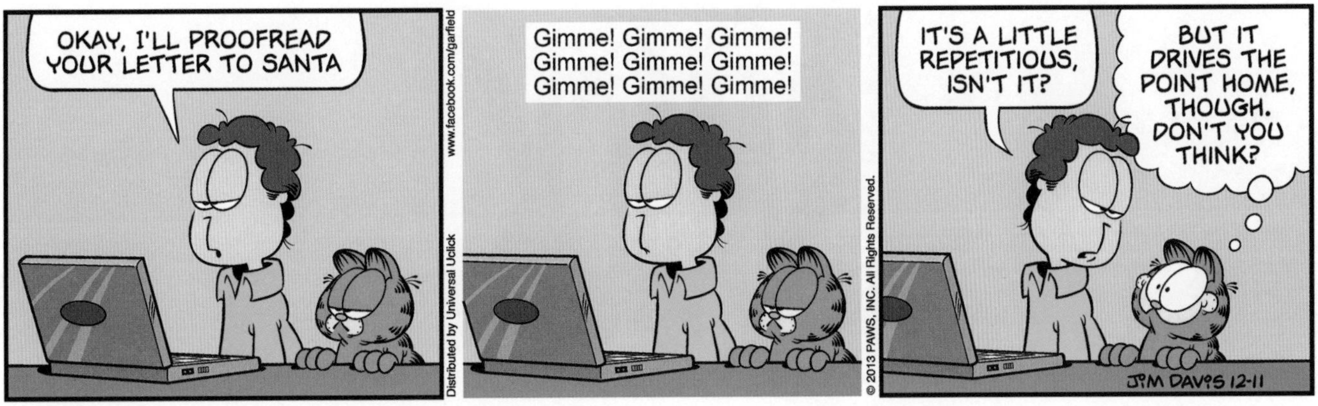
OKAY, I'LL PROOFREAD YOUR LETTER TO SANTA
Distributed by Universal Uclick www.facebook.com/garfield
Gimme! Gimme! Gimme! Gimme! Gimme! Gimme! Gimme! Gimme! Gimme!
© 2013 PAWS, INC. All Rights Reserved.
IT'S A LITTLE REPETITIOUS, ISN'T IT?
BUT IT DRIVES THE POINT HOME, THOUGH. DON'T YOU THINK?
JIM DAVIS 12-11

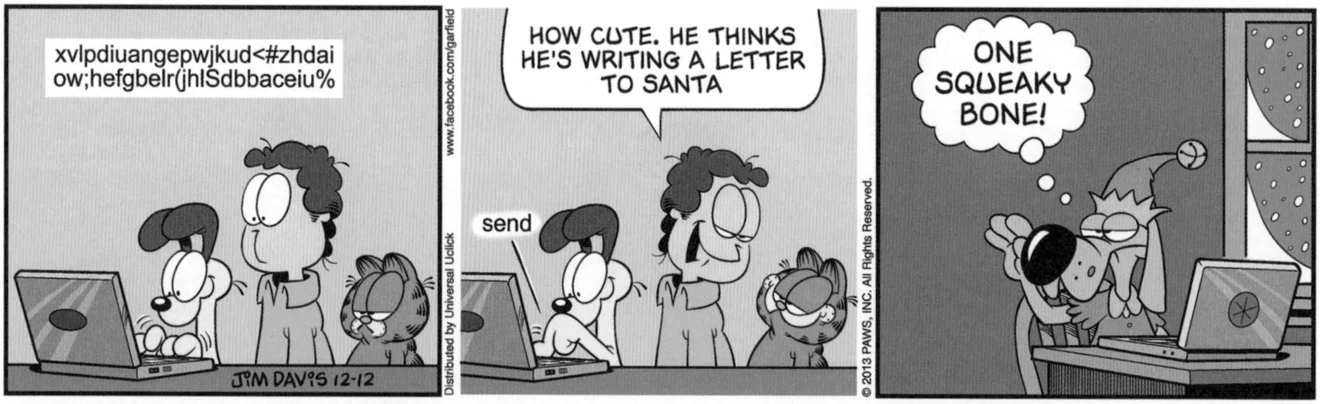
xvlpdiuangepwjkud<#zhdai
ow;hefgbelr(jhlSdbbaceiu%
JIM DAVIS 12-12
Distributed by Universal Uclick
www.facebook.com/garfield
send
HOW CUTE. HE THINKS HE'S WRITING A LETTER TO SANTA
© 2013 PAWS, INC. All Rights Reserved.
ONE SQUEAKY BONE!

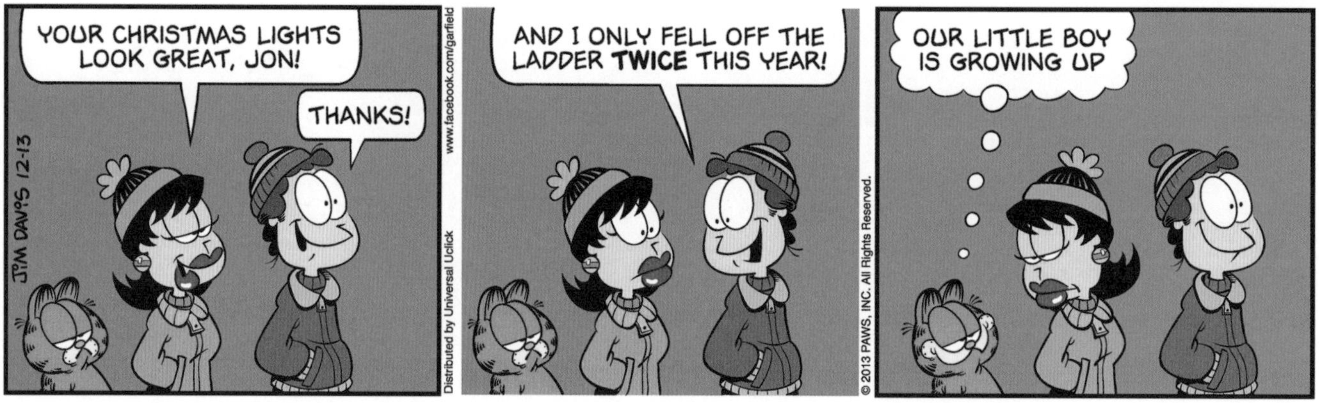
YOUR CHRISTMAS LIGHTS LOOK GREAT, JON!
THANKS!
JIM DAVIS 12-13
Distributed by Universal Uclick
www.facebook.com/garfield
AND I ONLY FELL OFF THE LADDER **TWICE** THIS YEAR!
© 2013 PAWS, INC. All Rights Reserved.
OUR LITTLE BOY IS GROWING UP

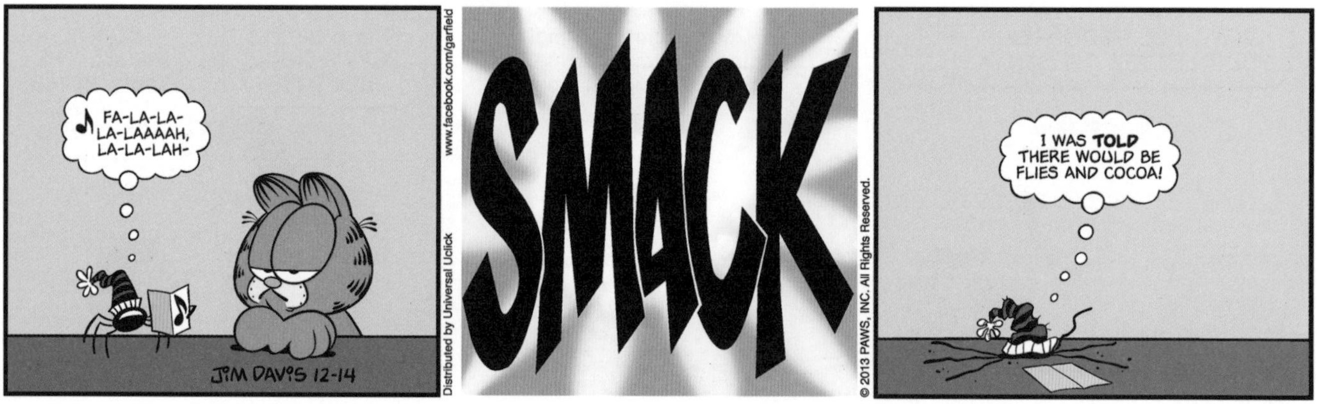
♪ FA-LA-LA-LA-LAAAAH, LA-LA-LAH-
JIM DAVIS 12-14
Distributed by Universal Uclick
www.facebook.com/garfield
SMACK
© 2013 PAWS, INC. All Rights Reserved.
I WAS **TOLD** THERE WOULD BE FLIES AND COCOA!

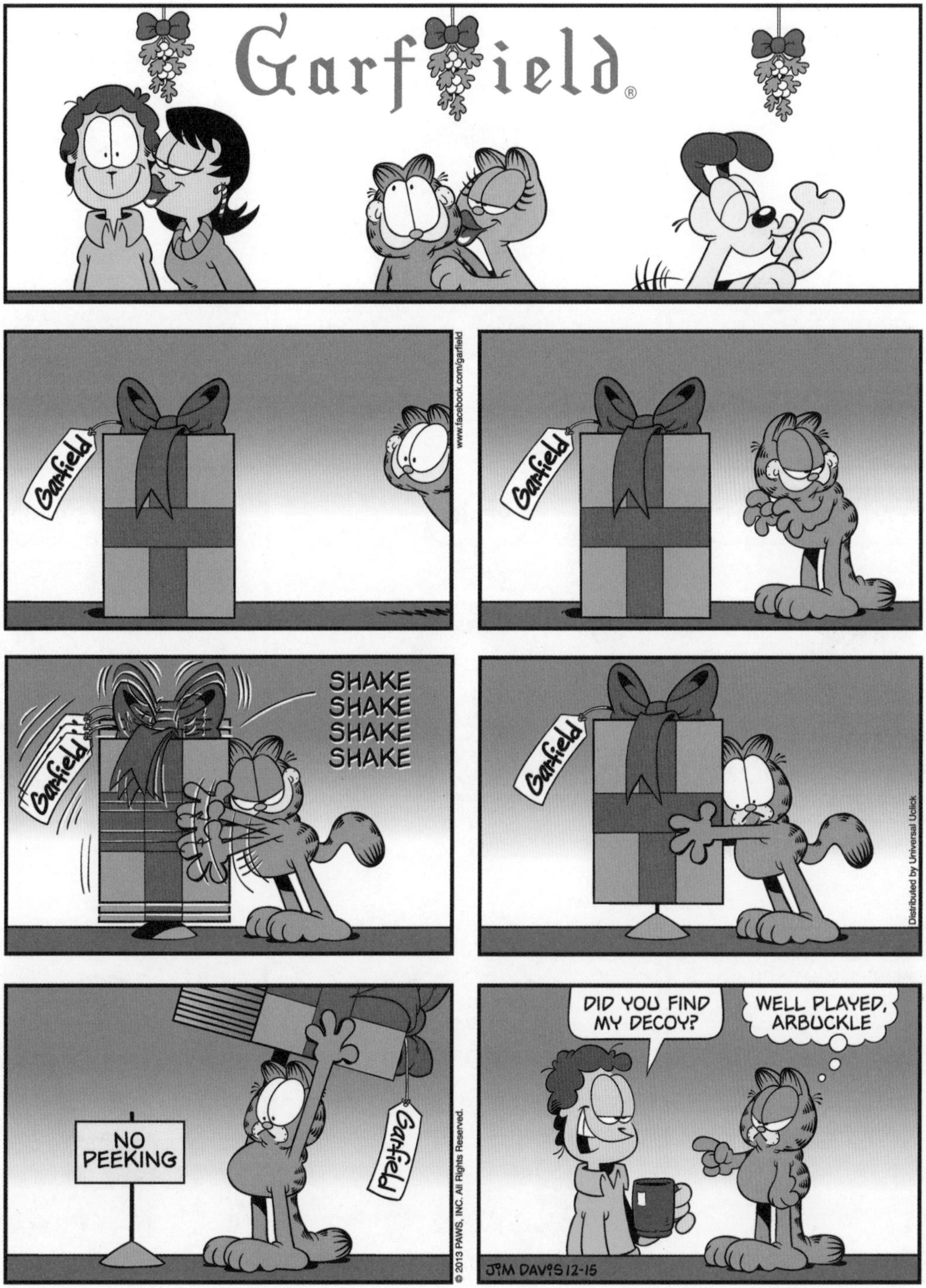

Garfield
www.facebook.com/garfield
Garfield
Garfield
SHAKE
SHAKE
SHAKE
SHAKE
Garfield
Garfield
Distributed by Universal Uclick
NO PEEKING
Garfield
© 2013 PAWS, INC. All Rights Reserved.
DID YOU FIND MY DECOY?
WELL PLAYED, ARBUCKLE
JIM DAVIS 12-15

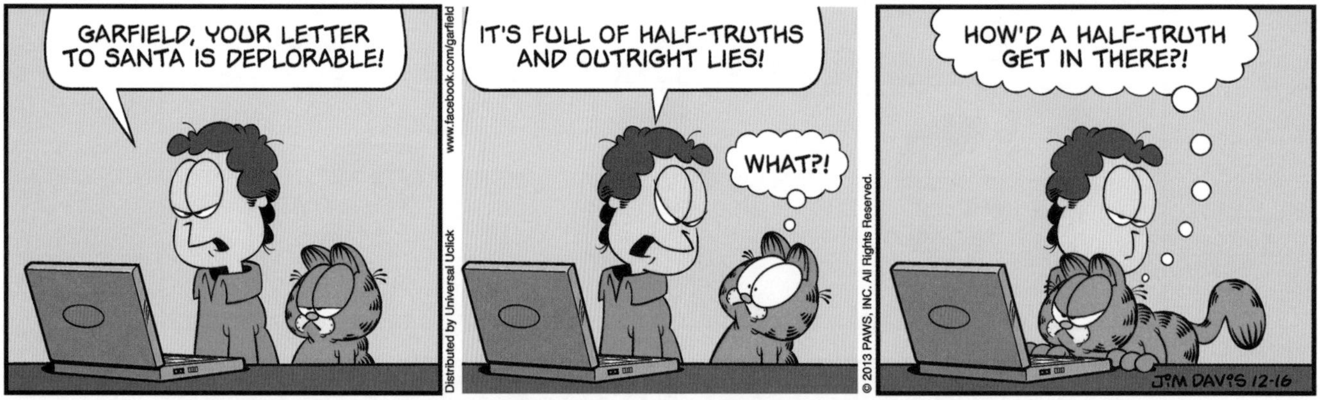
GARFIELD, YOUR LETTER TO SANTA IS DEPLORABLE!
IT'S FULL OF HALF-TRUTHS AND OUTRIGHT LIES!
WHAT?!
HOW'D A HALF-TRUTH GET IN THERE?!
JIM DAVIS 12-16
www.facebook.com/garfield
Distributed by Universal Uclick
© 2013 PAWS, INC. All Rights Reserved.

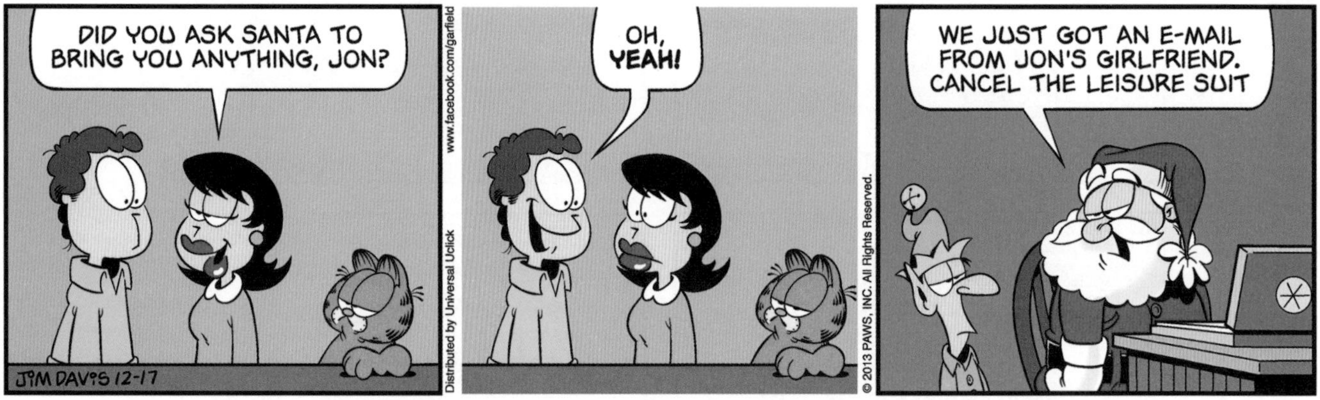
DID YOU ASK SANTA TO BRING YOU ANYTHING, JON?
OH, **YEAH!**
WE JUST GOT AN E-MAIL FROM JON'S GIRLFRIEND. CANCEL THE LEISURE SUIT
JIM DAVIS 12-17
www.facebook.com/garfield
Distributed by Universal Uclick
© 2013 PAWS, INC. All Rights Reserved.

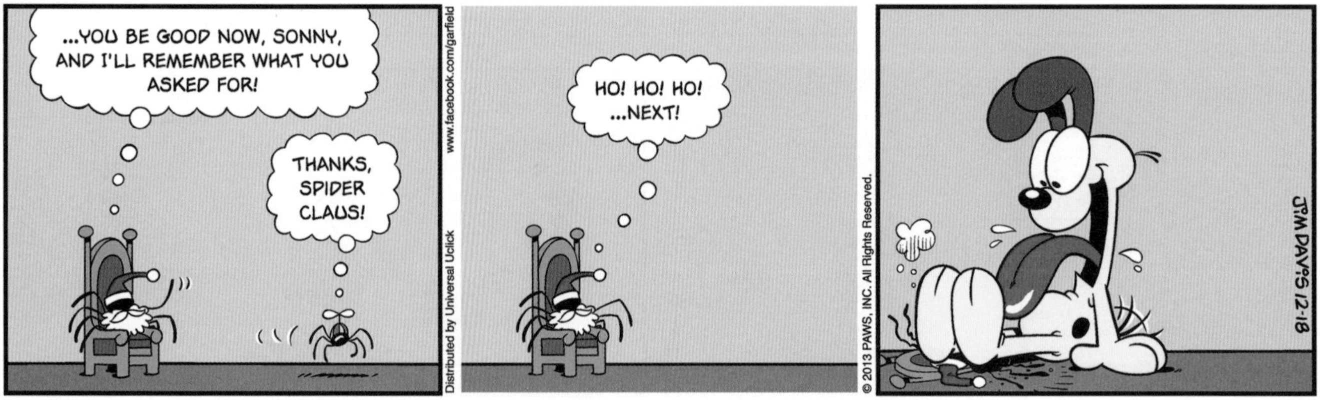
...YOU BE GOOD NOW, SONNY, AND I'LL REMEMBER WHAT YOU ASKED FOR!
THANKS, SPIDER CLAUS!
HO! HO! HO! ...NEXT!
JIM DAVIS 12-18
www.facebook.com/garfield
Distributed by Universal Uclick
© 2013 PAWS, INC. All Rights Reserved.

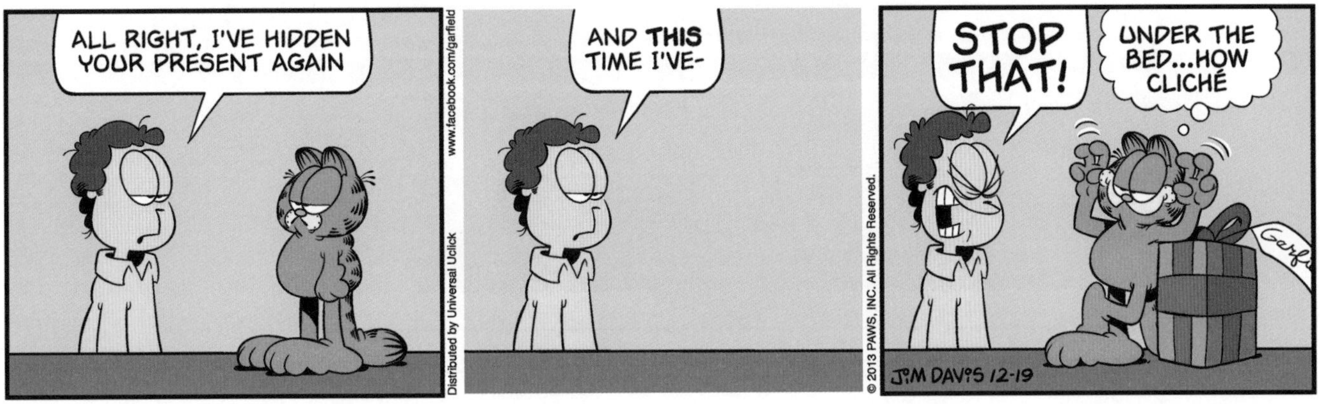
ALL RIGHT, I'VE HIDDEN YOUR PRESENT AGAIN
www.facebook.com/garfield
Distributed by Universal Uclick
AND **THIS** TIME I'VE-
STOP THAT!
UNDER THE BED...HOW CLICHÉ
Garfi
© 2013 PAWS, INC. All Rights Reserved.
JIM DAVIS 12-19

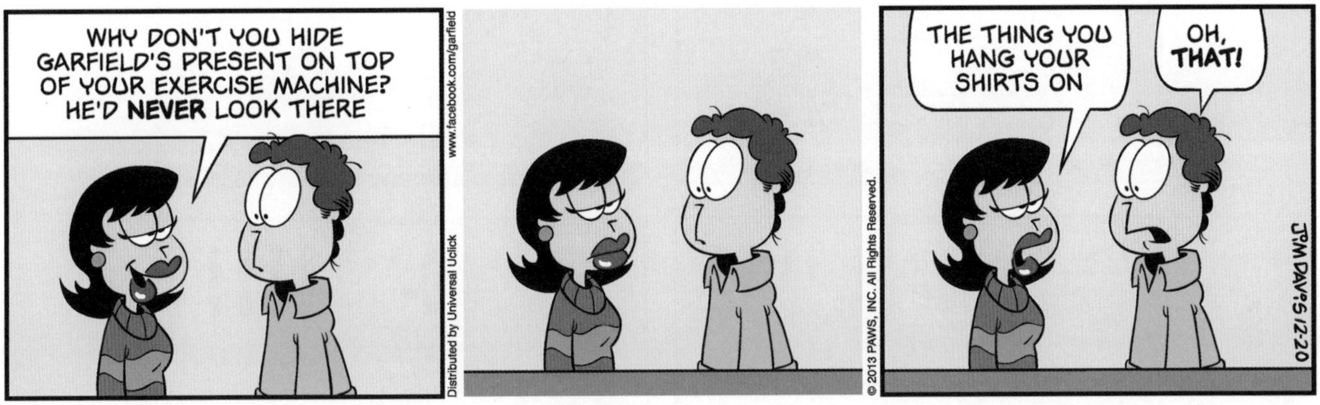
WHY DON'T YOU HIDE GARFIELD'S PRESENT ON TOP OF YOUR EXERCISE MACHINE? HE'D **NEVER** LOOK THERE
www.facebook.com/garfield
Distributed by Universal Uclick
© 2013 PAWS, INC. All Rights Reserved.
THE THING YOU HANG YOUR SHIRTS ON
OH, **THAT!**
JIM DAVIS 12-20

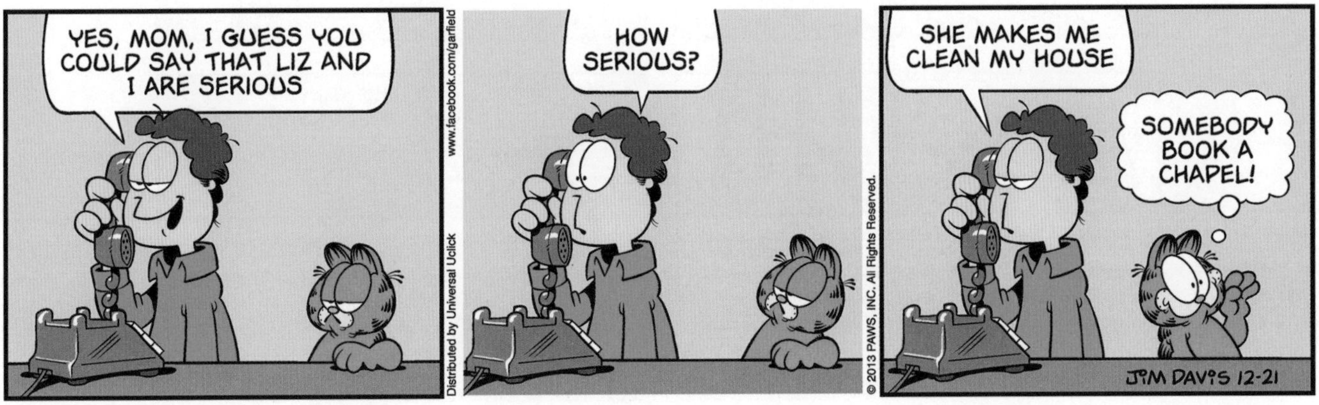
YES, MOM, I GUESS YOU COULD SAY THAT LIZ AND I ARE SERIOUS
www.facebook.com/garfield
Distributed by Universal Uclick
HOW SERIOUS?
© 2013 PAWS, INC. All Rights Reserved.
SHE MAKES ME CLEAN MY HOUSE
SOMEBODY BOOK A CHAPEL!
JIM DAVIS 12-21

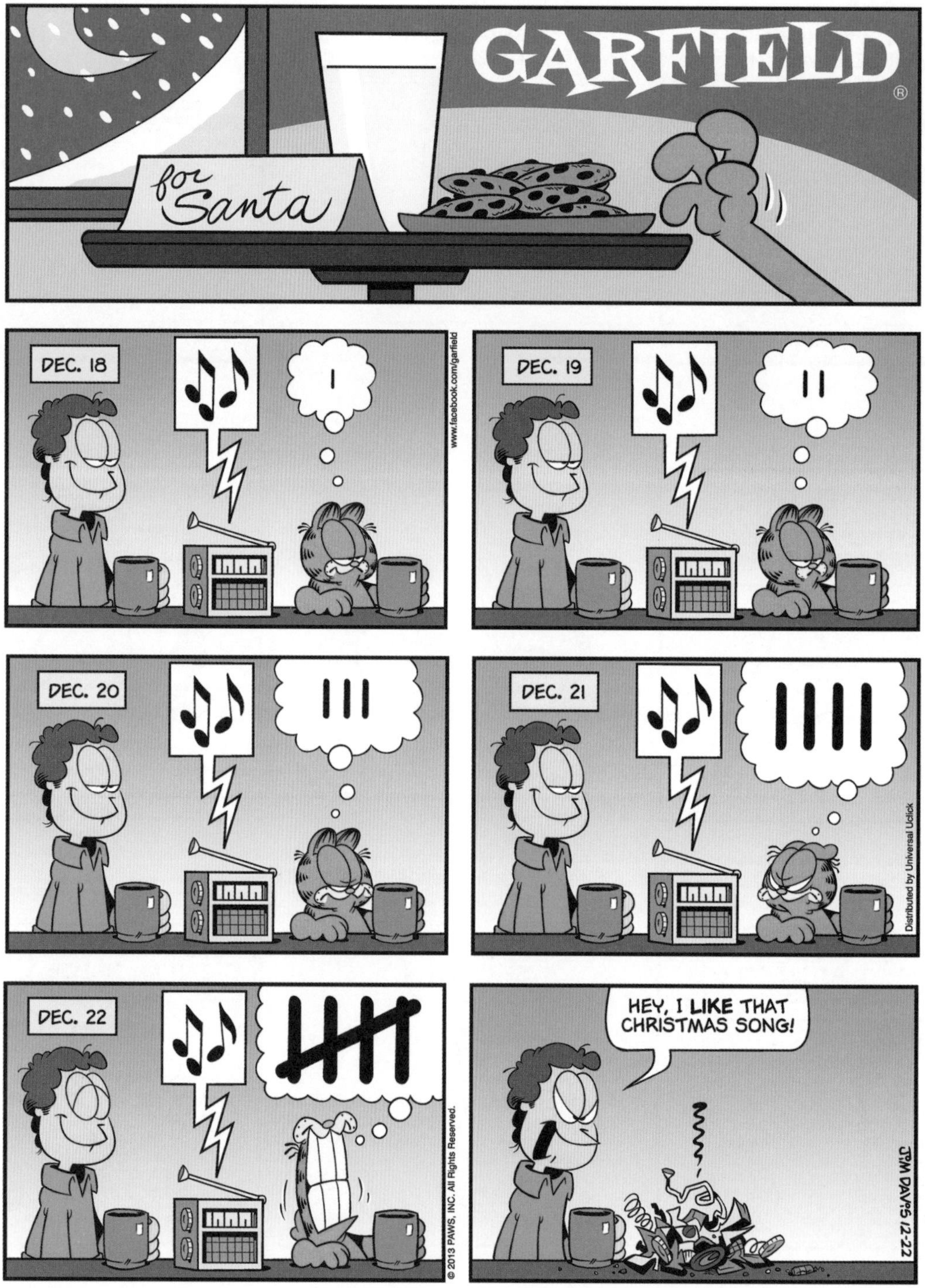
GARFIELD
for Santa
DEC. 18
I
www.facebook.com/garfield
DEC. 19
II
DEC. 20
III
DEC. 21
IIII
Distributed by Universal Uclick
DEC. 22
© 2013 PAWS, INC. All Rights Reserved.
HEY, I LIKE THAT CHRISTMAS SONG!
JIM DAVIS 12-22

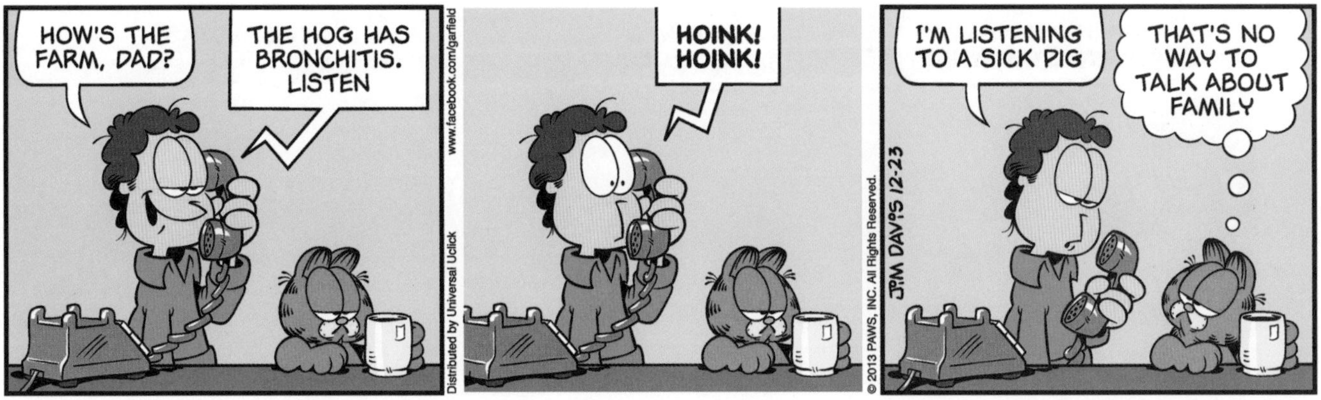
HOW'S THE FARM, DAD?
THE HOG HAS BRONCHITIS. LISTEN
Distributed by Universal Uclick
www.facebook.com/garfield
HOINK! HOINK!
© 2013 PAWS, INC. All Rights Reserved.
JIM DAVIS 12-23
I'M LISTENING TO A SICK PIG
THAT'S NO WAY TO TALK ABOUT FAMILY

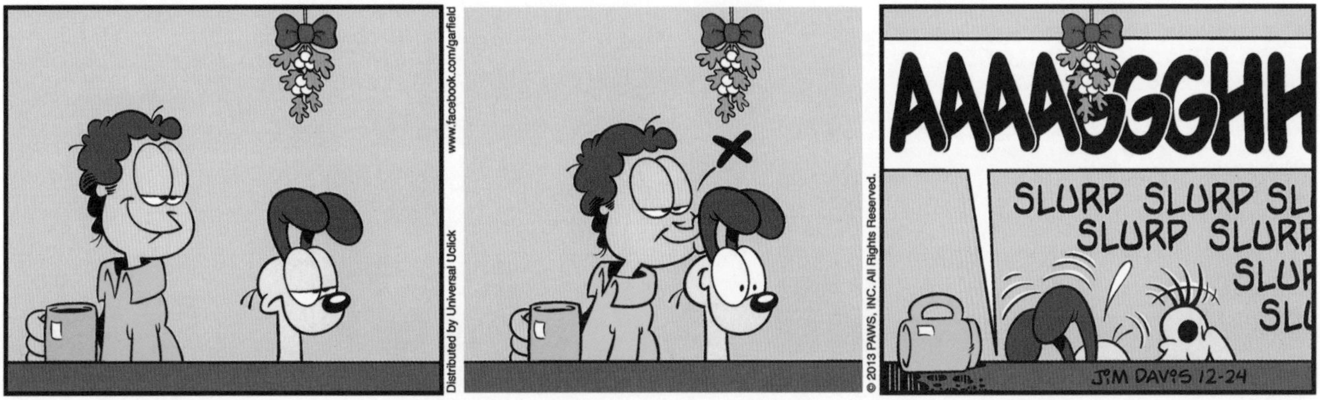
Distributed by Universal Uclick
www.facebook.com/garfield
© 2013 PAWS, INC. All Rights Reserved.
AAAAGGHH
SLURP SLURP SL
SLURP SLURP
SLUR
SL
JIM DAVIS 12-24

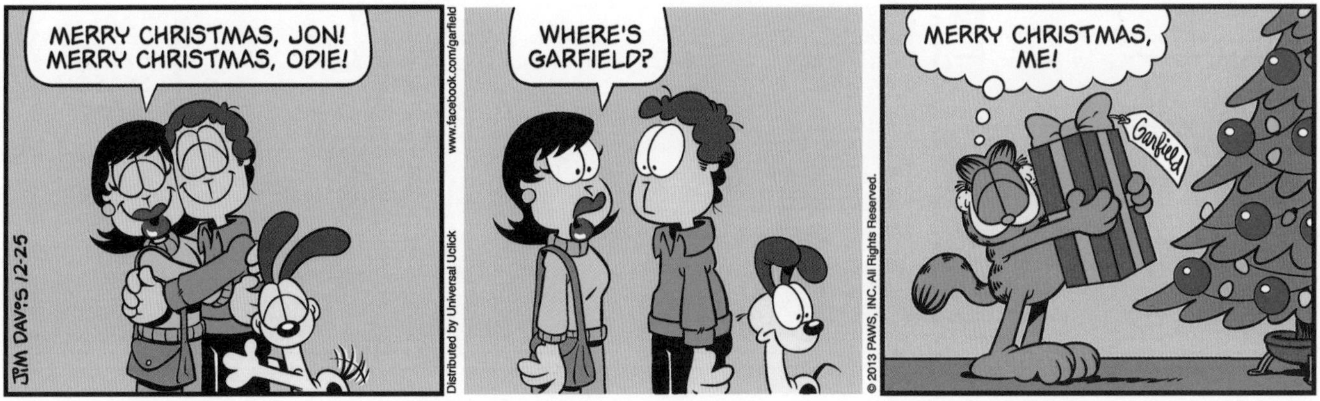
MERRY CHRISTMAS, JON! MERRY CHRISTMAS, ODIE!
JIM DAVIS 12-25
Distributed by Universal Uclick
www.facebook.com/garfield
WHERE'S GARFIELD?
© 2013 PAWS, INC. All Rights Reserved.
MERRY CHRISTMAS, ME!
Garfield

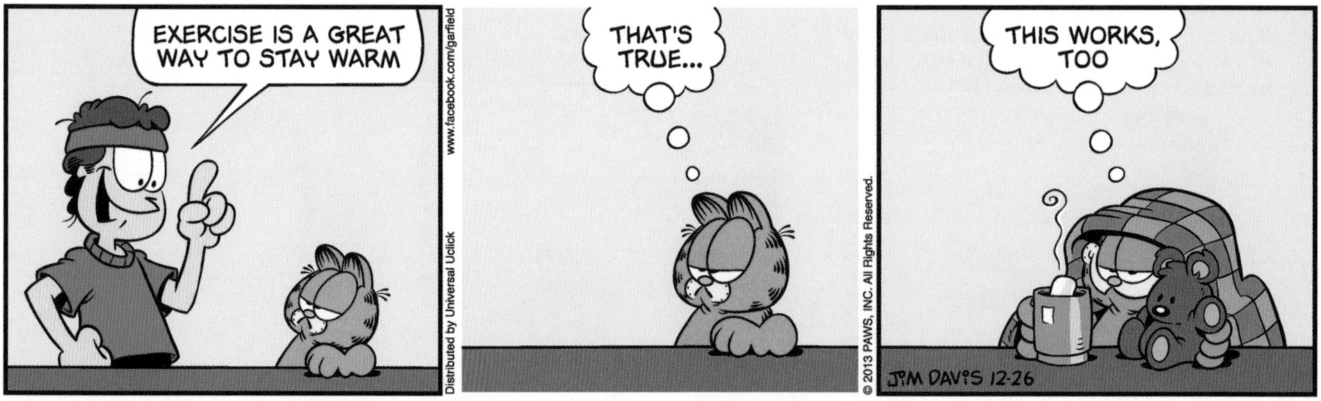
EXERCISE IS A GREAT WAY TO STAY WARM
Distributed by Universal Uclick www.facebook.com/garfield
THAT'S TRUE...
© 2013 PAWS, INC. All Rights Reserved.
THIS WORKS, TOO
JIM DAVIS 12-26

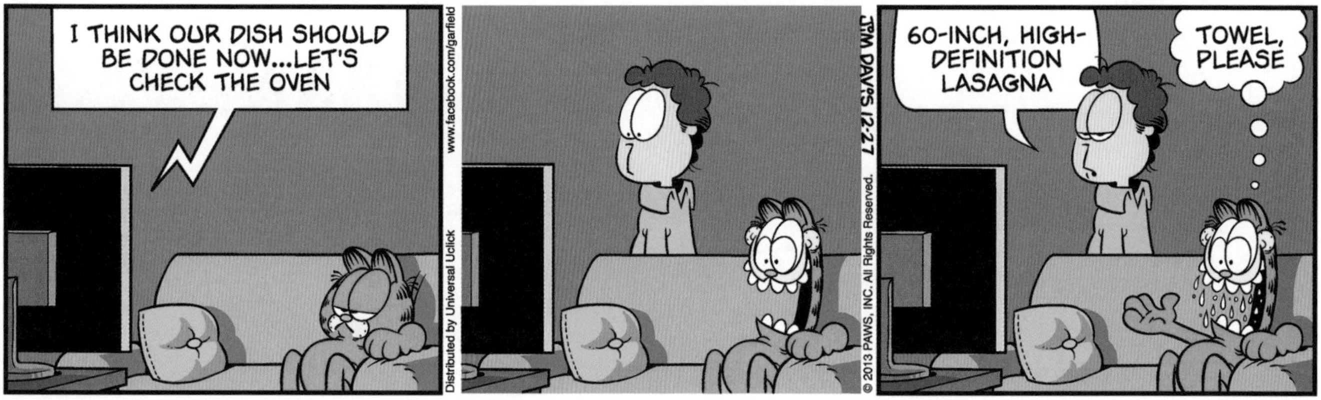
I THINK OUR DISH SHOULD BE DONE NOW...LET'S CHECK THE OVEN
Distributed by Universal Uclick www.facebook.com/garfield
JIM DAVIS 12-27
© 2013 PAWS, INC. All Rights Reserved.
60-INCH, HIGH-DEFINITION LASAGNA
TOWEL, PLEASE

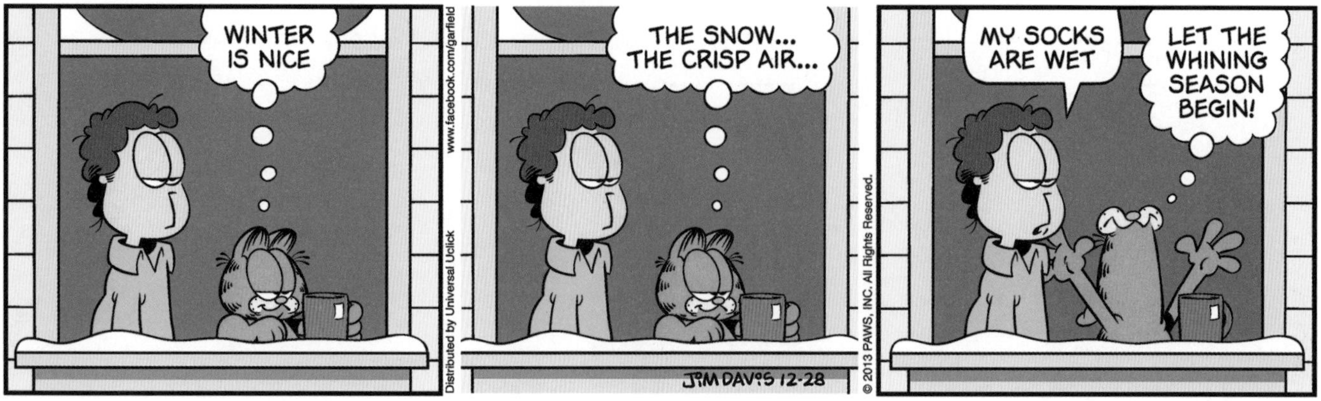
WINTER IS NICE
Distributed by Universal Uclick www.facebook.com/garfield
THE SNOW... THE CRISP AIR...
JIM DAVIS 12-28
© 2013 PAWS, INC. All Rights Reserved.
MY SOCKS ARE WET
LET THE WHINING SEASON BEGIN!

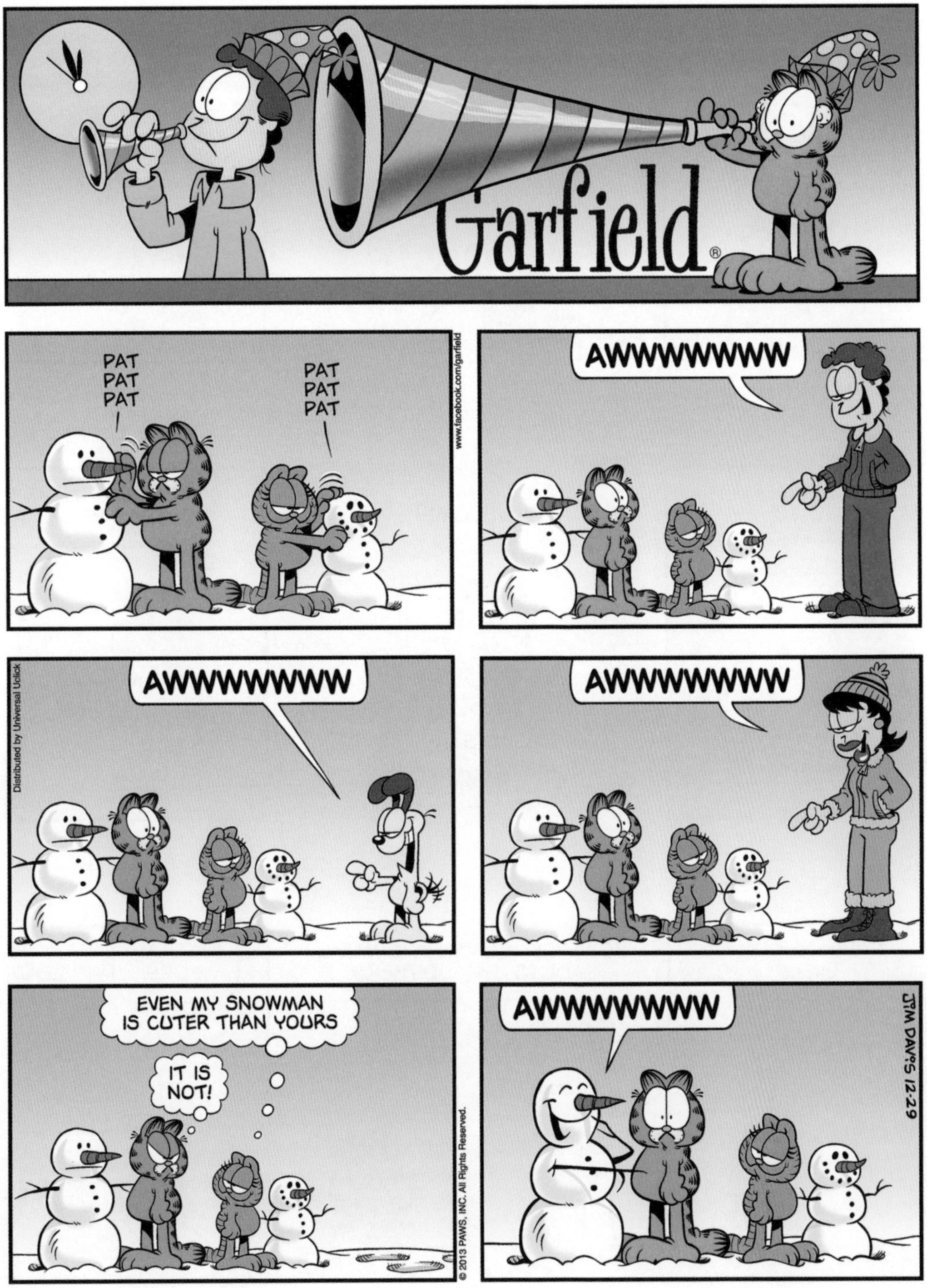
Garfield®
PAT PAT PAT
PAT PAT PAT
www.facebook.com/garfield
AWWWWWWW
Distributed by Universal Uclick
AWWWWWWW
AWWWWWWW
EVEN MY SNOWMAN IS CUTER THAN YOURS
IT IS NOT!
© 2013 PAWS, INC. All Rights Reserved.
AWWWWWWW
JPM DAVPS 12-29

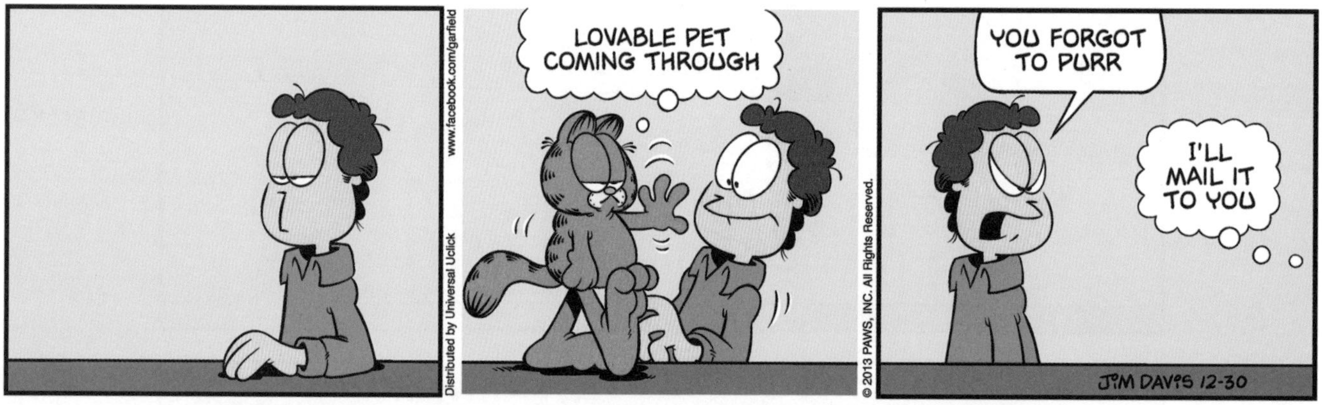
www.facebook.com/garfield
Distributed by Universal Uclick
LOVABLE PET COMING THROUGH
© 2013 PAWS, INC. All Rights Reserved.
YOU FORGOT TO PURR
I'LL MAIL IT TO YOU
JIM DAVIS 12-30

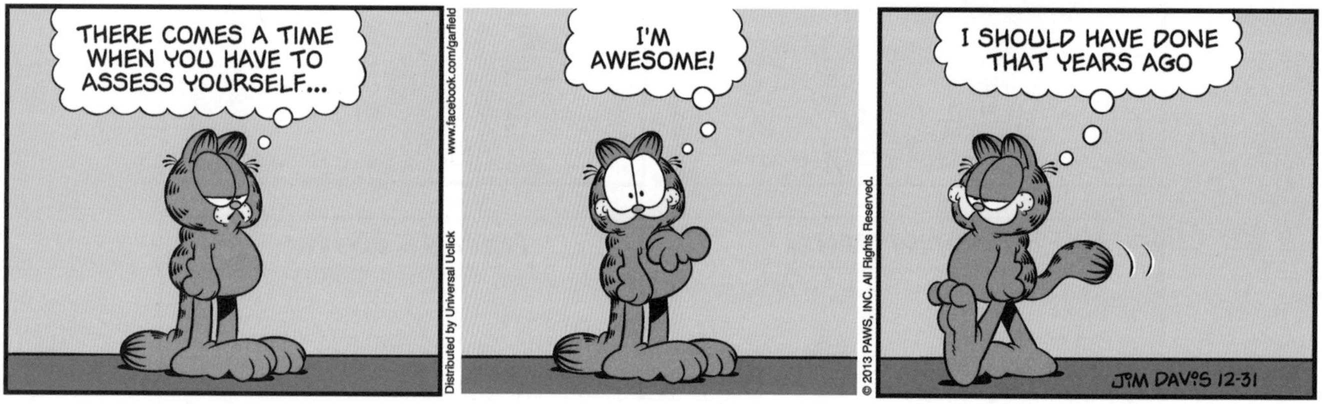
THERE COMES A TIME WHEN YOU HAVE TO ASSESS YOURSELF...
www.facebook.com/garfield
Distributed by Universal Uclick
I'M AWESOME!
© 2013 PAWS, INC. All Rights Reserved.
I SHOULD HAVE DONE THAT YEARS AGO
JIM DAVIS 12-31

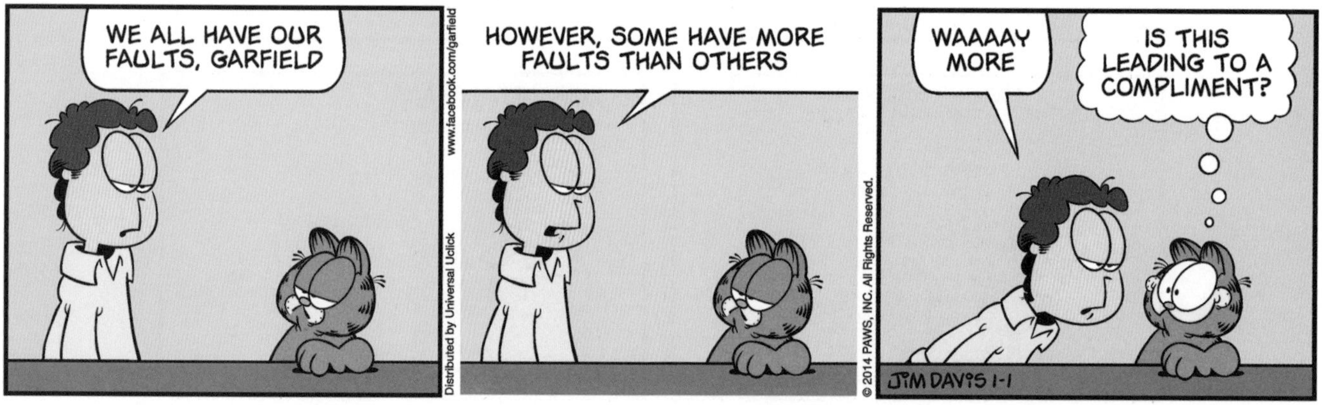
WE ALL HAVE OUR FAULTS, GARFIELD
www.facebook.com/garfield
Distributed by Universal Uclick
HOWEVER, SOME HAVE MORE FAULTS THAN OTHERS
© 2014 PAWS, INC. All Rights Reserved.
WAAAAY MORE
IS THIS LEADING TO A COMPLIMENT?
JIM DAVIS 1-1

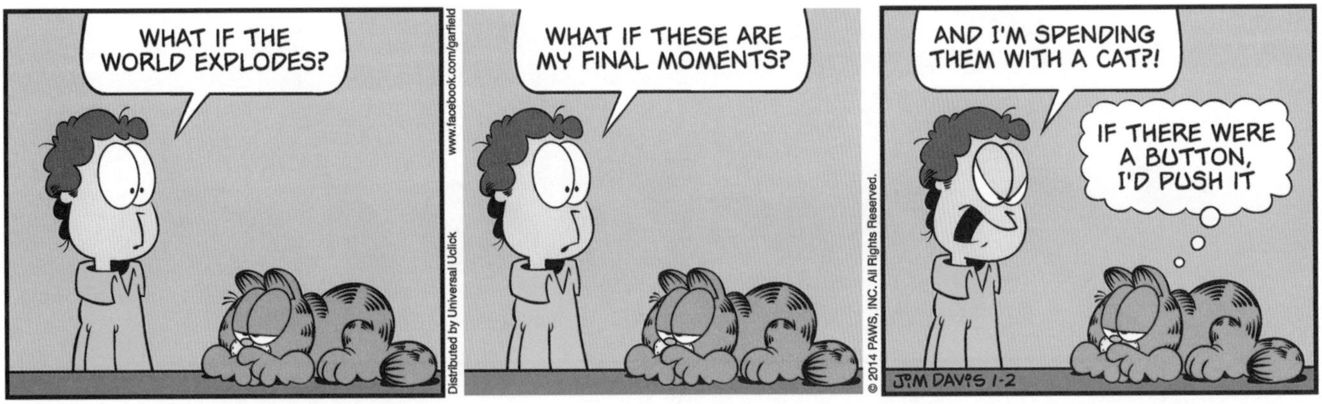
WHAT IF THE WORLD EXPLODES?
WHAT IF THESE ARE MY FINAL MOMENTS?
AND I'M SPENDING THEM WITH A CAT?!
IF THERE WERE A BUTTON, I'D PUSH IT
JIM DAVIS 1-2
www.facebook.com/garfield
Distributed by Universal Uclick
© 2014 PAWS, INC. All Rights Reserved.

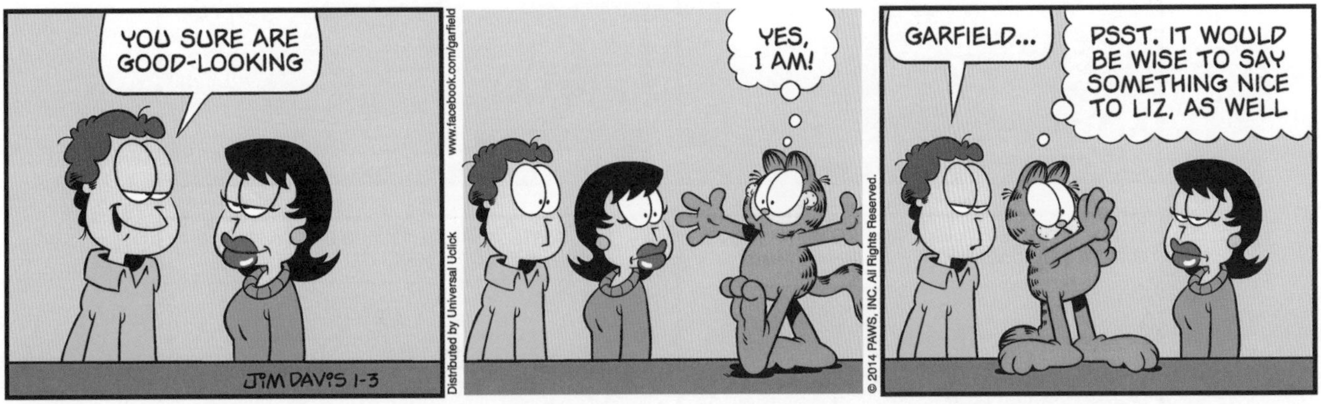
YOU SURE ARE GOOD-LOOKING
JIM DAVIS 1-3
YES, I AM!
GARFIELD...
PSST. IT WOULD BE WISE TO SAY SOMETHING NICE TO LIZ, AS WELL
www.facebook.com/garfield
Distributed by Universal Uclick
© 2014 PAWS, INC. All Rights Reserved.

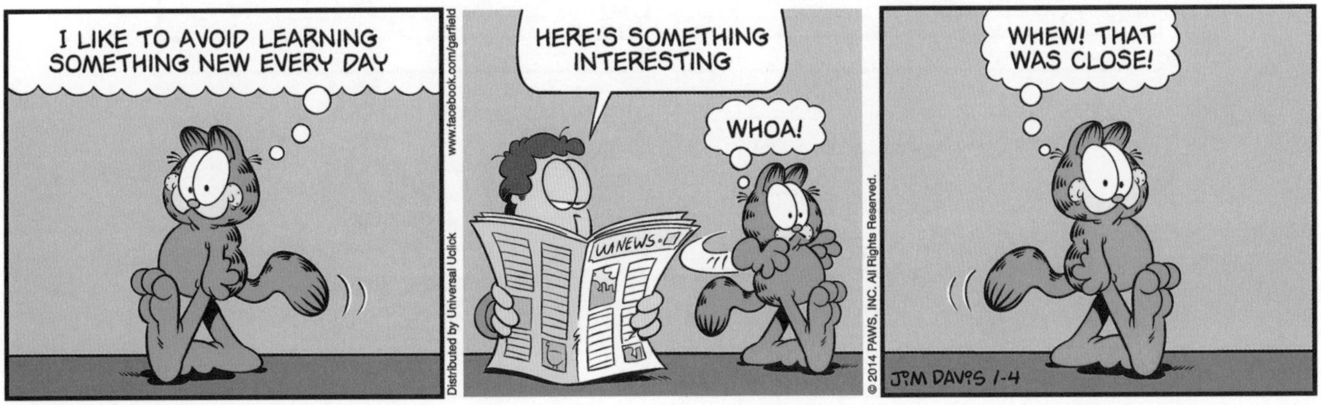
I LIKE TO AVOID LEARNING SOMETHING NEW EVERY DAY
HERE'S SOMETHING INTERESTING
WHOA!
NEWS
WHEW! THAT WAS CLOSE!
JIM DAVIS 1-4
www.facebook.com/garfield
Distributed by Universal Uclick
© 2014 PAWS, INC. All Rights Reserved.

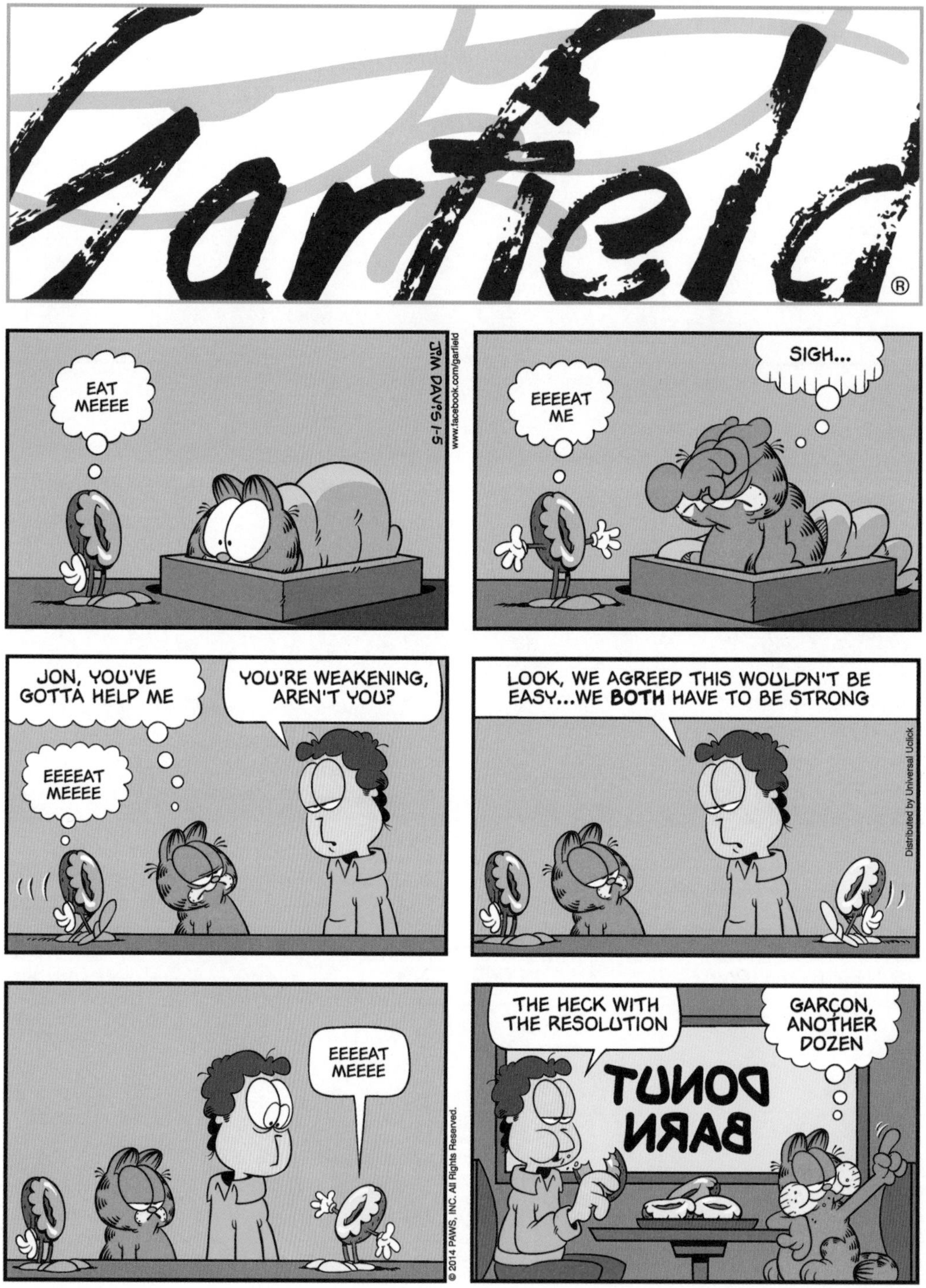
Garfield
JIM DAVIS 1-5
www.facebook.com/garfield
EAT MEEEE
EEEEAT ME
SIGH...
JON, YOU'VE GOTTA HELP ME
EEEEAT MEEEE
YOU'RE WEAKENING, AREN'T YOU?
LOOK, WE AGREED THIS WOULDN'T BE EASY...WE BOTH HAVE TO BE STRONG
Distributed by Universal Uclick
EEEEAT MEEEE
© 2014 PAWS, INC. All Rights Reserved.
THE HECK WITH THE RESOLUTION
GARÇON, ANOTHER DOZEN
DONUT BARN

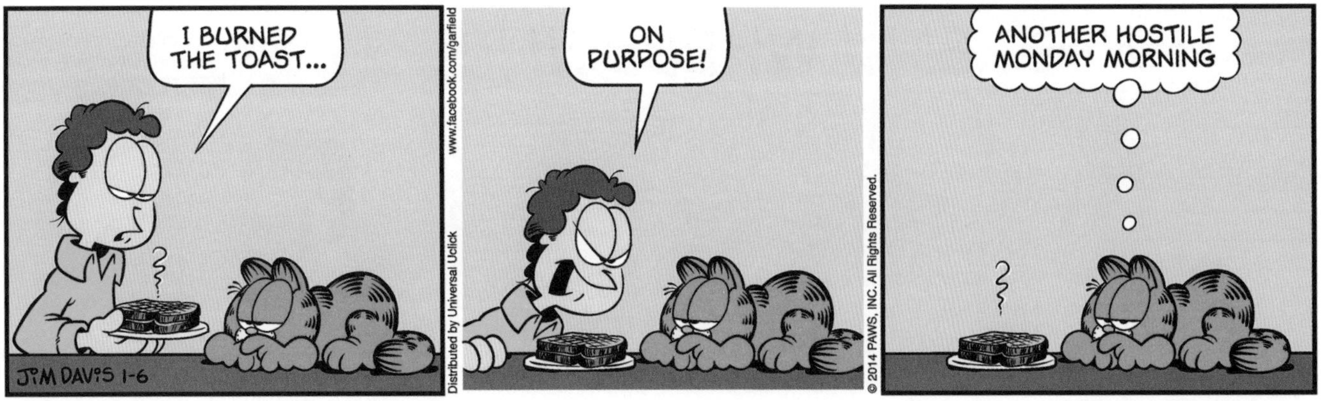
I BURNED THE TOAST...
JIM DAVIS 1-6
www.facebook.com/garfield
Distributed by Universal Uclick
ON PURPOSE!
© 2014 PAWS, INC. All Rights Reserved.
ANOTHER HOSTILE MONDAY MORNING

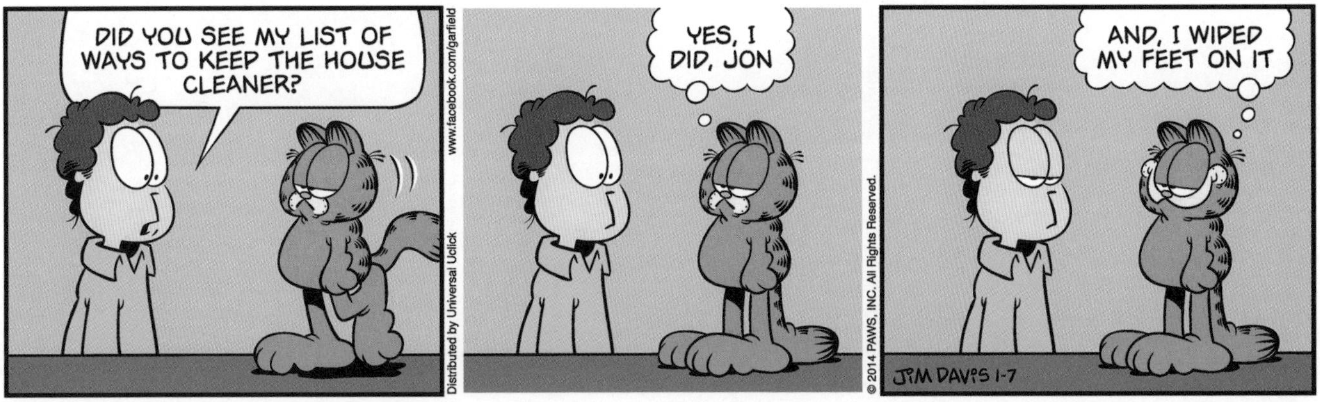
DID YOU SEE MY LIST OF WAYS TO KEEP THE HOUSE CLEANER?
www.facebook.com/garfield
Distributed by Universal Uclick
YES, I DID, JON
© 2014 PAWS, INC. All Rights Reserved.
AND, I WIPED MY FEET ON IT
JIM DAVIS 1-7

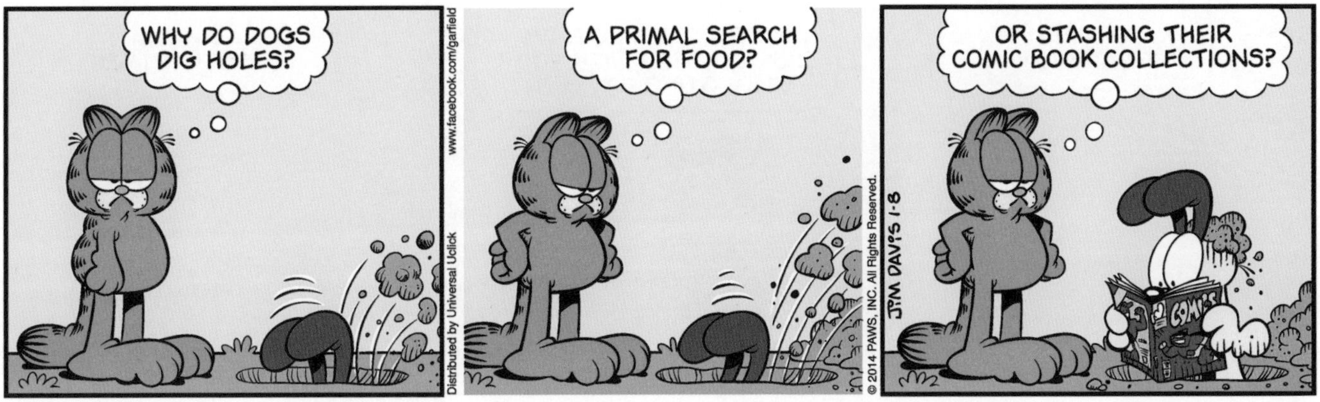
WHY DO DOGS DIG HOLES?
www.facebook.com/garfield
Distributed by Universal Uclick
A PRIMAL SEARCH FOR FOOD?
© 2014 PAWS, INC. All Rights Reserved.
JIM DAVIS 1-8
OR STASHING THEIR COMIC BOOK COLLECTIONS?
COMICS

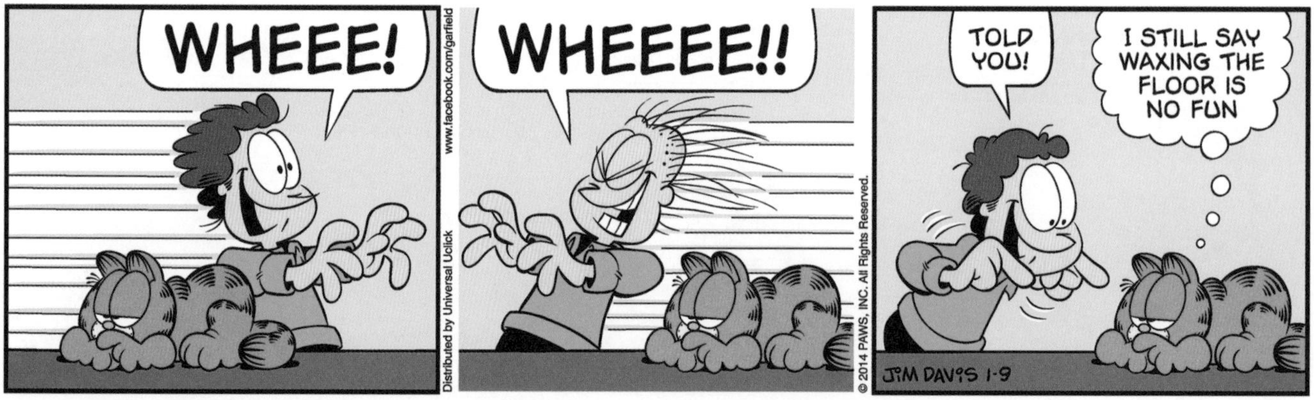
WHEEE!
www.facebook.com/garfield
Distributed by Universal Uclick
WHEEEE!!
© 2014 PAWS, INC. All Rights Reserved.
TOLD YOU!
I STILL SAY WAXING THE FLOOR IS NO FUN
JIM DAVIS 1-9

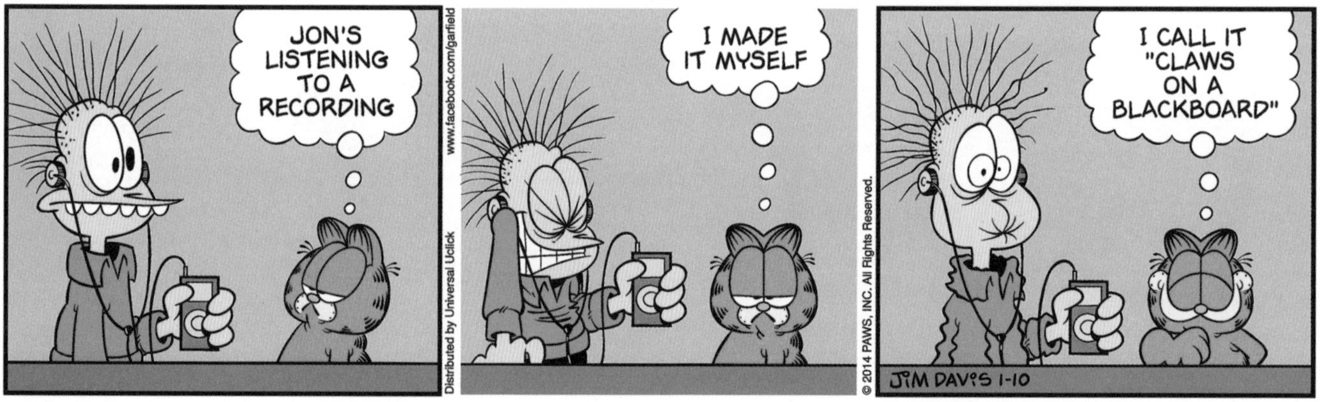
JON'S LISTENING TO A RECORDING
www.facebook.com/garfield
Distributed by Universal Uclick
I MADE IT MYSELF
© 2014 PAWS, INC. All Rights Reserved.
I CALL IT "CLAWS ON A BLACKBOARD"
JIM DAVIS 1-10

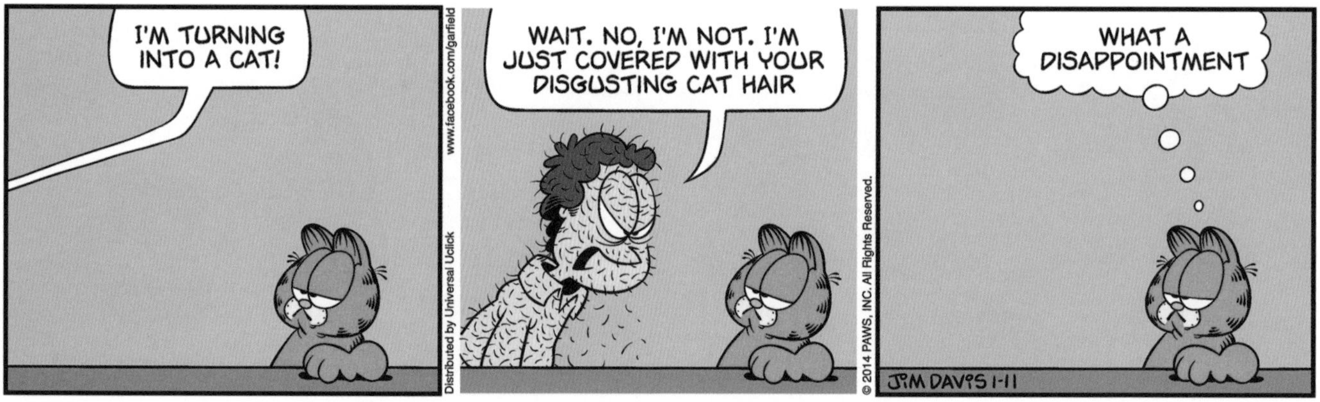
I'M TURNING INTO A CAT!
www.facebook.com/garfield
Distributed by Universal Uclick
WAIT. NO, I'M NOT. I'M JUST COVERED WITH YOUR DISGUSTING CAT HAIR
© 2014 PAWS, INC. All Rights Reserved.
WHAT A DISAPPOINTMENT
JIM DAVIS 1-11

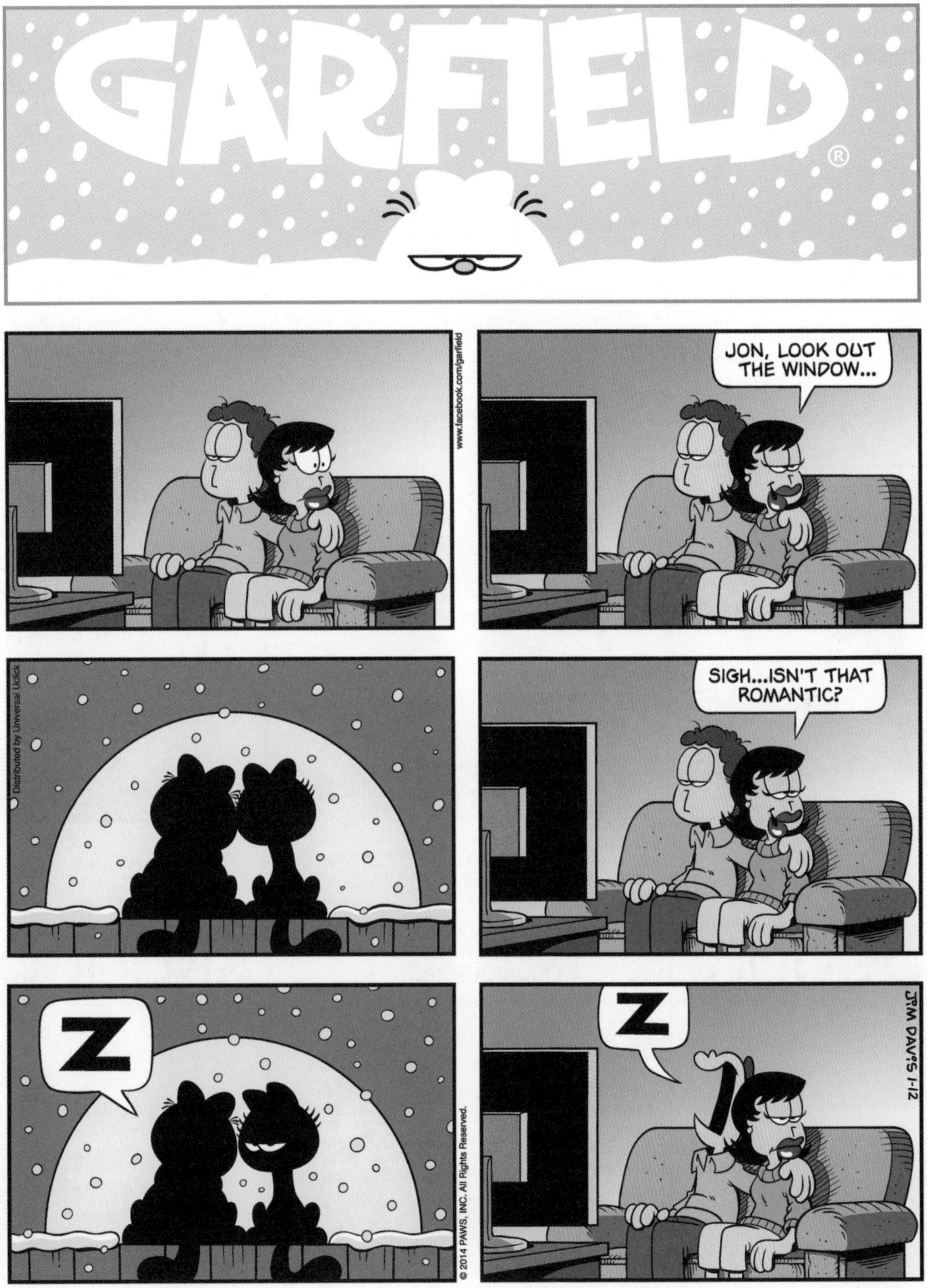
GARFIELD
www.facebook.com/garfield
JON, LOOK OUT THE WINDOW...
Distributed by Universal Uclick
SIGH...ISN'T THAT ROMANTIC?
Z
© 2014 PAWS, INC. All Rights Reserved.
Z
JIM DAVIS 1-12

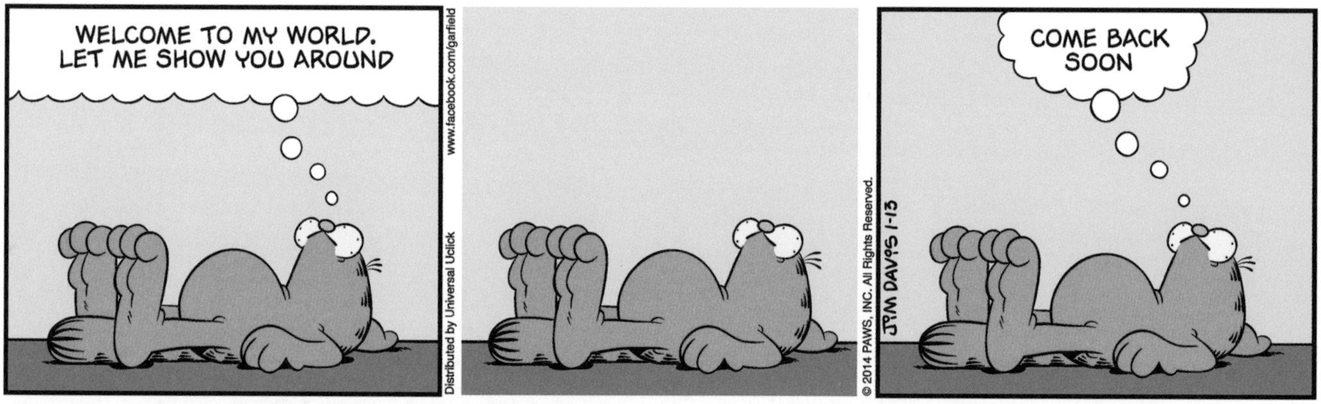
WELCOME TO MY WORLD. LET ME SHOW YOU AROUND
Distributed by Universal Uclick www.facebook.com/garfield
© 2014 PAWS, INC. All Rights Reserved.
JIM DAVIS 1-13
COME BACK SOON

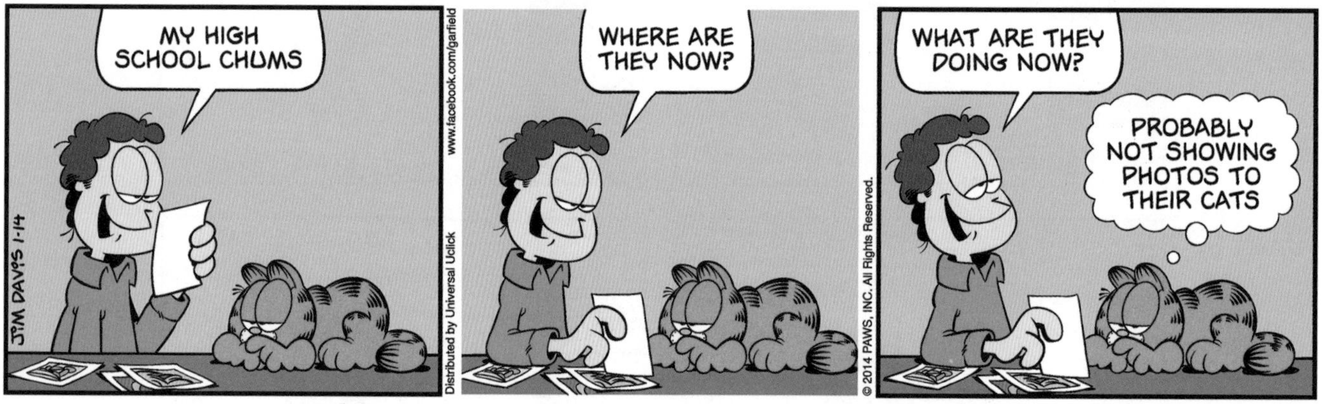
MY HIGH SCHOOL CHUMS
JIM DAVIS 1-14
Distributed by Universal Uclick www.facebook.com/garfield
WHERE ARE THEY NOW?
© 2014 PAWS, INC. All Rights Reserved.
WHAT ARE THEY DOING NOW?
PROBABLY NOT SHOWING PHOTOS TO THEIR CATS

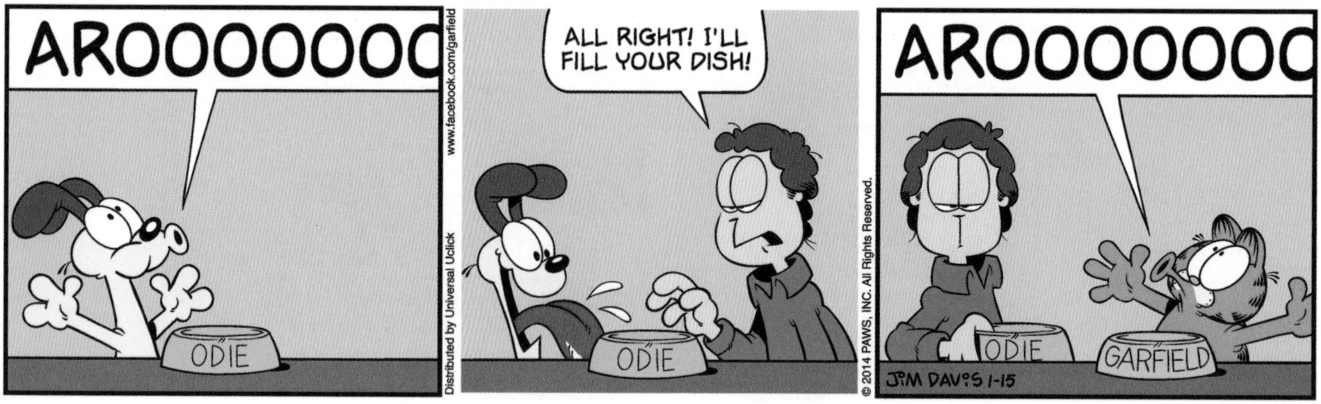
AROOOOOOO
ODIE
Distributed by Universal Uclick www.facebook.com/garfield
ALL RIGHT! I'LL FILL YOUR DISH!
ODIE
© 2014 PAWS, INC. All Rights Reserved.
AROOOOOOO
ODIE
GARFIELD
JIM DAVIS 1-15

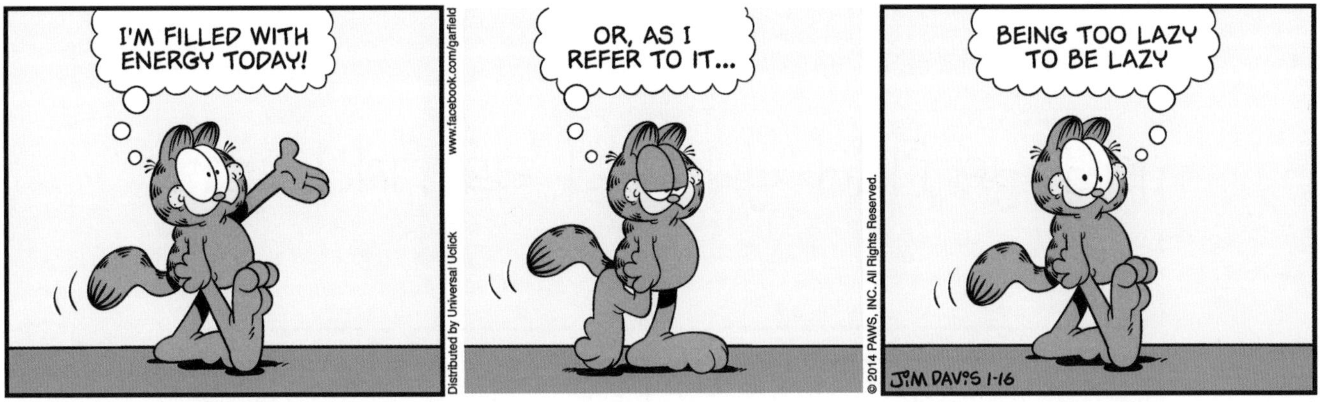
I'M FILLED WITH ENERGY TODAY!
OR, AS I REFER TO IT...
BEING TOO LAZY TO BE LAZY
JIM DAVIS 1-16
Distributed by Universal Uclick
www.facebook.com/garfield
© 2014 PAWS, INC. All Rights Reserved.

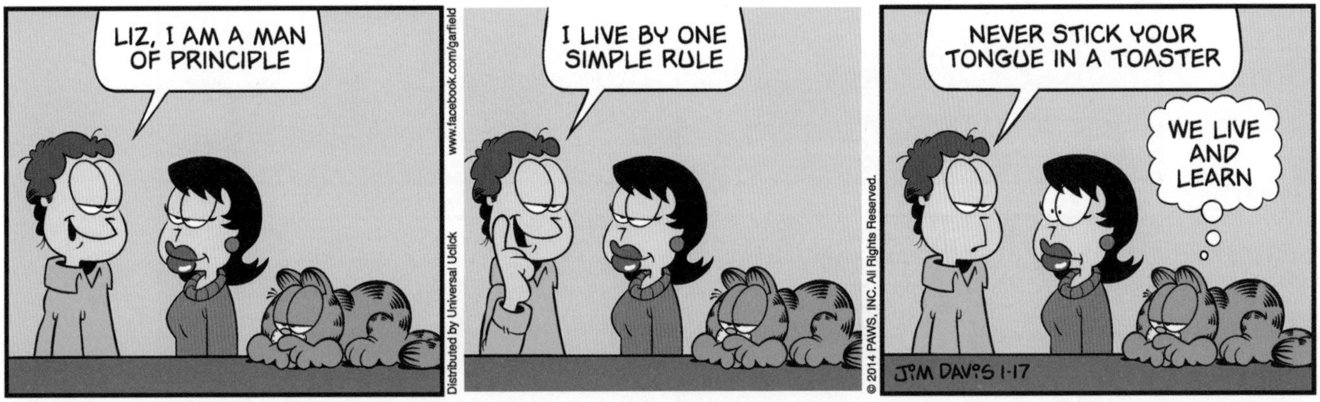
LIZ, I AM A MAN OF PRINCIPLE
I LIVE BY ONE SIMPLE RULE
NEVER STICK YOUR TONGUE IN A TOASTER
WE LIVE AND LEARN
JIM DAVIS 1-17
Distributed by Universal Uclick
www.facebook.com/garfield
© 2014 PAWS, INC. All Rights Reserved.

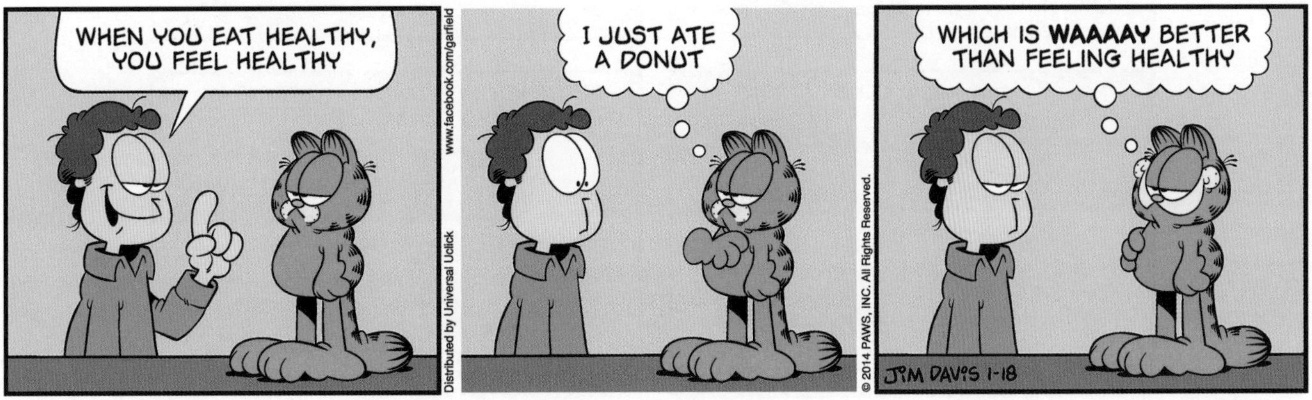
WHEN YOU EAT HEALTHY, YOU FEEL HEALTHY
I JUST ATE A DONUT
WHICH IS **WAAAAY** BETTER THAN FEELING HEALTHY
JIM DAVIS 1-18
Distributed by Universal Uclick
www.facebook.com/garfield
© 2014 PAWS, INC. All Rights Reserved.

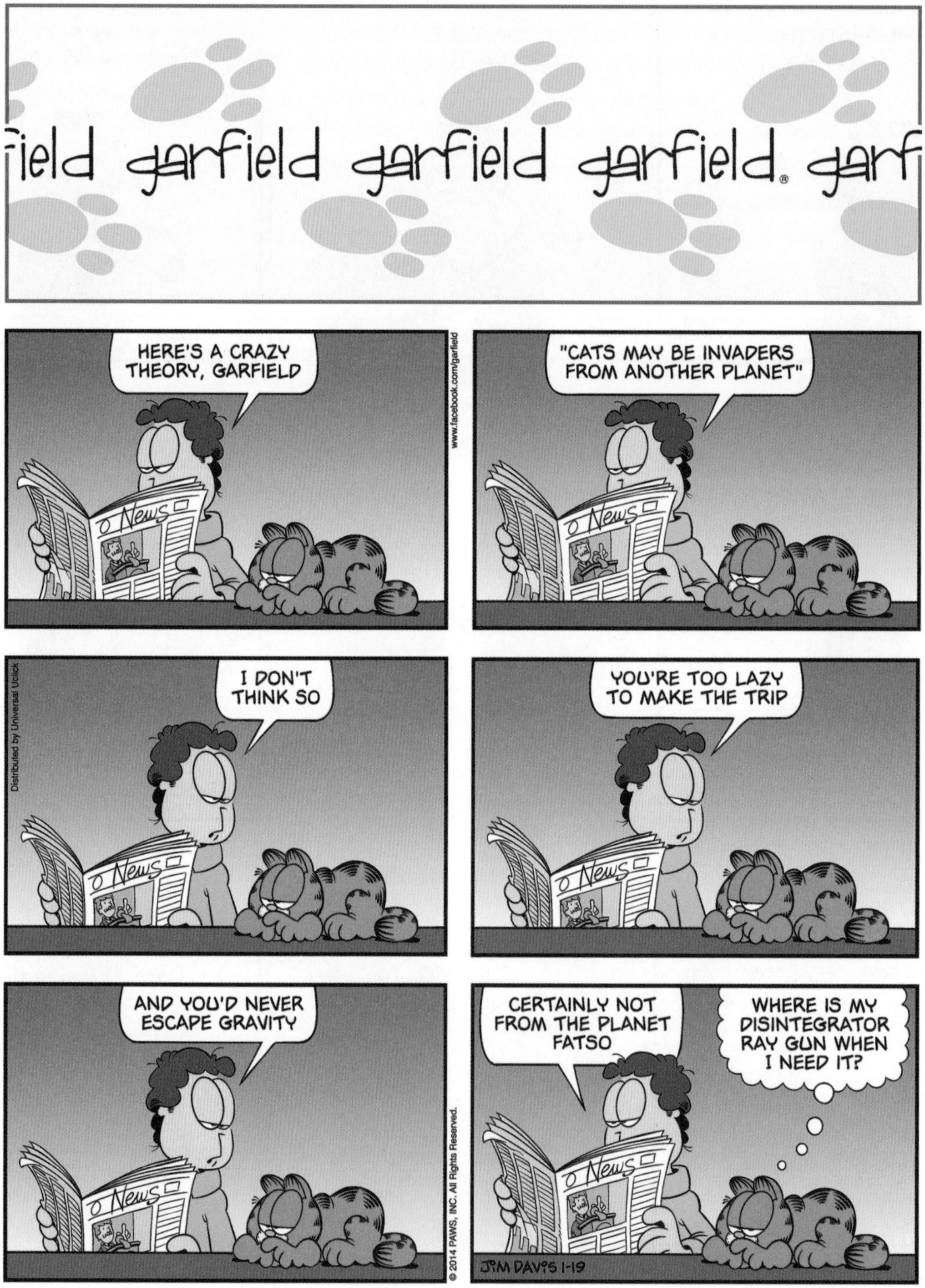
garfield
HERE'S A CRAZY THEORY, GARFIELD
"CATS MAY BE INVADERS FROM ANOTHER PLANET"
I DON'T THINK SO
YOU'RE TOO LAZY TO MAKE THE TRIP
AND YOU'D NEVER ESCAPE GRAVITY
CERTAINLY NOT FROM THE PLANET FATSO
WHERE IS MY DISINTEGRATOR RAY GUN WHEN I NEED IT?
www.facebook.com/garfield
Distributed by Universal Uclick
© 2014 PAWS, INC. All Rights Reserved.
JIM DAVIS 1-19

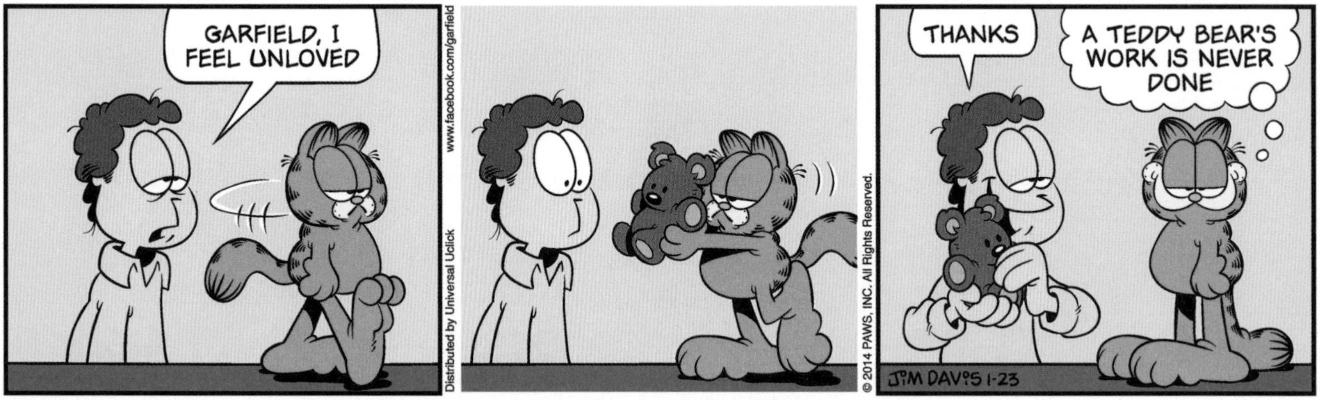
GARFIELD, I FEEL UNLOVED
THANKS
A TEDDY BEAR'S WORK IS NEVER DONE
JIM DAVIS 1-23
Distributed by Universal Uclick
www.facebook.com/garfield
© 2014 PAWS, INC. All Rights Reserved.

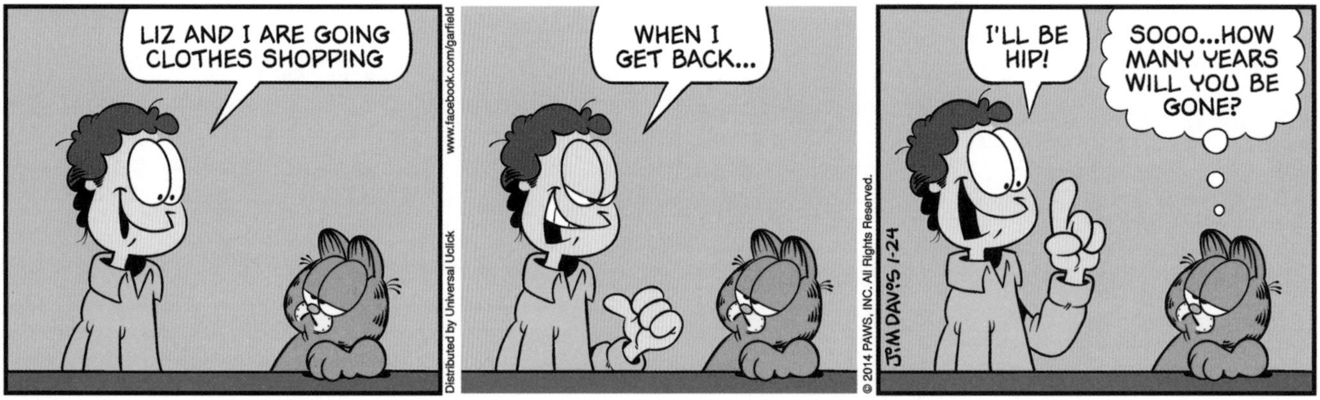
LIZ AND I ARE GOING CLOTHES SHOPPING
WHEN I GET BACK...
I'LL BE HIP!
SOOO...HOW MANY YEARS WILL YOU BE GONE?
JIM DAVIS 1-24
Distributed by Universal Uclick
www.facebook.com/garfield
© 2014 PAWS, INC. All Rights Reserved.

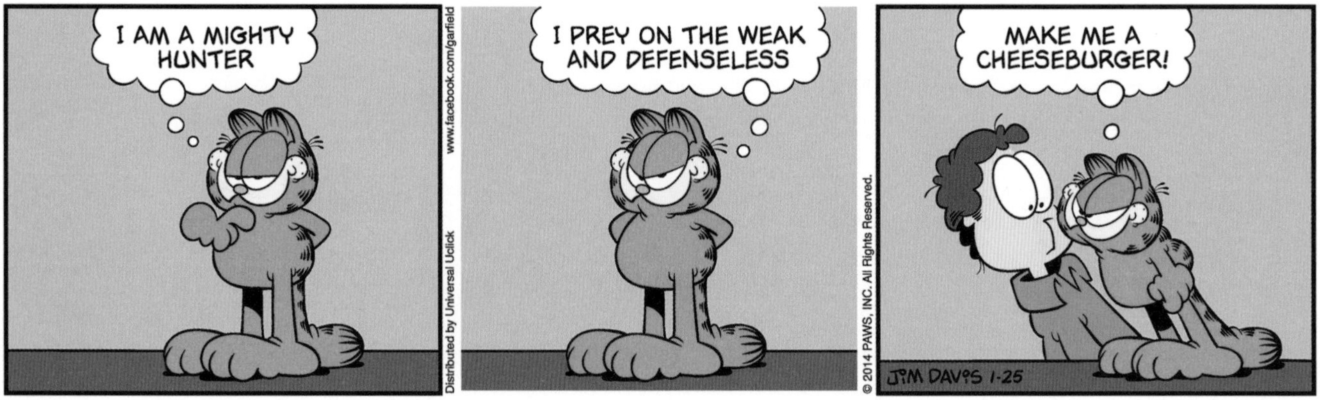
I AM A MIGHTY HUNTER
I PREY ON THE WEAK AND DEFENSELESS
MAKE ME A CHEESEBURGER!
JIM DAVIS 1-25
Distributed by Universal Uclick
www.facebook.com/garfield
© 2014 PAWS, INC. All Rights Reserved.

More TRUTH about cats

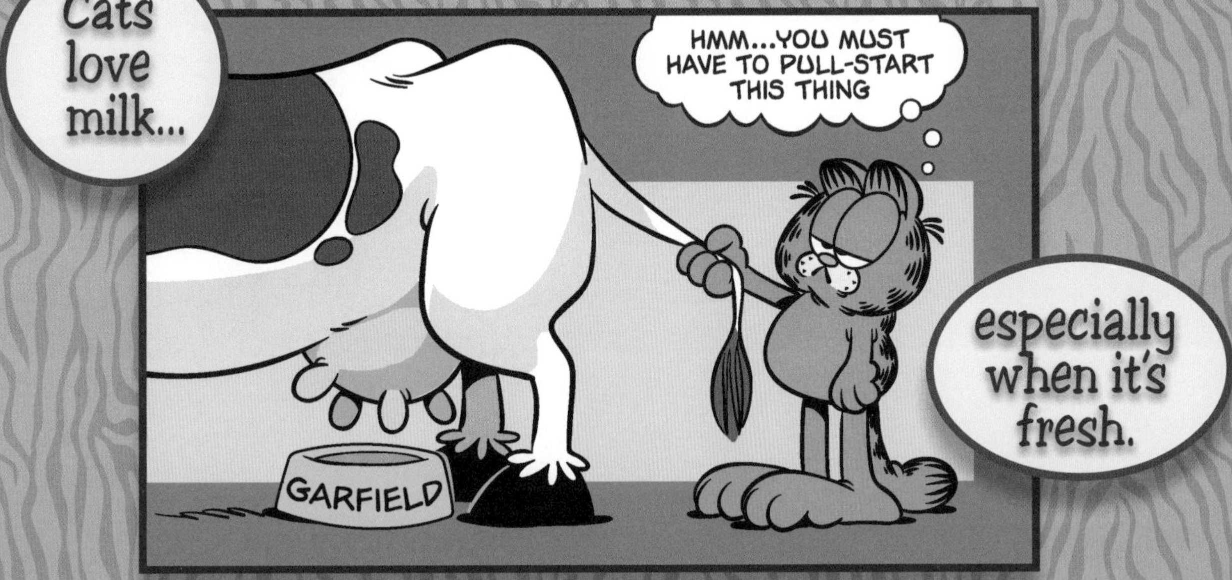
Cats love milk...
HMM...YOU MUST HAVE TO PULL-START THIS THING
GARFIELD
especially when it's fresh.

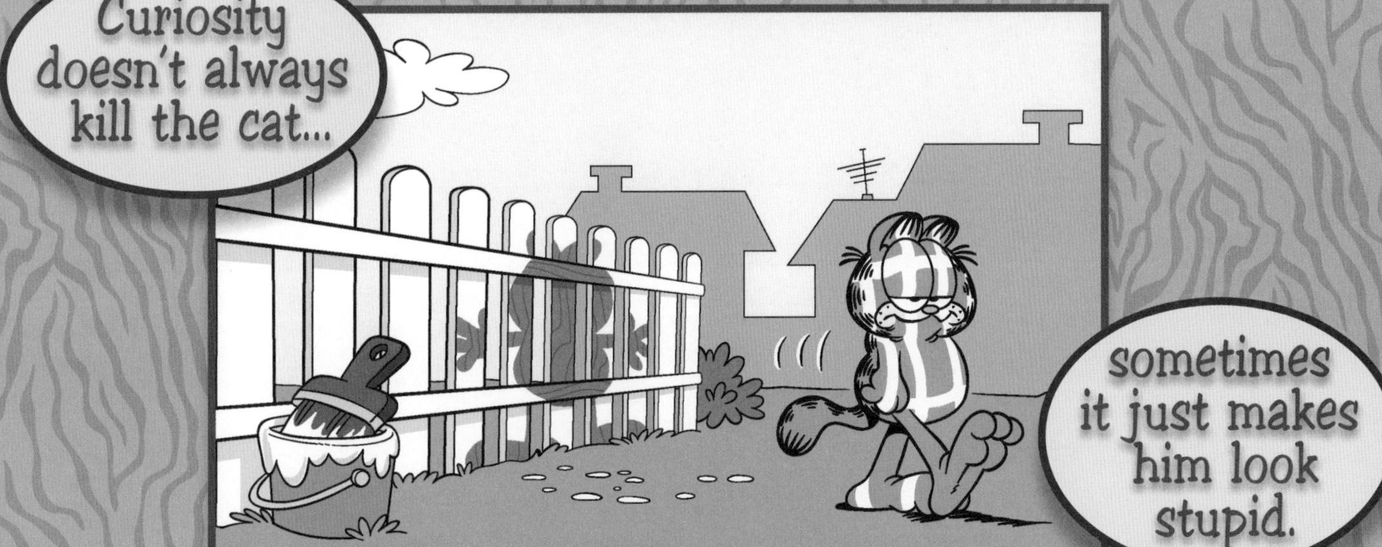
Curiosity doesn't always kill the cat...
sometimes it just makes him look stupid.

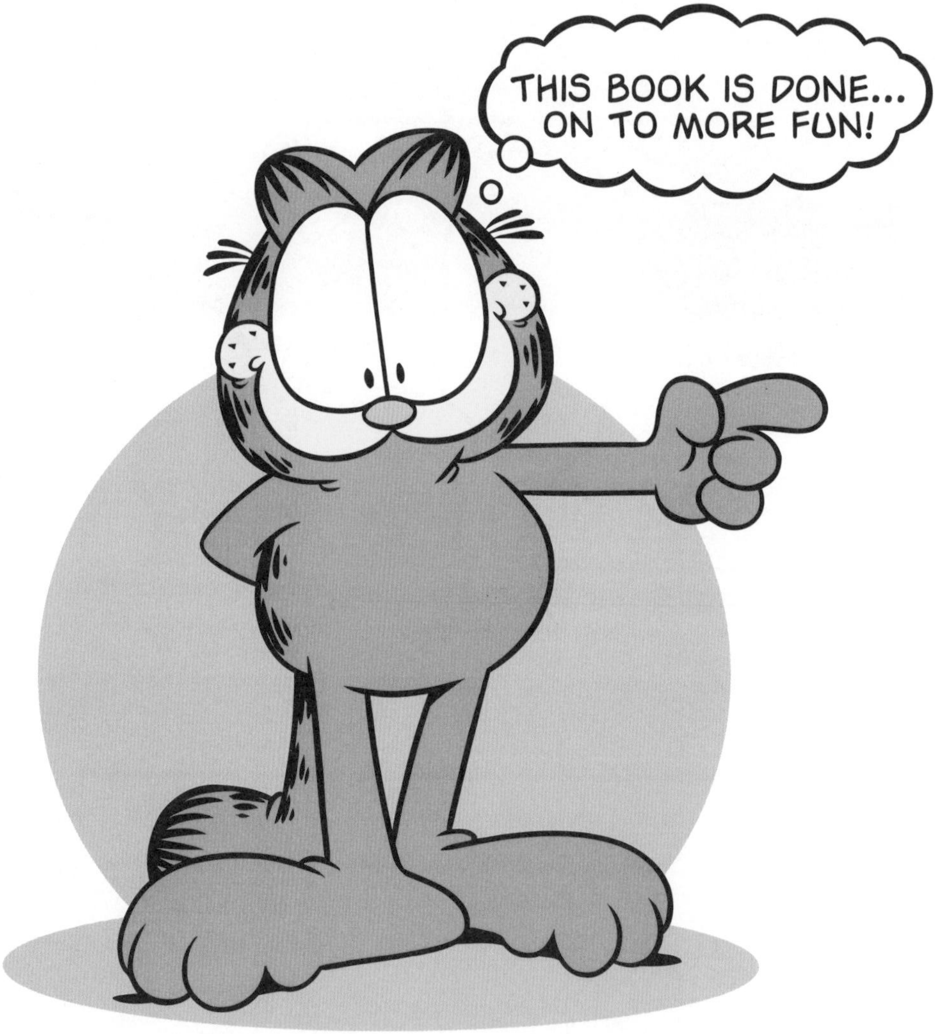
THIS BOOK IS DONE... ON TO MORE FUN!

Garfield
LISTENS TO HIS GUT

BY JIM DAVIS

FEEED MEEE

Ballantine Books • New York

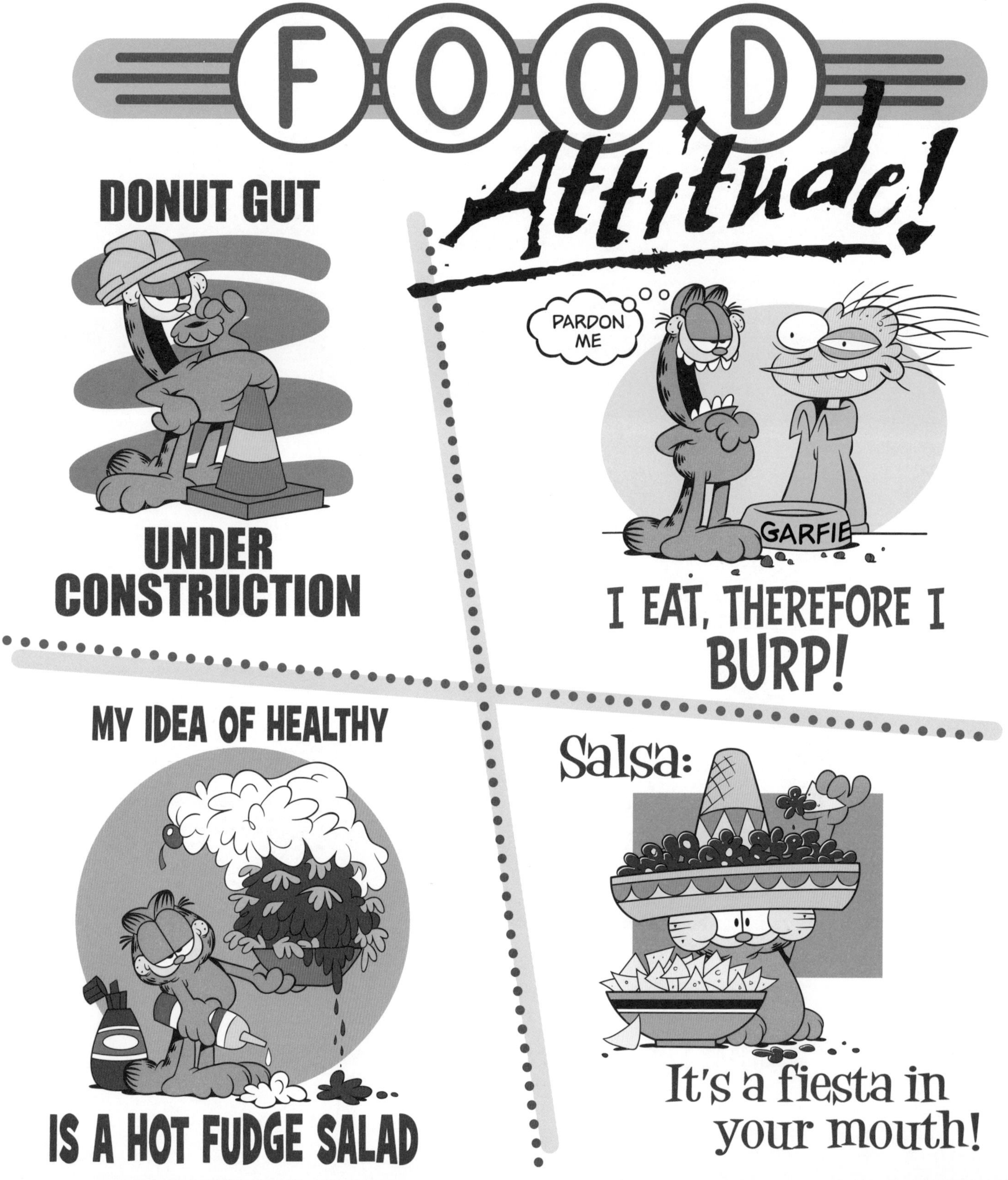
FOOD
Attitude!
DONUT GUT
UNDER CONSTRUCTION
PARDON ME
GARFIE
I EAT, THEREFORE I BURP!
MY IDEA OF HEALTHY
IS A HOT FUDGE SALAD
Salsa:
It's a fiesta in your mouth!

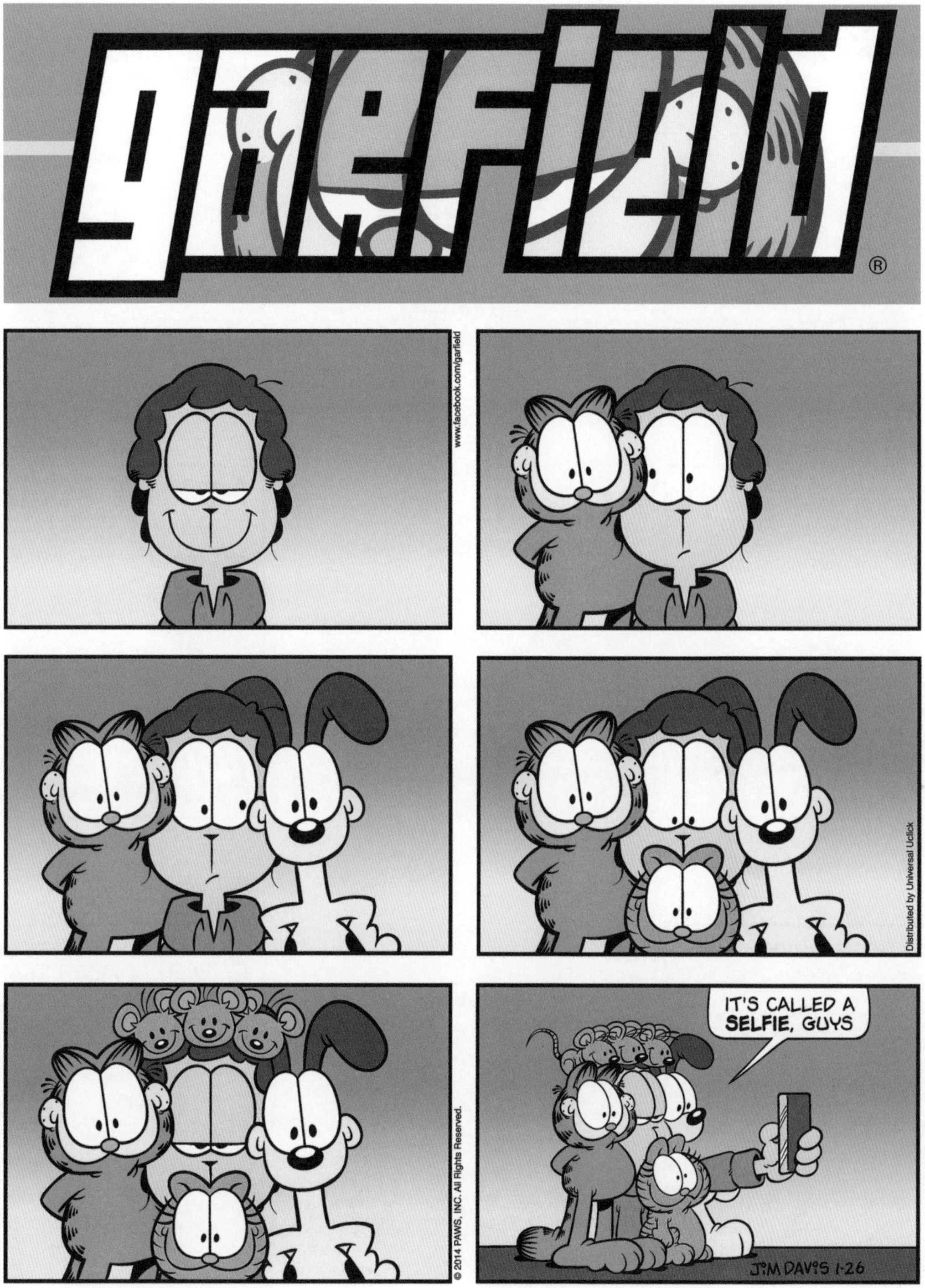
www.facebook.com/garfield
Distributed by Universal Uclick
© 2014 PAWS, INC. All Rights Reserved.
IT'S CALLED A SELFIE, GUYS
JIM DAVIS 1-26

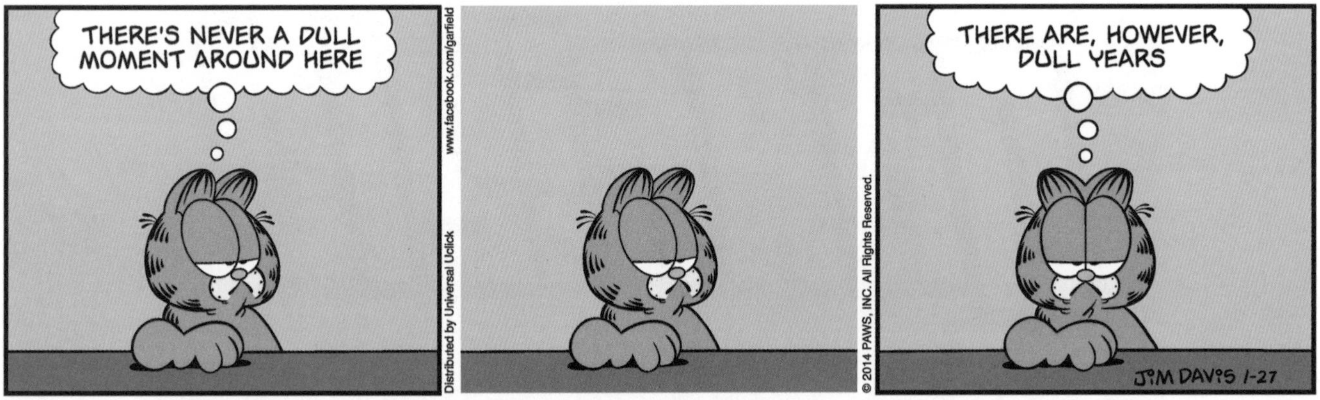
THERE'S NEVER A DULL MOMENT AROUND HERE
www.facebook.com/garfield
Distributed by Universal Uclick
© 2014 PAWS, INC. All Rights Reserved.
THERE ARE, HOWEVER, DULL YEARS
JIM DAVIS 1-27

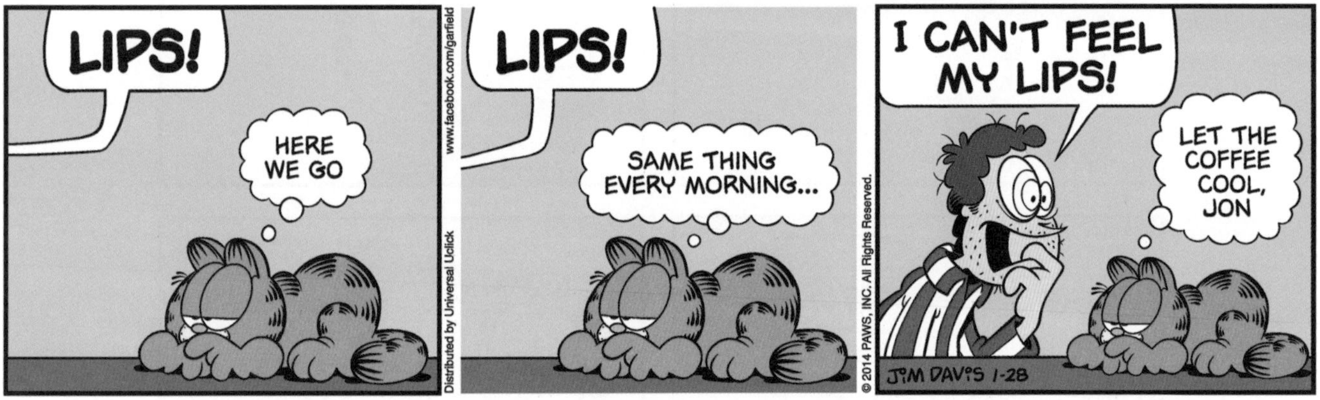
LIPS!
HERE WE GO
www.facebook.com/garfield
Distributed by Universal Uclick
LIPS!
SAME THING EVERY MORNING...
© 2014 PAWS, INC. All Rights Reserved.
I CAN'T FEEL MY LIPS!
LET THE COFFEE COOL, JON
JIM DAVIS 1-28

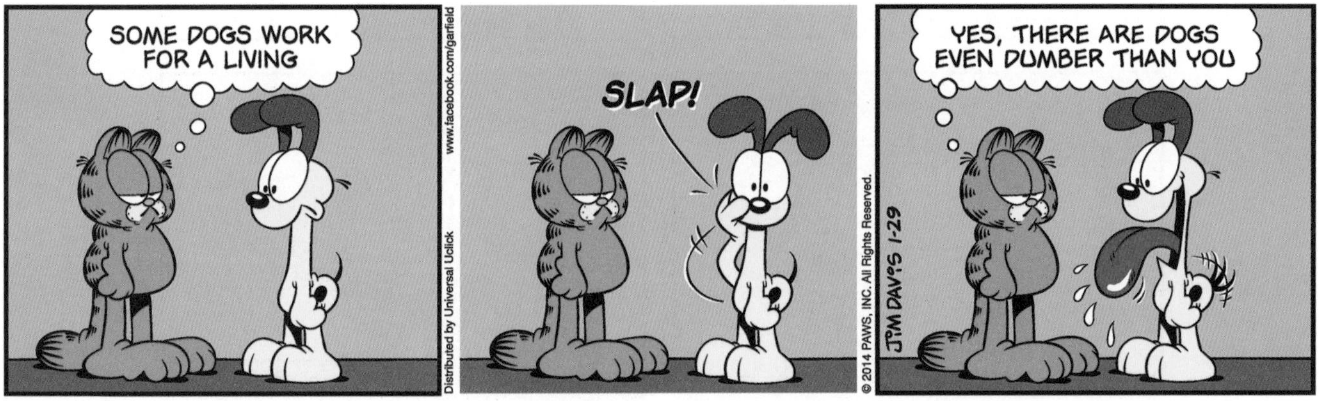
SOME DOGS WORK FOR A LIVING
www.facebook.com/garfield
Distributed by Universal Uclick
SLAP!
© 2014 PAWS, INC. All Rights Reserved.
JIM DAVIS 1-29
YES, THERE ARE DOGS EVEN DUMBER THAN YOU

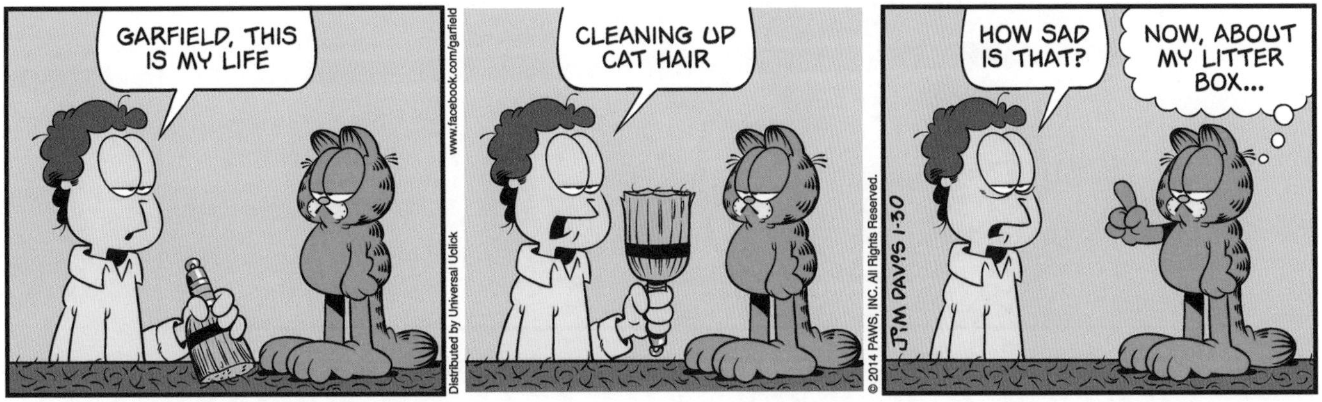
GARFIELD, THIS IS MY LIFE
Distributed by Universal Uclick
www.facebook.com/garfield
CLEANING UP CAT HAIR
© 2014 PAWS, INC. All Rights Reserved.
JIM DAVIS 1-30
HOW SAD IS THAT?
NOW, ABOUT MY LITTER BOX...

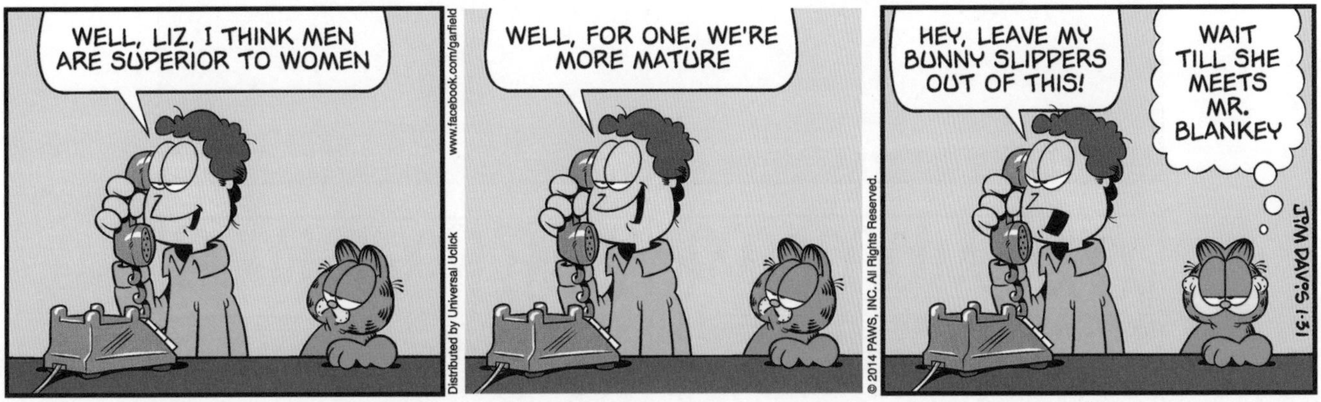
WELL, LIZ, I THINK MEN ARE SUPERIOR TO WOMEN
Distributed by Universal Uclick
www.facebook.com/garfield
WELL, FOR ONE, WE'RE MORE MATURE
© 2014 PAWS, INC. All Rights Reserved.
HEY, LEAVE MY BUNNY SLIPPERS OUT OF THIS!
WAIT TILL SHE MEETS MR. BLANKEY
JIM DAVIS 1-31

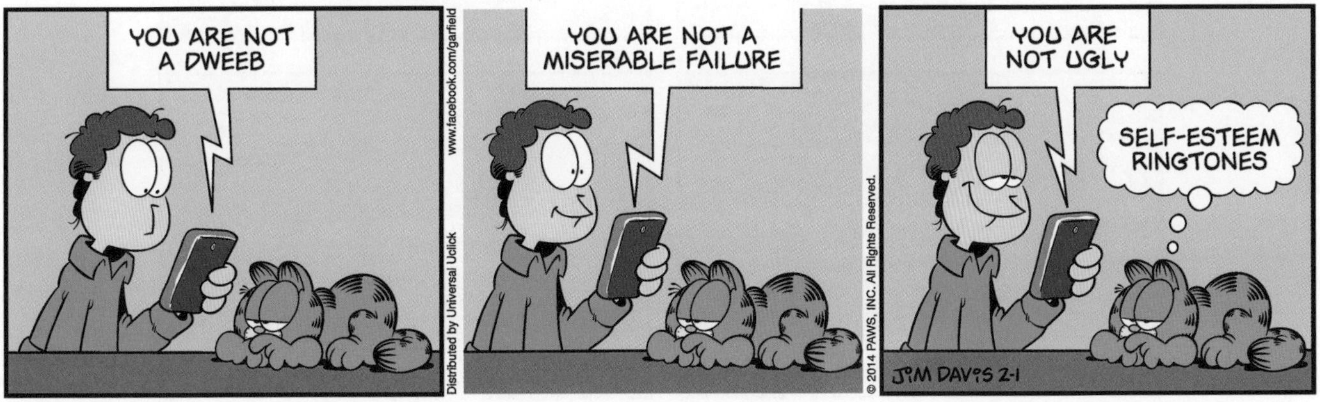
YOU ARE NOT A DWEEB
Distributed by Universal Uclick
www.facebook.com/garfield
YOU ARE NOT A MISERABLE FAILURE
© 2014 PAWS, INC. All Rights Reserved.
YOU ARE NOT UGLY
SELF-ESTEEM RINGTONES
JIM DAVIS 2-1

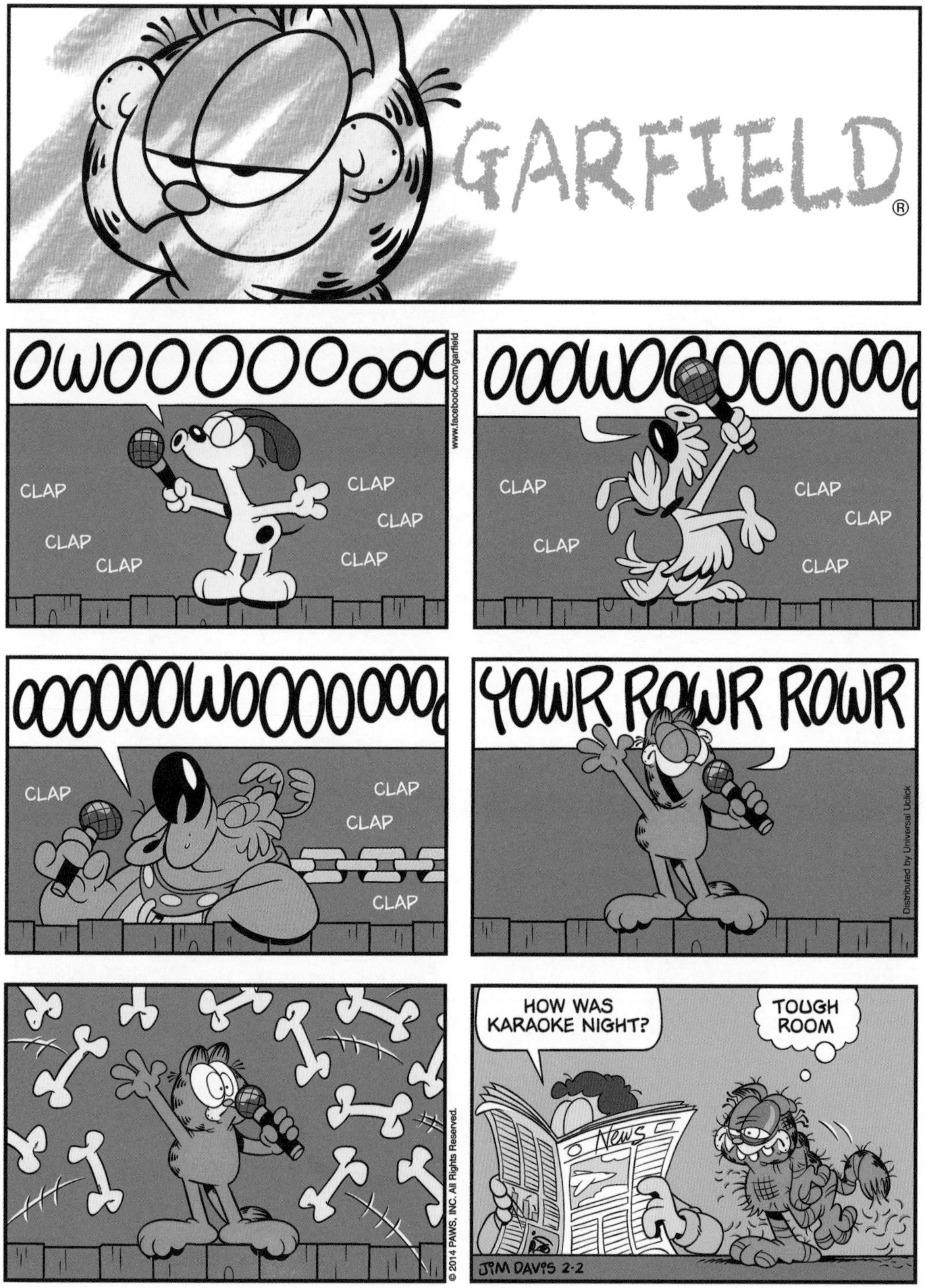
GARFIELD®
OWOOOOOOOOO
CLAP CLAP CLAP CLAP CLAP CLAP
www.facebook.com/garfield
OOOWOOOOOOOOO
CLAP CLAP CLAP CLAP CLAP
OOOOOOWOOOOOOOO
CLAP CLAP CLAP CLAP
YOWR ROWR ROWR
Distributed by Universal Uclick
© 2014 PAWS, INC. All Rights Reserved.
HOW WAS KARAOKE NIGHT?
TOUGH ROOM
NEWS
JIM DAVIS 2-2

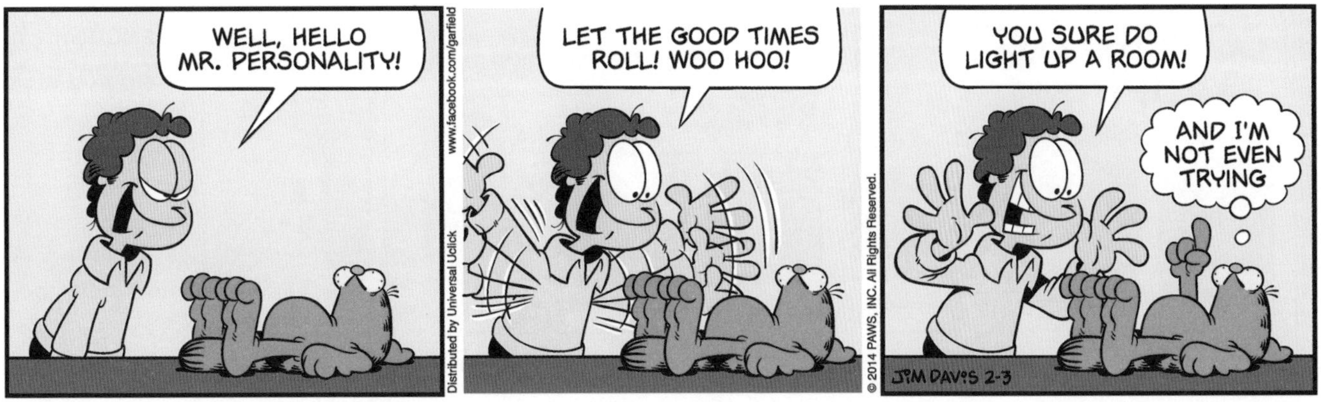
WELL, HELLO MR. PERSONALITY!
LET THE GOOD TIMES ROLL! WOO HOO!
YOU SURE DO LIGHT UP A ROOM!
AND I'M NOT EVEN TRYING
Distributed by Universal Uclick www.facebook.com/garfield
© 2014 PAWS, INC. All Rights Reserved.
JIM DAVIS 2-3

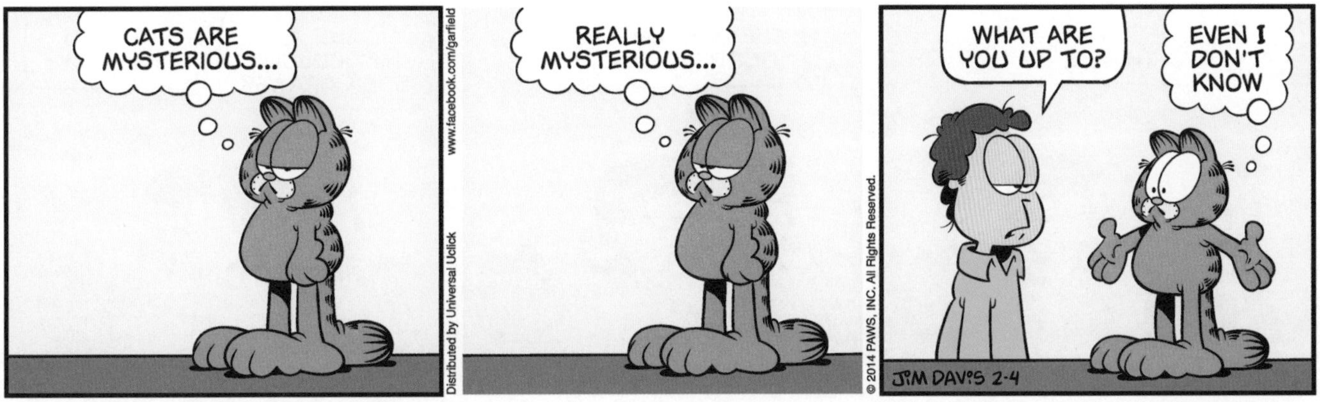
CATS ARE MYSTERIOUS...
REALLY MYSTERIOUS...
WHAT ARE YOU UP TO?
EVEN I DON'T KNOW
Distributed by Universal Uclick www.facebook.com/garfield
© 2014 PAWS, INC. All Rights Reserved.
JIM DAVIS 2-4

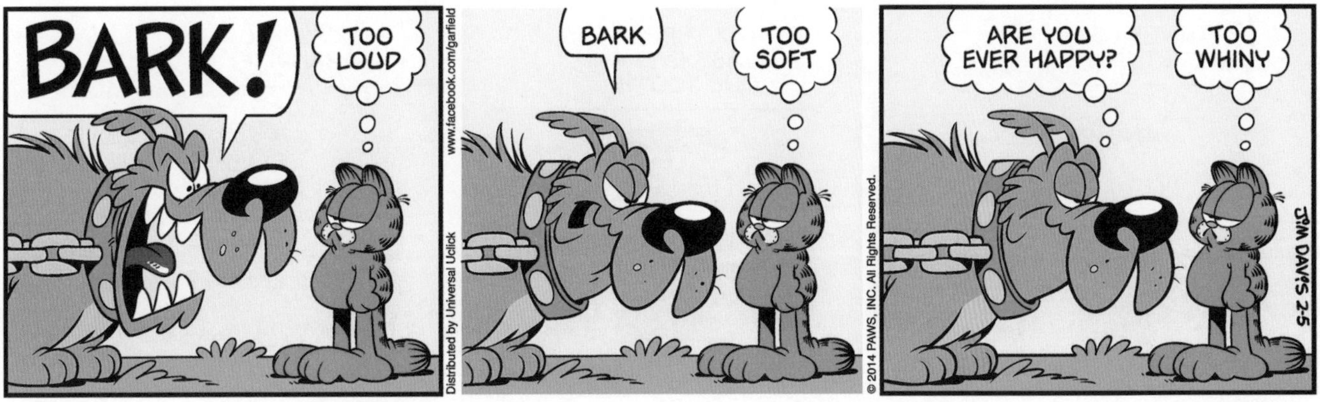
BARK!
TOO LOUD
BARK
TOO SOFT
ARE YOU EVER HAPPY?
TOO WHINY
Distributed by Universal Uclick www.facebook.com/garfield
© 2014 PAWS, INC. All Rights Reserved.
JIM DAVIS 2-5

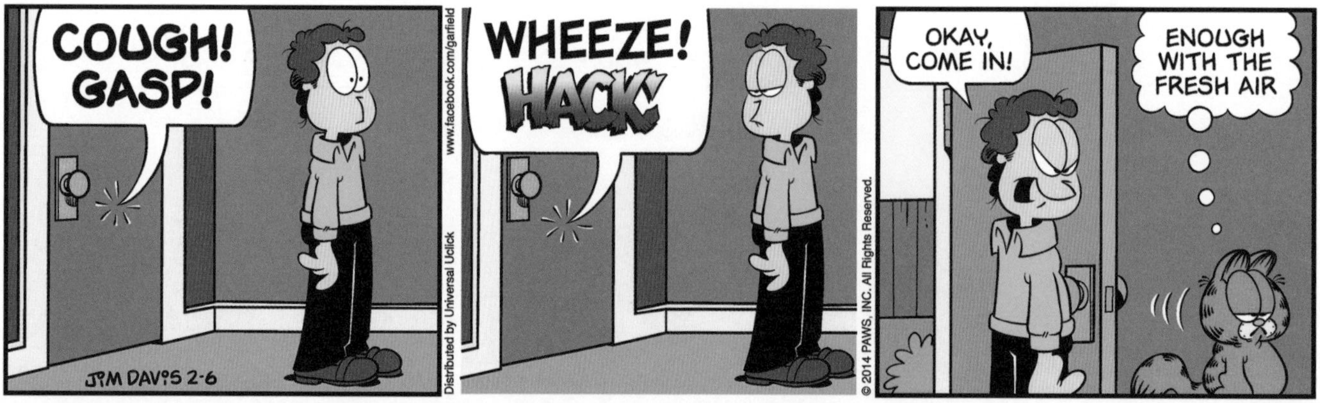
COUGH! GASP!
JIM DAVIS 2-6
Distributed by Universal Uclick www.facebook.com/garfield
WHEEZE! HACK!
© 2014 PAWS, INC. All Rights Reserved.
OKAY, COME IN!
ENOUGH WITH THE FRESH AIR

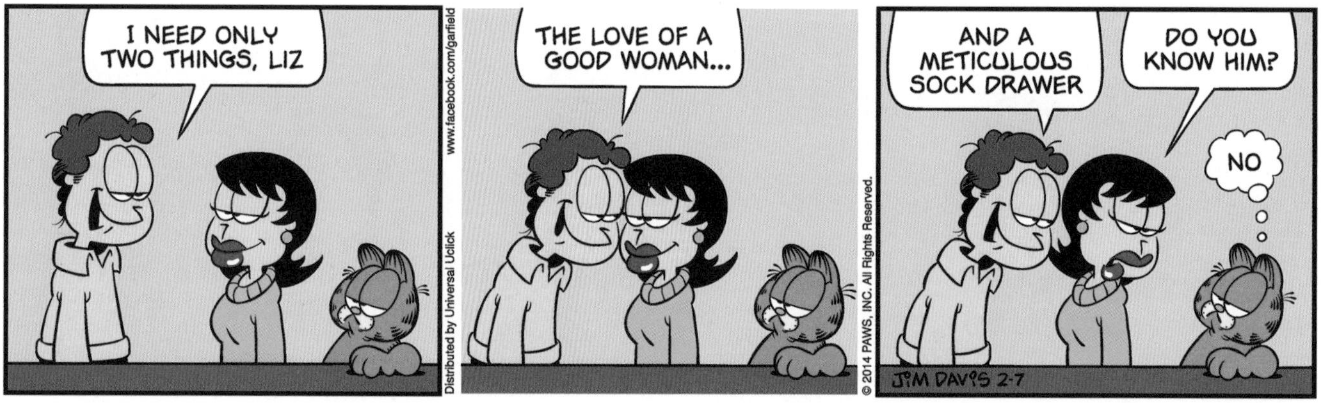
I NEED ONLY TWO THINGS, LIZ
Distributed by Universal Uclick www.facebook.com/garfield
THE LOVE OF A GOOD WOMAN...
© 2014 PAWS, INC. All Rights Reserved.
AND A METICULOUS SOCK DRAWER
DO YOU KNOW HIM?
NO
JIM DAVIS 2-7

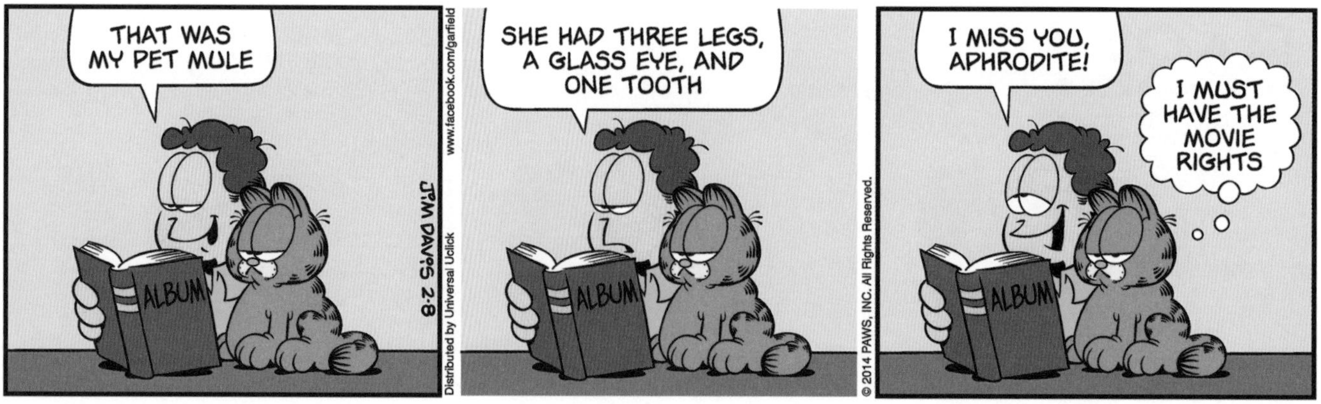
THAT WAS MY PET MULE
ALBUM
JIM DAVIS 2-8
Distributed by Universal Uclick www.facebook.com/garfield
SHE HAD THREE LEGS, A GLASS EYE, AND ONE TOOTH
ALBUM
© 2014 PAWS, INC. All Rights Reserved.
I MISS YOU, APHRODITE!
I MUST HAVE THE MOVIE RIGHTS
ALBUM

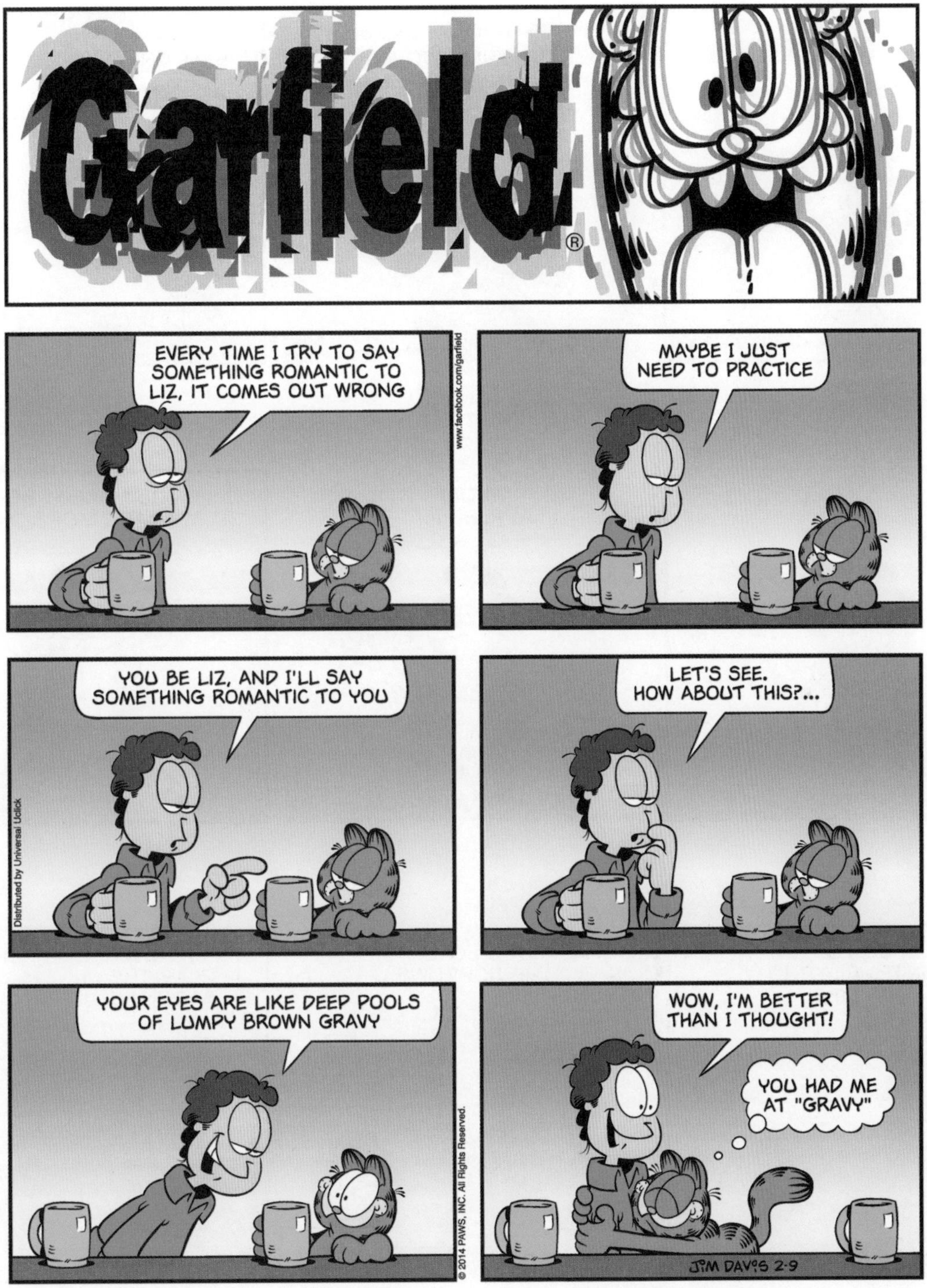
Garfield®
www.facebook.com/garfield
EVERY TIME I TRY TO SAY SOMETHING ROMANTIC TO LIZ, IT COMES OUT WRONG
MAYBE I JUST NEED TO PRACTICE
Distributed by Universal Uclick
YOU BE LIZ, AND I'LL SAY SOMETHING ROMANTIC TO YOU
LET'S SEE. HOW ABOUT THIS?...
YOUR EYES ARE LIKE DEEP POOLS OF LUMPY BROWN GRAVY
© 2014 PAWS, INC. All Rights Reserved.
WOW, I'M BETTER THAN I THOUGHT!
YOU HAD ME AT "GRAVY"
JIM DAVIS 2-9

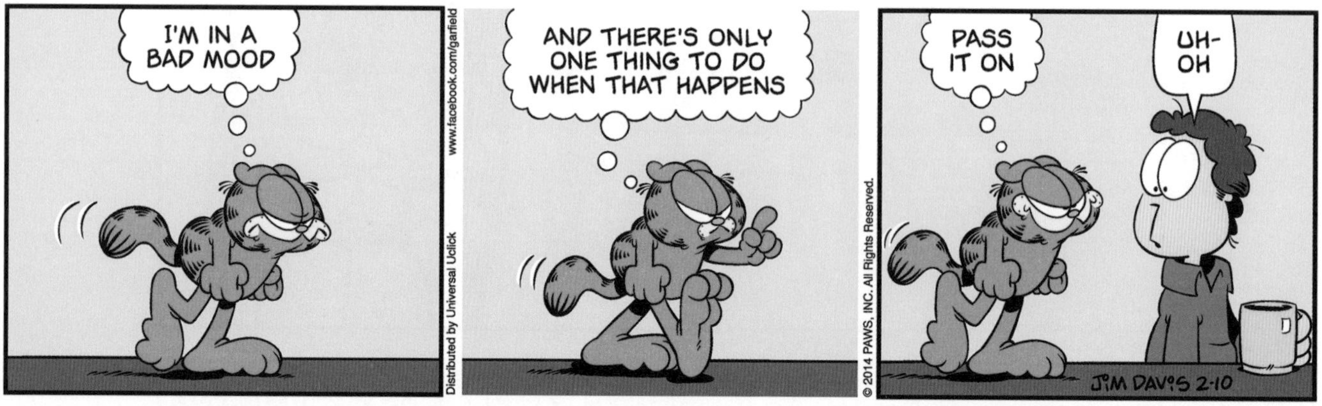
I'M IN A BAD MOOD
AND THERE'S ONLY ONE THING TO DO WHEN THAT HAPPENS
PASS IT ON
UH-OH
JIM DAVIS 2-10
Distributed by Universal Uclick
www.facebook.com/garfield
© 2014 PAWS, INC. All Rights Reserved.

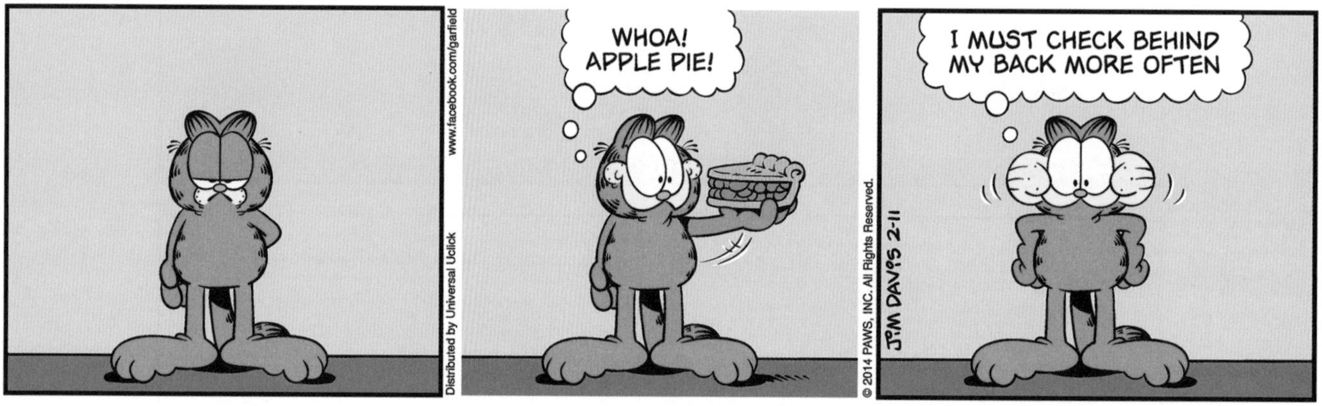
WHOA! APPLE PIE!
I MUST CHECK BEHIND MY BACK MORE OFTEN
JIM DAVIS 2-11
Distributed by Universal Uclick
www.facebook.com/garfield
© 2014 PAWS, INC. All Rights Reserved.

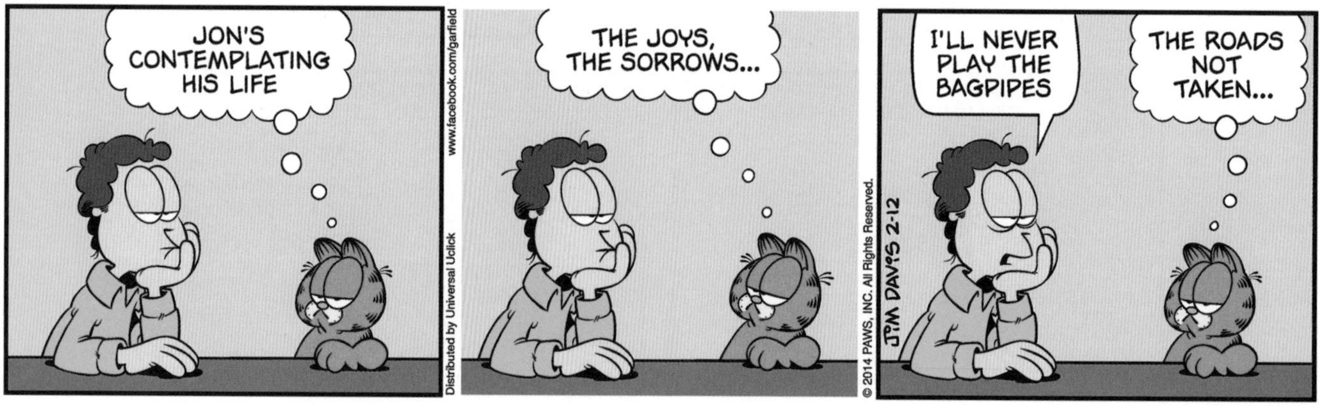
JON'S CONTEMPLATING HIS LIFE
THE JOYS, THE SORROWS...
I'LL NEVER PLAY THE BAGPIPES
THE ROADS NOT TAKEN...
JIM DAVIS 2-12
Distributed by Universal Uclick
www.facebook.com/garfield
© 2014 PAWS, INC. All Rights Reserved.

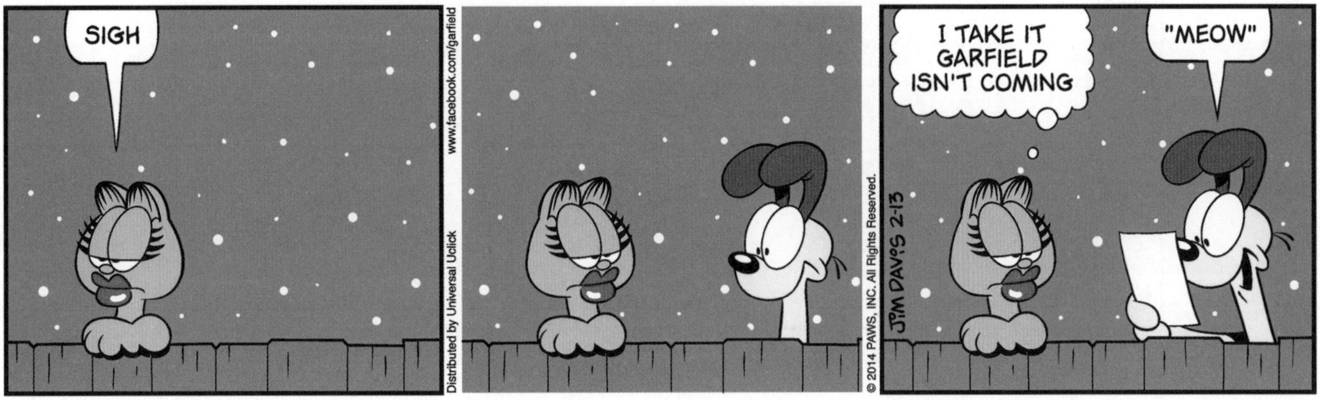
SIGH
www.facebook.com/garfield
Distributed by Universal Uclick
I TAKE IT GARFIELD ISN'T COMING
"MEOW"
JIM DAVIS 2-13
© 2014 PAWS, INC. All Rights Reserved.

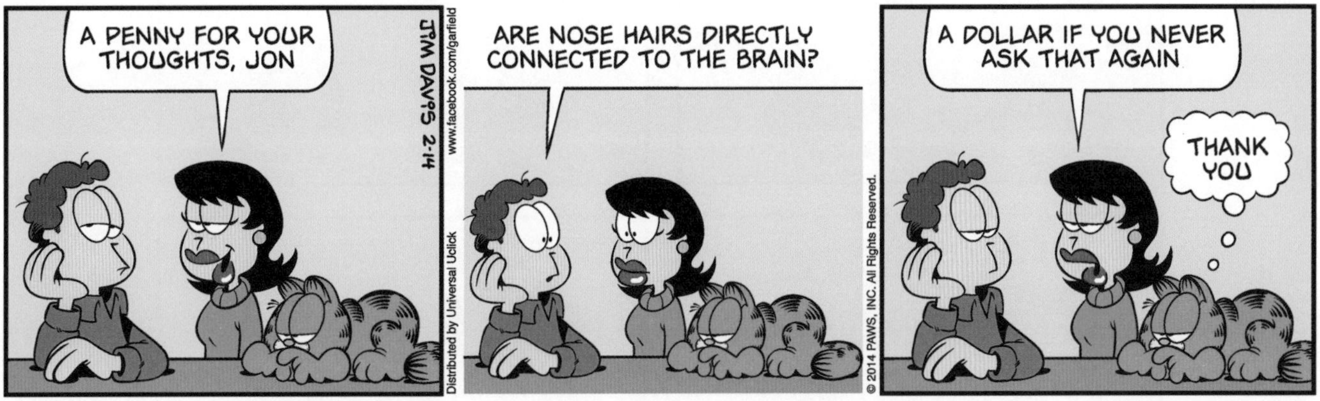
A PENNY FOR YOUR THOUGHTS, JON
JIM DAVIS 2-14
www.facebook.com/garfield
Distributed by Universal Uclick
ARE NOSE HAIRS DIRECTLY CONNECTED TO THE BRAIN?
© 2014 PAWS, INC. All Rights Reserved.
A DOLLAR IF YOU NEVER ASK THAT AGAIN
THANK YOU

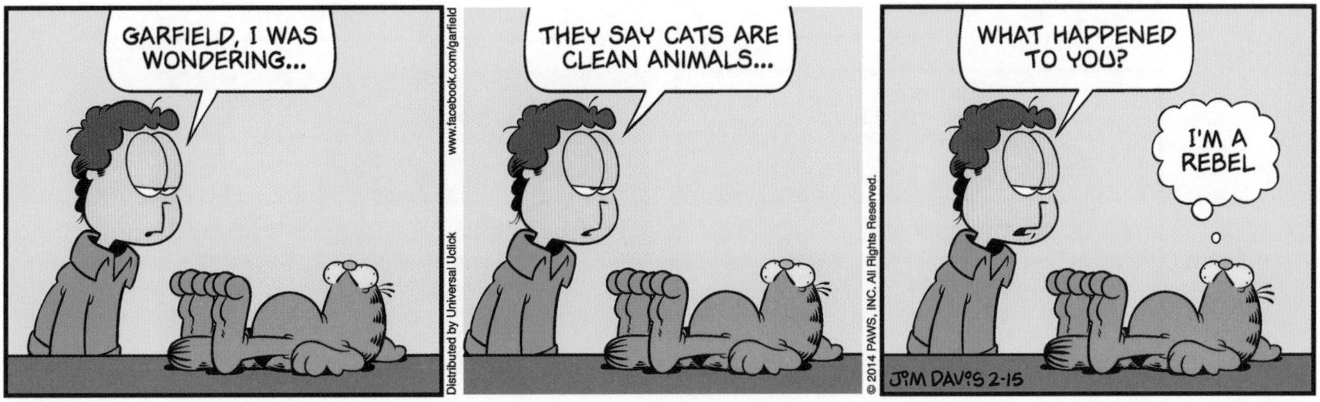
GARFIELD, I WAS WONDERING...
www.facebook.com/garfield
Distributed by Universal Uclick
THEY SAY CATS ARE CLEAN ANIMALS...
© 2014 PAWS, INC. All Rights Reserved.
WHAT HAPPENED TO YOU?
I'M A REBEL
JIM DAVIS 2-15

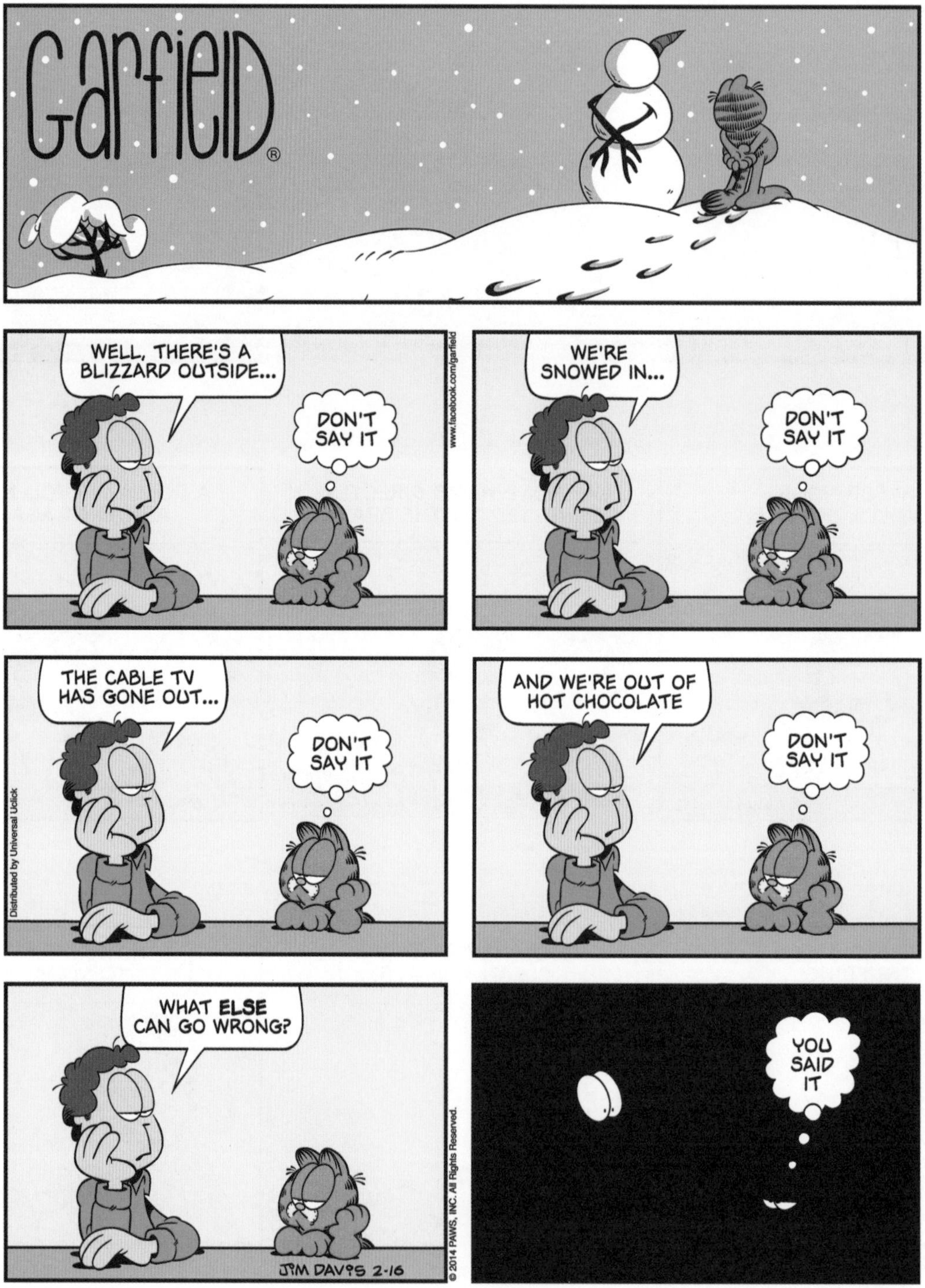

GARFIELD®
WELL, THERE'S A BLIZZARD OUTSIDE...
DON'T SAY IT
WE'RE SNOWED IN...
DON'T SAY IT
THE CABLE TV HAS GONE OUT...
DON'T SAY IT
AND WE'RE OUT OF HOT CHOCOLATE
DON'T SAY IT
WHAT **ELSE** CAN GO WRONG?
YOU SAID IT
JIM DAVIS 2-16
www.facebook.com/garfield
Distributed by Universal Uclick
© 2014 PAWS, INC. All Rights Reserved.

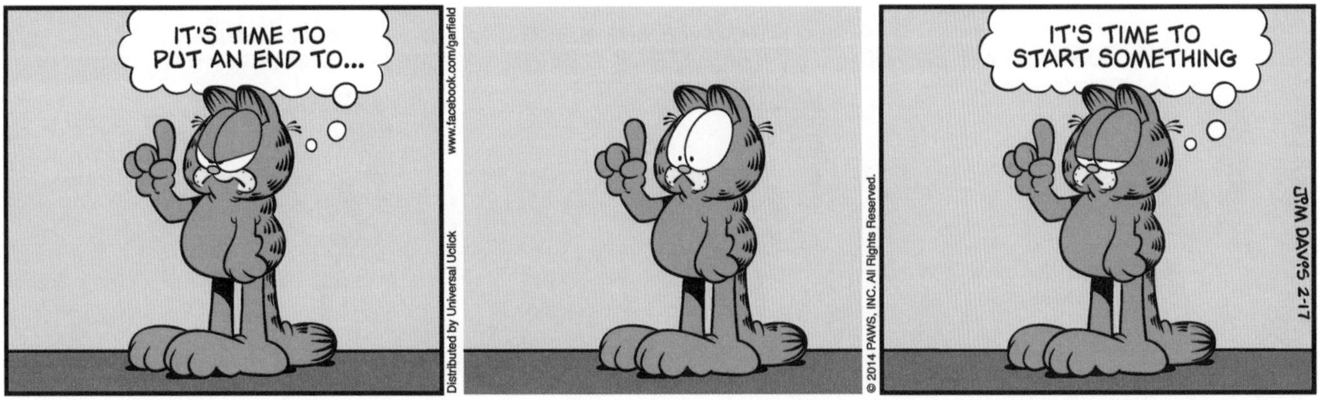
IT'S TIME TO PUT AN END TO...
IT'S TIME TO START SOMETHING
JIM DAVIS 2-17
Distributed by Universal Uclick
www.facebook.com/garfield
© 2014 PAWS, INC. All Rights Reserved.

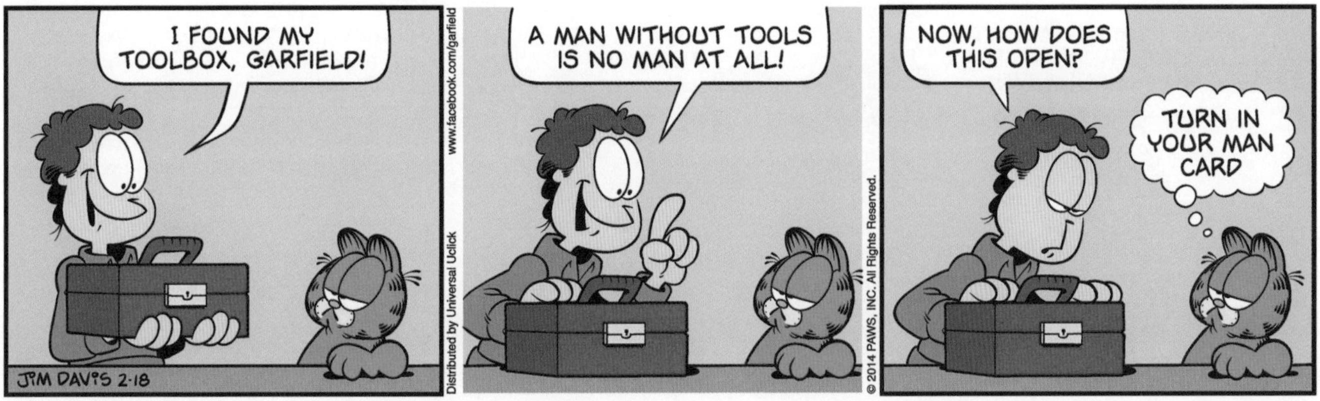
I FOUND MY TOOLBOX, GARFIELD!
A MAN WITHOUT TOOLS IS NO MAN AT ALL!
NOW, HOW DOES THIS OPEN?
TURN IN YOUR MAN CARD
JIM DAVIS 2-18
Distributed by Universal Uclick
www.facebook.com/garfield
© 2014 PAWS, INC. All Rights Reserved.

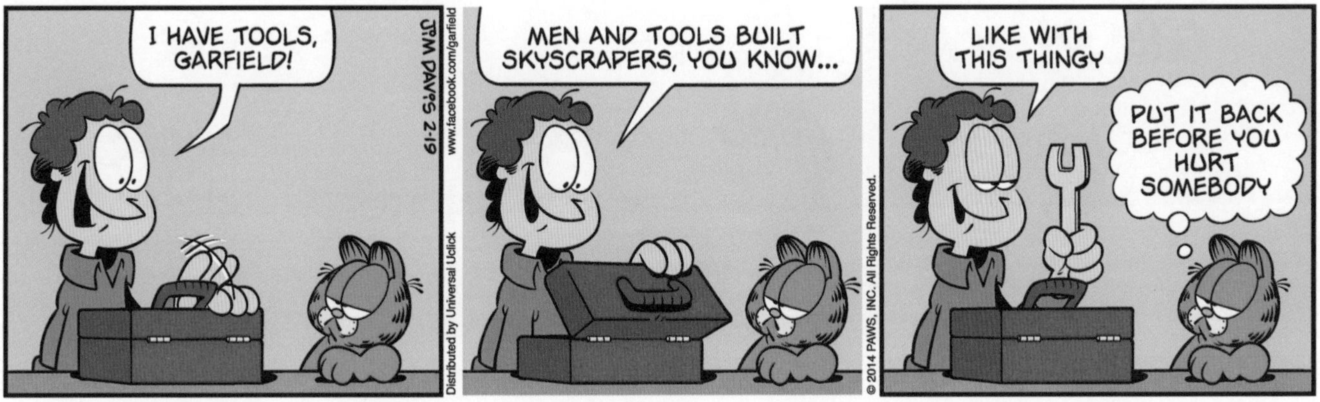
I HAVE TOOLS, GARFIELD!
MEN AND TOOLS BUILT SKYSCRAPERS, YOU KNOW...
LIKE WITH THIS THINGY
PUT IT BACK BEFORE YOU HURT SOMEBODY
JIM DAVIS 2-19
Distributed by Universal Uclick
www.facebook.com/garfield
© 2014 PAWS, INC. All Rights Reserved.

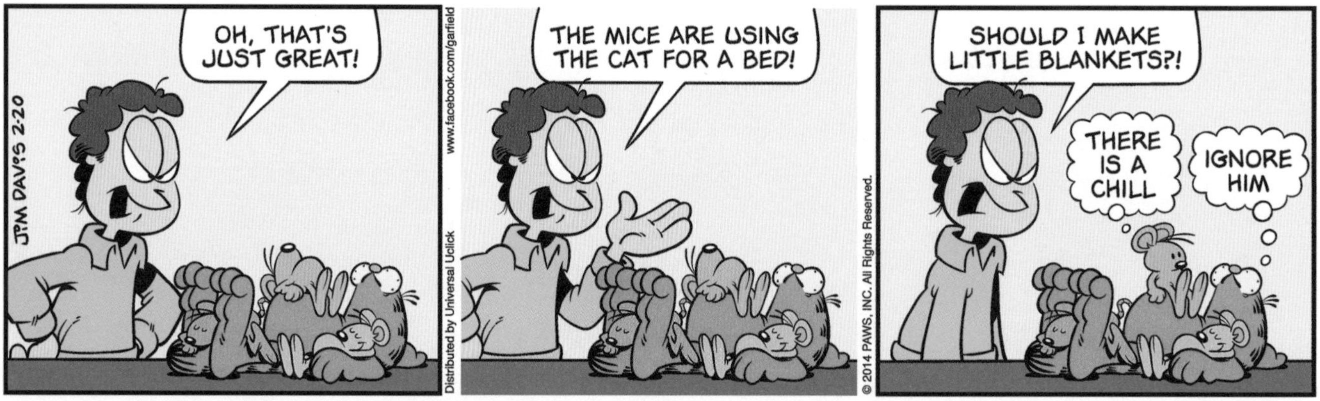
JIM DAVIS 2-20
OH, THAT'S JUST GREAT!
THE MICE ARE USING THE CAT FOR A BED!
SHOULD I MAKE LITTLE BLANKETS?!
THERE IS A CHILL
IGNORE HIM
Distributed by Universal Uclick www.facebook.com/garfield
© 2014 PAWS, INC. All Rights Reserved.

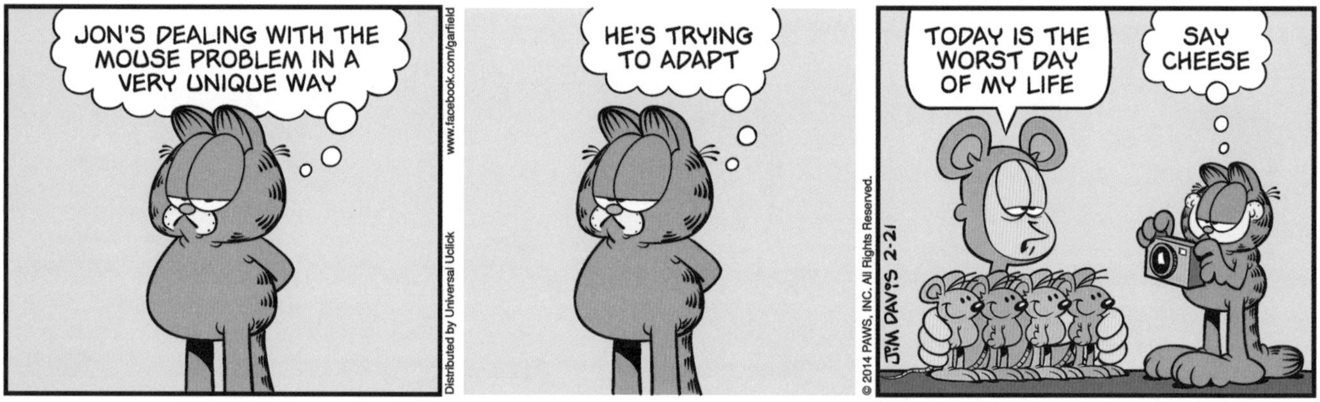
JON'S DEALING WITH THE MOUSE PROBLEM IN A VERY UNIQUE WAY
HE'S TRYING TO ADAPT
TODAY IS THE WORST DAY OF MY LIFE
SAY CHEESE
JIM DAVIS 2-21
Distributed by Universal Uclick www.facebook.com/garfield
© 2014 PAWS, INC. All Rights Reserved.

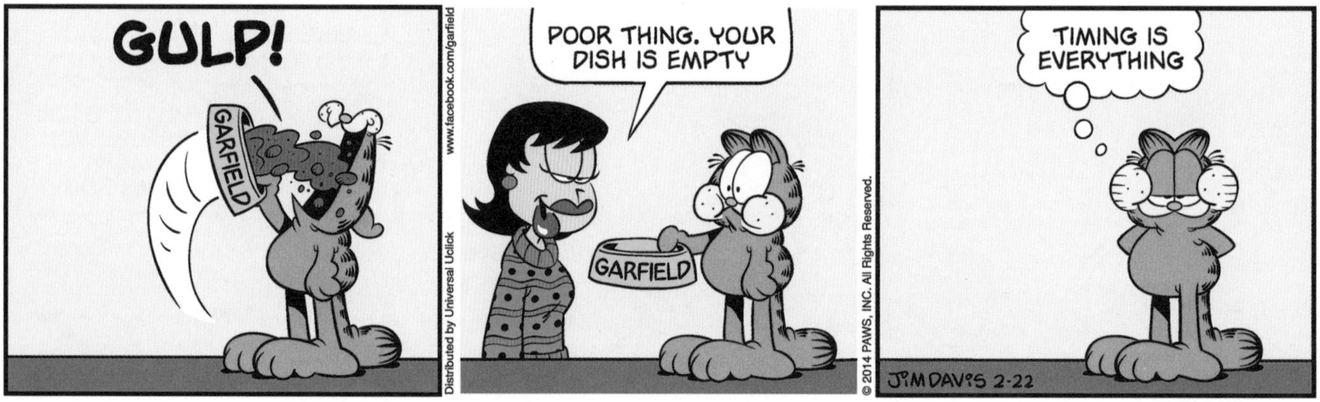
GULP!
GARFIELD
POOR THING. YOUR DISH IS EMPTY
GARFIELD
TIMING IS EVERYTHING
JIM DAVIS 2-22
Distributed by Universal Uclick www.facebook.com/garfield
© 2014 PAWS, INC. All Rights Reserved.

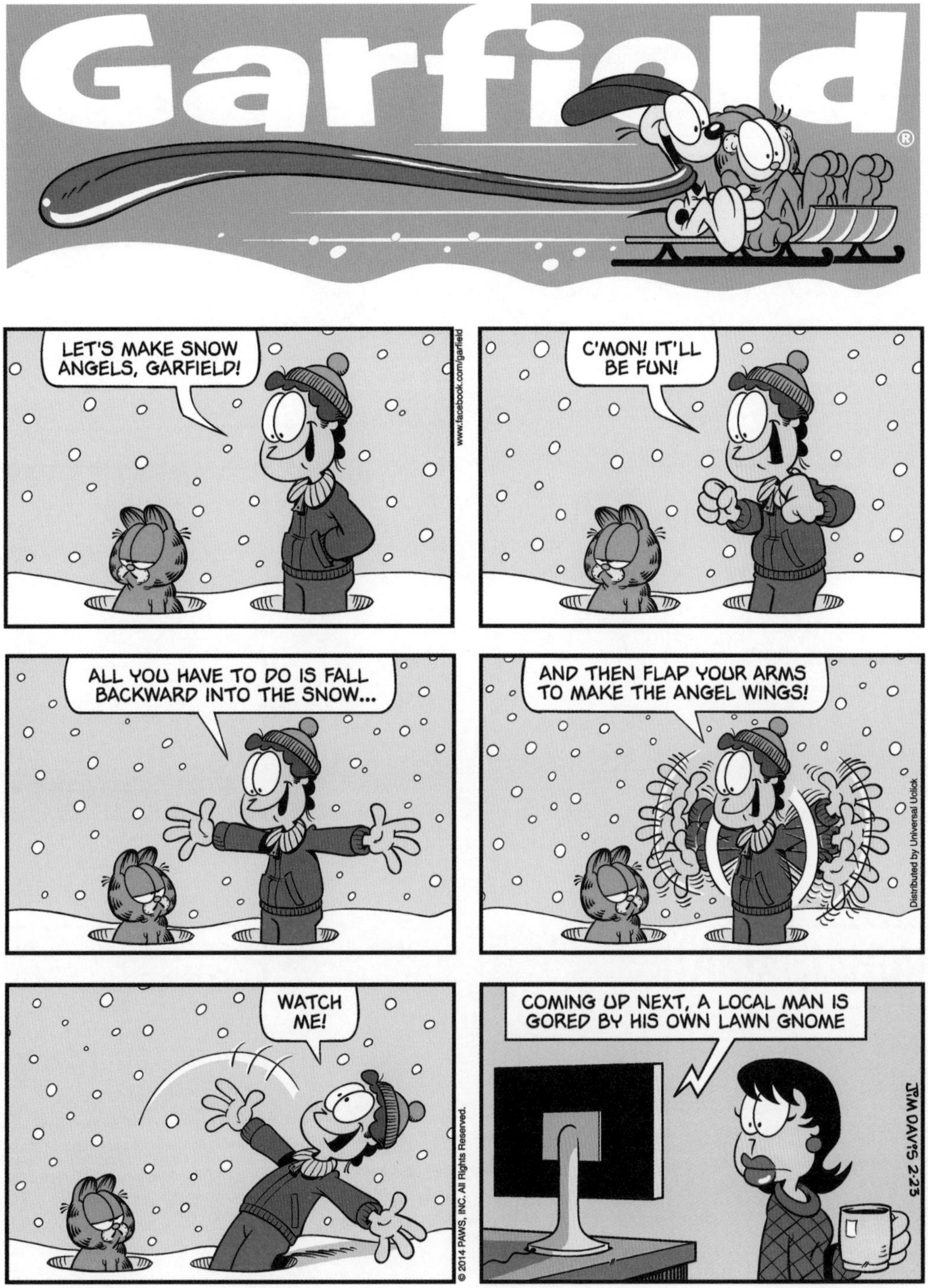
Garfield®
LET'S MAKE SNOW ANGELS, GARFIELD!
www.facebook.com/garfield
C'MON! IT'LL BE FUN!
ALL YOU HAVE TO DO IS FALL BACKWARD INTO THE SNOW...
AND THEN FLAP YOUR ARMS TO MAKE THE ANGEL WINGS!
Distributed by Universal Uclick
WATCH ME!
© 2014 PAWS, INC. All Rights Reserved.
COMING UP NEXT, A LOCAL MAN IS GORED BY HIS OWN LAWN GNOME
JIM DAVIS 2-23

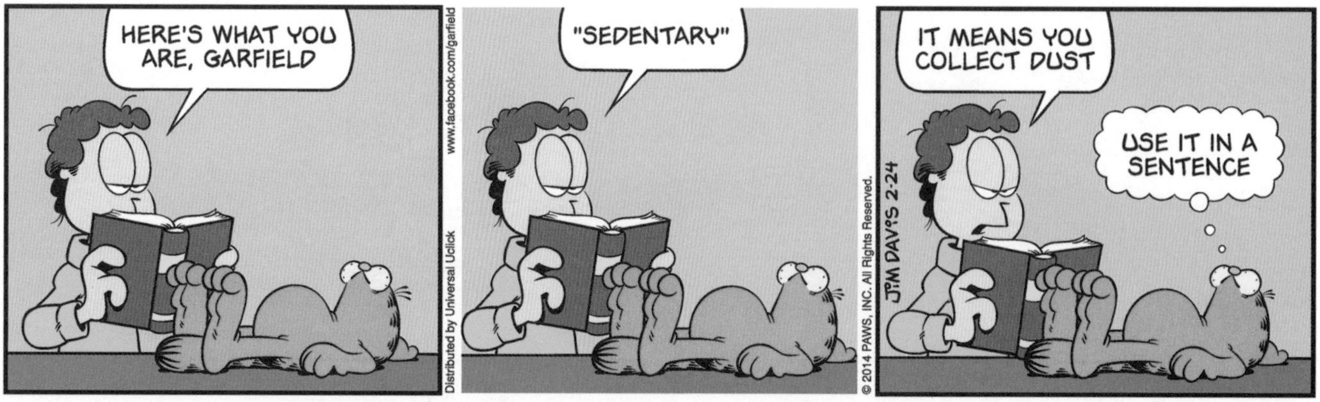
HERE'S WHAT YOU ARE, GARFIELD
"SEDENTARY"
IT MEANS YOU COLLECT DUST
USE IT IN A SENTENCE
Distributed by Universal Uclick
www.facebook.com/garfield
© 2014 PAWS, INC. All Rights Reserved.
JIM DAVIS 2-24

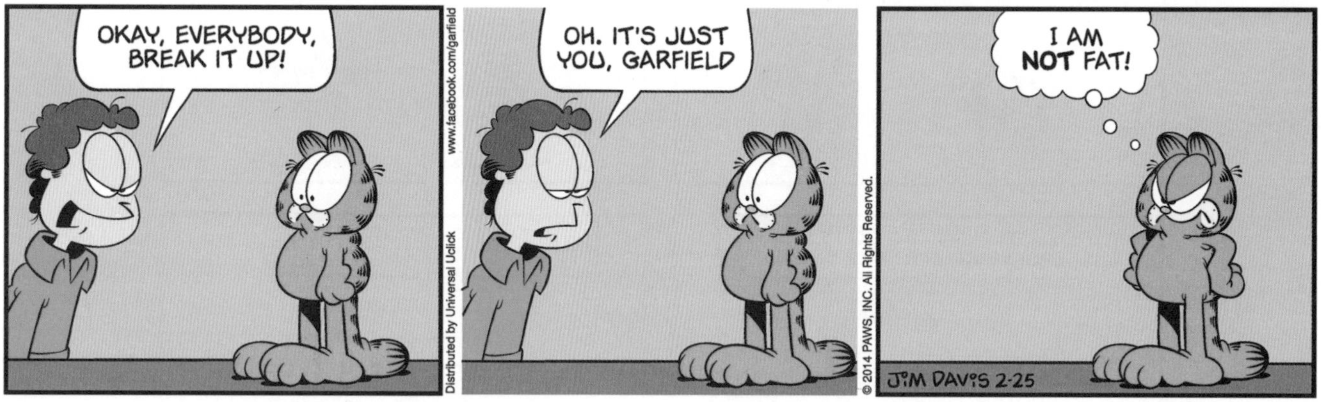
OKAY, EVERYBODY, BREAK IT UP!
OH. IT'S JUST YOU, GARFIELD
I AM **NOT** FAT!
Distributed by Universal Uclick
www.facebook.com/garfield
© 2014 PAWS, INC. All Rights Reserved.
JIM DAVIS 2-25

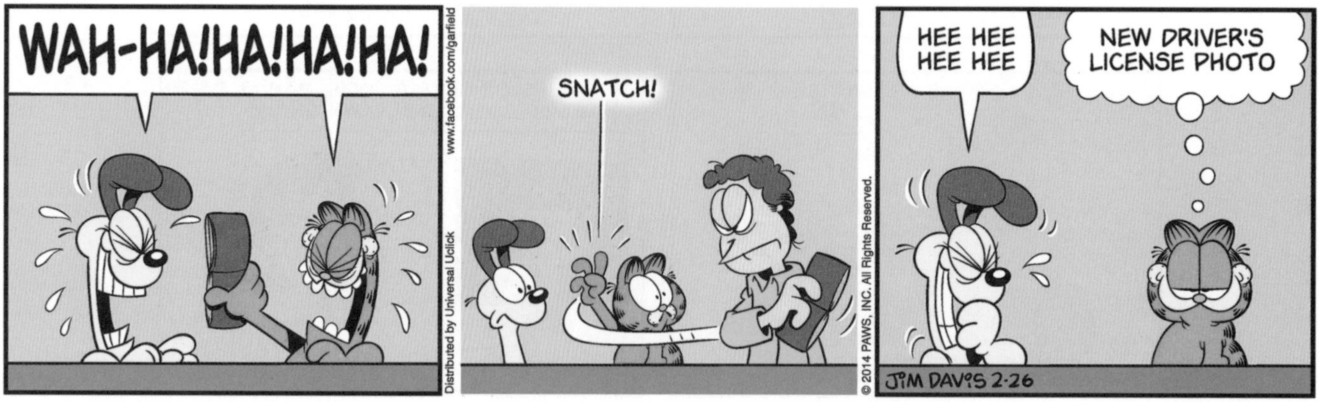
WAH-HA!HA!HA!HA!
SNATCH!
HEE HEE HEE HEE
NEW DRIVER'S LICENSE PHOTO
Distributed by Universal Uclick
www.facebook.com/garfield
© 2014 PAWS, INC. All Rights Reserved.
JIM DAVIS 2-26

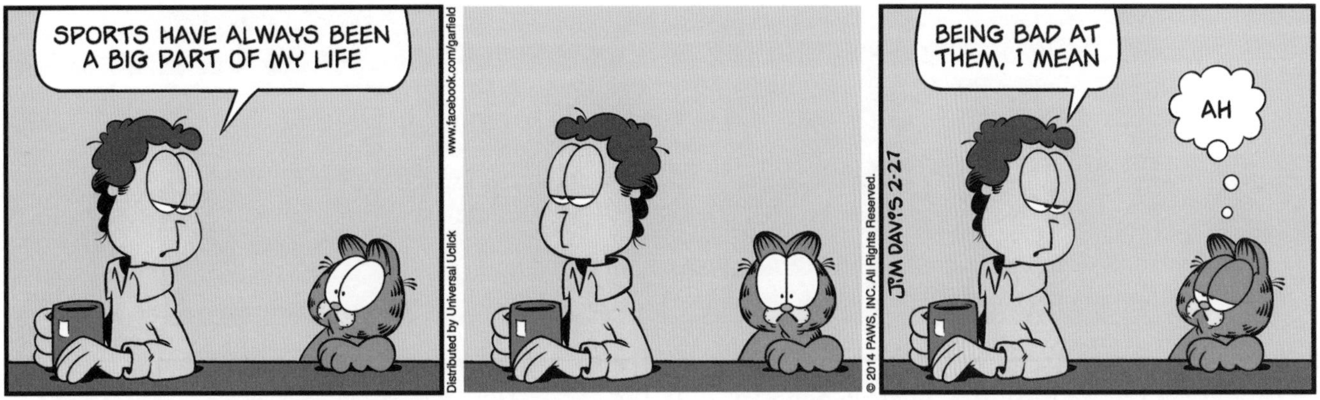
SPORTS HAVE ALWAYS BEEN A BIG PART OF MY LIFE
Distributed by Universal Uclick www.facebook.com/garfield
© 2014 PAWS, INC. All Rights Reserved.
JIM DAVIS 2-27
BEING BAD AT THEM, I MEAN
AH

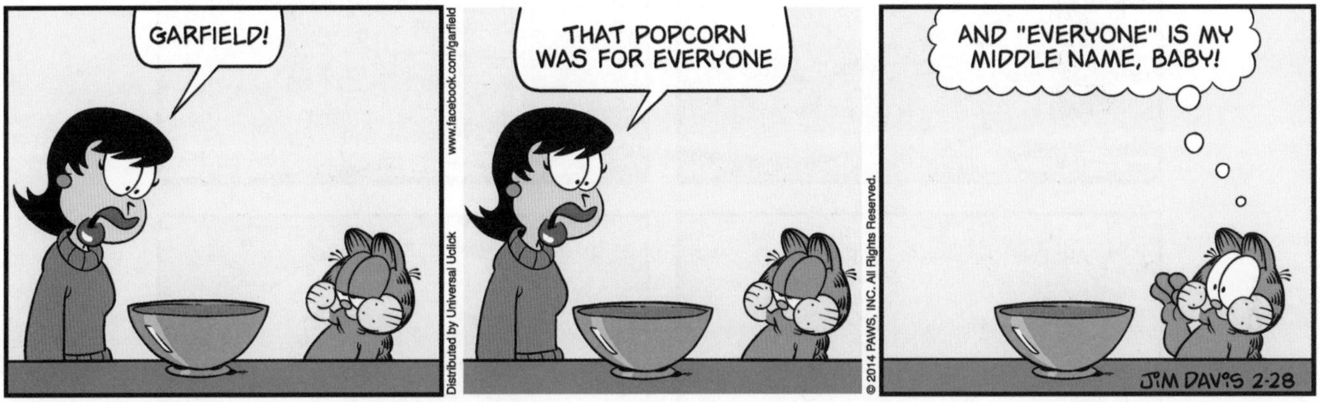
GARFIELD!
Distributed by Universal Uclick www.facebook.com/garfield
THAT POPCORN WAS FOR EVERYONE
© 2014 PAWS, INC. All Rights Reserved.
AND "EVERYONE" IS MY MIDDLE NAME, BABY!
JIM DAVIS 2-28

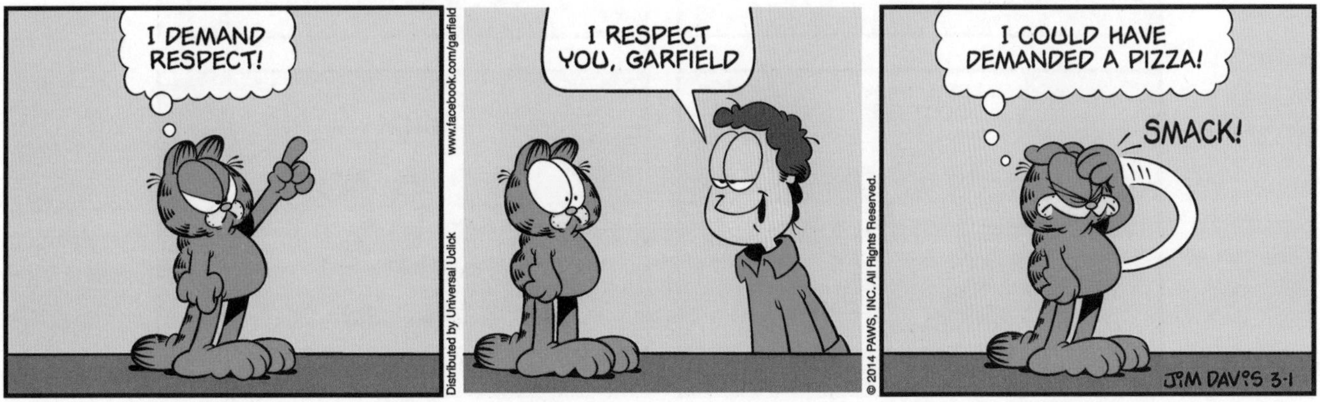
I DEMAND RESPECT!
Distributed by Universal Uclick www.facebook.com/garfield
I RESPECT YOU, GARFIELD
© 2014 PAWS, INC. All Rights Reserved.
I COULD HAVE DEMANDED A PIZZA!
SMACK!
JIM DAVIS 3-1

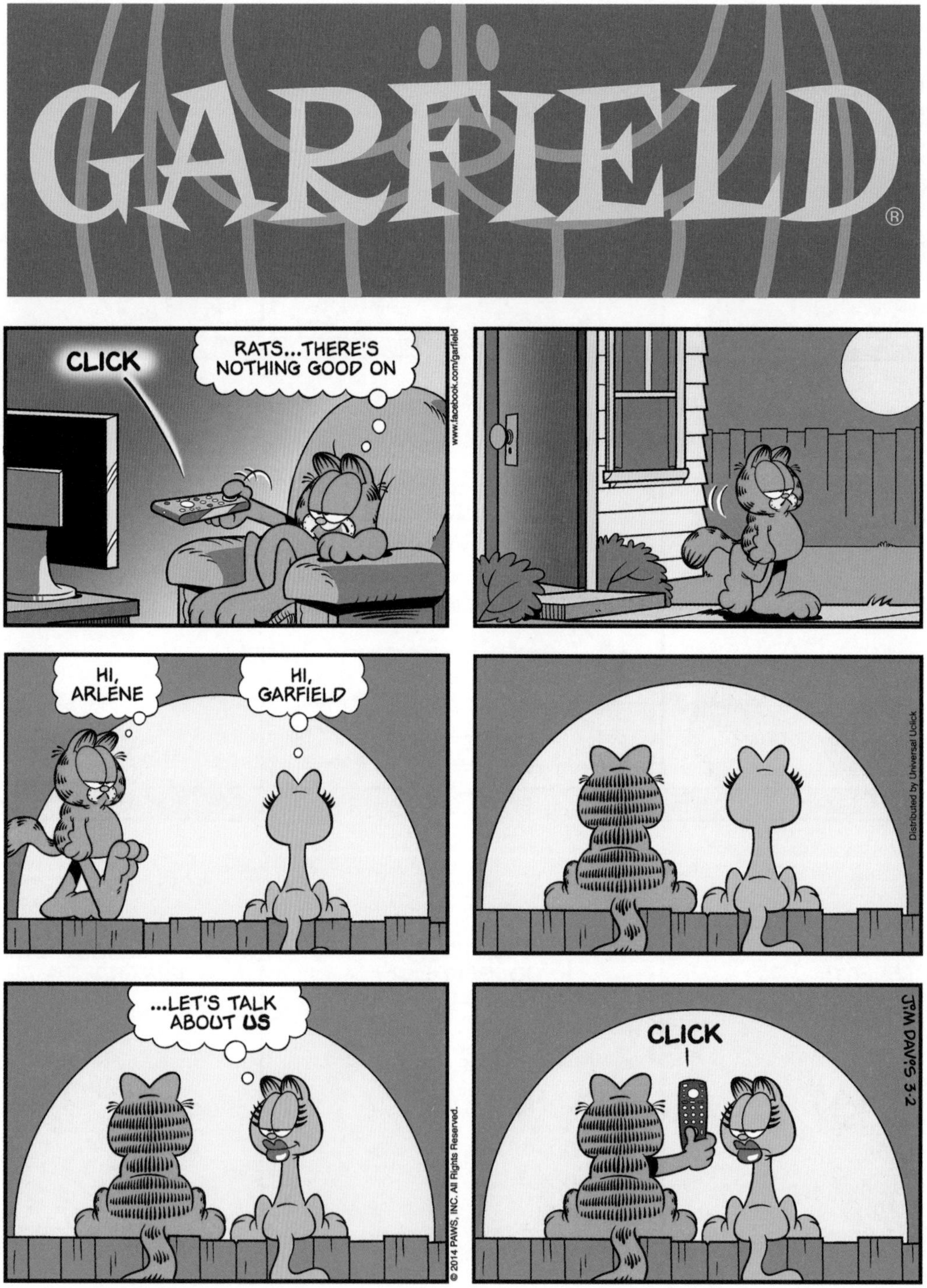
GARFIELD®
CLICK
RATS...THERE'S NOTHING GOOD ON
www.facebook.com/garfield
HI, ARLENE
HI, GARFIELD
Distributed by Universal Uclick
...LET'S TALK ABOUT US
© 2014 PAWS, INC. All Rights Reserved.
CLICK
JIM DAVIS 3-2

SORRY, GARFIELD
JIM DAVIS 3-3
www.facebook.com/garfield
Distributed by Universal Uclick
I'M TOO DEPRESSED TO COOK
© 2014 PAWS, INC. All Rights Reserved.
THAT DOESN'T HELP
WHAT IF I JUGGLE MICE?

I SHOULD NEVER HAVE TRIED TO MAKE PIZZA FROM SCRATCH!
www.facebook.com/garfield
Distributed by Universal Uclick
ME PIZZA. ME WANT MORE PEPPERONI
© 2014 PAWS, INC. All Rights Reserved.
MWA-HA-HA!
TOO MUCH YEAST
JIM DAVIS 3-4

BEWARE...
www.facebook.com/garfield
Distributed by Universal Uclick
OF THE CONDESCENDING DOG
© 2014 PAWS, INC. All Rights Reserved.
JIM DAVIS 3-5
OKAY, NOW I AM ABOUT TO BARK AT YOU
I HATE HIM ALREADY

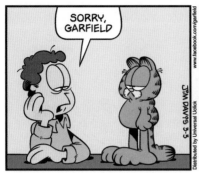

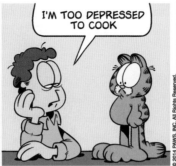

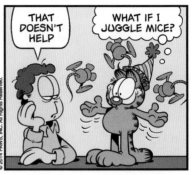

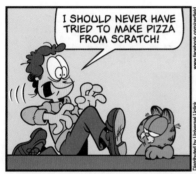

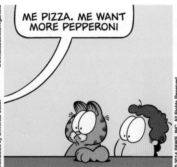

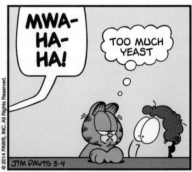

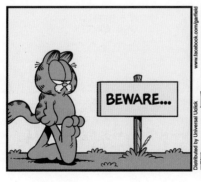

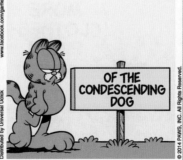

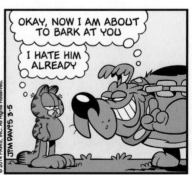

WHY, HELLO, GARFIELD
www.facebook.com/garfield
Distributed by Universal Uclick
MY, MY, HOW DISAPPOINTING...
© 2014 PAWS, INC. All Rights Reserved.
JIM DAVIS 3-6
I WANT THE REMOTE
NO CHEESE, NO REMOTE

THE FORECAST IS CLOUDY AND COLD
www.facebook.com/garfield
Distributed by Universal Uclick
SIGH...IT MIGHT SNOW...WHO KNOWS?...
JIM DAVIS 3-7
© 2014 PAWS, INC. All Rights Reserved.
WHO CARES!
IT'S BEEN A LONG WINTER

www.facebook.com/garfield
Distributed by Universal Uclick
MORE CLOTHES-PINS!!
© 2014 PAWS, INC. All Rights Reserved.
IT'S BEEN A LONG WINTER
JIM DAVIS 3-8

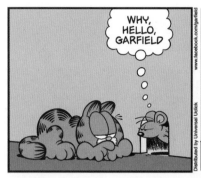

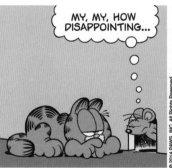

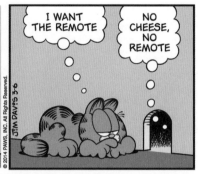

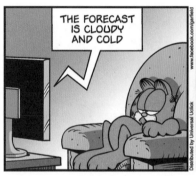

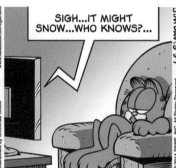

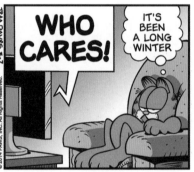

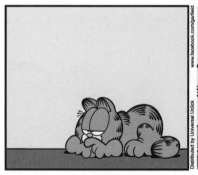

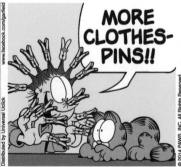

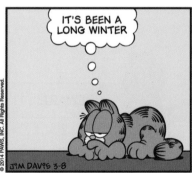

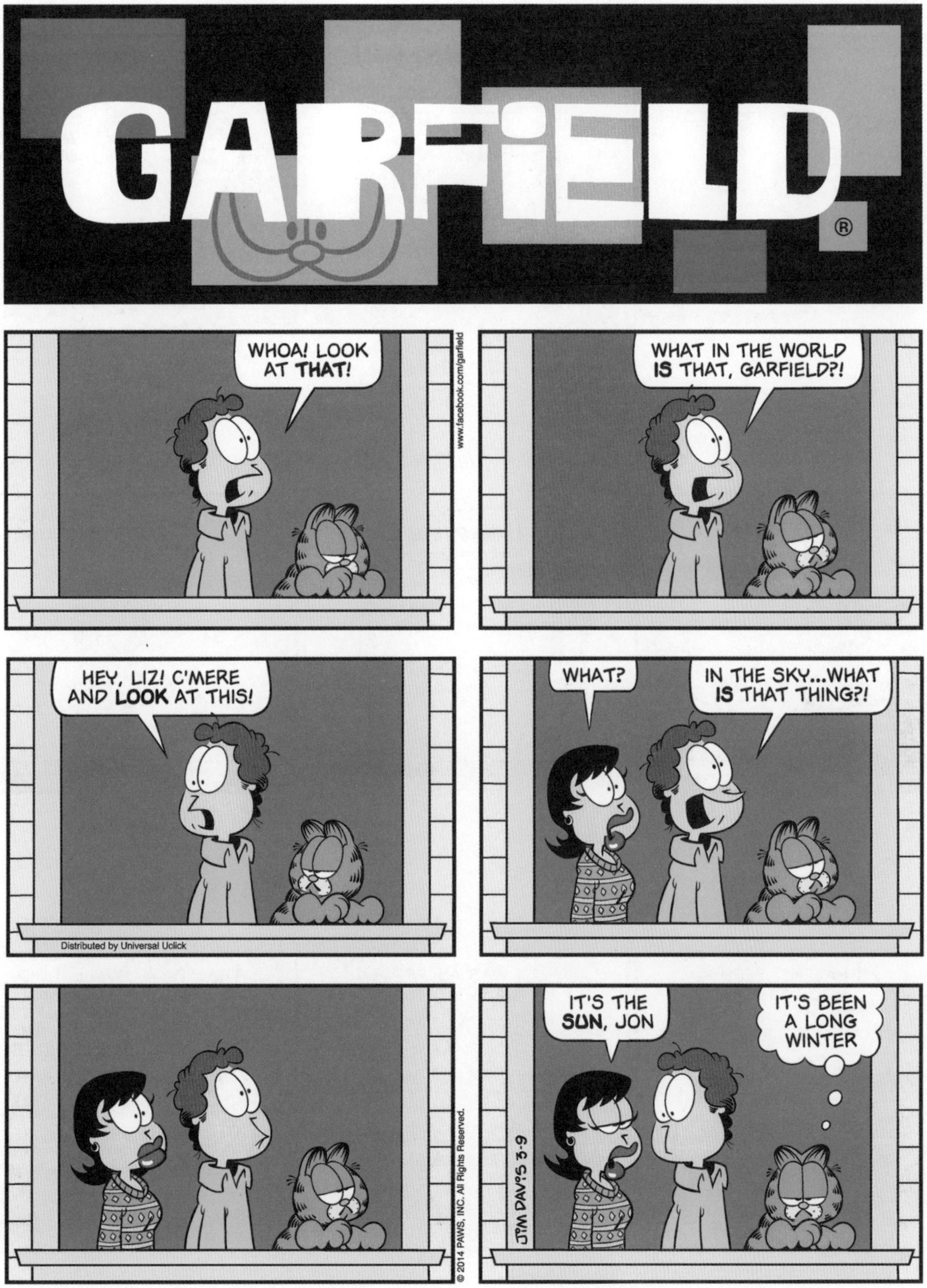
GARFIELD®
WHOA! LOOK AT THAT!
www.facebook.com/garfield
WHAT IN THE WORLD IS THAT, GARFIELD?!
HEY, LIZ! C'MERE AND LOOK AT THIS!
Distributed by Universal Uclick
WHAT?
IN THE SKY...WHAT IS THAT THING?!
© 2014 PAWS, INC. All Rights Reserved.
JIM DAVIS 3-9
IT'S THE SUN, JON
IT'S BEEN A LONG WINTER

WE NEED SOME ENTERTAINMENT, GARFIELD
www.facebook.com/garfield
Distributed by Universal Uclick
LET'S LIP-SYNCH TO OLD OPERA RECORDS!
© 2014 PAWS, INC. All Rights Reserved.
WE'LL NEED VIKING HELMETS!
MAY YOU SIT UPON ONE
JIM DAVIS 3-10

JIM DAVIS 3-11
www.facebook.com/garfield
Distributed by Universal Uclick
STOP SHEDDING!
© 2014 PAWS, INC. All Rights Reserved.
LIKE CATS HAVE PAUSE BUTTONS

JIM DAVIS 3-12
I HAVEN'T SEEN YOU LATELY
www.facebook.com/garfield
Distributed by Universal Uclick
I WAS ASLEEP LAST MONTH
© 2014 PAWS, INC. All Rights Reserved.
THE WHOLE MONTH?
WELL, I DID TOSS AND TURN A LITTLE AROUND THE TWENTY-THIRD

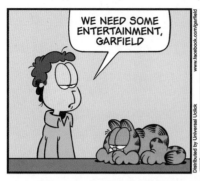

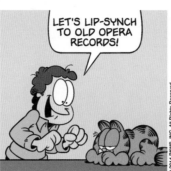

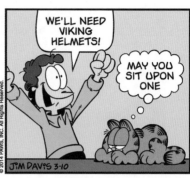

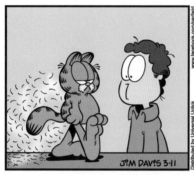

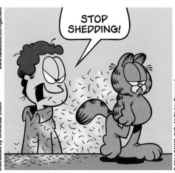

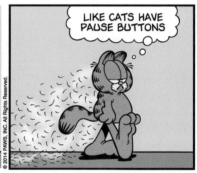

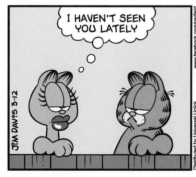

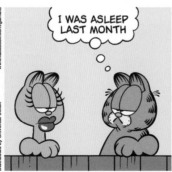

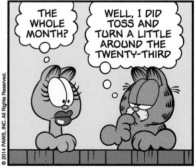

OH, A SPIDER'S LIFE FOR MEEEE...
CATCH A JUICY FLY...
CATCH THAT FLY, AND SUCK IT DRY...
REVIEW TIME
JIM DAVIS 3-13
www.facebook.com/garfield
Distributed by Universal Uclick
© 2014 PAWS, INC. All Rights Reserved.

WE'RE A LITTLE TIRED THIS MORNING, LIZ
ALL-NIGHT CARTOON MARATHON
SHE THINKS WE'RE NUTS
THE WOMAN'S PRIORITIES ARE OBVIOUSLY OUT OF WHACK
JIM DAVIS 3-14
www.facebook.com/garfield
Distributed by Universal Uclick
© 2014 PAWS, INC. All Rights Reserved.

WHOA...
WHAT IF YOU COULD SEE THROUGH YOUR EYELIDS?
WE'LL RETURN TO "DEEP, DUMB THOUGHTS" AFTER THIS MESSAGE
JIM DAVIS 3-15
www.facebook.com/garfield
Distributed by Universal Uclick
© 2014 PAWS, INC. All Rights Reserved.

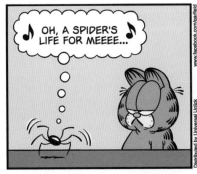

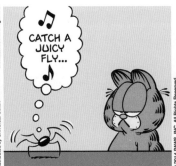

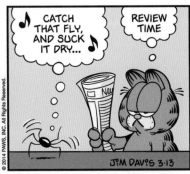

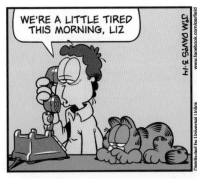

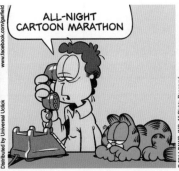

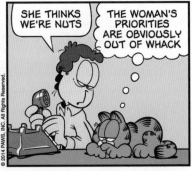

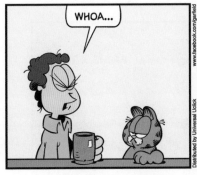

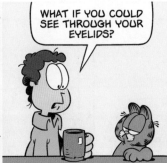

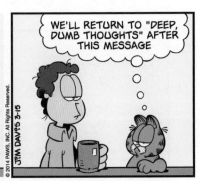

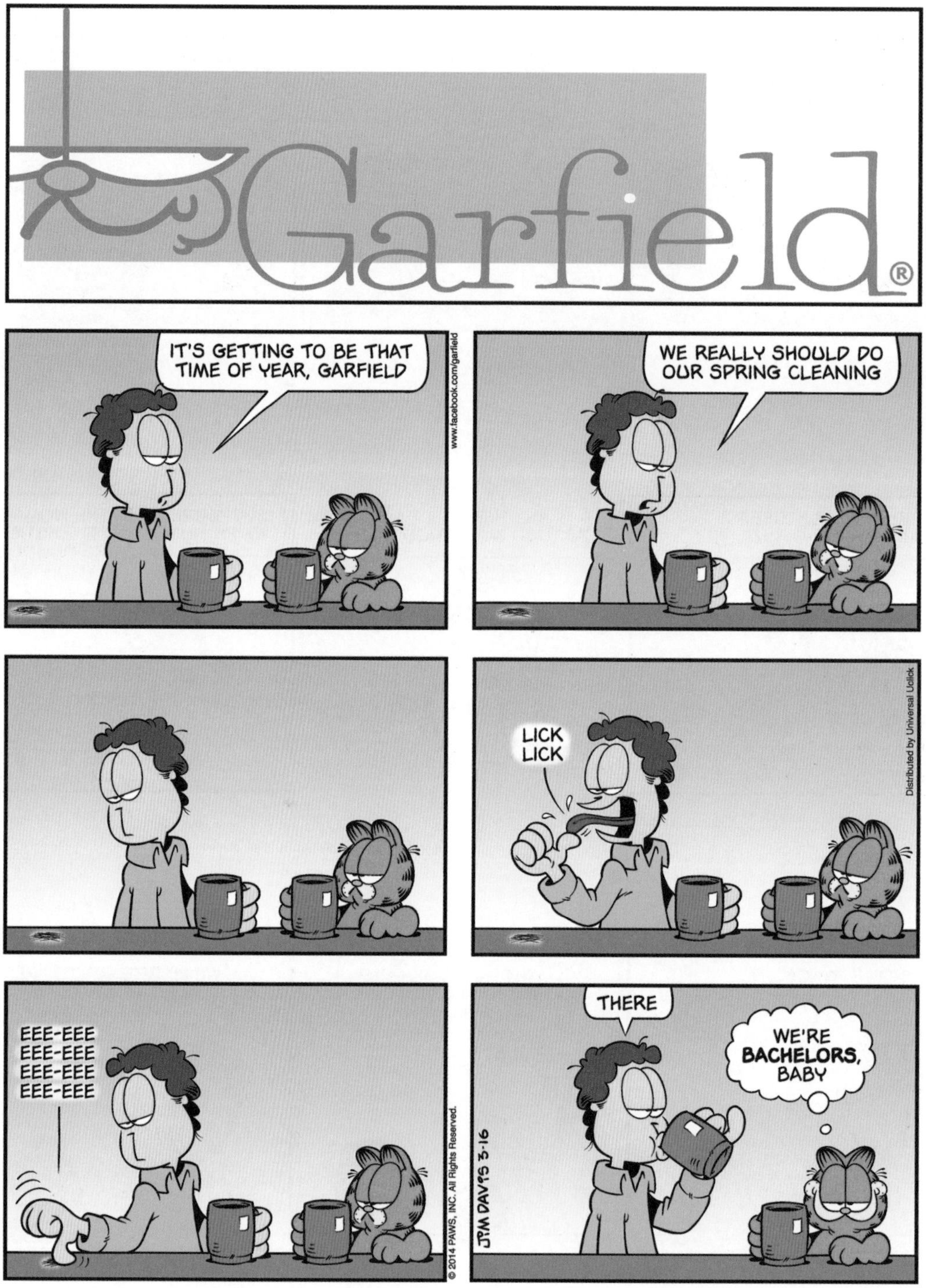
Garfield®
IT'S GETTING TO BE THAT TIME OF YEAR, GARFIELD
www.facebook.com/garfield
WE REALLY SHOULD DO OUR SPRING CLEANING
LICK LICK
Distributed by Universal Uclick
EEE-EEE EEE-EEE EEE-EEE EEE-EEE
© 2014 PAWS, INC. All Rights Reserved.
JPM DAVIS 3-16
THERE
WE'RE **BACHELORS,** BABY

I HAVE SWEPT AND VACUUMED UP ALL THE CAT HAIR IN THE HOUSE
JIM DAVIS 3-17
Distributed by Universal Uclick www.facebook.com/garfield
© 2014 PAWS, INC. All Rights Reserved.
AH, THE CYCLE OF LIFE!

MAN, I LOOK GOOD TODAY!
Distributed by Universal Uclick www.facebook.com/garfield
OH, WAIT...
© 2014 PAWS, INC. All Rights Reserved.
I FORGOT TO TAKE THE HANGER OUT OF MY SHIRT
YOU'RE GOING TO LEAVE IT IN THERE, AREN'T YOU?
JIM DAVIS 3-18

ODIE
Distributed by Universal Uclick www.facebook.com/garfield
ODIE
© 2014 PAWS, INC. All Rights Reserved.
ARE YOU LOSING WEIGHT?
ODIE
JIM DAVIS 3-19

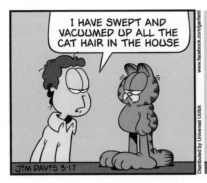

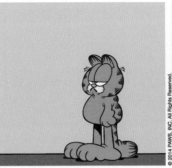

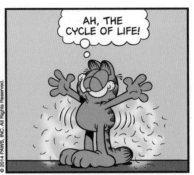

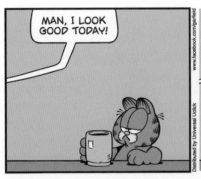

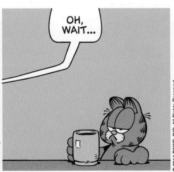

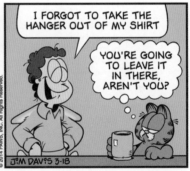

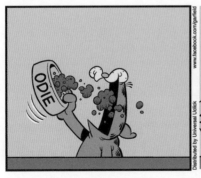

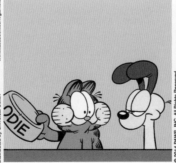

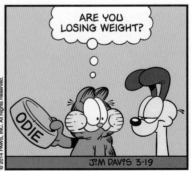

JIM DAVIS 3-20
www.facebook.com/garfield
Distributed by Universal Uclick
© 2014 PAWS, INC. All Rights Reserved.
SPRING IS HERE

THE SUN IS SHINING, GARFIELD
www.facebook.com/garfield
Distributed by Universal Uclick
THE AIR IS FRESH!
© 2014 PAWS, INC. All Rights Reserved.
NOT AN INSIDE DAY, PAL
ARE YOU IMPLYING MOVEMENT?
JIM DAVIS 3-21

SOMEDAY I'LL BE A MIGHTY TREE!
www.facebook.com/garfield
Distributed by Universal Uclick
YOU'RE A FLOWER. YOU BLOOM, AND THEN YOU DIE
© 2014 PAWS, INC. All Rights Reserved.
I SHOULD'VE STAYED IN SCHOOL
JIM DAVIS 3-22

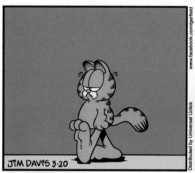

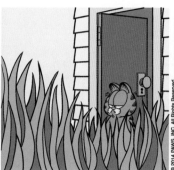

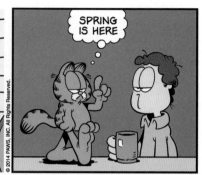

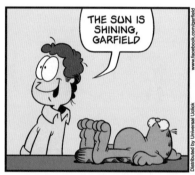

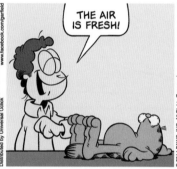

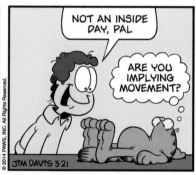

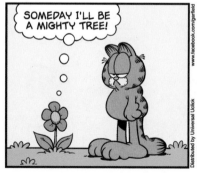

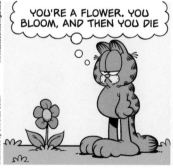

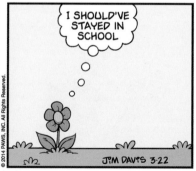

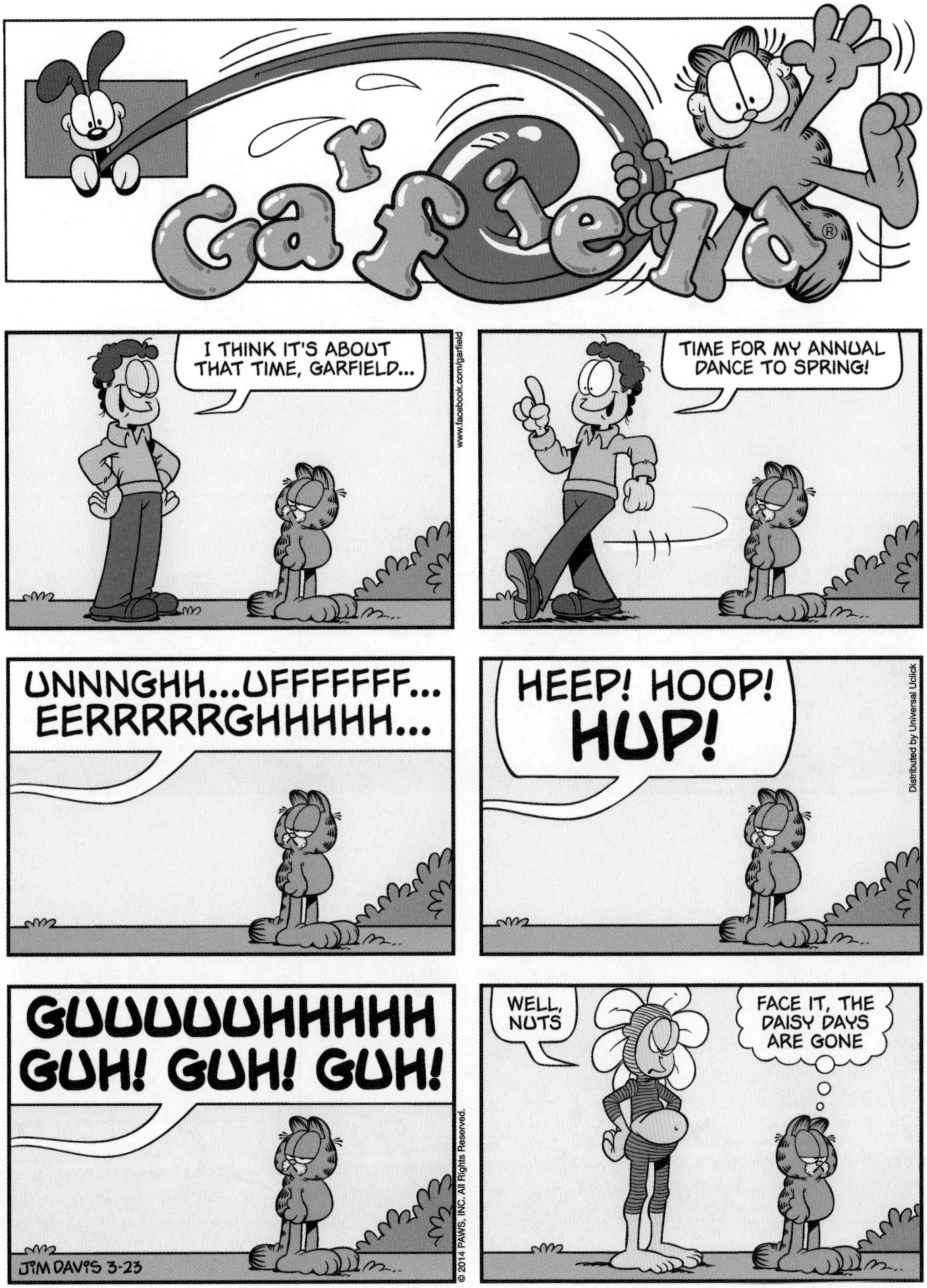
Garfield®
I THINK IT'S ABOUT THAT TIME, GARFIELD...
www.facebook.com/garfield
TIME FOR MY ANNUAL DANCE TO SPRING!
UNNNGHH...UFFFFFFF... EERRRRRGHHHHH...
HEEP! HOOP! HUP!
Distributed by Universal Uclick
GUUUUUHHHHH GUH! GUH! GUH!
JIM DAVIS 3-23
© 2014 PAWS, INC. All Rights Reserved.
WELL, NUTS
FACE IT, THE DAISY DAYS ARE GONE

YOU KNOW, GARFIELD...
www.facebook.com/garfield
Distributed by Universal Uclick
IT WOULD BE A SHAME IF I WERE ALLERGIC TO CAT HAIR
YEAH
© 2014 PAWS, INC. All Rights Reserved.
I'D HAVE TO GET RID OF YOU
JIM DAVIS 3-24

I'M GOING TO BE A BUTTERFLY
www.facebook.com/garfield
Distributed by Universal Uclick
AND JUST HOW ARE YOU GOING TO DO THAT?
UH...
© 2014 PAWS, INC. All Rights Reserved.
JIM DAVIS 3-25
I KNOW A GUY

HEY THERE, BUDDY!
www.facebook.com/garfield
Distributed by Universal Uclick
HAVE SOME PUDDING, OL' PAL, OL' PAL!
© 2014 PAWS, INC. All Rights Reserved.
THERE'S A PILL IN THERE, ISN'T THERE?
JIM DAVIS 3-26

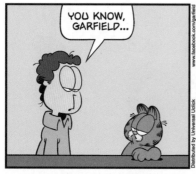

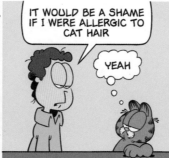

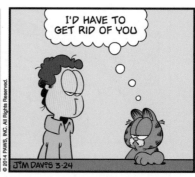

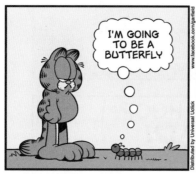

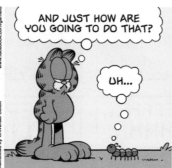

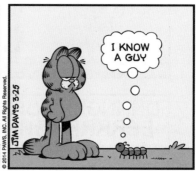

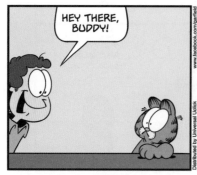

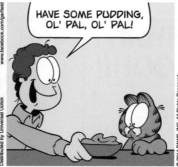

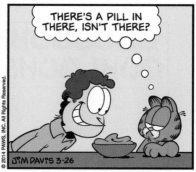

THINGS ARE LOOKING UP
www.facebook.com/garfield
Distributed by Universal Uclick
© 2014 PAWS, INC. All Rights Reserved.
THAT'S JUST HOW AWFUL THINGS HAVE BEEN LATELY
JIM DAVIS 3-27

LIZ, WHY DO YOU GO OUT WITH ME?
JIM DAVIS 3-28
www.facebook.com/garfield
Distributed by Universal Uclick
© 2014 PAWS, INC. All Rights Reserved.
WELL, THIS IS AN AWKWARD PAUSE
I'M GATHERING MY THOUGHTS

GARFIELD, I HAD A PROFOUND THOUGHT
www.facebook.com/garfield
Distributed by Universal Uclick
© 2014 PAWS, INC. All Rights Reserved.
GONE
LOCK THAT DOOR, PLEASE
JIM DAVIS 3-29

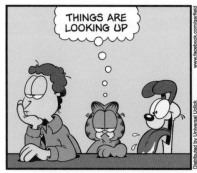

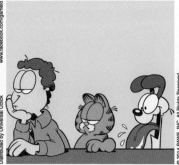

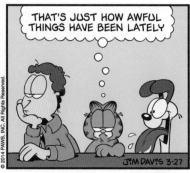

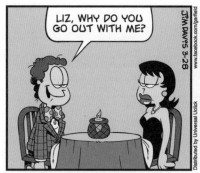

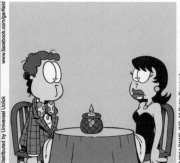

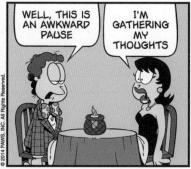

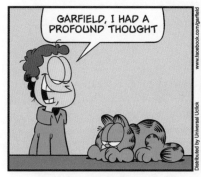

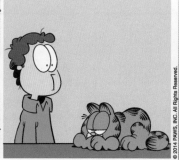

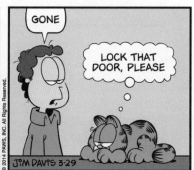

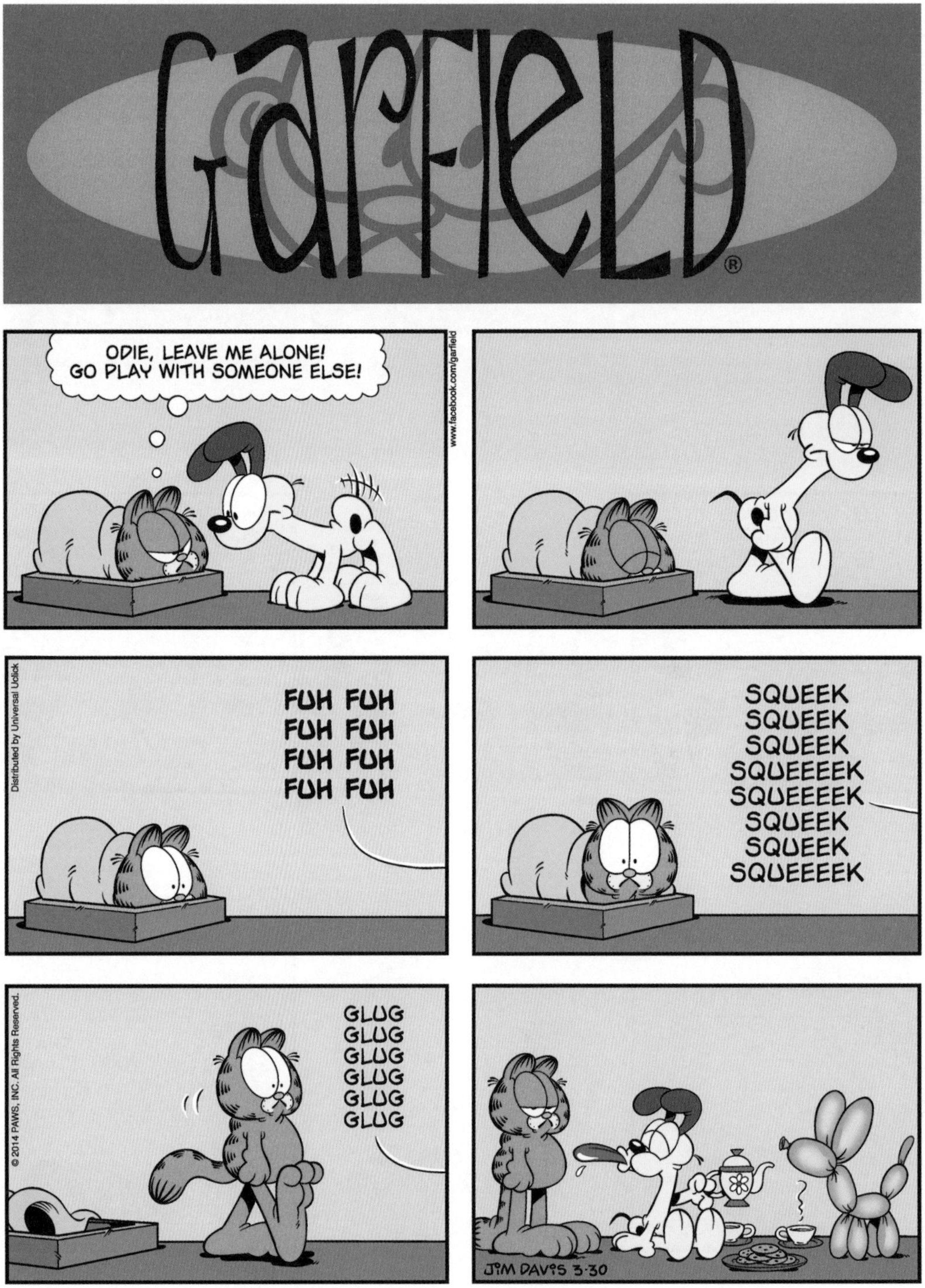
GARFIELD
ODIE, LEAVE ME ALONE! GO PLAY WITH SOMEONE ELSE!
www.facebook.com/garfield
Distributed by Universal Uclick
FUH FUH FUH FUH FUH FUH FUH FUH
SQUEEK SQUEEK SQUEEK SQUEEEEK SQUEEEEK SQUEEK SQUEEK SQUEEEEK
© 2014 PAWS, INC. All Rights Reserved.
GLUG GLUG GLUG GLUG GLUG GLUG
JIM DAVIS 3-30

I LIKE LIVING HERE
JIM DAVIS 3-31
www.facebook.com/garfield
Distributed by Universal Uclick
WE'RE LAID-BACK
© 2014 PAWS, INC. All Rights Reserved.
NO ONE'S GOING TO STEAL **MY** BRAIN!
AND SOMEWHAT INSANE

BARK! BARK! BARK!
JIM DAVIS 4-1
www.facebook.com/garfield
Distributed by Universal Uclick
© 2014 PAWS, INC. All Rights Reserved.
WOULD YOU MIND NOT LISTENING TO MUSIC WHILE I'M BARKING AT YOU?
HUH?

JON'S WHISTLING
www.facebook.com/garfield
Distributed by Universal Uclick
LA LA LA!
NOW HE'S SINGING
© 2014 PAWS, INC. All Rights Reserved.
CARE TO JOIN ME FOR A RUN?
NOW HE'S DOING STAND-UP COMEDY
JIM DAVIS 4-2

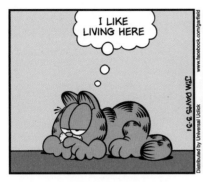

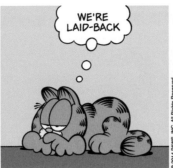

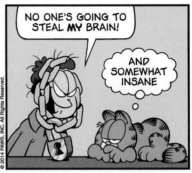

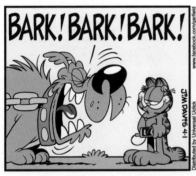

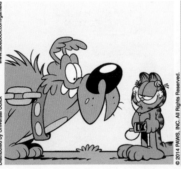

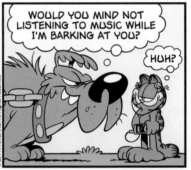

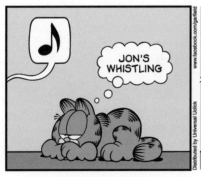

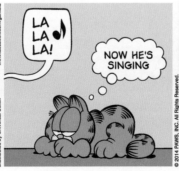

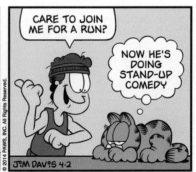

MOUSE!
KILL IT AND EAT IT, GARFIELD!
KILL AND EAT!
SORRY, I'M MORE OF A THAW-AND-MICROWAVE GUY
Distributed by Universal Uclick www.facebook.com/garfield
© 2014 PAWS, INC. All Rights Reserved.
JIM DAVIS 4-3

WHAT IF LIZ BREAKS UP WITH ME?
I CAN'T HANDLE REJECTION
RIDICULE AND SCORN, BUT NOT REJECTION
YOU ALSO DO LOATHING WELL
Distributed by Universal Uclick www.facebook.com/garfield
© 2014 PAWS, INC. All Rights Reserved.
JIM DAVIS 4-4

WELCOME TO "HEALTHY KIDS"
NOW ANOTHER EPISODE OF...
"BILLY, THE HAPPY INTESTINE"!
BILLY CREEPS ME OUT
JIM DAVIS 4-5
Distributed by Universal Uclick www.facebook.com/garfield
© 2014 PAWS, INC. All Rights Reserved.

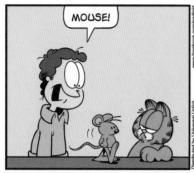

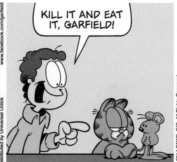

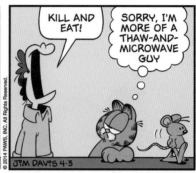

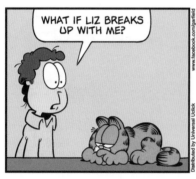

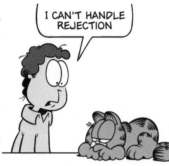

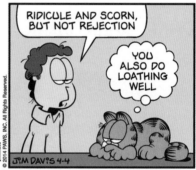

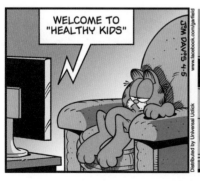

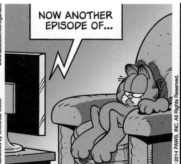

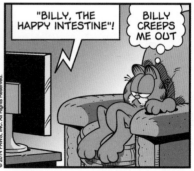

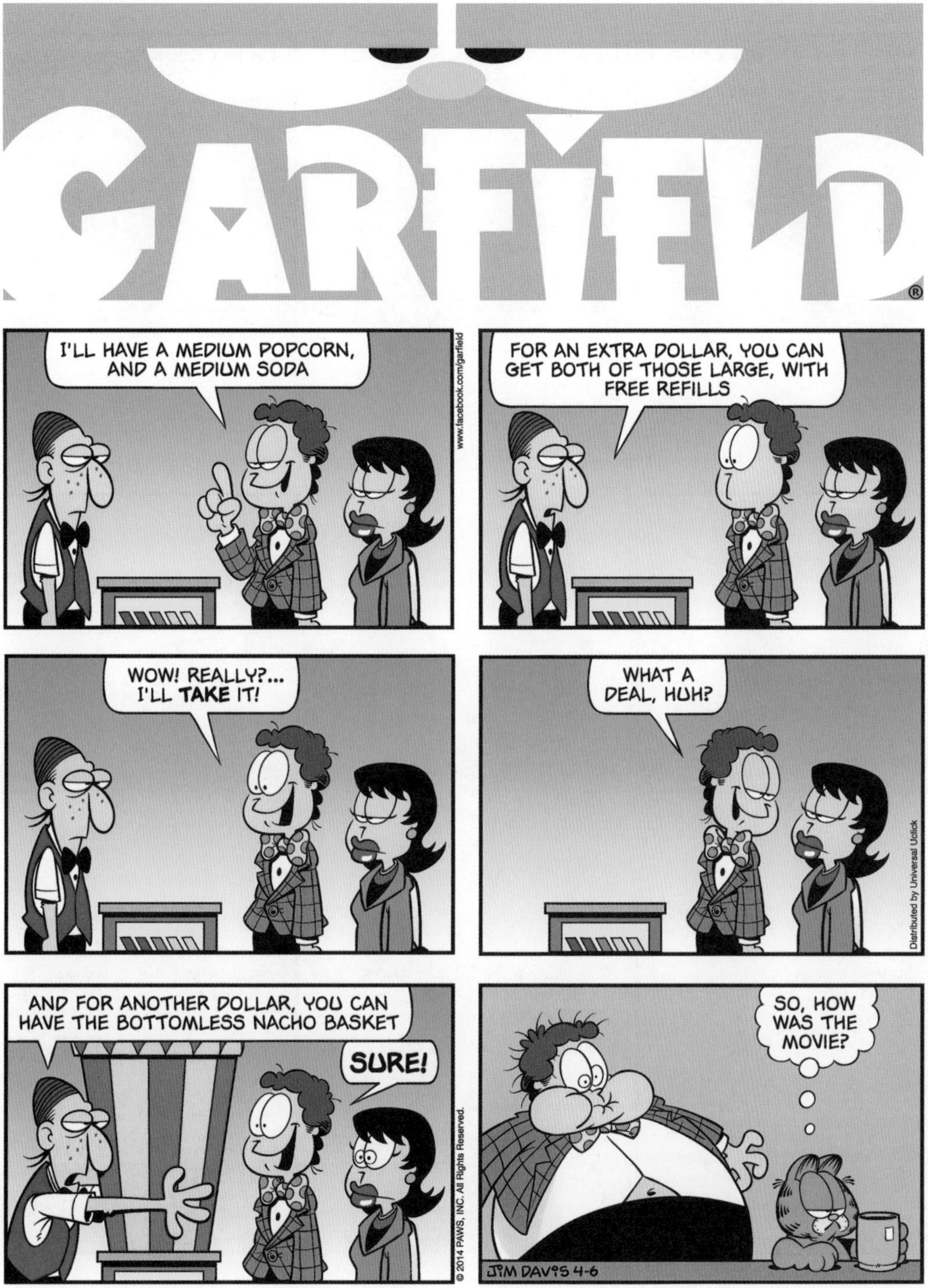
GARFIELD®
I'LL HAVE A MEDIUM POPCORN, AND A MEDIUM SODA
www.facebook.com/garfield
FOR AN EXTRA DOLLAR, YOU CAN GET BOTH OF THOSE LARGE, WITH FREE REFILLS
WOW! REALLY?... I'LL **TAKE** IT!
WHAT A DEAL, HUH?
Distributed by Universal Uclick
AND FOR ANOTHER DOLLAR, YOU CAN HAVE THE BOTTOMLESS NACHO BASKET
SURE!
© 2014 PAWS, INC. All Rights Reserved.
SO, HOW WAS THE MOVIE?
JIM DAVIS 4-6

GARFIELD, I FEEL LAZY
YES, COME TO THE DARK SIDE
MAYBE I NEED TO EXERCISE
NO! NO! COME BACK!
OR EAT COOKIES AND WATCH TV
YES, COME TO ME, MY SON
JIM DAVIS 4-7
Distributed by Universal Uclick
www.facebook.com/garfield
© 2014 PAWS, INC. All Rights Reserved.

THE ANCIENTS BELIEVED CATS WERE GOOD LUCK
THEY DIED OUT
WHO'S FEEDING THE CATS?!
JIM DAVIS 4-8
Distributed by Universal Uclick
www.facebook.com/garfield
© 2014 PAWS, INC. All Rights Reserved.

BEFORE YOU EAT ME...
MAY I BORROW A MARKER?
SURE
OKAY, I'M READY
HMMM. I DIDN'T SEE THAT COMING
IT WAS THE CAT
JIM DAVIS 4-9
Distributed by Universal Uclick
www.facebook.com/garfield
© 2014 PAWS, INC. All Rights Reserved.

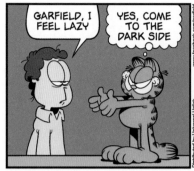

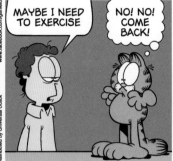

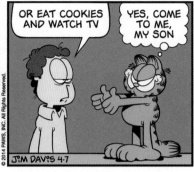

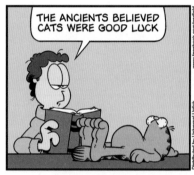

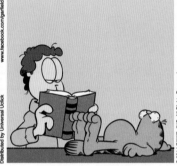

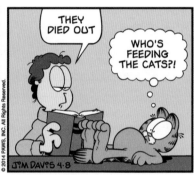

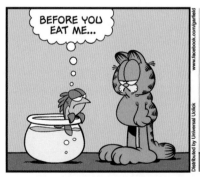

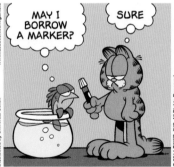

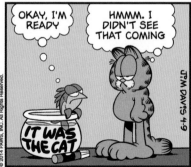

HERE WE GO...
JIM DAVIS 4-10
MOMMY, LOOK!
WAIT FOR IT...
IT'S A HAIRY HOG!
...AND, IT'S BITING TIME
Distributed by Universal Uclick www.facebook.com/garfield
© 2014 PAWS, INC. All Rights Reserved.

WALKING IN THE RAIN IS SO ROMANTIC
RUNNING THROUGH THE SPRINKLERS IS FUN, TOO
THAT'S NOT AS ROMANTIC
YEAH, BUT THERE'S LESS CHANCE OF A LIGHTNING STRIKE
SCORE ONE FOR THE PARANOID
JIM DAVIS 4-11
Distributed by Universal Uclick www.facebook.com/garfield
© 2014 PAWS, INC. All Rights Reserved.

LIFE IS GOING ON OUT THERE...
AND HERE I SIT EATING DONUTS AND WATCHING CARTOONS
REALITY IS OVERRATED
JIM DAVIS 4-12
Distributed by Universal Uclick www.facebook.com/garfield
© 2014 PAWS, INC. All Rights Reserved.

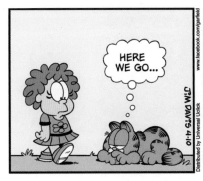

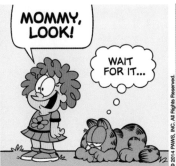

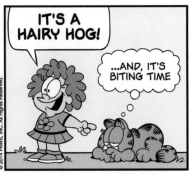

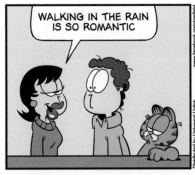

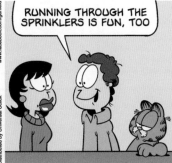

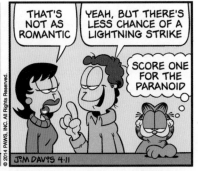

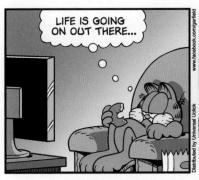

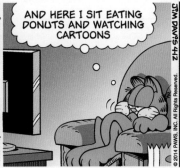

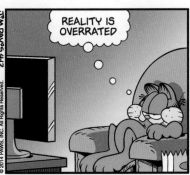

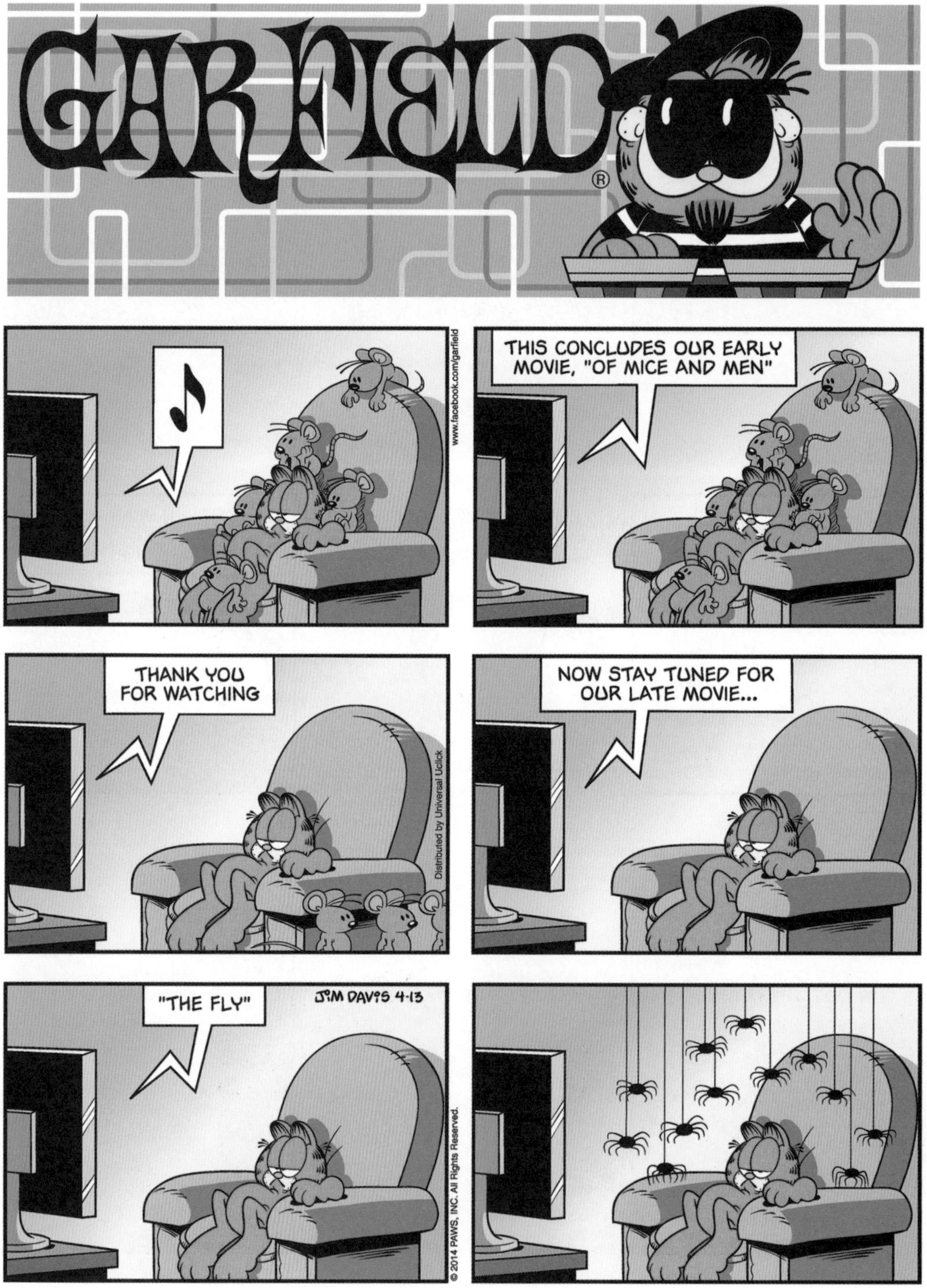
GARFIELD®
♪
www.facebook.com/garfield
THIS CONCLUDES OUR EARLY MOVIE, "OF MICE AND MEN"
THANK YOU FOR WATCHING
Distributed by Universal Uclick
NOW STAY TUNED FOR OUR LATE MOVIE...
"THE FLY"
JIM DAVIS 4-13
© 2014 PAWS, INC. All Rights Reserved.

GOOD MORNING! BAGEL OR TOAST?
Distributed by Universal Uclick www.facebook.com/garfield
EITHER WAY, I'M GONNA BURN IT!
© 2014 PAWS, INC. All Rights Reserved.
BWA-HA-HA-HAAAH!
TECHNOLOGY HATES ME
JIM DAVIS 4-14

I'M BACK, GARFIELD
Distributed by Universal Uclick www.facebook.com/garfield
YOU HAVEN'T MOVED, HAVE YOU?
© 2014 PAWS, INC. All Rights Reserved.
EXACTLY WHAT DO YOU DO WHEN I'M GONE?
OH, GEE! YOU JUST MISSED THE PONY RIDE!
JIM DAVIS 4-15

STILL SLEEPING WITH YOUR TEDDY BEAR, I SEE
Distributed by Universal Uclick www.facebook.com/garfield
THAT'S KIND OF IMMATURE, YOU KNOW...
© 2014 PAWS, INC. All Rights Reserved.
TIME TO GROW UP
THANK YOU, MR. BUNNY SLIPPERS
JIM DAVIS 4-16

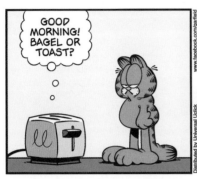

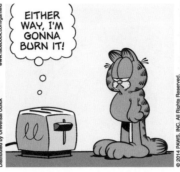

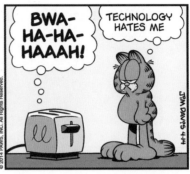

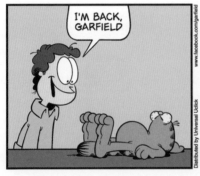

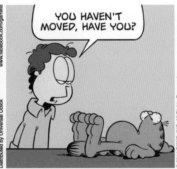

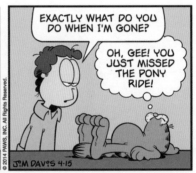

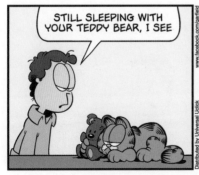

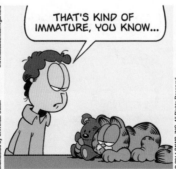

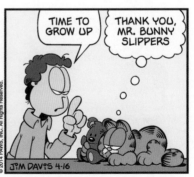

SPIDERWEBS ARE OKAY, BUT I'M THINKING OF GETTING MY OWN APARTMENT
JIM DAVIS 4-17
www.facebook.com/garfield
Distributed by Universal Uclick
SMACK!
© 2014 PAWS, INC. All Rights Reserved.
OR AN ENVELOPE

MY PROM WAS TRAUMATIC
JIM DAVIS 4-18
www.facebook.com/garfield
Distributed by Universal Uclick
I HAD TO WEAR DAD'S TUXEDO
YEAR BOOK
© 2014 PAWS, INC. All Rights Reserved.
WE COULDN'T FIND THE PANTS
NICE KILT

I BOUGHT CAT FOOD, GARFIELD
LIFE IS GOOD
www.facebook.com/garfield
Distributed by Universal Uclick
IT'S A SPECIAL FORMULA FOR "LAZY CATS"
COOL
© 2014 PAWS, INC. All Rights Reserved.
PRE-CHEWED
LIFE IS **VERY** GOOD
JIM DAVIS 4-19

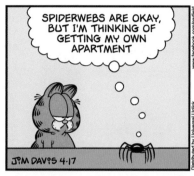

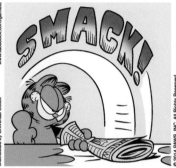

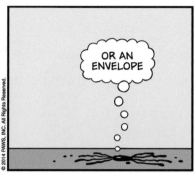

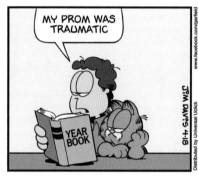

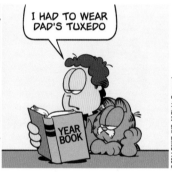

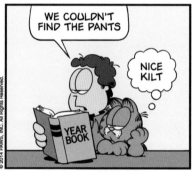

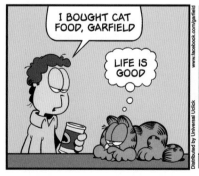

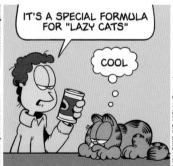

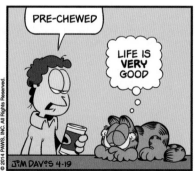

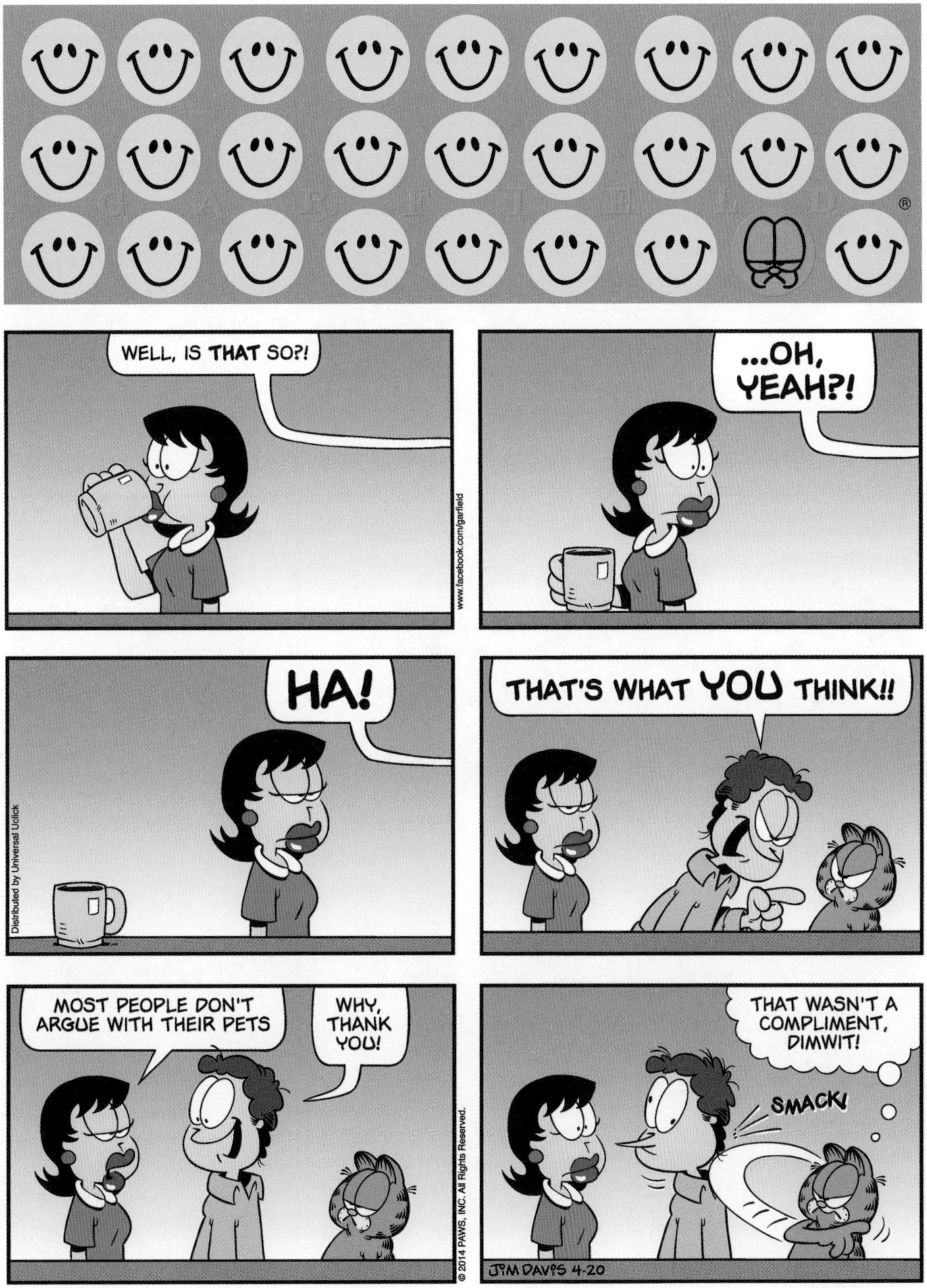
GARFIELD®
WELL, IS THAT SO?!
...OH, YEAH?!
HA!
THAT'S WHAT YOU THINK!!
MOST PEOPLE DON'T ARGUE WITH THEIR PETS
WHY, THANK YOU!
THAT WASN'T A COMPLIMENT, DIMWIT!
SMACK!
JIM DAVIS 4-20
www.facebook.com/garfield
Distributed by Universal Uclick
© 2014 PAWS, INC. All Rights Reserved.

www.facebook.com/garfield
Distributed by Universal Uclick
ROLL OVER
© 2014 PAWS, INC. All Rights Reserved.
I'M NOT DOING THIS AGAIN
YOU WANT ME TO GET FLAT ON ONE SIDE?
JIM DAVIS 4-21

YOU NEVER RESPOND TO MY BARKING
JIM DAVIS 4-22
www.facebook.com/garfield
Distributed by Universal Uclick
WHAT IF I LIE DOWN AND PLAY DEAD?
© 2014 PAWS, INC. All Rights Reserved.
GEE, I FEEL SO DOG-LIKE!
WAKE ME IN AN HOUR

CATCH ME, JON!
www.facebook.com/garfield
Distributed by Universal Uclick
© 2014 PAWS, INC. All Rights Reserved.
JIM DAVIS 4-23
DIDN'T YOU USED TO BE TALLER?

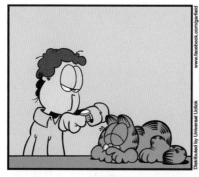

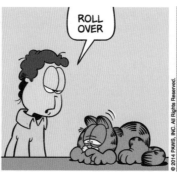

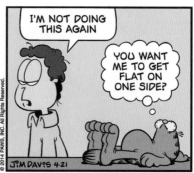

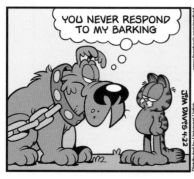

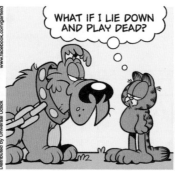

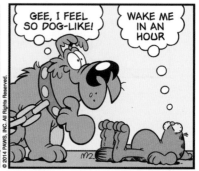

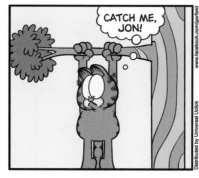

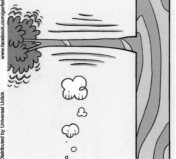

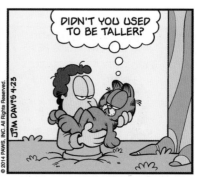

YUP, YEARS AGO I OFFENDED AN OLD GYPSY WOMAN
Distributed by Universal Uclick www.facebook.com/garfield
SHE PUT A CURSE ON ME
© 2014 PAWS, INC. All Rights Reserved.
"TAKE THIS CAT," SHE SAID!
I'M SENSING NEGATIVITY HERE
JIM DAVIS 4-24

I'M BORED, GARFIELD
Distributed by Universal Uclick www.facebook.com/garfield
LET'S DO SOMETHING
© 2014 PAWS, INC. All Rights Reserved.
WANNA GO TO THE AIRPORT AND PRETEND WE'RE GOING SOMEWHERE?
LIKE TO A PLACE WITH A LIFE?
JIM DAVIS 4-25

JIM DAVIS 4-26
WHIPPED CREAM?
JUST WHEN IT CAN'T GET ANY BETTER
Distributed by Universal Uclick www.facebook.com/garfield
PSSSST
© 2014 PAWS, INC. All Rights Reserved.
DARN!
IT DOES

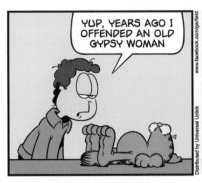

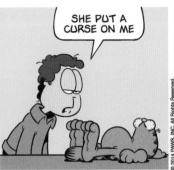

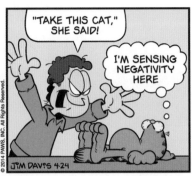

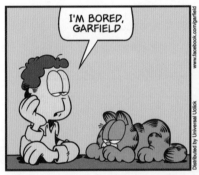

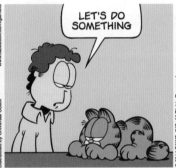

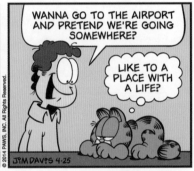

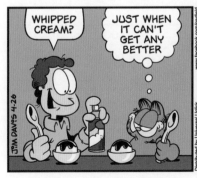

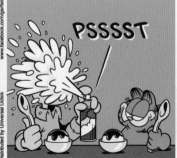

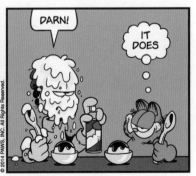

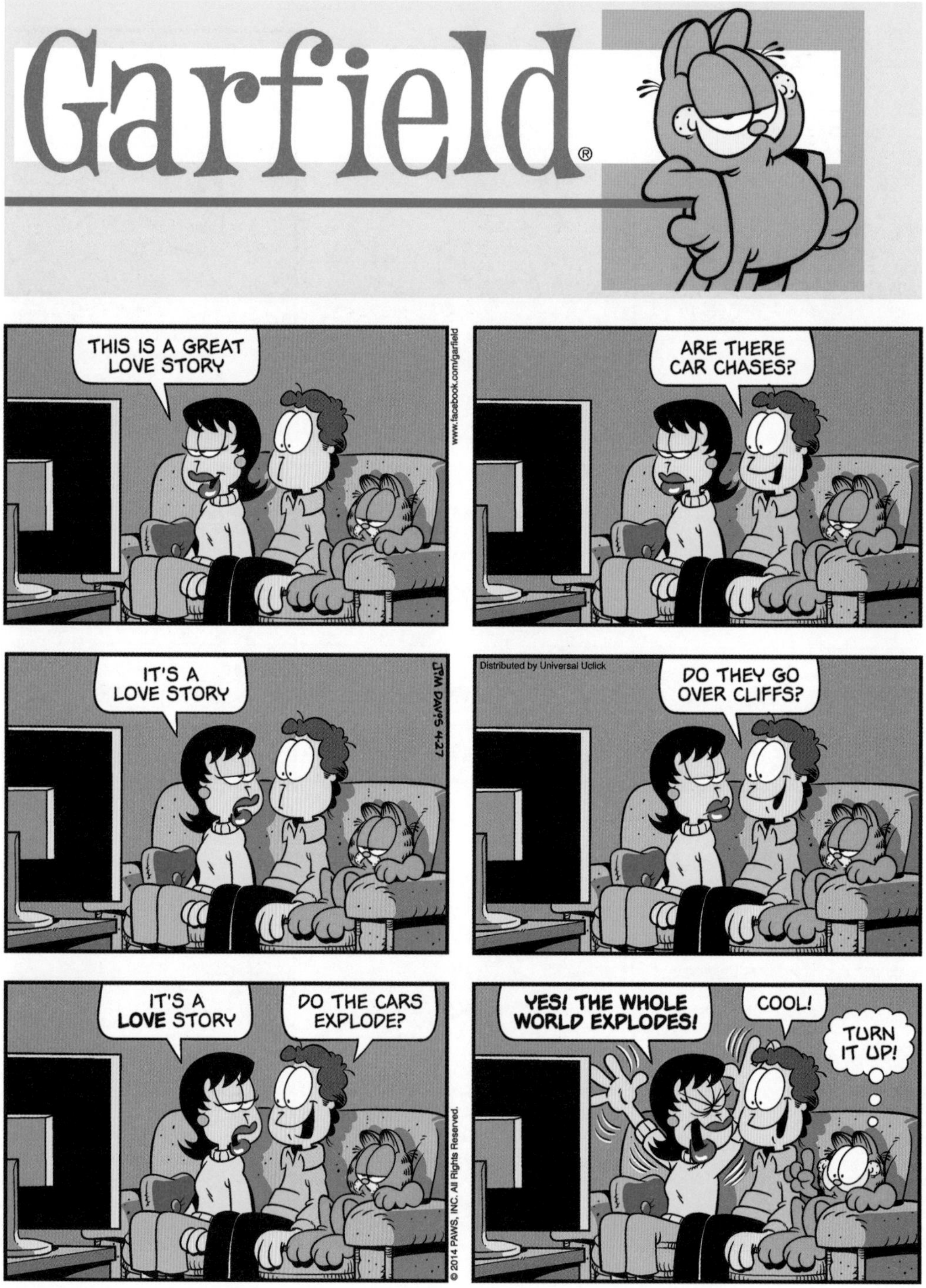
Garfield®
THIS IS A GREAT LOVE STORY
www.facebook.com/garfield
ARE THERE CAR CHASES?
IT'S A LOVE STORY
JIM DAVIS 4-27
Distributed by Universal Uclick
DO THEY GO OVER CLIFFS?
IT'S A LOVE STORY
DO THE CARS EXPLODE?
© 2014 PAWS, INC. All Rights Reserved.
YES! THE WHOLE WORLD EXPLODES!
COOL!
TURN IT UP!

AM I TOO LATE FOR FUN?!
TOO EARLY?!
JIM DAVIS 4-28
© 2014 PAWS, INC. All Rights Reserved.
Distributed by Universal Uclick www.facebook.com/garfield

I AM A MIGHTY OAK!
YOU'RE A TWIG
I AM A MIGHTY TWIG!
JIM DAVIS 4-29
© 2014 PAWS, INC. All Rights Reserved.
Distributed by Universal Uclick www.facebook.com/garfield

THE PET CHANNEL PRESENTS...
"THE CAT'S PAJAMAS"!
HERE'S FLUFFY MODELING A LOVELY ENSEMBLE
OH, PLEASE
I NEVER GET NICE THINGS
JIM DAVIS 4-30
© 2014 PAWS, INC. All Rights Reserved.
Distributed by Universal Uclick www.facebook.com/garfield

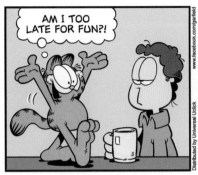

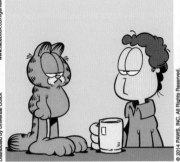

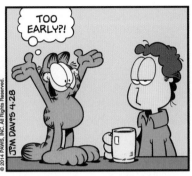

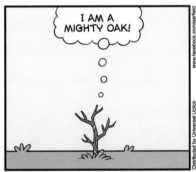

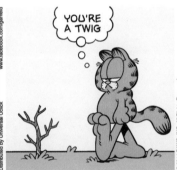

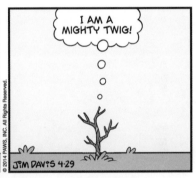

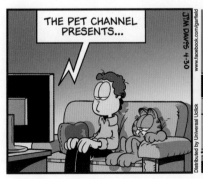

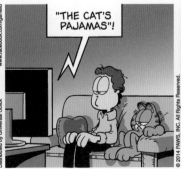

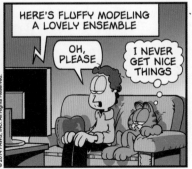

OH, GARFIELD...
SURPRISE! IT'S AN APPLE!
I PREFER MY SURPRISES IN PIE FORM!
JIM DAVIS 5-1
Distributed by Universal Uclick
www.facebook.com/garfield
© 2014 PAWS, INC. All Rights Reserved.

LIZ IS COMING OVER TONIGHT
MAYBE I SHOULD TIDY UP
THINK SHE'LL WANT A CLEAN FORK?
LET'S NOT GET CRAZY, HERE...
JIM DAVIS 5-2
Distributed by Universal Uclick
www.facebook.com/garfield
© 2014 PAWS, INC. All Rights Reserved.

WHAT DO YOU THINK OF THESE FANGS, HUH?
THEY COULD BE WHITER
MMMM!
AND BARKING WITH YOUR MOUTH CLOSED IS JUST HUMMING
JIM DAVIS 5-3
Distributed by Universal Uclick
www.facebook.com/garfield
© 2014 PAWS, INC. All Rights Reserved.

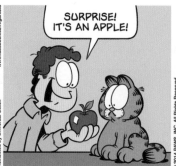

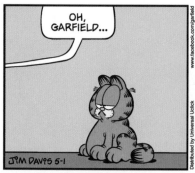

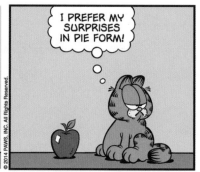

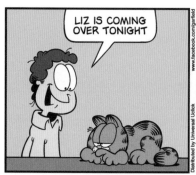

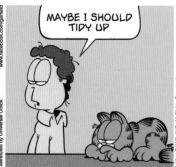

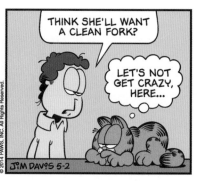

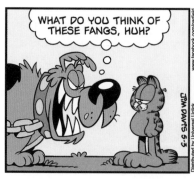

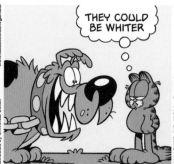

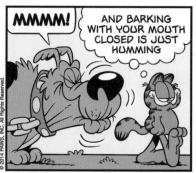

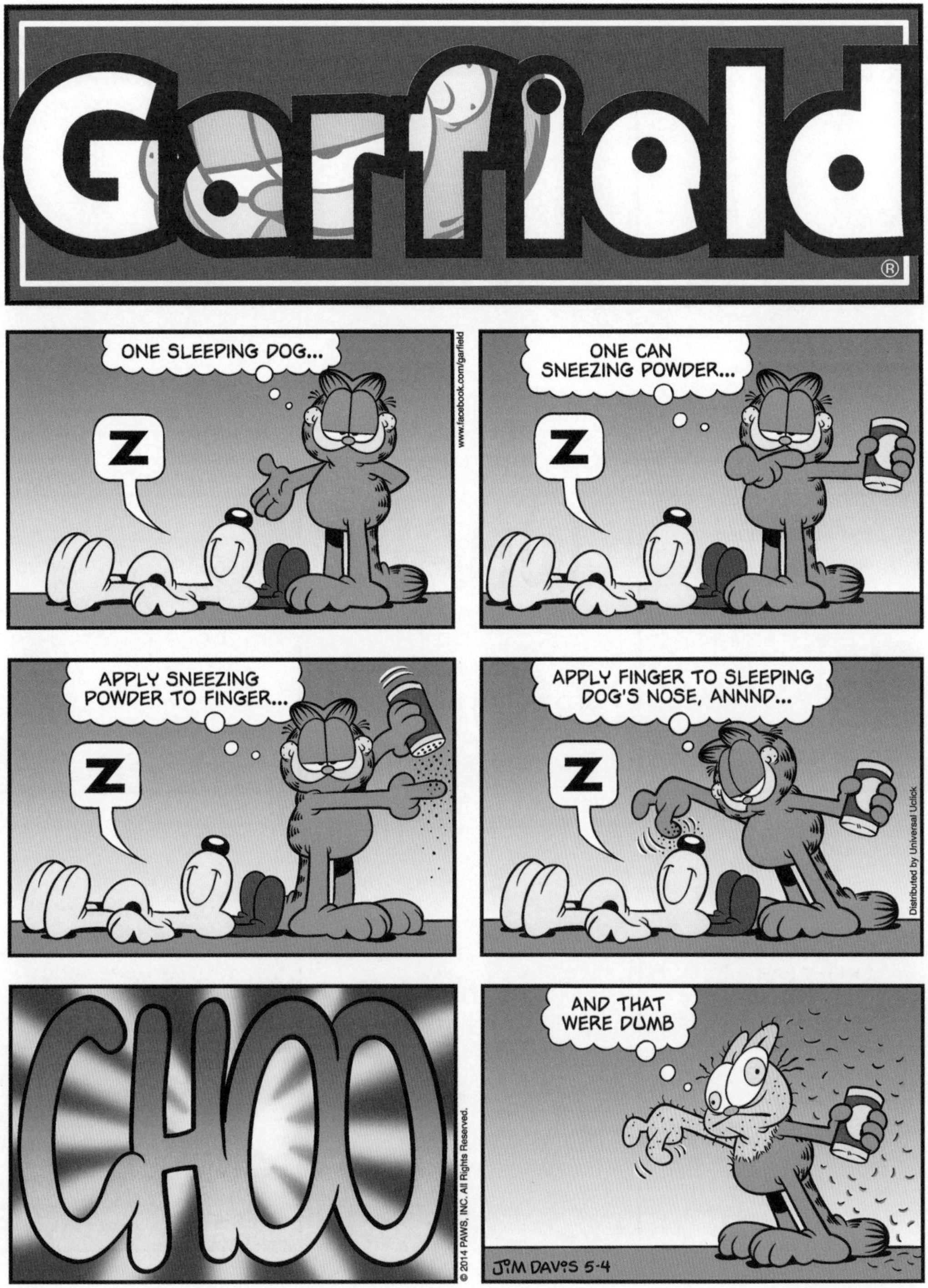
Garfield®
ONE SLEEPING DOG...
Z
www.facebook.com/garfield
ONE CAN SNEEZING POWDER...
Z
APPLY SNEEZING POWDER TO FINGER...
Z
APPLY FINGER TO SLEEPING DOG'S NOSE, ANNND...
Z
Distributed by Universal Uclick
CHOO
© 2014 PAWS, INC. All Rights Reserved.
AND THAT WERE DUMB
JIM DAVIS 5-4

I KNOW WHAT I WANT TO DO WITH THE REST OF MY LIFE
www.facebook.com/garfield
Distributed by Universal Uclick
© 2014 PAWS, INC. All Rights Reserved.
JIM DAVIS 5-5
YES, THIS IS IT. AND NO, I DON'T NEED AN ASSISTANT

TODAY IS GOING TO BE MY LUCKY DAY!
JIM DAVIS 5-6
www.facebook.com/garfield
Distributed by Universal Uclick
WHAP!
© 2014 PAWS, INC. All Rights Reserved.
OF COURSE, IT'S EARLY YET!
ALWAYS THE OPTIMIST...

I MIGHT HAVE A FLAW OR TWO
www.facebook.com/garfield
Distributed by Universal Uclick
I'M PERFECT
© 2014 PAWS, INC. All Rights Reserved.
TELL ME MORE ABOUT YOUR MANY WEAKNESSES
JIM DAVIS 5-7

I VACUUMED TODAY, GARFIELD...
AND I DISCOVERED SOMETHING
THE RUG ISN'T GREEN
SO IT'S NOT EVOLVING?
www.facebook.com/garfield
Distributed by Universal Uclick
© 2014 PAWS, INC. All Rights Reserved.
JIM DAVIS 5-8

HI, SWEETIE
YOU'RE SO SWEET
IT'S LIZ
I FIGURED IT WAS THAT OR YOU WERE TALKING TO A DONUT
www.facebook.com/garfield
Distributed by Universal Uclick
© 2014 PAWS, INC. All Rights Reserved.
JIM DAVIS 5-9

I INVITED SALLY TO THE PROM
I DON'T THINK SHE WANTED TO GO WITH ME
SHE BURNED HER GOWN ON MY FRONT LAWN
SUBTLE
www.facebook.com/garfield
Distributed by Universal Uclick
© 2014 PAWS, INC. All Rights Reserved.
JIM DAVIS 5-10

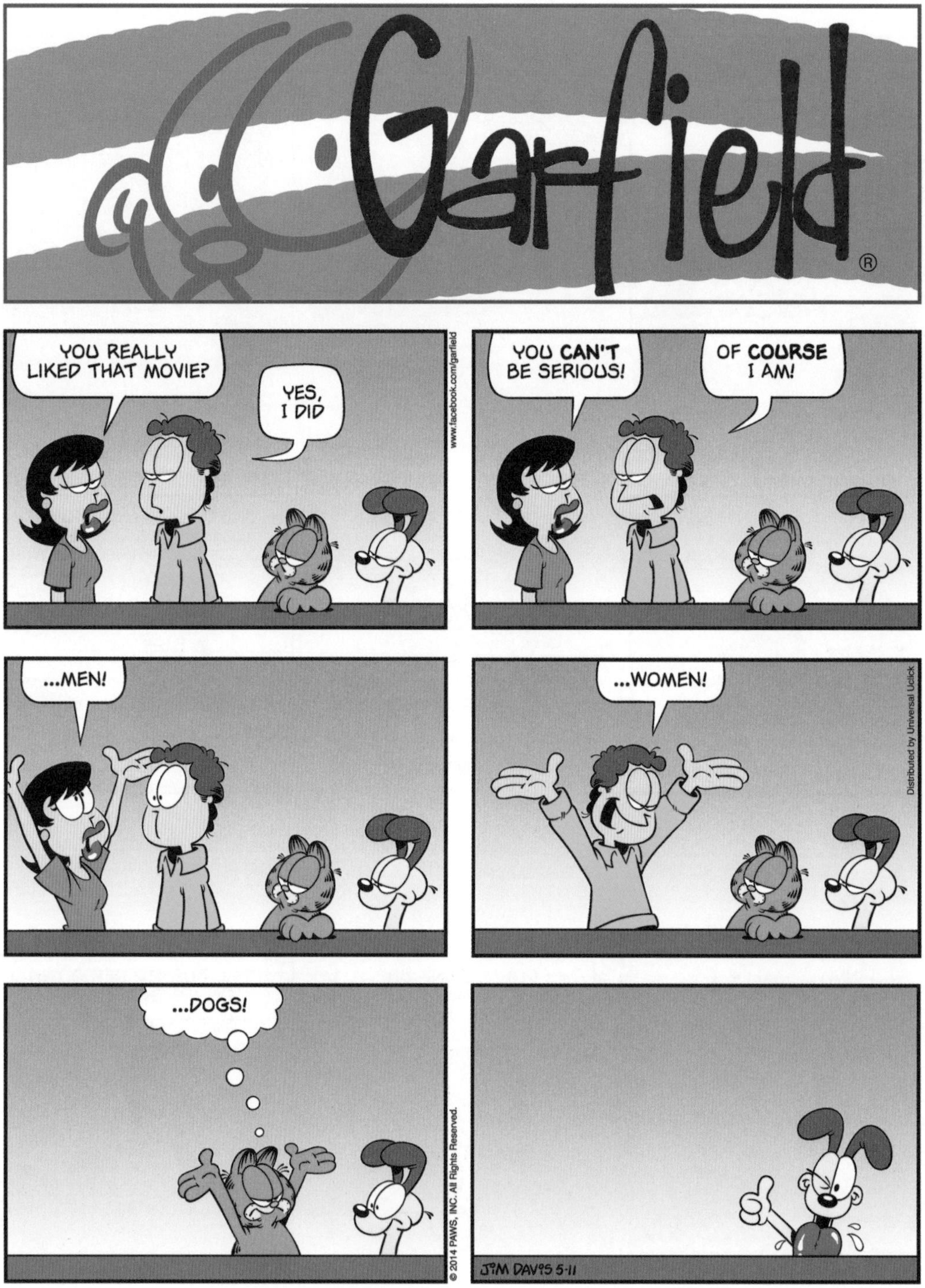
Garfield®
YOU REALLY LIKED THAT MOVIE?
YES, I DID
www.facebook.com/garfield
YOU **CAN'T** BE SERIOUS!
OF **COURSE** I AM!
...MEN!
...WOMEN!
Distributed by Universal Uclick
...DOGS!
© 2014 PAWS, INC. All Rights Reserved.
JIM DAVIS 5-11

IT SAYS HERE THAT YOU SHOULD GREET MONDAY MORNING WITH A SMILE
NEWS
OR NOT
HOW ABOUT A GUT-WRENCHING SCREAM OF DESPERATION?
JIM DAVIS 5-12
Distributed by Universal Uclick
www.facebook.com/garfield
© 2014 PAWS, INC. All Rights Reserved.

GOOD THINGS COME TO THOSE WHO WAIT
OF COURSE THERE'S SOMETHING TO BE SAID FOR THAT INSTANT GRATIFICATION THING, TOO
JIM DAVIS 5-13
Distributed by Universal Uclick
www.facebook.com/garfield
© 2014 PAWS, INC. All Rights Reserved.

LIFE IS A MYSTERY, GARFIELD
SO MANY QUESTIONS
LIKE, WHAT DAY IS THIS?
YOU ARE SO COSMIC
JIM DAVIS 5-14
Distributed by Universal Uclick
www.facebook.com/garfield
© 2014 PAWS, INC. All Rights Reserved.

LIFE IS A REFLECTING POOL, GARFIELD
WHERE ONE CAN SEE ONE'S TRUE SELF
I HAVE COOL HAIR
THE WATER MUST BE MURKY TODAY
JIM DAVIS 5-15
www.facebook.com/garfield
Distributed by Universal Uclick
© 2014 PAWS, INC. All Rights Reserved.

WHAT'S YOUR FAVORITE POLKA SONG, LIZ?
UH...
I DON'T THINK I HAVE ONE
TOO HARD TO CHOOSE, HUH?
JUST NOD YOUR HEAD AND BACK AWAY SLOWLY
JIM DAVIS 5-16
www.facebook.com/garfield
Distributed by Universal Uclick
© 2014 PAWS, INC. All Rights Reserved.

I'M WRITING MY MEMOIRS, GARFIELD
CHAPTER TWO...
THAT'S WHERE I GET KIDNAPPED BY ALIENS
I SUSPECTED AS MUCH...
JIM DAVIS 5-17
www.facebook.com/garfield
Distributed by Universal Uclick
© 2014 PAWS, INC. All Rights Reserved.

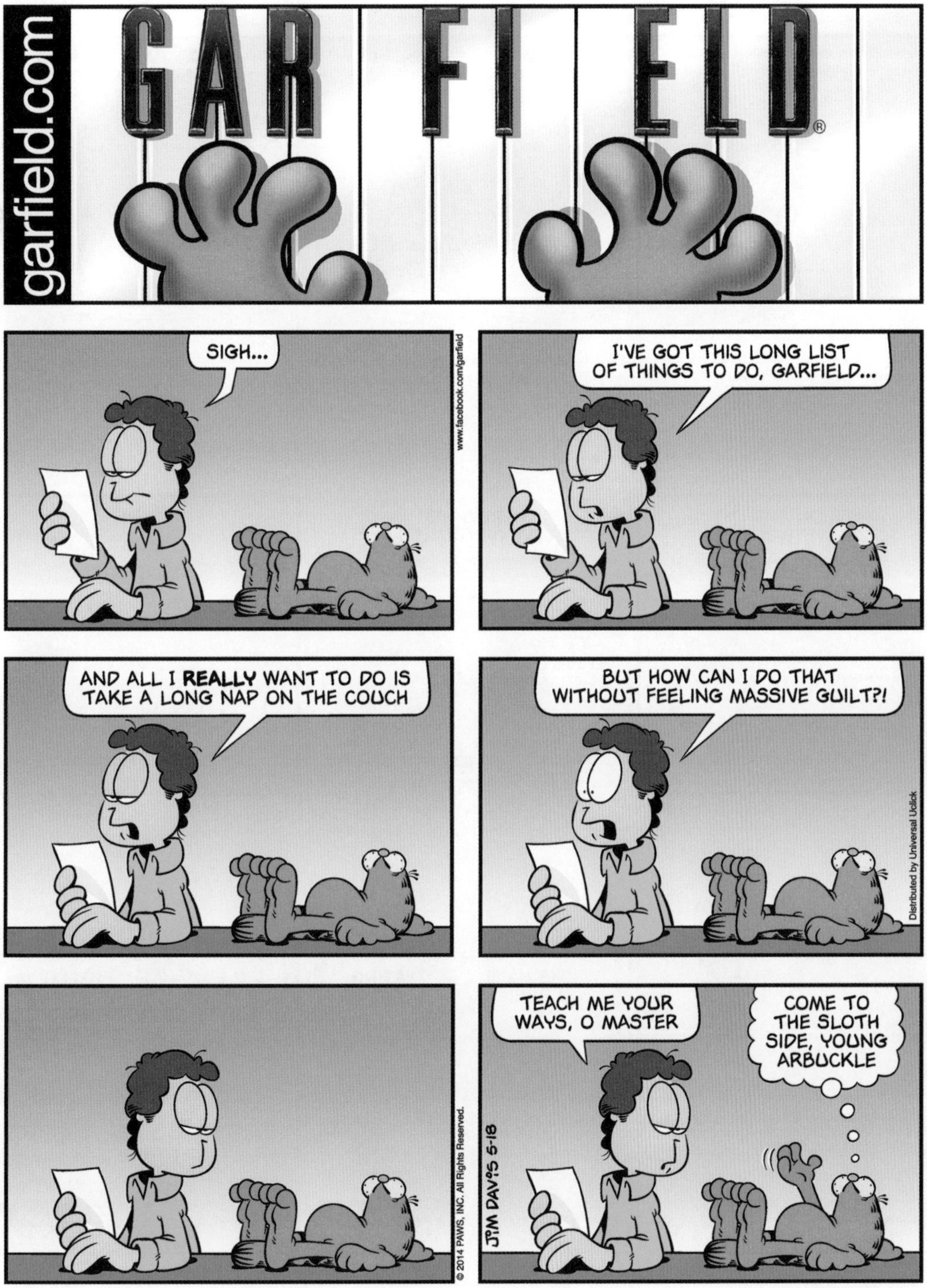
garfield.com
GARFIELD®
SIGH...
www.facebook.com/garfield
I'VE GOT THIS LONG LIST OF THINGS TO DO, GARFIELD...
AND ALL I REALLY WANT TO DO IS TAKE A LONG NAP ON THE COUCH
BUT HOW CAN I DO THAT WITHOUT FEELING MASSIVE GUILT?!
Distributed by Universal Uclick
© 2014 PAWS, INC. All Rights Reserved.
JIM DAVIS 5-18
TEACH ME YOUR WAYS, O MASTER
COME TO THE SLOTH SIDE, YOUNG ARBUCKLE

I HATE MORNINGS
JIM DAVIS 5-19
www.facebook.com/garfield
Distributed by Universal Uclick
I HATE CHEERFUL MORNING PEOPLE
© 2014 PAWS, INC. All Rights Reserved.
AND I HATE THE OLD RUBBER OMELET GAG

JON'S ON THE SOCIAL NETWORK
JIM DAVIS 5-20
www.facebook.com/garfield
Distributed by Universal Uclick
HERE'S HIS LIST OF FRIENDS
© 2014 PAWS, INC. All Rights Reserved.
"BOB"

JIM DAVIS 5-21
www.facebook.com/garfield
Distributed by Universal Uclick
WHERE HAVE YOU BEEN?
EATING LASAGNA
© 2014 PAWS, INC. All Rights Reserved.
DID YOU SAVE ME SOME?
HELLO, MY NAME IS GARFIELD. I DON'T BELIEVE WE'VE MET

AH, MY HIGH SCHOOL GRADUATION
YEAR BOOK
I REMEMBER WHEN THEY CALLED MY NAME
"RON ARBUNKLE"
THANKS FOR SHARING, RON
Distributed by Universal Uclick
www.facebook.com/garfield
© 2014 PAWS, INC. All Rights Reserved.
JIM DAVIS 5-22

I LIKE HAVING LIZ AROUND, GARFIELD
SHE'S VERY THOUGHTFUL
AND SHE DOESN'T SHRED THE CURTAINS
JUST WAIT
Distributed by Universal Uclick
www.facebook.com/garfield
© 2014 PAWS, INC. All Rights Reserved.
JIM DAVIS 5-23

HERE'S A DELICIOUS BURGER THAT I'M LEAVING NEXT TO YOU
I HOPE YOU DON'T EAT IT!
WHY DON'T YOU JUST THROW THE TOFU AWAY?
Distributed by Universal Uclick
www.facebook.com/garfield
© 2014 PAWS, INC. All Rights Reserved.
JIM DAVIS 5-24

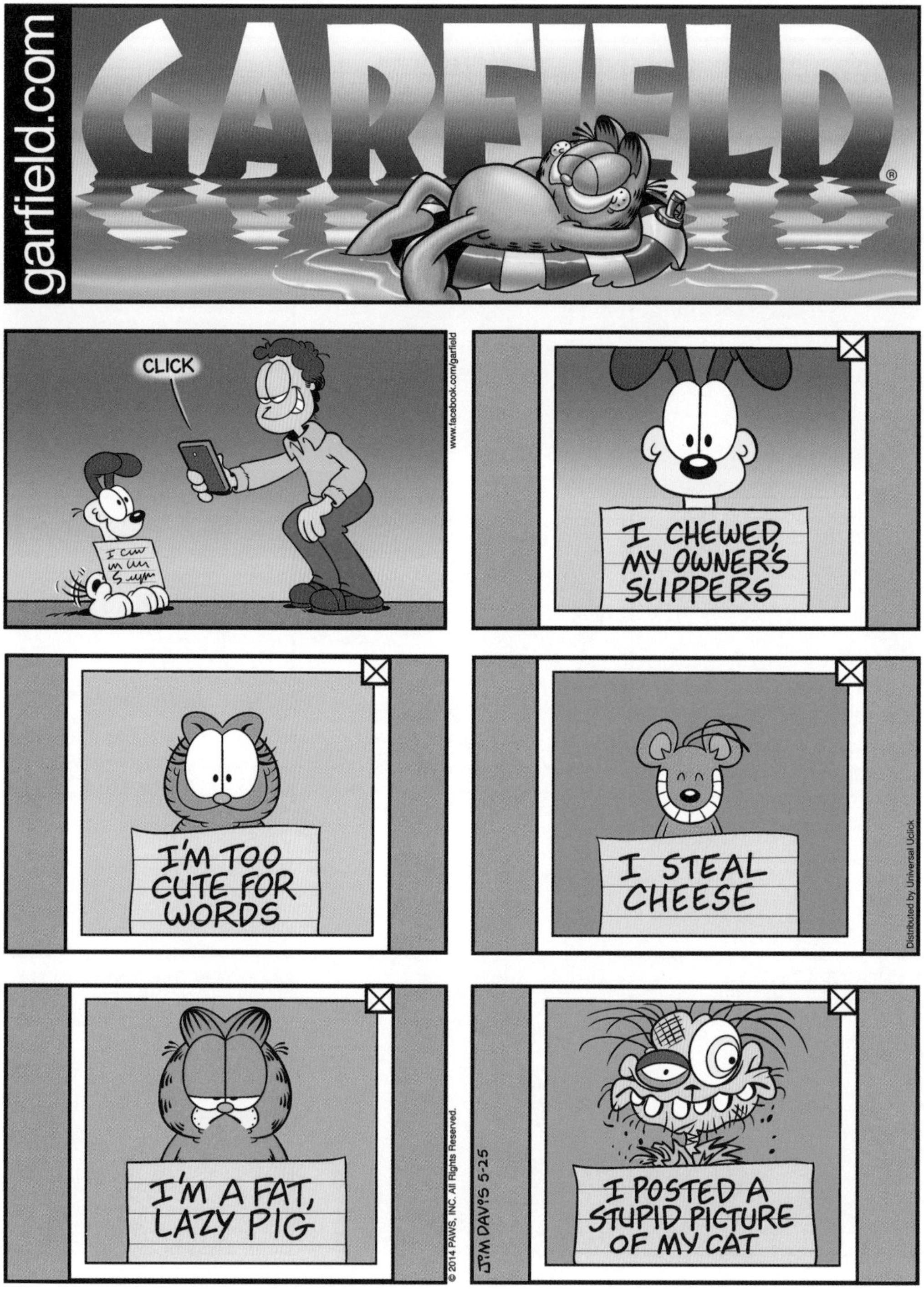
garfield.com
GARFIELD
CLICK
www.facebook.com/garfield
I CHEWED MY OWNER'S SLIPPERS
I'M TOO CUTE FOR WORDS
I STEAL CHEESE
Distributed by Universal Uclick
I'M A FAT, LAZY PIG
© 2014 PAWS, INC. All Rights Reserved.
JIM DAVIS 5-25
I POSTED A STUPID PICTURE OF MY CAT

WE'LL SAVE YOU!
www.facebook.com/garfield
Distributed by Universal Uclick
THAT ISN'T NECESSARY! I'M FINE, THANK YOU!
© 2014 PAWS, INC. All Rights Reserved.
ARE YOU SURE?!
NEVER TRUST DOGS WITH LADDERS
JIM DAVIS 5-29

GARFIELD, WHAT ARE YOU TRYING TO TELL ME?
www.facebook.com/garfield
Distributed by Universal Uclick
IS THERE DANGER?
© 2014 PAWS, INC. All Rights Reserved.
DO **NOT** GO TO THE BEACH!
JIM DAVIS 5-30

TONIGHT'S HORROR MOVIE...
www.facebook.com/garfield
Distributed by Universal Uclick
"CLAWS OF DEATH!"
JIM DAVIS 5-31
© 2014 PAWS, INC. All Rights Reserved.
OH, LOOK, HOWARD, A LITTLE KITTEN!
RUN, HOWARD, RUN

garfield.com
Garfield®
www.facebook.com/garfield
Z
MMMPH!
Distributed by Universal Uclick
MMMMPH!
STOP IT!
© 2014 PAWS, INC. All Rights Reserved.
I'LL STOP IT WHEN YOUR FACE STOPS BEING WARM
JIM DAVIS 6-1

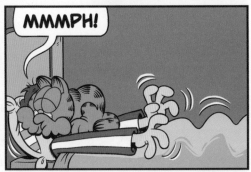

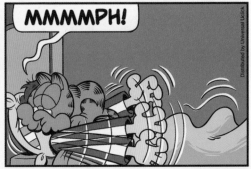

YOU HAVE A CHOICE OF ALARMS THIS MORNING
7:00
www.facebook.com/garfield
Distributed by Universal Uclick
DO YOU PREFER HUMOROUS OR PRACTICAL?
HUMOROUS
7:00
© 2014 PAWS, INC. All Rights Reserved.
JIM DAVIS 6-2
DID YOU HEAR THE ONE ABOUT THE CAT AND THE LAWN MOWER?
I HATE MORNINGS
7:00

I NEED A NEW HOBBY
BOTTLE CAP COLLECTING WASN'T EXCITING ENOUGH FOR YOU?
www.facebook.com/garfield
Distributed by Universal Uclick
MAYBE I CAN TAKE UP BIRD WATCHING!
I CAN SEE THE HEADLINE NOW...
© 2014 PAWS, INC. All Rights Reserved.
OR IDENTIFY DIFFERENT TYPES OF WOOD!
"LOCAL CAT FOUND BORED TO DEATH NEAR BINOCULARS"
JIM DAVIS 6-3

BEWARE OF THE DOG
www.facebook.com/garfield
Distributed by Universal Uclick
© 2014 PAWS, INC. All Rights Reserved.
YOU SAW THE SIGN, RIGHT?
THIS IS HOW I BEWARE
JIM DAVIS 6-4

GARFIELD, WHERE IS MY FISH?
BY NOW? SOMEWHERE BETWEEN THE ESOPHAGUS AND THE DUODENUM
JIM DAVIS 6-5
Distributed by Universal Uclick
www.facebook.com/garfield
© 2014 PAWS, INC. All Rights Reserved.

ALL WE HAVE IS NOODLES, SO WE'RE HAVING NOODLES TONIGHT, GARFIELD
THE FORKS ARE DIRTY, BUT WE CAN USE THESE PENCILS LIKE CHOPSTICKS
AND THE NAPKINS ARE STILL IN THE LAUNDRY, SO...
WILL YOU PLEASE GET MARRIED!
JIM DAVIS 6-6
Distributed by Universal Uclick
www.facebook.com/garfield
© 2014 PAWS, INC. All Rights Reserved.

JIM DAVIS 6-7
I LIKE IT BETTER WHEN WE HAVE MICE
Distributed by Universal Uclick
www.facebook.com/garfield
© 2014 PAWS, INC. All Rights Reserved.

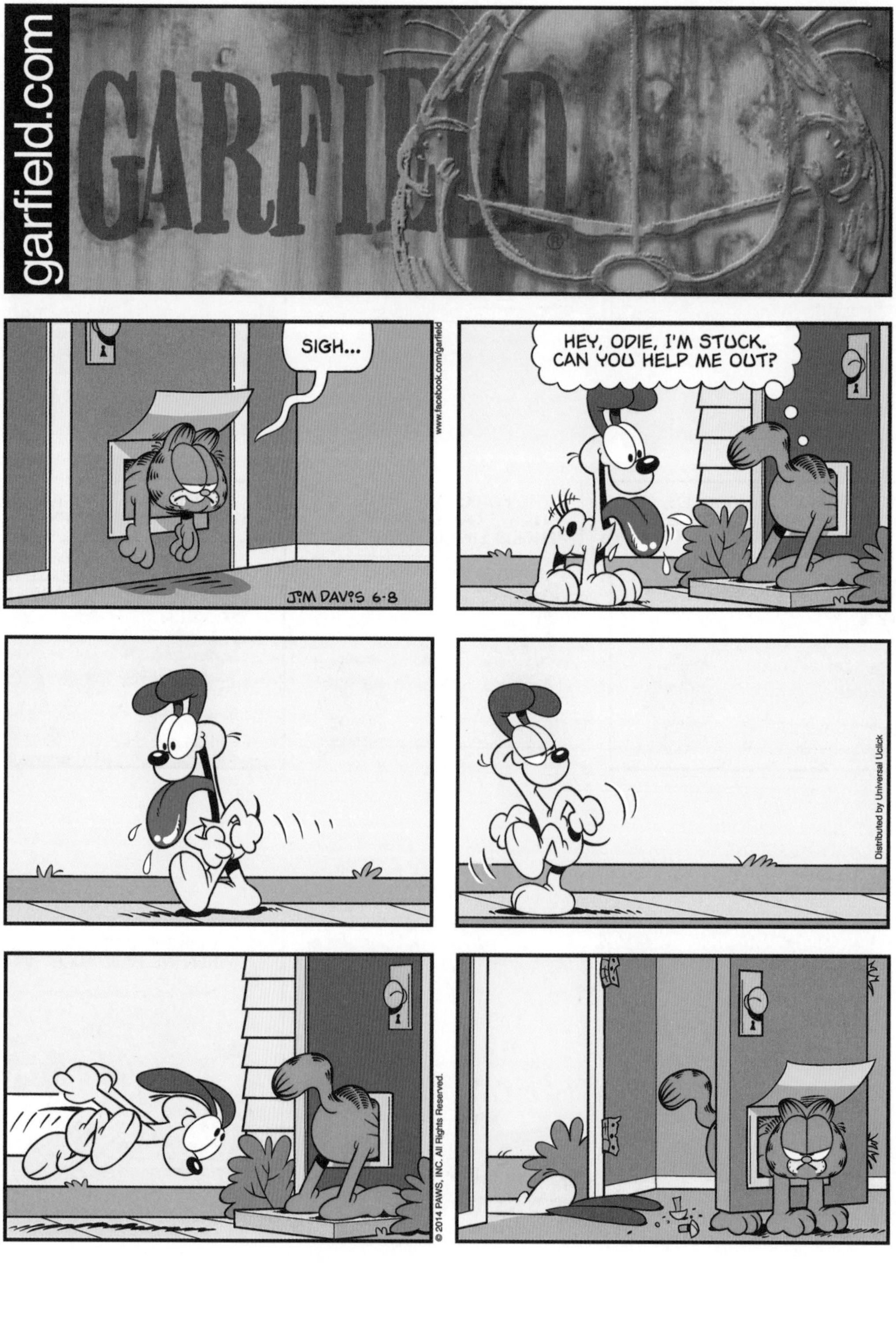
garfield.com
GARFIELD®
SIGH...
www.facebook.com/garfield
JIM DAVIS 6-8
HEY, ODIE, I'M STUCK. CAN YOU HELP ME OUT?
Distributed by Universal Uclick
© 2014 PAWS, INC. All Rights Reserved.

I'M IN CHARGE AROUND HERE
NOBODY ELSE WANTED THE JOB
JIM DAVIS 6-9
Distributed by Universal Uclick
www.facebook.com/garfield
© 2014 PAWS, INC. All Rights Reserved.

MOSS ALWAYS GROWS ON THE NORTH SIDE OF A TREE
WHO CARES?
WHICH SIDE DOES THE TAFFY GROW ON?
JIM DAVIS 6-10
Distributed by Universal Uclick
www.facebook.com/garfield
© 2014 PAWS, INC. All Rights Reserved.

ODIE ISN'T GOING OUTSIDE TODAY
THE TOUGH SQUIRRELS ARE OUT THERE
LAST TIME, THEY FORCED HIM TO GATHER ACORNS
JIM DAVIS 6-11
Distributed by Universal Uclick
www.facebook.com/garfield
© 2014 PAWS, INC. All Rights Reserved.

SOMEDAY I'LL GET WHAT I DESERVE
WAIT!
I WANT SOMETHING **WAY** BETTER THAN THAT
JIM DAVIS 6-12
www.facebook.com/garfield
Distributed by Universal Uclick
© 2014 PAWS, INC. All Rights Reserved.

ANOTHER AGE NIGHTMARE?
YEP
YOU DON'T LOOK VERY SCARY TO ME
OH?
I'M THE MENU YOU CAN'T READ WITHOUT THE GLASSES YOU CAN'T FIND
I STAND CORRECTED
JIM DAVIS 6-13
www.facebook.com/garfield
Distributed by Universal Uclick
© 2014 PAWS, INC. All Rights Reserved.

YOU?...
YOU CAN'T **POSSIBLY** BE AN AGE NIGHTMARE
OH, BUT I AM...
I'M THAT AWFUL MUSIC THAT KIDS TODAY LISTEN TO!
GO AWAY
JIM DAVIS 6-14
www.facebook.com/garfield
Distributed by Universal Uclick
© 2014 PAWS, INC. All Rights Reserved.

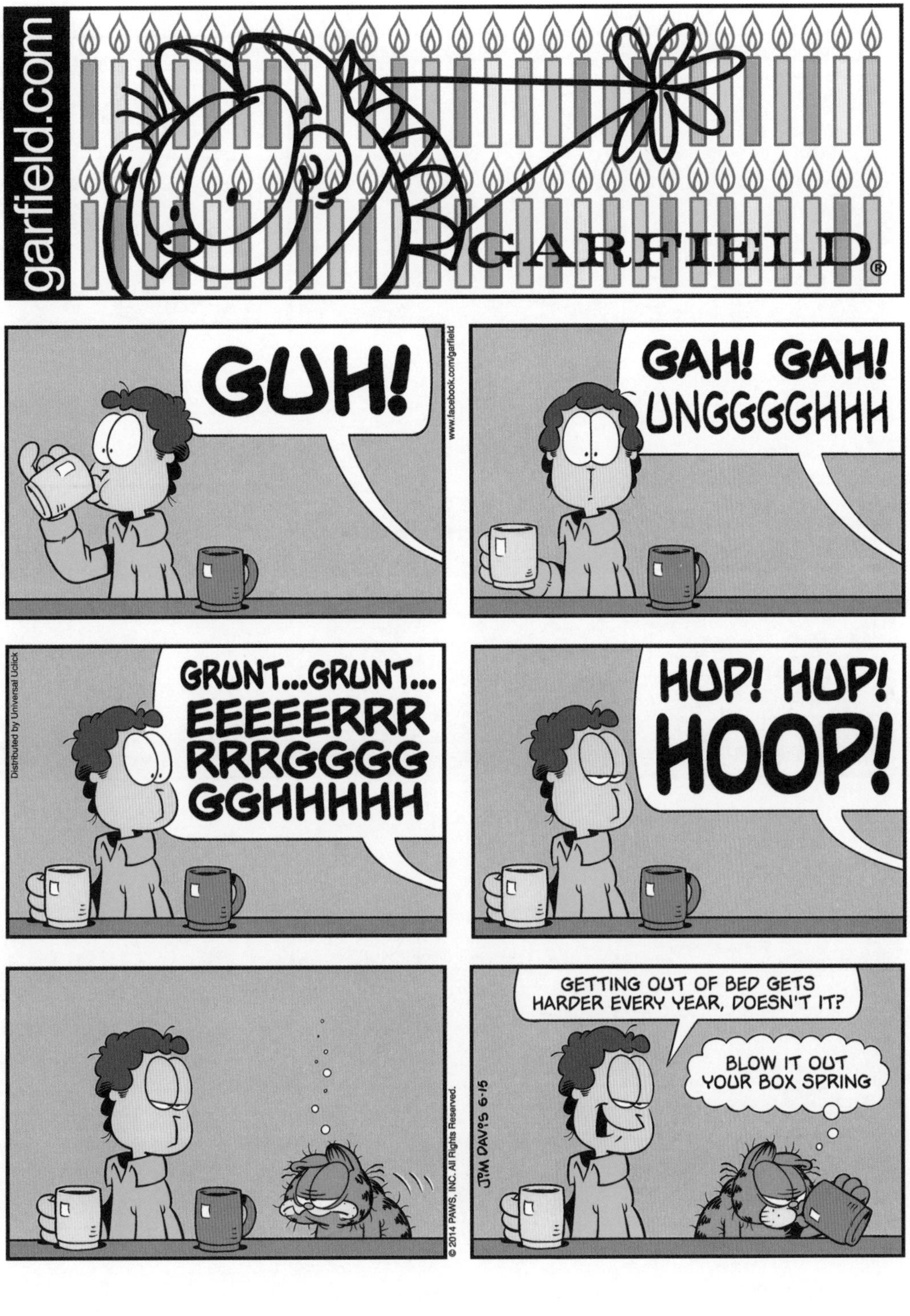
garfield.com
GARFIELD®
GUH!
www.facebook.com/garfield
GAH! GAH! UNGGGGHHH
Distributed by Universal Uclick
GRUNT...GRUNT... EEEEERRR RRRGGGG GGHHHHH
HUP! HUP! HOOP!
© 2014 PAWS, INC. All Rights Reserved.
JIM DAVIS 6-15
GETTING OUT OF BED GETS HARDER EVERY YEAR, DOESN'T IT?
BLOW IT OUT YOUR BOX SPRING

YOU'RE TONIGHT'S AGE NIGHTMARE?
YUPPER-DOO
JIM DAVIS 6-16
www.facebook.com/garfield
Distributed by Universal Uclick
BUT YOU'RE COFFEE. COFFEE'S NOT SCARY
OH, NO?
© 2014 PAWS, INC. All Rights Reserved.
I'M DECAF, WITH NONFAT MILK AND ARTIFICIAL SWEETENER
YAAHH

...SO YOU'RE MY AGE NIGHTMARE TONIGHT? WHAT ARE YOU?
www.facebook.com/garfield
Distributed by Universal Uclick
I'M FINE PRINT!
BWAH-HA-HA-HAAAH!
© 2014 PAWS, INC. All Rights Reserved.
JIM DAVIS 6-17
MMMFFF! MMMFFFF!

LET ME GUESS... TONIGHT'S AGE NIGHTMARE?
THAT'S ME!
www.facebook.com/garfield
Distributed by Universal Uclick
I'M THE JAR OF PICKLES THAT YOU CAN'T OPEN ANYMORE!
© 2014 PAWS, INC. All Rights Reserved.
JIM DAVIS 6-18
AND YOU?
I'M THE PACKAGE OF BATTERIES YOU NEVER **COULD** OPEN

I DON'T FEEL LIKE GETTING OLDER
JUNE
JIM DAVIS 6-19
www.facebook.com/garfield
Distributed by Universal Uclick
MAYBE IF I CHANGE THE YEAR, I'LL GET YOUNGER ON MY BIRTHDAY
© 2014 PAWS, INC. All Rights Reserved.
GARFIELD, HAVE YOU SEEN MY PACIFIER?

I'M IN THE MOOD FOR ROMANCE
I'M IN THE MOOD FOR PANCAKES!
www.facebook.com/garfield
Distributed by Universal Uclick
© 2014 PAWS, INC. All Rights Reserved.
ROMANTIC PANCAKES!
GOOD SAVE, ROMEO
JIM DAVIS 6-20

YOU KNOW WHAT WOULD BE FUN?
LETTING YOUR CAT SLEEP?
www.facebook.com/garfield
Distributed by Universal Uclick
WE COULD LIE ON THE FRONT PORCH...
AND SLEEP?
© 2014 PAWS, INC. All Rights Reserved.
AND PRETEND THAT WE'RE DOORMATS!
THAT SAY "BEWARE OF SLEEPING CAT"
JIM DAVIS 6-21

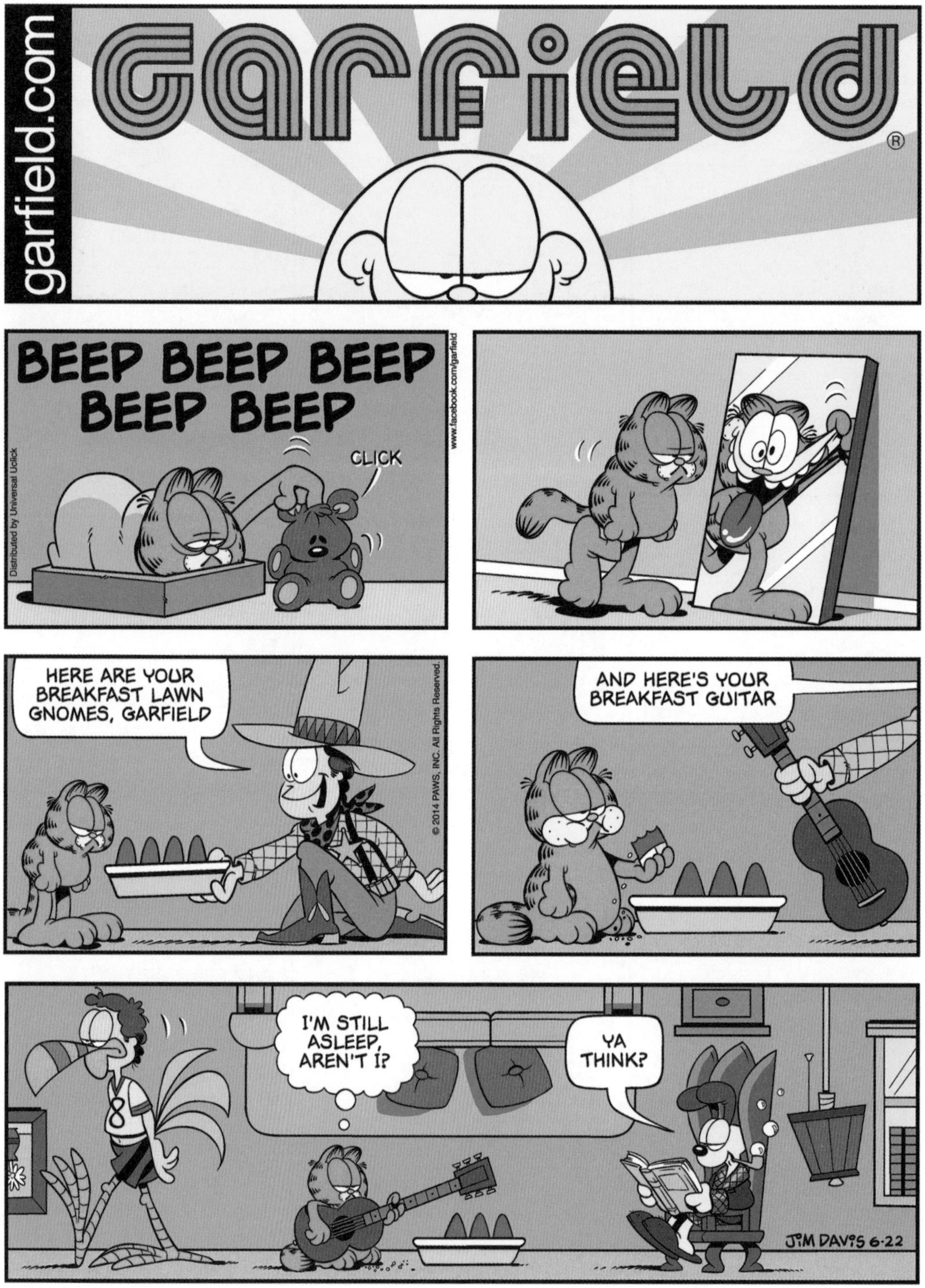
garfield.com
GARFIELD®
BEEP BEEP BEEP
BEEP BEEP
CLICK
Distributed by Universal Uclick
www.facebook.com/garfield
HERE ARE YOUR BREAKFAST LAWN GNOMES, GARFIELD
© 2014 PAWS, INC. All Rights Reserved.
AND HERE'S YOUR BREAKFAST GUITAR
I'M STILL ASLEEP, AREN'T I?
YA THINK?
JIM DAVIS 6-22

I'M TIRED OF THE DAILY GRIND
JIM DAVIS 6-23
www.facebook.com/garfield
Distributed by Universal Uclick
OH, ME, TOO
© 2014 PAWS, INC. All Rights Reserved.
YOU PROBABLY DON'T EVEN KNOW WHAT THAT MEANS
I'M TIRED OF HEARING ABOUT IT

ANOTHER WILDLIFE SHOW
www.facebook.com/garfield
Distributed by Universal Uclick
ALWAYS THE SAME THING
© 2014 PAWS, INC. All Rights Reserved.
I GET A CRAVING FOR ANTELOPE
JIM DAVIS 6-24

BARK! BARK! BARK! BARK!
JIM DAVIS 6-25
www.facebook.com/garfield
Distributed by Universal Uclick
HEY! I'M NOT DONE YET!
© 2014 PAWS, INC. All Rights Reserved.
BARK! BARK! BARK! BARK!
YOU DIDN'T HAVE TO GO BACK TO THE BEGINNING

WE INSECTS HAVE SIX LEGS
JIM DAVIS 6-26
www.facebook.com/garfield
Distributed by Universal Uclick
YOU HAVE EIGHT LEGS
TECHNICALLY, YES...
IF YOU COUNT THE SPARES
© 2014 PAWS, INC. All Rights Reserved.

TODAY I PUT HATS ON MY FEET AND A SHOE ON MY HEAD
www.facebook.com/garfield
Distributed by Universal Uclick
ON PURPOSE?
I TOLD YOU SHE'D ASK!
© 2014 PAWS, INC. All Rights Reserved.
JIM DAVIS 6-27

DING DING
ICE CREAM MAN!
www.facebook.com/garfield
Distributed by Universal Uclick
HOW?...
HERE'S YOUR WALLET
© 2014 PAWS, INC. All Rights Reserved.
JIM DAVIS 6-28

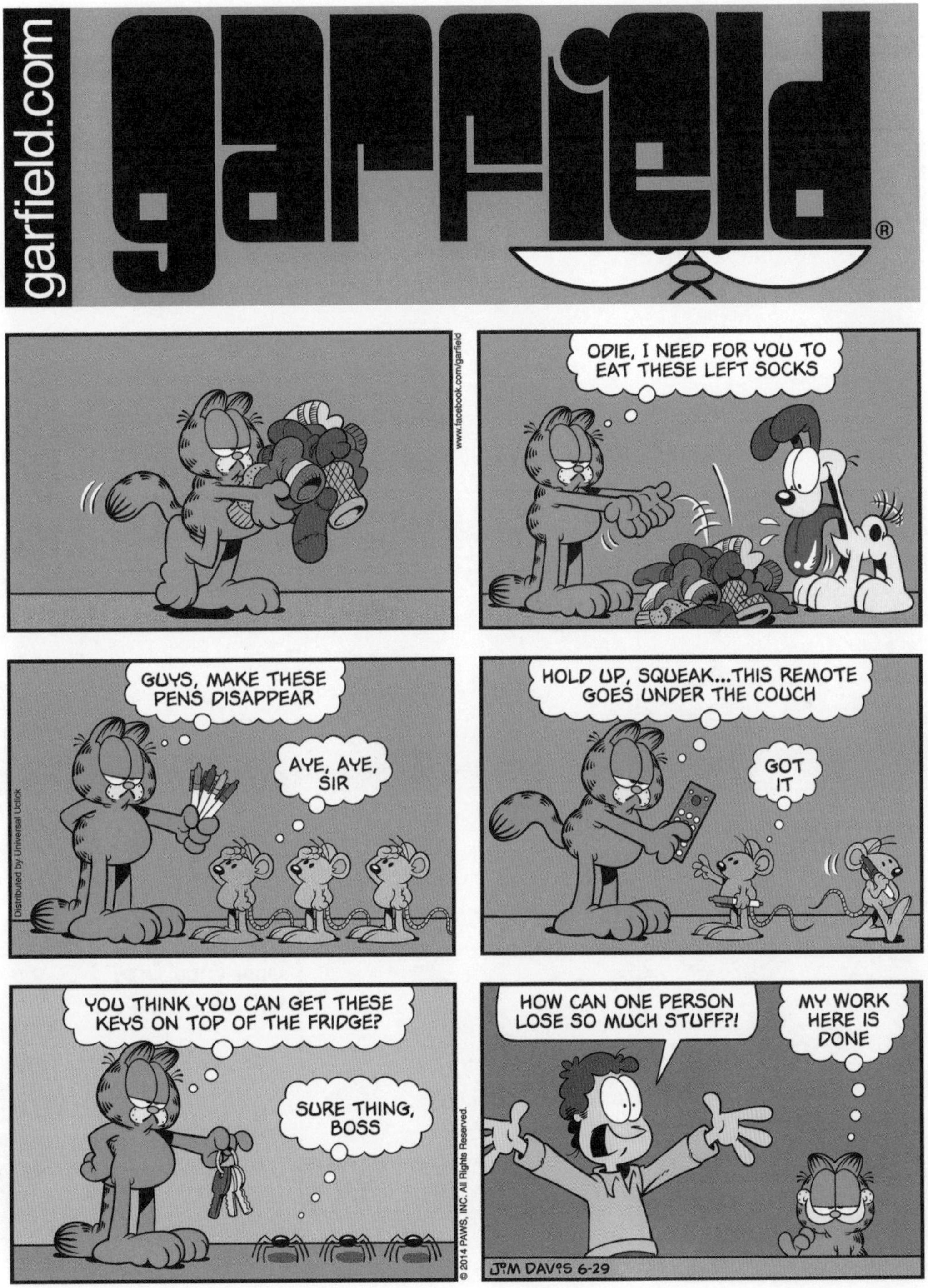
garfield.com
garfield
www.facebook.com/garfield
ODIE, I NEED FOR YOU TO EAT THESE LEFT SOCKS
GUYS, MAKE THESE PENS DISAPPEAR
AYE, AYE, SIR
Distributed by Universal Uclick
HOLD UP, SQUEAK...THIS REMOTE GOES UNDER THE COUCH
GOT IT
YOU THINK YOU CAN GET THESE KEYS ON TOP OF THE FRIDGE?
SURE THING, BOSS
© 2014 PAWS, INC. All Rights Reserved.
HOW CAN ONE PERSON LOSE SO MUCH STUFF?!
MY WORK HERE IS DONE
JIM DAVIS 6-29

THERE'S A WHOLE WORLD OUT THERE, GARFIELD...
JUST WAITING TO BE EXPERIENCED
BUT THAT WOULD REQUIRE GOING OUTSIDE
ALWAYS A CATCH!
JIM DAVIS 6-30
www.facebook.com/garfield
Distributed by Universal Uclick
© 2014 PAWS, INC. All Rights Reserved.

I HELPED AN ELDERLY LADY ACROSS THE STREET TODAY
I LOOKED BOTH WAYS BEFORE CROSSING, BUT I DIDN'T LOOK DOWN...
THERE WAS THIS OPEN MANHOLE...
STOP RIGHT THERE!
JIM DAVIS 7-1
www.facebook.com/garfield
Distributed by Universal Uclick
© 2014 PAWS, INC. All Rights Reserved.

DIG
DIG
DIG
DIG
JIM DAVIS 7-2
MMMMM
YIP! YIP! YIP! YIP! YIP! YIP!
IT'S WAR
www.facebook.com/garfield
Distributed by Universal Uclick
© 2014 PAWS, INC. All Rights Reserved.

M
I DIDN'T HAVE THE ENERGY FOR A WHOLE "MEOW"
JIM DAVIS 7-3
www.facebook.com/garfield
Distributed by Universal Uclick
© 2014 PAWS, INC. All Rights Reserved.

WE HAD A GREAT TIME AT THE AMUSEMENT PARK
THE HOT DOGS... THE POPCORN...
...THE ROLLER COASTERS...
JIM DAVIS 7-4
www.facebook.com/garfield
Distributed by Universal Uclick
© 2014 PAWS, INC. All Rights Reserved.

I KNEW THAT CUPCAKE WOULD COME UNSTUCK FROM THE CEILING EVENTUALLY
JIM DAVIS 7-5
www.facebook.com/garfield
Distributed by Universal Uclick
© 2014 PAWS, INC. All Rights Reserved.

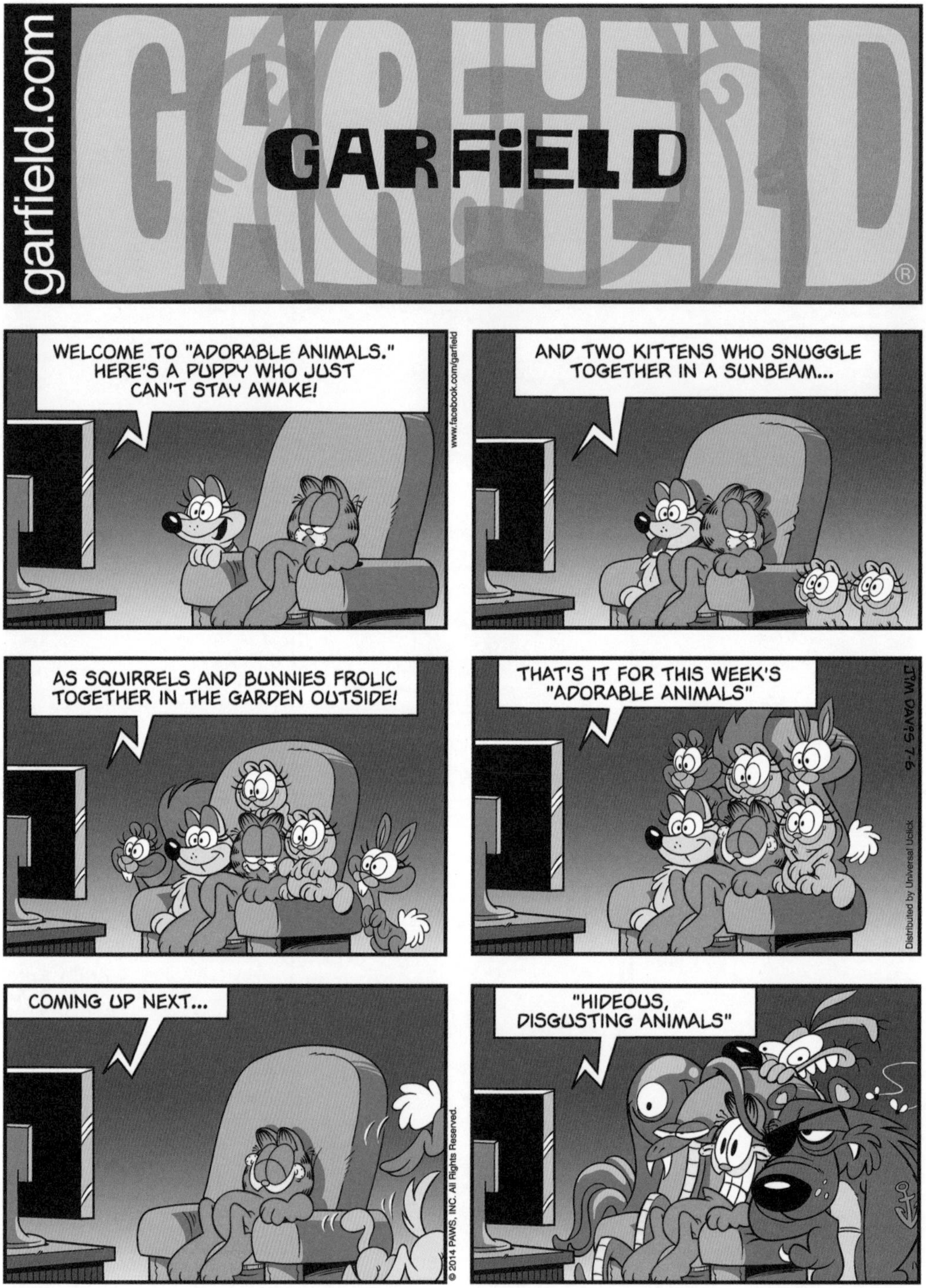
garfield.com
GARFIELD
WELCOME TO "ADORABLE ANIMALS." HERE'S A PUPPY WHO JUST CAN'T STAY AWAKE!
www.facebook.com/garfield
AND TWO KITTENS WHO SNUGGLE TOGETHER IN A SUNBEAM...
AS SQUIRRELS AND BUNNIES FROLIC TOGETHER IN THE GARDEN OUTSIDE!
THAT'S IT FOR THIS WEEK'S "ADORABLE ANIMALS"
JIM DAVIS 7-6
Distributed by Universal Uclick
COMING UP NEXT...
© 2014 PAWS, INC. All Rights Reserved.
"HIDEOUS, DISGUSTING ANIMALS"

WELL, IT'S MONDAY, AND YOU KNOW WHAT THAT MEANS...
MON. 7
JIM DAVIS 7-7
www.facebook.com/garfield
Distributed by Universal Uclick
SOMETHING BAD'S BOUND TO HAPPEN SOONER OR...
MON. 7
© 2014 PAWS, INC. All Rights Reserved.
MON. 7

ARE YOU SAYING NICE THINGS ABOUT ME IN YOUR MEMOIR?
www.facebook.com/garfield
Distributed by Universal Uclick
© 2014 PAWS, INC. All Rights Reserved.
I'LL GIVE YOU A CANDY BAR
"JON ARBUCKLE, MY HERO"
JIM DAVIS 7-8

www.facebook.com/garfield
Distributed by Universal Uclick
ZOOM
© 2014 PAWS, INC. All Rights Reserved.
SEEMED APPROPRIATE
JIM DAVIS 7-9

I HAVE A SORE THROAT
JIM DAVIS 7-10
www.facebook.com/garfield
Distributed by Universal Uclick
SO...
BARK
© 2014 PAWS, INC. All Rights Reserved.
AND...
BARK
NOT SCARED

LIZ AND I ARE GOING TO THE MUSEUM
www.facebook.com/garfield
Distributed by Universal Uclick
AND CATS AREN'T ALLOWED
© 2014 PAWS, INC. All Rights Reserved.
THAT WAS OUR IDEA
JIM DAVIS 7-11

GARFIELD! IT'S GOOD TO BE BACK HOME!
www.facebook.com/garfield
Distributed by Universal Uclick
WAIT A MINUTE!
© 2014 PAWS, INC. All Rights Reserved.
I NEVER WENT ANYWHERE!
CUE THE SCARY MUSIC
JIM DAVIS 7-12

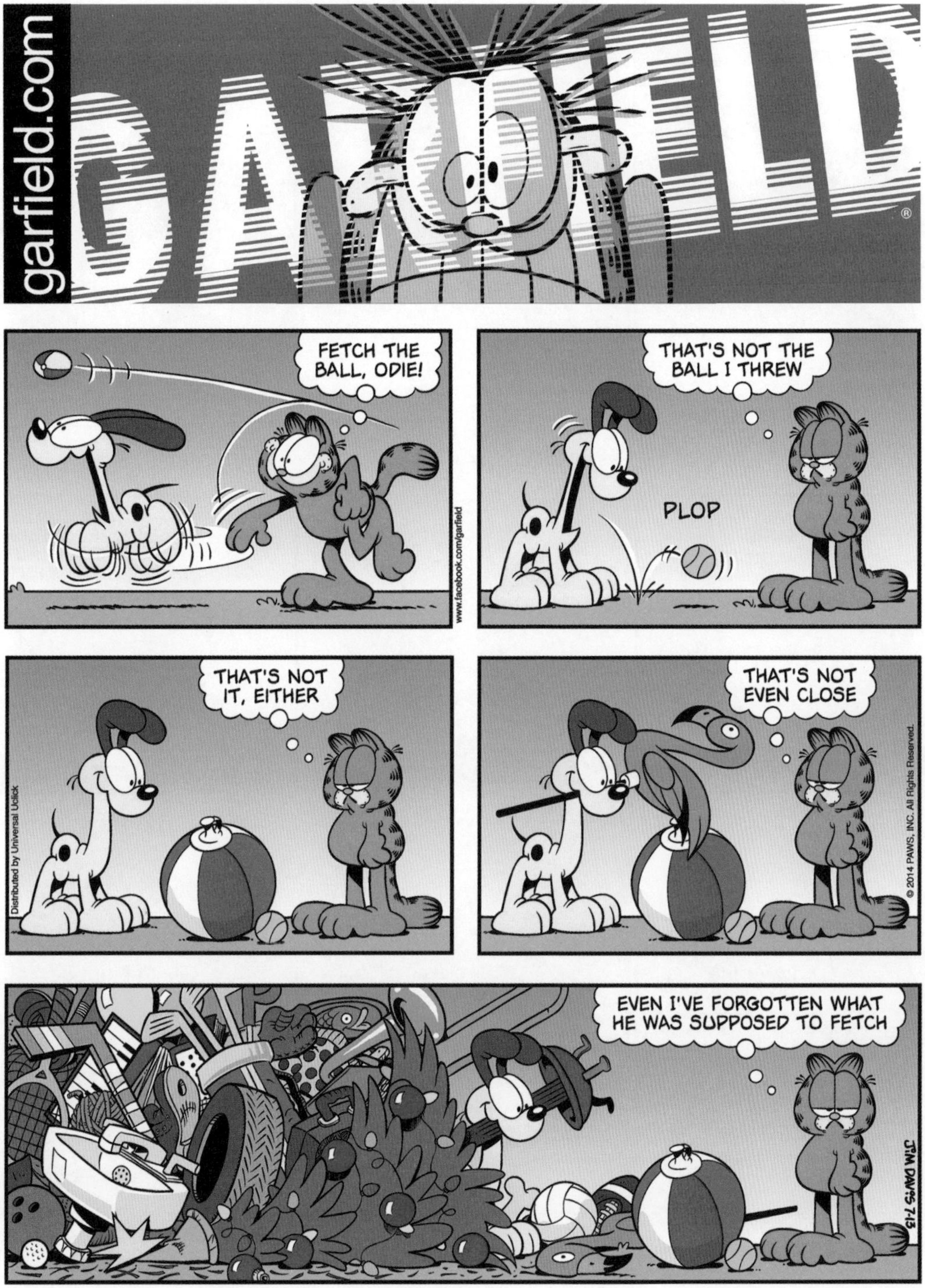
garfield.com
GARFIELD®
FETCH THE BALL, ODIE!
www.facebook.com/garfield
THAT'S NOT THE BALL I THREW
PLOP
Distributed by Universal Uclick
THAT'S NOT IT, EITHER
THAT'S NOT EVEN CLOSE
© 2014 PAWS, INC. All Rights Reserved.
EVEN I'VE FORGOTTEN WHAT HE WAS SUPPOSED TO FETCH
JIM DAVIS 7-13

JIM DAVIS 7-14
Distributed by Universal Uclick www.facebook.com/garfield
© 2014 PAWS, INC. All Rights Reserved.
WHAT WILL IT TAKE TO MAKE YOU GO AWAY?
FOOD HAS HISTORICALLY PROVEN TO BE AN EFFECTIVE MOTIVATOR

I'M A PRETTY HIP DUDE
Distributed by Universal Uclick www.facebook.com/garfield
© 2014 PAWS, INC. All Rights Reserved.
SO...
WAIT. I'M STILL PROCESSING THAT LAST COMMENT
JIM DAVIS 7-15

I'M GOING HANG GLIDING!
Distributed by Universal Uclick www.facebook.com/garfield
© 2014 PAWS, INC. All Rights Reserved.
THE HOUSE IS MINE!
JIM DAVIS 7-16

I'M STARTING TO SUSPECT THAT THIS ISN'T MY HAT
Distributed by Universal Uclick www.facebook.com/garfield
I WOULDN'T JUMP TO CONCLUSIONS, JON
© 2014 PAWS, INC. All Rights Reserved.
MAYBE THAT'S NOT YOUR HEAD
JIM DAVIS 7-17

BARKBARKBARK BARKBARKBARK
Distributed by Universal Uclick www.facebook.com/garfield
THAT'S IT. GOTTA GO!
© 2014 PAWS, INC. All Rights Reserved.
AND THE WEEKEND BEGINS
JIM DAVIS 7-18

MY, THIS IS INTERESTING
Distributed by Universal Uclick www.facebook.com/garfield
THERE WAS A FISH IN THIS BOWL...
© 2014 PAWS, INC. All Rights Reserved.
AND NOW THERE ISN'T
HE SAID SOMETHING ABOUT GETTING A CONDO
JIM DAVIS 7-19

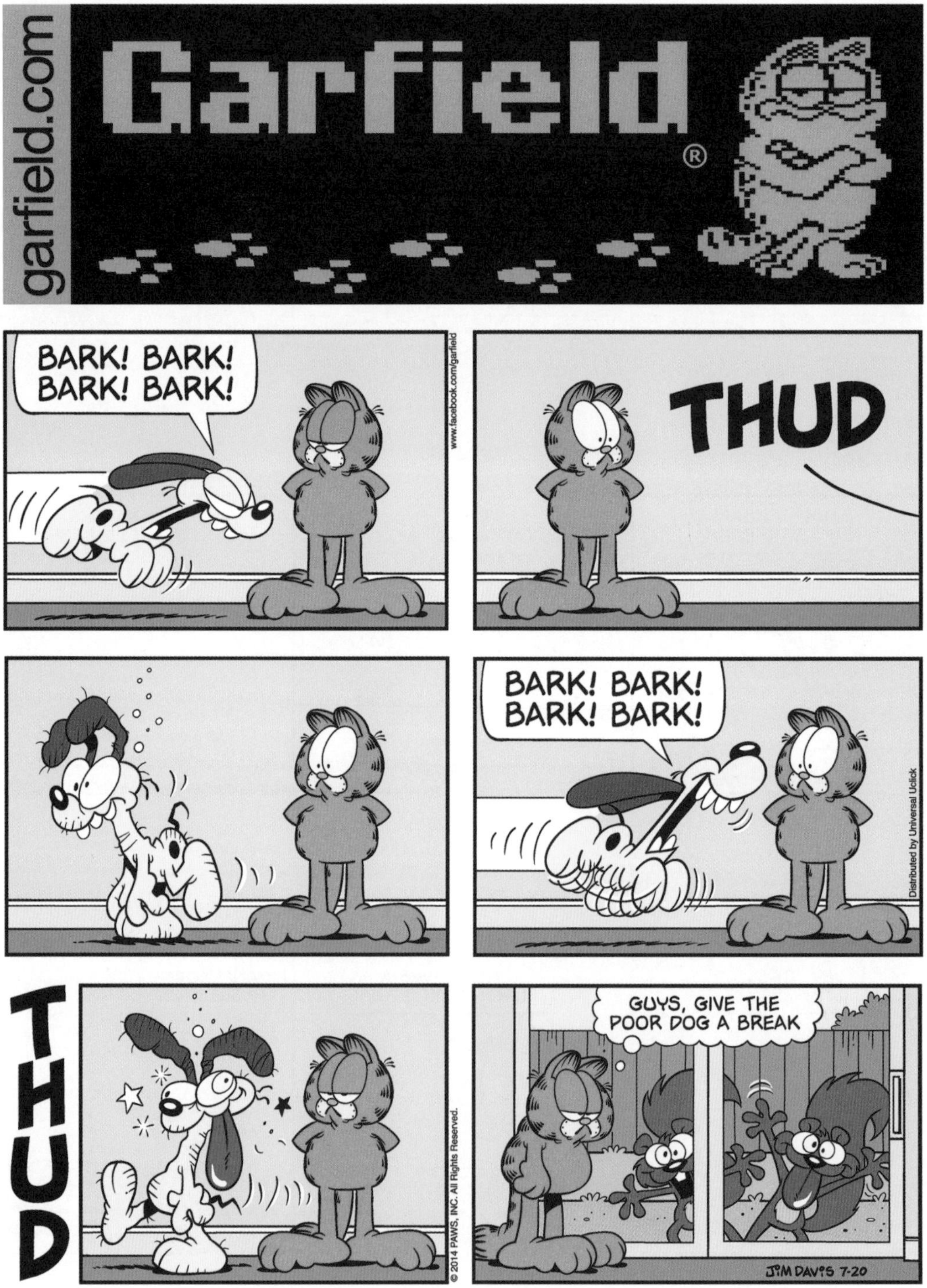
garfield.com
Garfield®
BARK! BARK! BARK! BARK!
www.facebook.com/garfield
THUD
BARK! BARK! BARK! BARK!
Distributed by Universal Uclick
THUD
© 2014 PAWS, INC. All Rights Reserved.
GUYS, GIVE THE POOR DOG A BREAK
JIM DAVIS 7-20

www.facebook.com/garfield
Distributed by Universal Uclick
BLAT
© 2014 PAWS, INC. All Rights Reserved.
COFFEE WORE OFF, EH?
WHO TOLD?
JIM DAVIS 7-21

MY NEW GIRLFRIEND IS FROM ANOTHER COUNTRY
www.facebook.com/garfield
Distributed by Universal Uclick
ANOTHER COUNTRY?
© 2014 PAWS, INC. All Rights Reserved.
SHE LIVES IN THE BASEMENT
DOES SHE SPEAK ENGLISH?
JIM DAVIS 7-22

SOMEDAY WE MAY BE VISITED BY CREATURES FROM ANOTHER PLANET
www.facebook.com/garfield
Distributed by Universal Uclick
© 2014 PAWS, INC. All Rights Reserved.
I HID THE COOKIE JAR
JIM DAVIS 7-23

MMM
WHOLE WHEAT!
MMM
WHOLE BACON!
www.facebook.com/garfield
Distributed by Universal Uclick
© 2014 PAWS, INC. All Rights Reserved.
JIM DAVIS 7-24

WHAT HAVE YOU BEEN UP TO, JON?
I'VE BEEN DATING YOU
I ALREADY KNEW THAT
THAT'S ALL HE'S GOT, LADY
www.facebook.com/garfield
Distributed by Universal Uclick
© 2014 PAWS, INC. All Rights Reserved.
JIM DAVIS 7-25

WE'RE OUT OF KETCHUP...
SO I PUT WHIPPED CREAM ON YOUR SANDWICH
HE KNOWS ME WELL
www.facebook.com/garfield
Distributed by Universal Uclick
© 2014 PAWS, INC. All Rights Reserved.
JIM DAVIS 7-26

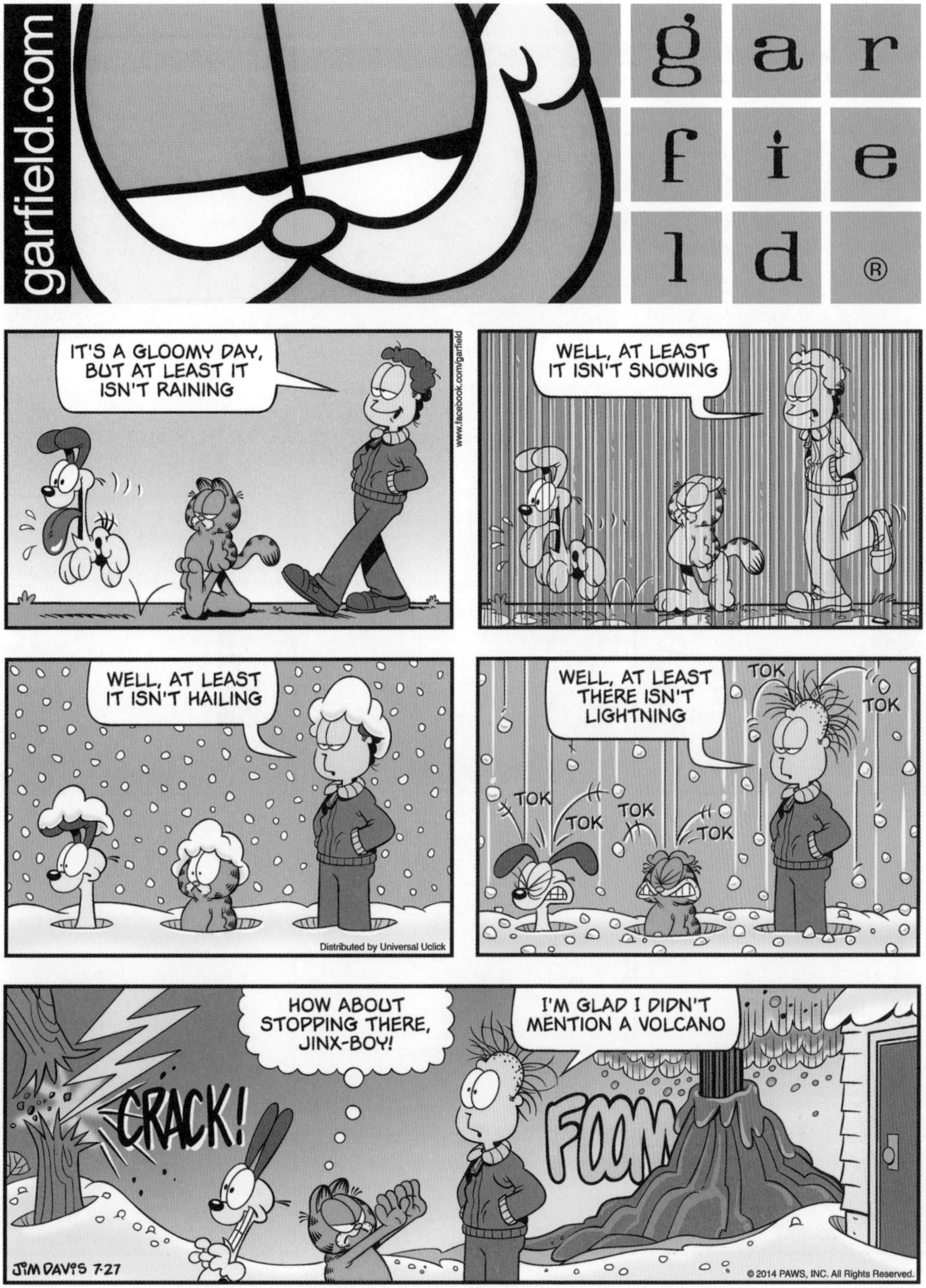

garfield.com
garfield®
IT'S A GLOOMY DAY, BUT AT LEAST IT ISN'T RAINING
www.facebook.com/garfield
WELL, AT LEAST IT ISN'T SNOWING
WELL, AT LEAST IT ISN'T HAILING
Distributed by Universal Uclick
WELL, AT LEAST THERE ISN'T LIGHTNING
TOK
TOK
TOK
TOK
TOK
TOK
HOW ABOUT STOPPING THERE, JINX-BOY!
CRACK!
I'M GLAD I DIDN'T MENTION A VOLCANO
FOOM
JIM DAVIS 7-27
© 2014 PAWS, INC. All Rights Reserved.

GARFIELD, I JUST HAD A PROFOUND THOUGHT!...
DARN!
MAY IT REST IN PEACE
JIM DAVIS 7-28
Distributed by Universal Uclick www.facebook.com/garfield
© 2014 PAWS, INC. All Rights Reserved.

WELCOME TO "PRACTICAL JOKES!"
TED HAS PUT A SQUIRREL IN HIS WIFE CINDY'S PURSE. LET'S WATCH...
UH, CINDY, DO YOU HAVE ANY GUM?
AND THE NUMBER OF A GOOD DIVORCE LAWYER?
JIM DAVIS 7-29
Distributed by Universal Uclick www.facebook.com/garfield
© 2014 PAWS, INC. All Rights Reserved.

ARF
ARF
ARF
ARF
PRIVATE CONVERSATION
JIM DAVIS 7-30
Distributed by Universal Uclick www.facebook.com/garfield
© 2014 PAWS, INC. All Rights Reserved.

CATS CAN SENSE WHEN SOMETHING IS WRONG
SMACK!
OW!
THAT HURT!
I KNEW THAT...
www.facebook.com/garfield
Distributed by Universal Uclick
© 2014 PAWS, INC. All Rights Reserved.
JIM DAVIS 7-31

LIZ AND I RODE A ROLLER COASTER TODAY. IT WENT WAY UP IN THE AIR...
AND THEN WENT WAY DOWN
AM I BLINKING?
NOT YET
www.facebook.com/garfield
Distributed by Universal Uclick
© 2014 PAWS, INC. All Rights Reserved.
JIM DAVIS 8-1

HARD-CORE SPORTS FANS ARE CRAZY
© 2014 PAWS, INC. All Rights Reserved.
JIM DAVIS 8-2
www.facebook.com/garfield
Distributed by Universal Uclick
BUT HARD-CORE GAME SHOW FANS ARE EVEN CRAZIER
AARDVARK! AARDVARK! AARDVARK!
AND THE ANSWER IS "PLATYPUS"

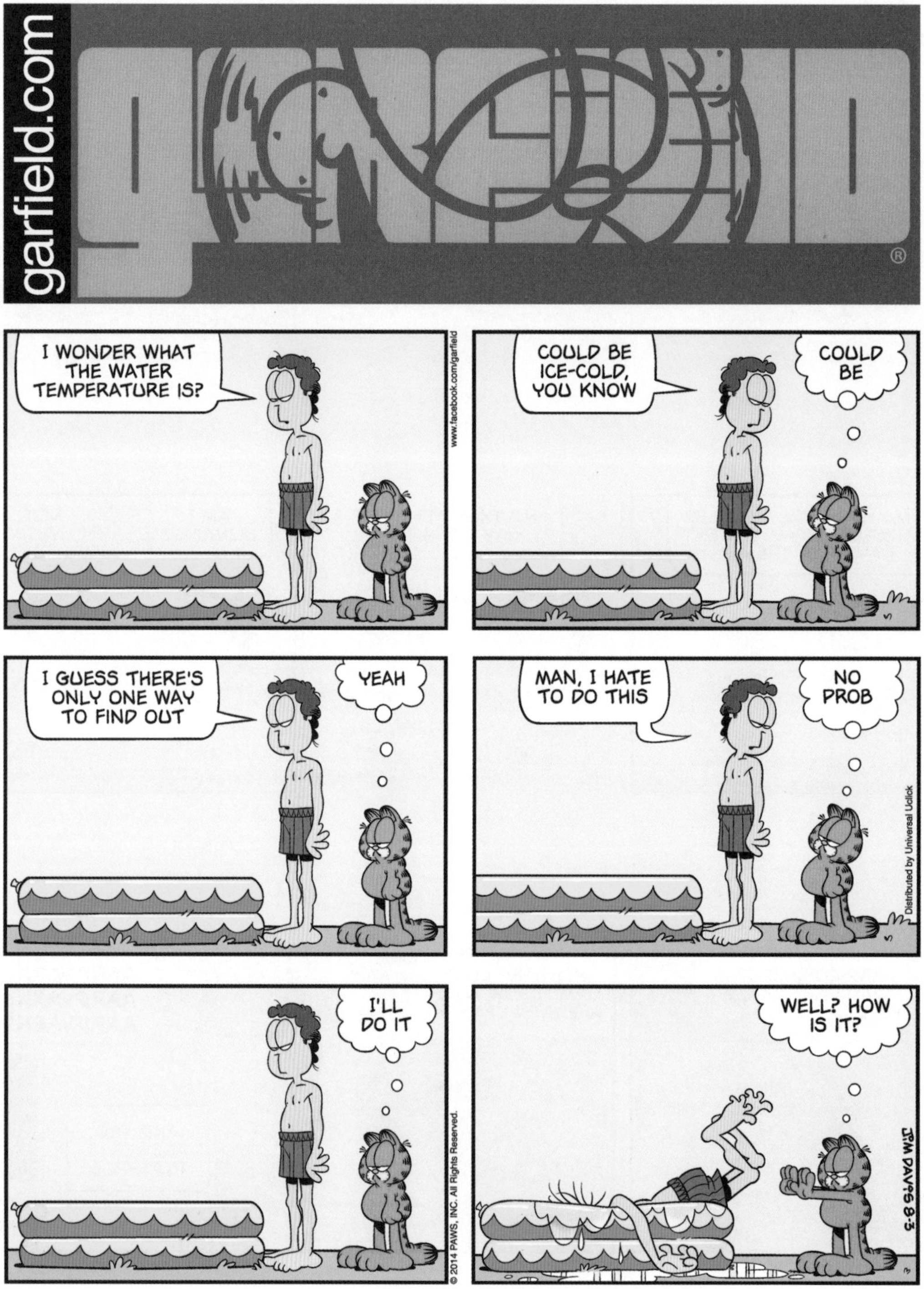
garfield.com
GARFIELD®
I WONDER WHAT THE WATER TEMPERATURE IS?
www.facebook.com/garfield
COULD BE ICE-COLD, YOU KNOW
COULD BE
I GUESS THERE'S ONLY ONE WAY TO FIND OUT
YEAH
MAN, I HATE TO DO THIS
NO PROB
Distributed by Universal Uclick
I'LL DO IT
© 2014 PAWS, INC. All Rights Reserved.
WELL? HOW IS IT?
JIM DAVIS 8-3

DO SOMETHING WITH THE MICE, GARFIELD!
OKAY
JIM DAVIS 8-4
www.facebook.com/garfield
Distributed by Universal Uclick
HAVING DINNER IS NOT WHAT I MEANT!
WELL, THEN, I GUESS THAT WE SHOULD BE A LITTLE MORE SPECIFIC, SHOULDN'T WE?
© 2014 PAWS, INC. All Rights Reserved.

I HEARD OF A CURE FOR STRESS
JIM DAVIS 8-5
www.facebook.com/garfield
Distributed by Universal Uclick
RELAXING YOUR FACIAL MUSCLES
AH, THAT'S BETTER
FOR YOU, MAYBE
© 2014 PAWS, INC. All Rights Reserved.

WHY DO DOGS BURY BONES?...
JIM DAVIS 8-6
www.facebook.com/garfield
Distributed by Universal Uclick
NOBODY KNOWS
DIG DIG DIG
HANG ON...
© 2014 PAWS, INC. All Rights Reserved.

I THINK IT'S FLEA SEASON
I FEEL ITCHY
AND I SEE TINY LADDERS
JIM DAVIS 8-7
Distributed by Universal Uclick
www.facebook.com/garfield
© 2014 PAWS, INC. All Rights Reserved.

HAVE YOU EVER PUT YOUR SHOES ON BEFORE YOUR SOCKS?
NO
OH, ME NEITHER!
UH-HUH
JIM DAVIS 8-8
Distributed by Universal Uclick
www.facebook.com/garfield
© 2014 PAWS, INC. All Rights Reserved.

HELP WANTED
JUST WHAT I NEED!
HELP WANTED
BRING ME A CHEESEBURGER AND A STRAWBERRY MILK SHAKE
HELP WANTED
JIM DAVIS 8-9
Distributed by Universal Uclick
www.facebook.com/garfield
© 2014 PAWS, INC. All Rights Reserved.

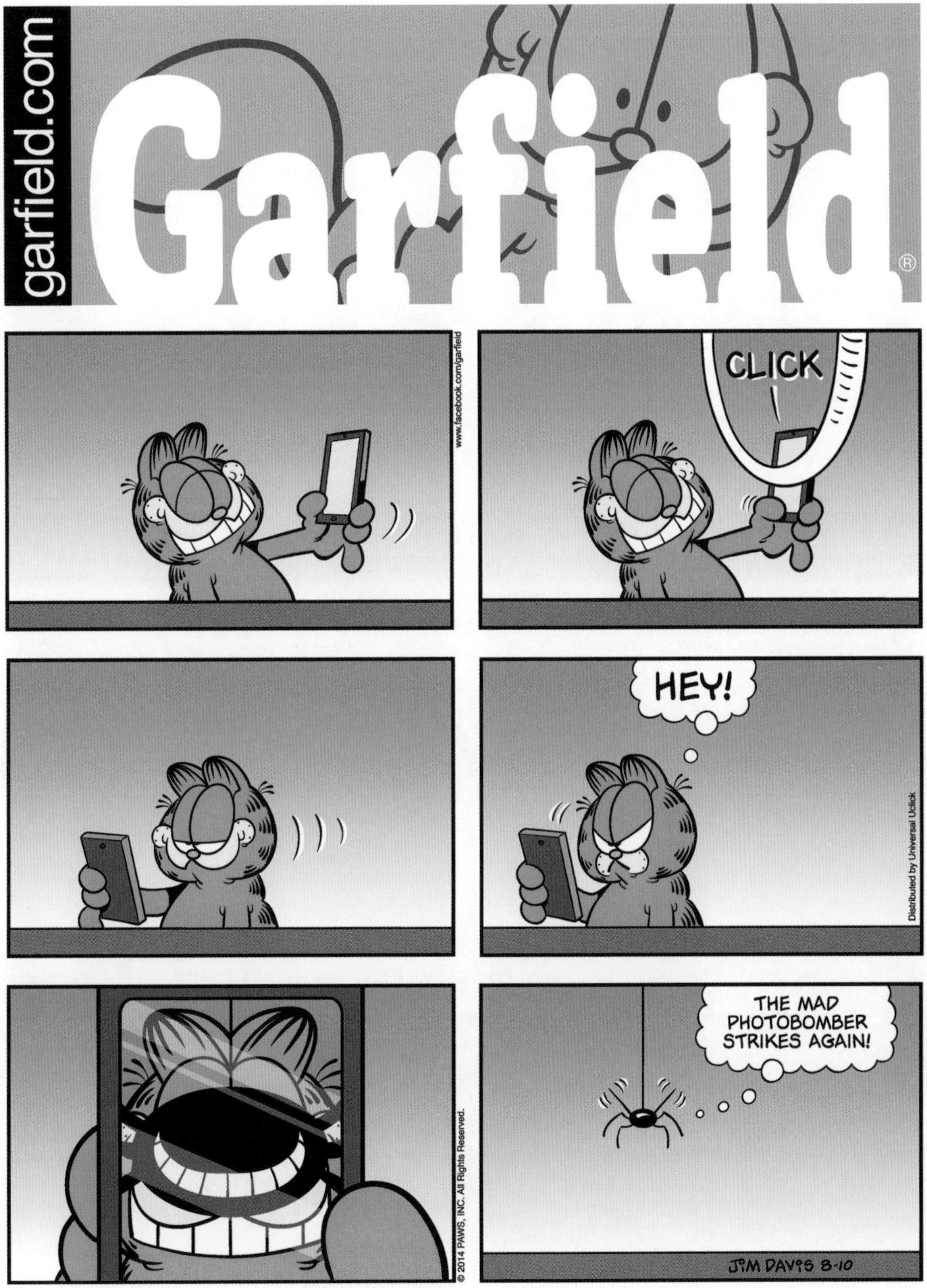
garfield.com
Garfield®
www.facebook.com/garfield
CLICK
HEY!
Distributed by Universal Uclick
© 2014 PAWS, INC. All Rights Reserved.
THE MAD PHOTOBOMBER STRIKES AGAIN!
JIM DAVIS 8-10

FEAR ME, WORLD!
TOING!
ALMOST FORGOT THAT PART
JIM DAVIS 8-11
www.facebook.com/garfield
Distributed by Universal Uclick
© 2014 PAWS, INC. All Rights Reserved.

HELLO, SWINDELL PIZZA? I'D LIKE A LARGE PEPPERONI
NO, I DON'T NEED A TWO-LITER OF SODA. JUST...
NO, I DON'T NEED ANY WINGS WITH THAT
NO, I DON'T WANT ANY BREADSTICKS, EITHER. JUST THE PIZZA
AND JUST WHY WOULD I NEED A SERVICE PLAN FOR A PIZZA?!
THE OLD UPSELL
JIM DAVIS 8-12
www.facebook.com/garfield
Distributed by Universal Uclick
© 2014 PAWS, INC. All Rights Reserved.

I'M ORDERING A PIZZA. WHAT SHOULD I GET?
YES, COULD I GET A LARGE...MUSHROOM PIZZA...
WITH FROGS... AND MAKE IT SAD
SO MUCH FOR CHICKEN AND ONION
JIM DAVIS 8-13
www.facebook.com/garfield
Distributed by Universal Uclick
© 2014 PAWS, INC. All Rights Reserved.

HAPPY SLAP-IN-THE-BACK-OF-THE-HEAD DAY!
www.facebook.com/garfield
Distributed by Universal Uclick
SLAP!
© 2014 PAWS, INC. All Rights Reserved.
NOT ONE OF JON'S FAVORITE HOLIDAYS
JIM DAVIS 8-14

LIZ PUT ME ON A HEALTHY DIET
www.facebook.com/garfield
Distributed by Universal Uclick
SHE THINKS I'M STICKING TO IT, BUT I'M NOT
© 2014 PAWS, INC. All Rights Reserved.
I FEEL SO GUILTY
DONUTS HELP
JIM DAVIS 8-15

I'M GOING TO SPEND THE DAY SEEING THE WORLD LIKE YOU!
WELCOME
www.facebook.com/garfield
Distributed by Universal Uclick
THERE'S NOT MUCH TO DO DOWN HERE, IS THERE?
NOW YOU'RE GETTING IT...
© 2014 PAWS, INC. All Rights Reserved.
JIM DAVIS 8-16
Z
AND NOW YOU'VE GOT IT

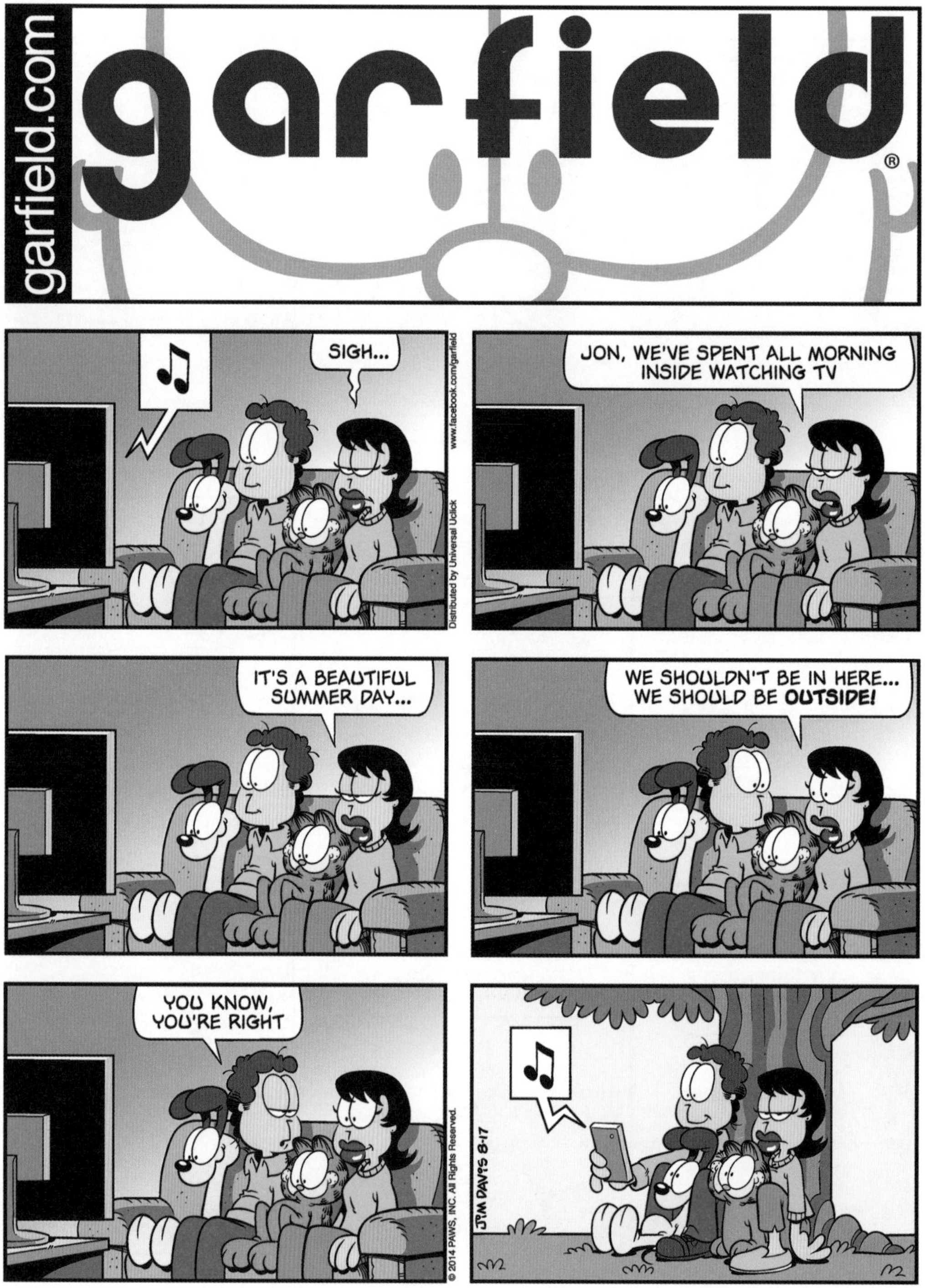
garfield.com
garfield
♫
SIGH...
www.facebook.com/garfield
Distributed by Universal Uclick
JON, WE'VE SPENT ALL MORNING INSIDE WATCHING TV
IT'S A BEAUTIFUL SUMMER DAY...
WE SHOULDN'T BE IN HERE... WE SHOULD BE **OUTSIDE!**
YOU KNOW, YOU'RE RIGHT
© 2014 PAWS, INC. All Rights Reserved.
JIM DAVIS 8-17
♫

SIP
SIP
JIM DAVIS 8-18
Distributed by Universal Uclick
www.facebook.com/garfield
ZANG
ZONG
© 2014 PAWS, INC. All Rights Reserved.
OWOOO
WE LIKE OUR COFFEE STRONG ENOUGH TO FIGHT CRIME

HELLO, MIME PIZZA? I'D LIKE A LARGE PEPPERONI
Distributed by Universal Uclick
www.facebook.com/garfield
HELLO?
© 2014 PAWS, INC. All Rights Reserved.
JIM DAVIS 8-19
I'M NOT SURE WHETHER I JUST ORDERED A PIZZA OR NOT
LET'S HOPE THE DELIVERY BOY DOESN'T HAVE TO WALK HERE AGAINST THE WIND

OKAY, ODIE... FETCH THE STICK!
Distributed by Universal Uclick
www.facebook.com/garfield
CHOMP
© 2014 PAWS, INC. All Rights Reserved.
JIM DAVIS 8-20
AFTER I THROW IT, IF YOU PLEASE...

TIME TO LIFT WEIGHTS, GARFIELD
www.facebook.com/garfield
Distributed by Universal Uclick
© 2014 PAWS, INC. All Rights Reserved.
OOPS, TOO LATE NOW
THAT WAS CLOSE
JIM DAVIS 8-21

HOW'S MY SWEETY, WEETY, WIZZY LIZ?
CLICK CLICK CLICK
www.facebook.com/garfield
Distributed by Universal Uclick
HOW'S MY WIDDLE LOVE PUMPKIN?
CLICK CLICK CLICK CLICK
© 2014 PAWS, INC. All Rights Reserved.
EXCUSE ME ONE MOMENT
STUPID REMOTE
CLICK CLICK CLICK
JIM DAVIS 8-22

I'M GOING TO SPEND THE DAY ON ALL FOURS, SO I CAN SEE THE WORLD AS YOU DO!
BE MY GUEST
JIM DAVIS 8-23
www.facebook.com/garfield
Distributed by Universal Uclick
WOW, EVERYTHING LOOKS SO BIG...
© 2014 PAWS, INC. All Rights Reserved.
AND YOU HAVE A **LOT** OF LINT IN YOUR WORLD
YEAH, PEOPLE SHED, TOO

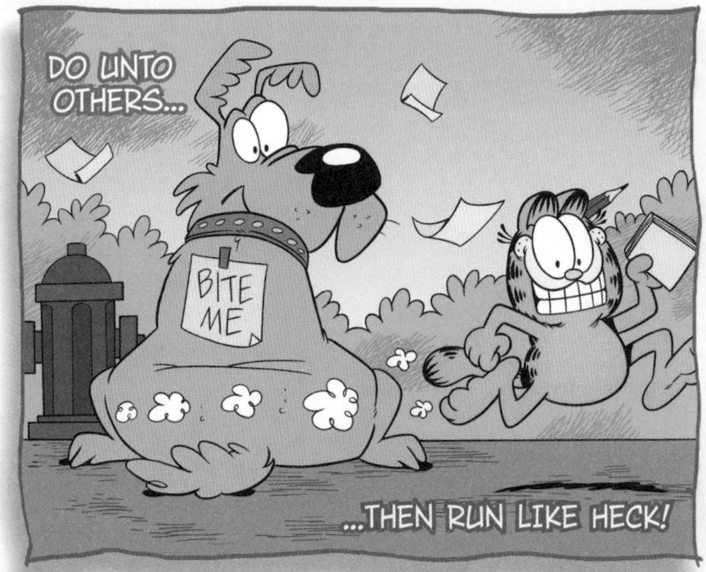
DO UNTO OTHERS...
BITE ME
...THEN RUN LIKE HECK!

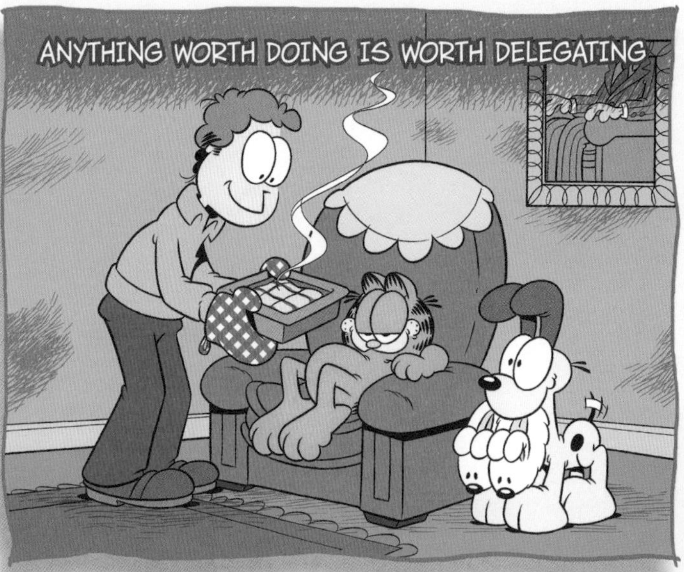
ANYTHING WORTH DOING IS WORTH DELEGATING

THOUGHTS TO CHEW ON

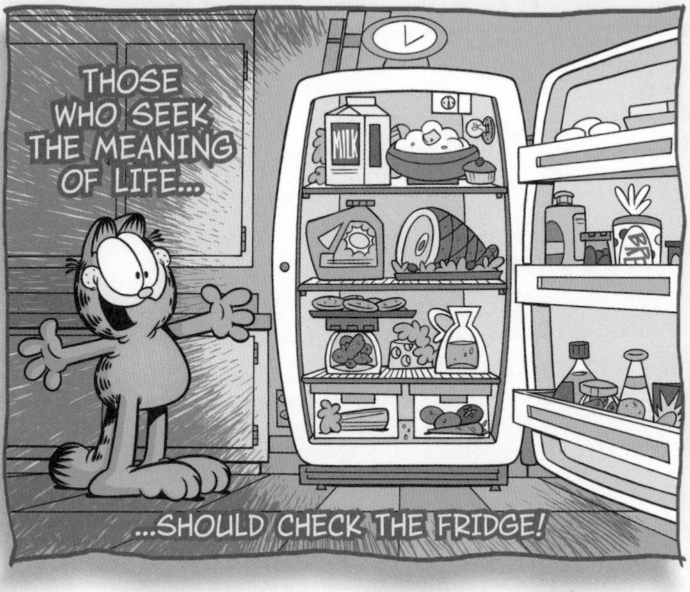
THOSE WHO SEEK THE MEANING OF LIFE...
MILK
...SHOULD CHECK THE FRIDGE!

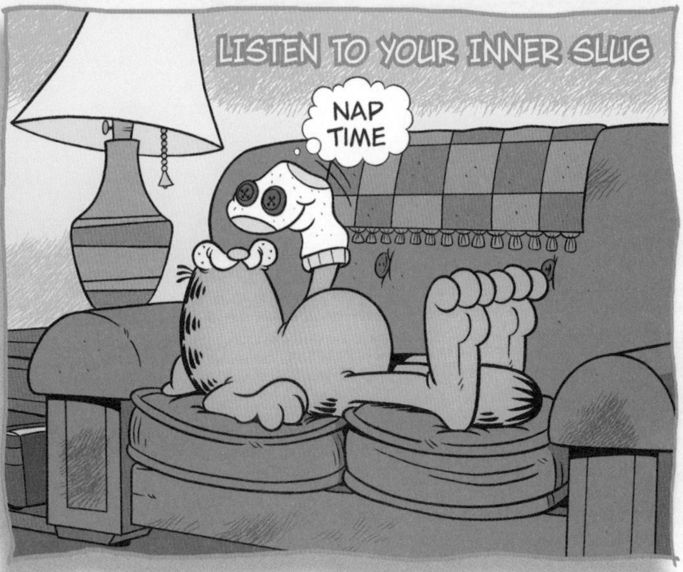
LISTEN TO YOUR INNER SLUG
NAP TIME

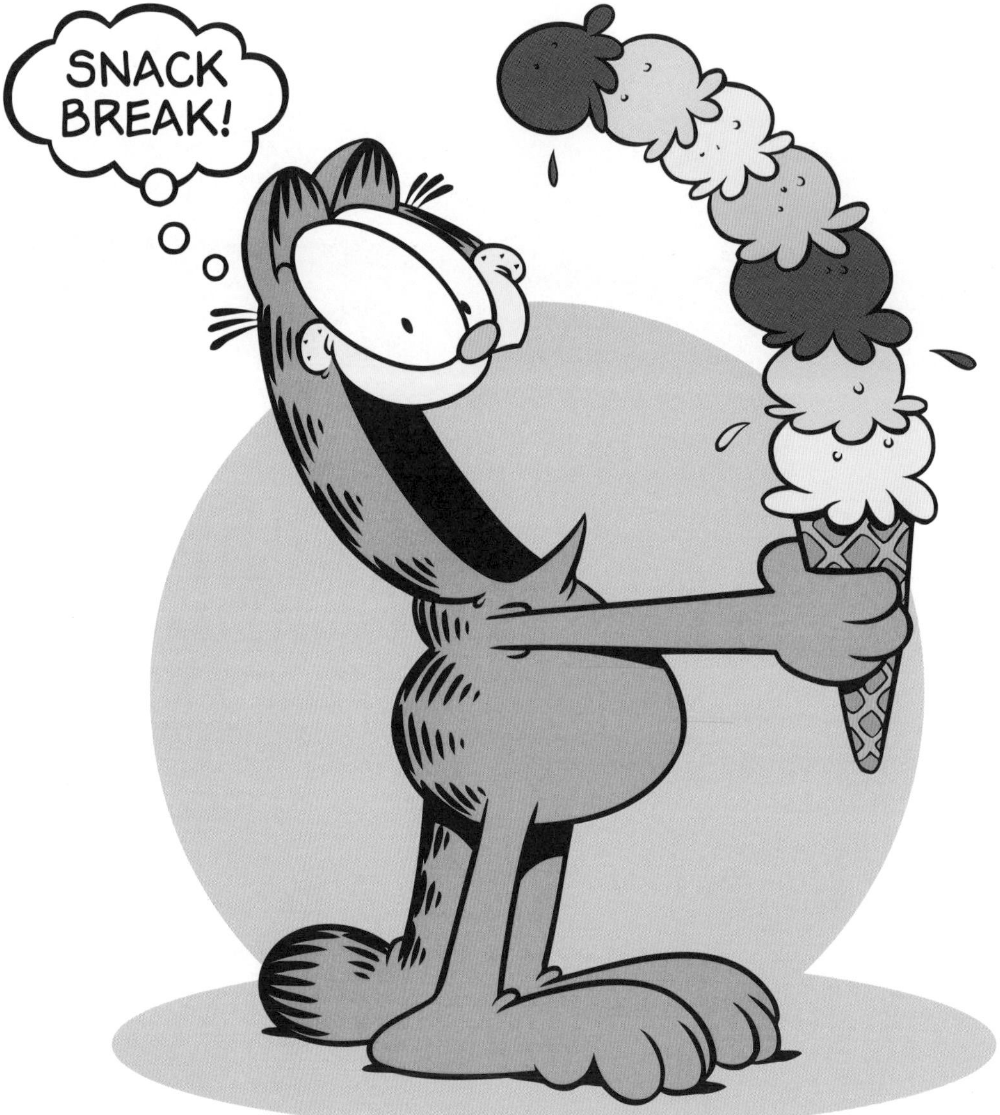
SNACK BREAK!

Garfield
Cooks Up Trouble

BY JIM DAVIS

Ballantine Books • New York

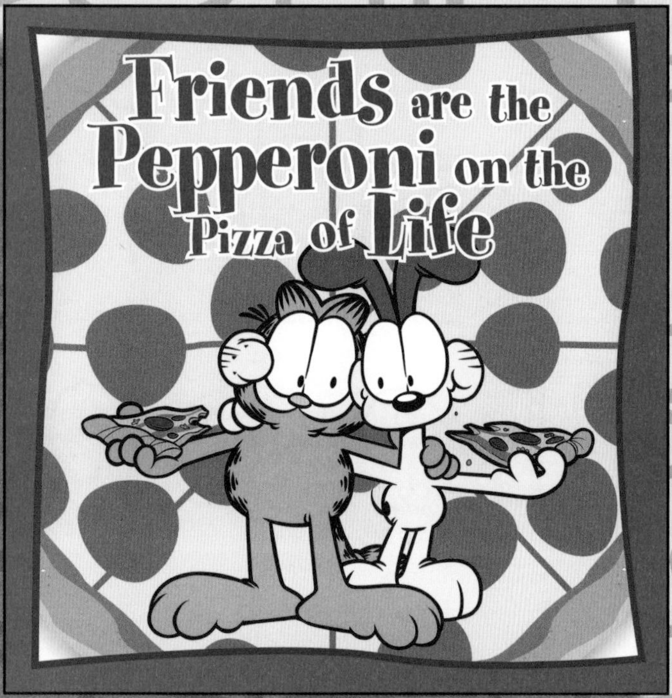
Friends are the Pepperoni on the Pizza of Life

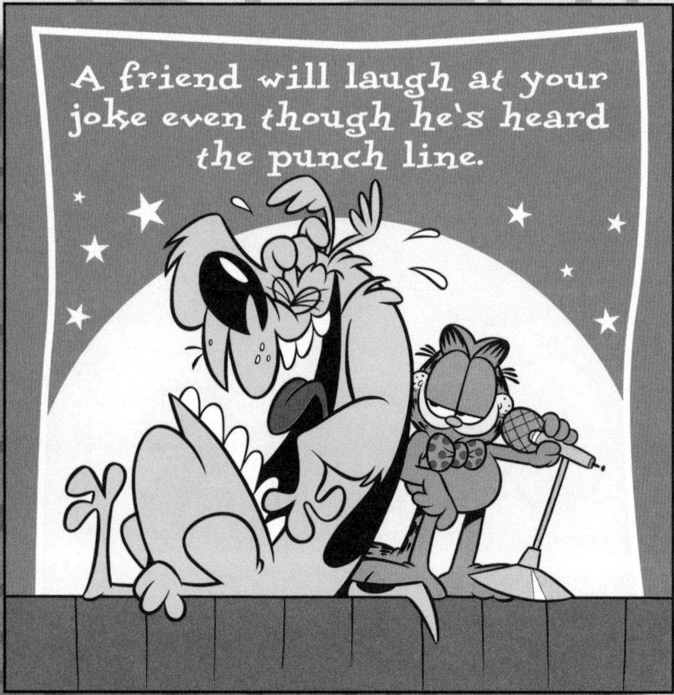
A friend will laugh at your joke even though he's heard the punch line.

FRIENDSHIP

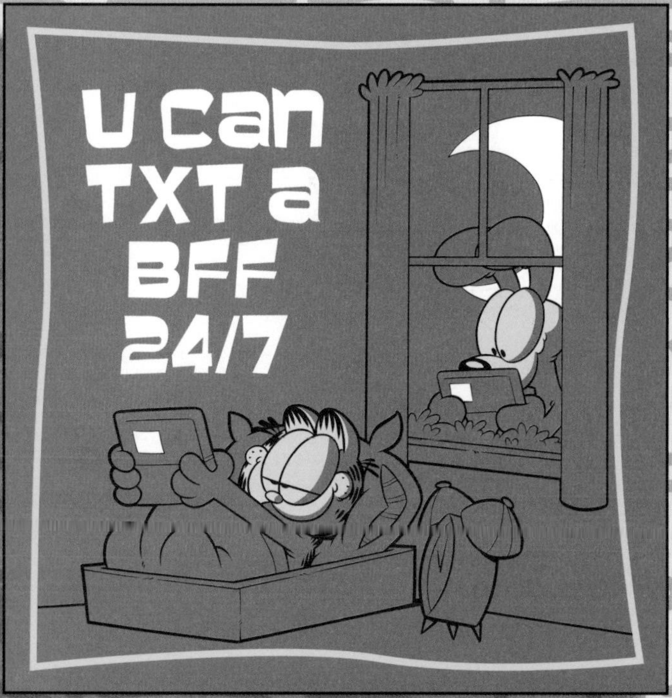
U can TXT a BFF 24/7

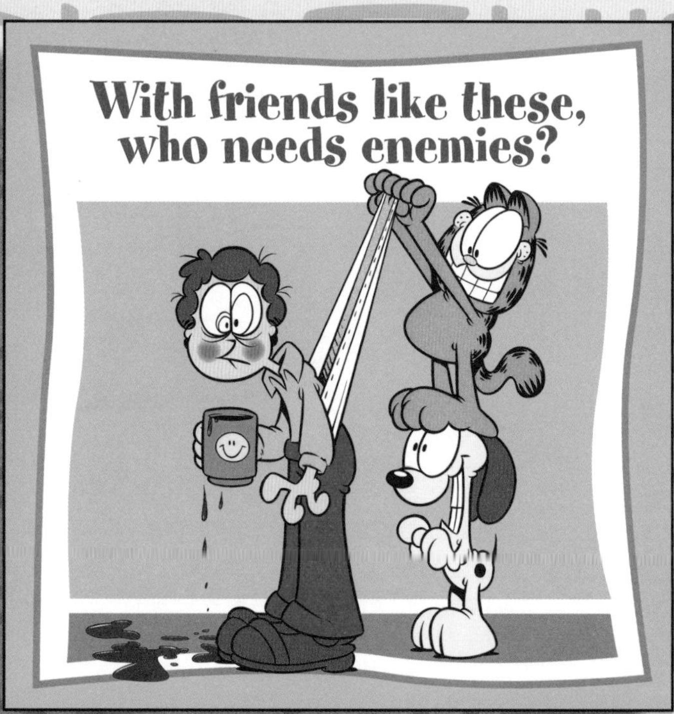
With friends like these, who needs enemies?

garfield.com
GARFIELD
www.facebook.com/garfield
Precious
Garfield
Mittens
Pumpkin
AH, YOUR OBEDIENCE SCHOOL YEARBOOK...
I REMEMBER MITTENS
YEAH, THERE'S A WEIRDO IN EVERY CLASS
© 2014 PAWS, INC. All Rights Reserved.
JIM DAVIS 8-24
Distributed by Universal Uclick

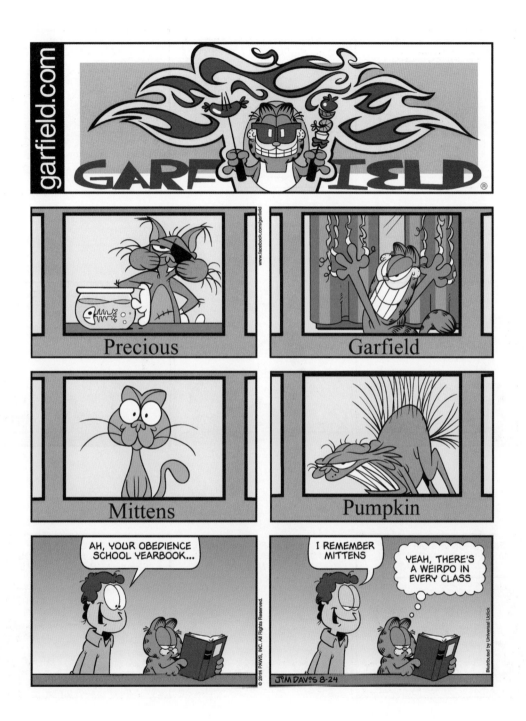

SOMETIMES, WHEN I WATCH THE NEWS, I THINK THAT HUMANITY MIGHT BE IN TROUBLE
JIM DAVIS 8-25
www.facebook.com/garfield
Distributed by Universal Uclick
BUT THEN I LOOK OUT THE WINDOW ON A BRIGHT, SUNNY DAY...
© 2014 PAWS, INC. All Rights Reserved.
AND I **KNOW** IT'S IN TROUBLE

GARFIELD
JIM DAVIS 8-26
www.facebook.com/garfield
Distributed by Universal Uclick
FOOD
GARFIELD
© 2014 PAWS, INC. All Rights Reserved.
THANKS FOR POINTING THAT OUT
GARFIELD

ONCE UPON A TIME THERE WAS A HOUSE WITH A MAN, A DOG, AND A CAT
JIM DAVIS 8-27
www.facebook.com/garfield
Distributed by Universal Uclick
THE MAN WAS THIN, THE DOG WAS HAPPY, AND THE CAT WAS FAT
© 2014 PAWS, INC. All Rights Reserved.
THEN THE CAT ATE MY BREAKFAST, AND THE DOG CHEWED UP MY SLIPPERS THIS MORNING!
THIS SOUNDS FAMILIAR

DO NOT BE JEALOUS OF MY AWESOMENESS
www.facebook.com/garfield
Distributed by Universal Uclick
OH, OKAY. GO AHEAD!
© 2014 PAWS, INC. All Rights Reserved.
JIM DAVIS 8-28

LIZ CARES ABOUT ME
www.facebook.com/garfield
Distributed by Universal Uclick
SHE PUT ME ON A HEALTHY DIET
NOW I'M GOING TO CARE ABOUT YOU
VENT YOUR HOSTILITY ELSEWHERE, SLIM
© 2014 PAWS, INC. All Rights Reserved.
JIM DAVIS 8-29

www.facebook.com/garfield
Distributed by Universal Uclick
© 2014 PAWS, INC. All Rights Reserved.
JIM DAVIS 8-30
IF YOU WANT ME TO MOVE, JUST SAY SO

garfield.com
GARFIELD
MMMMM...A NICE NAP OUTSIDE. WHY DON'T I DO THIS MORE OFTEN?
www.facebook.com/garfield
FOO!
PLIP
Distributed by Universal Uclick
SMACK!
BEAT IT!
JIM DAVIS 8-31
© 2014 PAWS, INC. All Rights Reserved.
IT WAS HIM, DADDY!
AH, YES. THIS IS WHY

WELL, AT LEAST MONDAY'S OVER
MON.
JIM DAVIS 9-1
Distributed by Universal Uclick
www.facebook.com/garfield
RIP
MON.
© 2014 PAWS, INC. All Rights Reserved.
I'LL BE GOING BACK TO BED NOW
MON.

JIM DAVIS 9-2
Distributed by Universal Uclick
www.facebook.com/garfield
STOP RIGHT THERE!
© 2014 PAWS, INC. All Rights Reserved.
YOU ARE LOOKIN' **GREAT** TODAY!
BACK ATCHA!

OKAY, ODIE. GET READY, ANNND...
Distributed by Universal Uclick
www.facebook.com/garfield
FETCH YOURSELF!
© 2014 PAWS, INC. All Rights Reserved.
GARFIELD!
JIM DAVIS 9-3

HELLO, WORLD'S FASTEST PIZZA? I'D LIKE A LARGE PEPPERONI...
Distributed by Universal Uclick www.facebook.com/garfield
UM...
ZHOOP
© 2014 PAWS, INC. All Rights Reserved.
WITH EXTRA CHEESE
THESE GUYS ARE GOOD
JIM DAVIS 9-4

I'M NOT SURE LIZ THINKS THAT I'M SUAVE
NONSENSE!
Distributed by Universal Uclick www.facebook.com/garfield
BURP!
SCRATCH SCRATCH SCRATCH
SNIFF SNIFF
© 2014 PAWS, INC. All Rights Reserved.
JIM DAVIS 9-5
YOU SEEM SUAVE TO ME

I'VE GOT NOTHING TO DO
Distributed by Universal Uclick www.facebook.com/garfield
NOPE...NOTHING... NOTHING AT ALL...
© 2014 PAWS, INC. All Rights Reserved.
DID I MENTION THAT I'VE GOT NOTHING TO DO?
YOU COULD SHUT UP!
JIM DAVIS 9-6

garfield.com
GARFIELD®
SNIFF SNIFF SNIFF SNIFF SNIFF SNIFF
www.facebook.com/garfield
Distributed by Universal Uclick
SNIFF SNIFF SNIFF SNIFF SNIFF SNIFF SNIFF SNIFF
THIS HAS BEEN "THE DOG SHOW"
JIM DAVIS 9-7
CLICK
WELCOME TO "THE CAT SHOW"
© 2014 PAWS, INC. All Rights Reserved.
Z
Z

ARE YOU GOING TO LIE THERE ALL DAY?
THAT'S THE PLAN
Distributed by Universal Uclick www.facebook.com/garfield
YOU WON'T GET ANYTHING DONE LIKE THAT
ALSO PART OF THE PLAN
© 2014 PAWS, INC. All Rights Reserved.
YOU'RE GOING TO DISINTEGRATE INTO A BIG PILE OF DUST AND JUST BLOW AWAY!
SOMEONE'S LEAKED THE PLAN!
JIM DAVIS 9-8

AND NOW, TO EXPLAIN THE MEANING OF LIFE, HERE'S ODIE
Distributed by Universal Uclick www.facebook.com/garfield
Z
© 2014 PAWS, INC. All Rights Reserved.
I'VE NEVER FELT CLOSER TO YOU
JIM DAVIS 9-9

WHAT A GREAT NIGHT, HUH, GARFIELD?
Distributed by Universal Uclick www.facebook.com/garfield
MY AUNT WALBURGA USED TO SAY THE STARS WERE TINY FAIRIES WHO WATCH OVER US AND BRING US GOOD LUCK
© 2014 PAWS, INC. All Rights Reserved.
JIM DAVIS 9-10
THEN SHE STEPPED RIGHT OFF THE EDGE OF THE CANYON
I'M GOING HOME NOW

LIVERWURST...HORSERADISH... AND ANCHOVY PASTE! VOILÀ! THE PERFECT SANDWICH!
Distributed by Universal Uclick
www.facebook.com/garfield
© 2014 PAWS, INC. All Rights Reserved.
HOW COME YOU'RE NOT ANSWERING YOUR PHONE?
JIM DAVIS 9-11

WHERE CAN WE GO ON VACATION THIS YEAR, GARFIELD?
Distributed by Universal Uclick
www.facebook.com/garfield
ASIDE FROM A LASAGNA FACTORY
© 2014 PAWS, INC. All Rights Reserved.
JIM DAVIS 9-12
THAT'S A STUMPER

YAH!
Distributed by Universal Uclick
www.facebook.com/garfield
THIS PUDDLE WAS DEEPER THAN IT LOOKED!
© 2014 PAWS, INC. All Rights Reserved.
LIKE HE NEEDED TO POINT THAT OUT
A LITTLE HELP...
JIM DAVIS 9-13

garfield.com
Garfield®
www.facebook.com/garfield
1989
1995
2004
2011
JIM DAVIS 9-14
Distributed by Universal Uclick
© 2014 PAWS, INC. All Rights Reserved.
ALBUM
ALBUM
BOY, HAVE WE EVER HAD BORING LIVES
OH, I DON'T KNOW... REMEMBER THE MOUSTACHE?

I'M GOING TO READ JON'S MIND
HE WANTS ME TO EAT THE LAST COOKIE
JIM DAVIS 9-15
www.facebook.com/garfield
Distributed by Universal Uclick
© 2014 PAWS, INC. All Rights Reserved.

BEWARE OF SHY DOG
JIM DAVIS 9-16
YOU CAN COME OUT NOW
I CAN STILL HEAR YOU
www.facebook.com/garfield
Distributed by Universal Uclick
© 2014 PAWS, INC. All Rights Reserved.

NOW, TO ORDER THE PIZZA
JIM DAVIS 9-17
I'D LIKE A LARGE PEPPERONI WITH EXTRA CHEESE, PLEASE
NEXT, WE SIT ON THE COUCH, POP JELLY BEANS, AND WAIT
MY FAVORITE COOKING SHOW
www.facebook.com/garfield
Distributed by Universal Uclick
© 2014 PAWS, INC. All Rights Reserved.

JIM DAVIS 9-18
www.facebook.com/garfield
Distributed by Universal Uclick
BOY, IT'S DARK OUTSIDE!
THAT'S THE CLOSET
© 2014 PAWS, INC. All Rights Reserved.

I'M BORED
www.facebook.com/garfield
Distributed by Universal Uclick
LET'S GO SOMEPLACE WHERE WE CAN MEET SOME **GIRL** SOCK PUPPETS!
© 2014 PAWS, INC. All Rights Reserved.
I'LL DO ALL THE TALKING
I'LL TRY NOT TO PUT A CRIMP IN YOUR STYLE
JIM DAVIS 9-19

www.facebook.com/garfield
Distributed by Universal Uclick
HMMM
© 2014 PAWS, INC. All Rights Reserved.
JIM DAVIS 9-20
MUST BE LUNCHTIME

garfield.com
Garfield®
THUNK!
GAH!
www.facebook.com/garfield
YAAAHHH!
OW! OW!
OW! OW!
OW! OW!
Distributed by Universal Uclick
JIM DAVIS 9.21
© 2014 PAWS, INC. All Rights Reserved.
THUNK!
THAT'LL SHOW THAT OLD NAIL!
GAAHH HHHH

WELCOME TO "DEEP THOUGHTS"
DO SPACE ALIENS GET ACNE?
GOOD NIGHT FROM "DEEP THOUGHTS"
JIM DAVIS 9-22
www.facebook.com/garfield
Distributed by Universal Uclick
© 2014 PAWS, INC. All Rights Reserved.

MAYBE WE SHOULD TAKE SEPARATE VACATIONS THIS YEAR
I WILL GO SOMEWHERE FUN
BECAUSE YOU WILL NOT BE THERE
JIM DAVIS 9-23
www.facebook.com/garfield
Distributed by Universal Uclick
© 2014 PAWS, INC. All Rights Reserved.

BEWARE OF DOG
JIM DAVIS 9-24
AND I NEED TO BEWARE OF YOU BECAUSE...
BECAUSE I HAVE THE SNIFFLES!
AH-CHOO!
I GUESS A GUY'S GOTTA MAKE A LIVING
www.facebook.com/garfield
Distributed by Universal Uclick
© 2014 PAWS, INC. All Rights Reserved.

SEVERE WEATHER IS IN THE AREA
Distributed by Universal Uclick
www.facebook.com/garfield
DING-DONG!
© 2014 PAWS, INC. All Rights Reserved.
JIM DAVIS 9-25
DON'T ANSWER THAT!

DONUTS ARE BAD FOR YOU, YOU KNOW
Distributed by Universal Uclick
www.facebook.com/garfield
© 2014 PAWS, INC. All Rights Reserved.
JIM DAVIS 9-26
THEY AREN'T AS BAD FOR ME AS I AM FOR THEM

Distributed by Universal Uclick
www.facebook.com/garfield
© 2014 PAWS, INC. All Rights Reserved.
JIM DAVIS 9-27
I'VE HAD WORSE

garfield.com
GARFIELD
HI, MY NAME'S FINN! WHAT'S YOUR NAME?
www.facebook.com/garfield
I JUST MOVED IN TODAY! IS THIS A NICE PLACE? DO YOU LIKE IT HERE?
Distributed by Universal Uclick
IT LOOKS LIKE WE'RE GOING TO BE ROOMIES! I HOPE YOU DON'T SNORE, OR LIKE LOUD MUSIC...
© 2014 PAWS, INC. All Rights Reserved.
HE JUST MIGHT BE TOO STUPID TO EAT
YOU DON'T TALK MUCH, DO YOU?
JIM DAVIS 9-28

IT'S STRANGE, GARFIELD
EVERY TIME I GO INTO THE PET STORE...
THE GOLDFISH SCREAM
DID YOU PICK A BIG, JUICY ONE?
www.facebook.com/garfield
Distributed by Universal Uclick
© 2014 PAWS, INC. All Rights Reserved.
JIM DAVIS 9-29

SEE THIS FISH, GARFIELD?
THIS IS THE LAST FISH I'M BUYING
UNDERSTAND WHAT I'M SAYING?
I SHOULD SAVOR IT?
JIM DAVIS 9-30
www.facebook.com/garfield
Distributed by Universal Uclick
© 2014 PAWS, INC. All Rights Reserved.

UH-OH! I'M GOING TO MAKE A RUN FOR IT!
THERE SEEMS TO BE A TEENSY FLAW IN THAT PLAN
www.facebook.com/garfield
Distributed by Universal Uclick
© 2014 PAWS, INC. All Rights Reserved.
JIM DAVIS 10-1

JUST AS I THOUGHT!
THE LIFE SPAN OF A GOLDFISH IS SEVEN YEARS
NOT TWO MINUTES!
IT WAS A RICH AND FULL LIFE
FISH
JIM DAVIS 10-2
www.facebook.com/garfield
Distributed by Universal Uclick
© 2014 PAWS, INC. All Rights Reserved.

I REMEMBER A HAPPY FISHBOWL
I REMEMBER A FRISKY LITTLE FISH
WHERE HAVE ALL THE MEMORIES GONE?
IS THIS A COUNTRY SONG?
JIM DAVIS 10-3
www.facebook.com/garfield
Distributed by Universal Uclick
© 2014 PAWS, INC. All Rights Reserved.

HEY, GARFIELD, REMEMBER AUNT FRIEDA'S EGG SALAD FROM LAST CHRISTMAS?
AND THE APPLE COBBLER FROM YOUR BIRTHDAY, NEXT TO THE SUMMER SALAD?
OH, AND THERE'S A PIECE OF MOM AND DAD'S WEDDING CAKE!
TIME TO CLEAN OUT THE FRIDGE
JIM DAVIS 10-4
www.facebook.com/garfield
Distributed by Universal Uclick
© 2014 PAWS, INC. All Rights Reserved.

garfield.com
Garfield®
www.facebook.com/garfield
HOW CUTE...GARFIELD IS POSTING PHOTOS OF HIS DINNERS
JIM DAVIS 10-5
GARFIELD
GARFIELD
GARF
Distributed by Universal Uclick
© 2014 PAWS, INC. All Rights Reserved.
SAAAY, THAT ONE LOOKS LIKE MINE
BURP

YAWN!
CAN YOU TRY TO BE A LITTLE MORE PERSONABLE?
YES, I CAN
IF YOU CAN BE A LITTLE LESS DULL
Distributed by Universal Uclick
www.facebook.com/garfield
© 2014 PAWS, INC. All Rights Reserved.
JIM DAVIS 10-6

HOW WAS YOUR FOOD?
FORGETTABLE
GARFIELD
GARFIELD
MIND REFRESHING MY MEMORY?
GARFIELD
Distributed by Universal Uclick
www.facebook.com/garfield
© 2014 PAWS, INC. All Rights Reserved.
JIM DAVIS 10-7

BEWARE OF HIDDEN DOG
YOU DON'T LOOK VERY WELL-HIDDEN
I'M NOT
I'M ALSO NOT THE ONE TO BEWARE OF
Distributed by Universal Uclick
www.facebook.com/garfield
© 2014 PAWS, INC. All Rights Reserved.
JIM DAVIS 10-8

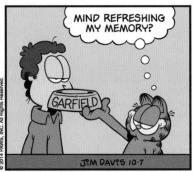

GARFIELD, I WANT TO WATCH TV
JIM DAVIS 10-9
www.facebook.com/garfield
Distributed by Universal Uclick
LET GO OF THE REMOTE
© 2014 PAWS, INC. All Rights Reserved.
YOU CAN DO THIS
COULD WE HAVE A MOMENT ALONE FIRST?

SOMEDAY I'D LIKE TO VISIT THE MOON
www.facebook.com/garfield
Distributed by Universal Uclick
© 2014 PAWS, INC. All Rights Reserved.
BUT YOU DON'T HAVE TO PACK MY THINGS JUST YET!
JIM DAVIS 10-10

GARFIELD ACTS MUCH NICER WHEN YOU'RE HERE, LIZ
www.facebook.com/garfield
Distributed by Universal Uclick
© 2014 PAWS, INC. All Rights Reserved.
REALLY?
ARE YOU LEAVING SOON?
JIM DAVIS 10-11

garfield.com
Garfield®
www.facebook.com/garfield
Distributed by Universal Uclick
I LOVE YOUR WORK!
© 2014 PAWS, INC. All Rights Reserved.
JIM DAVIS 10-12

GARFIELD, THESE ARE THE GOOD OLD DAYS
I'M GOING BACK TO BED
ALREADY THERE
JIM DAVIS 10-13
www.facebook.com/garfield
Distributed by Universal Uclick
© 2014 PAWS, INC. All Rights Reserved.

RUN FOR YOUR LIVES!
AND BRING ME BACK A MEATBALL SANDWICH!
JIM DAVIS 10-14
www.facebook.com/garfield
Distributed by Universal Uclick
© 2014 PAWS, INC. All Rights Reserved.

FREE PUPPIES
JIM DAVIS 10-15
FREE PUPPIES
STILL OVERPRICED
www.facebook.com/garfield
Distributed by Universal Uclick
© 2014 PAWS, INC. All Rights Reserved.

JON WENT TO THE DENTIST
I CAN ALWAYS TELL
THERE'S A SUBTLE CHANGE IN HIS DINING HABITS
JIM DAVIS 10-16
Distributed by Universal Uclick www.facebook.com/garfield
© 2014 PAWS, INC. All Rights Reserved.

IF YOU COULD LIVE IN ANOTHER TIME, WHEN WOULD IT BE, GARFIELD?
HMMM
I'D HAVE TO GO WITH THIS MORNING, WHEN WE HAD DONUTS
JIM DAVIS 10-17
Distributed by Universal Uclick www.facebook.com/garfield
© 2014 PAWS, INC. All Rights Reserved.

Z
MMMPH!
AND HAPPY DREAMS TO YOU, TOO, JON
JIM DAVIS 10-18
Distributed by Universal Uclick www.facebook.com/garfield
© 2014 PAWS, INC. All Rights Reserved.

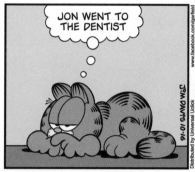

garfield.com
Garfield
WE INTERRUPT THIS PROGRAM TO BRING YOU A SPECIAL BULLETIN
JIM DAVIS 10-19
www.facebook.com/garfield
AUTHORITIES ARE REPORTING WHAT APPEARS TO BE A FREAK GARDENING ACCIDENT
Distributed by Universal Uclick
WE HAVE A REPORTER AT THE SCENE NOW...STU, WHAT CAN YOU TELL US?
WELL, LARRY, IT SEEMS THAT A LOCAL MAN HAS HIS HEAD STUCK INSIDE A WATERING CAN, AND IS WALKING DOWN THE MIDDLE OF THE STREET
I'LL SEE IF I CAN GET A WORD FROM HIM...SIR? CHANNEL SEVEN NEWS HERE...
CHANNEL SEVEN?! I'M ON TV?!
© 2014 PAWS, INC. All Rights Reserved.
HI, LIZ!
WE SHOULD DO SOMETHING
I'VE ALREADY LOCKED THE DOOR

I'M VERY SURE OF MYSELF
www.facebook.com/garfield
Distributed by Universal Uclick
SORT OF
KIND OF...MAYBE...UNLESS SOMEBODY'S AGAINST IT
JUST STOP TALKING
© 2014 PAWS, INC. All Rights Reserved.
JIM DAVIS 10-20

DON'T HIT ME. OR KICK ME. OR SCRATCH ME
www.facebook.com/garfield
Distributed by Universal Uclick
NO PROBLEM
OR BITE ME
OH, COME ON!
© 2014 PAWS, INC. All Rights Reserved.
JIM DAVIS 10-21

YIP! YIP! YIP! YIP! YIP! YIP! YIP! YIP!
www.facebook.com/garfield
Distributed by Universal Uclick
LIES! ALL LIES!
EXCEPT FOR THE FIFTH "YIP"
© 2014 PAWS, INC. All Rights Reserved.
JIM DAVIS 10-22

STOP CLAWING THE COUCH, GARFIELD!
CLAW CLAW CLAW
JIM DAVIS 10-23
www.facebook.com/garfield
Distributed by Universal Uclick
STOP CLAWING THE CURTAINS, GARFIELD!
CLAW CLAW CLAW
© 2014 PAWS, INC. All Rights Reserved.
I DIDN'T MEAN GO BACK TO THE COUCH!!
CLAW CLAW CLAW

MY LIPS ARE CHAPPED!
JIM DAVIS 10-24
www.facebook.com/garfield
Distributed by Universal Uclick
NOW I CAN'T KISS LIZ!
© 2014 PAWS, INC. All Rights Reserved.
GREAT NEWS!

www.facebook.com/garfield
Distributed by Universal Uclick
GARFIELD, THERE'S AN OLD SAYING...
© 2014 PAWS, INC. All Rights Reserved.
"A LAZY CAT GATHERS NO DONUTS"
THAT'S WHY YOU ARE HERE TO SERVE ME
JIM DAVIS 10-25

garfield.com
Garfield
I WISH I COULD JUST LIE THERE DOING NOTHING LIKE YOU, GARFIELD
www.facebook.com/garfield
LOOK AT ME... I'M A LAZY CAT!
I DON'T MOVE FOR HOURS AT A TIME...
STARING OFF INTO SPACE...
Distributed by Universal Uclick
TOTALLY USELESS
© 2014 PAWS, INC. All Rights Reserved.
WELL, I GUESS I'LL GO EAT MY LUNCH
THAT'S WHAT YOU (BURP) THINK
JIM DAVIS 10-26

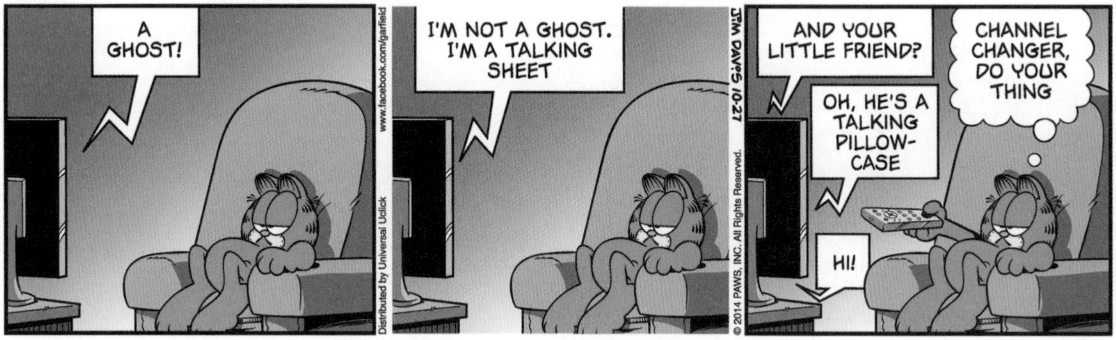
A GHOST!
www.facebook.com/garfield
Distributed by Universal Uclick
I'M NOT A GHOST. I'M A TALKING SHEET
JIM DAVIS 10-27
© 2014 PAWS, INC. All Rights Reserved.
AND YOUR LITTLE FRIEND?
OH, HE'S A TALKING PILLOW-CASE
HI!
CHANNEL CHANGER, DO YOUR THING

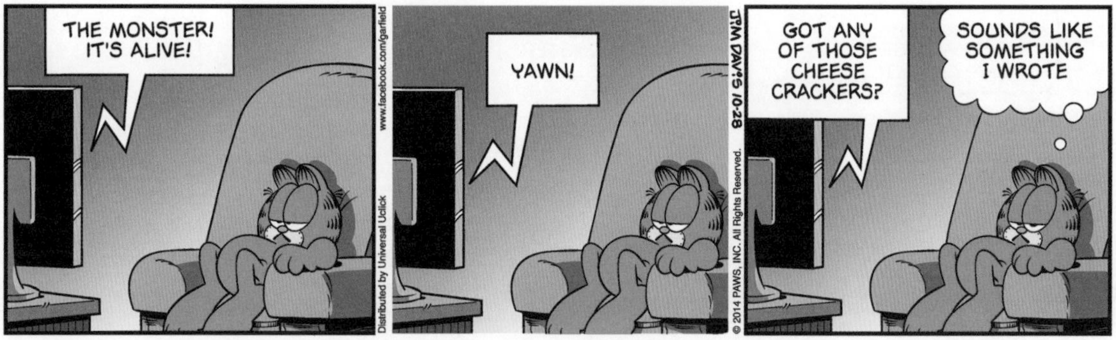
THE MONSTER! IT'S ALIVE!
www.facebook.com/garfield
Distributed by Universal Uclick
YAWN!
JIM DAVIS 10-28
© 2014 PAWS, INC. All Rights Reserved.
GOT ANY OF THOSE CHEESE CRACKERS?
SOUNDS LIKE SOMETHING I WROTE

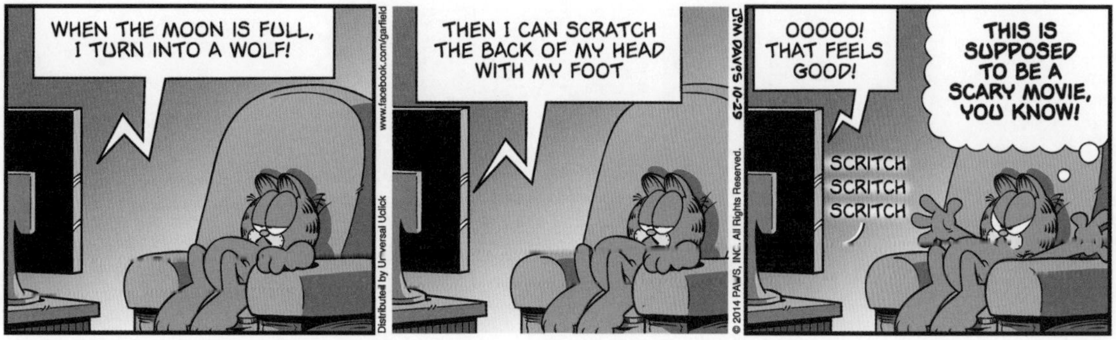
WHEN THE MOON IS FULL, I TURN INTO A WOLF!
www.facebook.com/garfield
Distributed by Universal Uclick
THEN I CAN SCRATCH THE BACK OF MY HEAD WITH MY FOOT
JIM DAVIS 10-29
© 2014 PAWS, INC. All Rights Reserved.
OOOOO! THAT FEELS GOOD!
SCRITCH
SCRITCH
SCRITCH
THIS IS SUPPOSED TO BE A SCARY MOVIE, YOU KNOW!

WELCOME TO "CAT CHANNEL CINEMA"
Distributed by Universal Uclick
www.facebook.com/garfield
TONIGHT'S FILM, "THE DAY THE CAN OPENER DIED"
© 2014 PAWS, INC. All Rights Reserved.
HOW WAS THE MOVIE LAST NIGHT?
IT WAS A WEEPER
JIM DAVIS 10-30

GARFIELD, THERE'S A CREEPY NOISE IN MY CLOSET!
Distributed by Universal Uclick
www.facebook.com/garfield
MAYBE IT'S A MONSTER!
NOT TO WORRY
© 2014 PAWS, INC. All Rights Reserved.
WHAT SHOULD WE DO?!
YOUR WARDROBE WILL KILL IT
JIM DAVIS 10-31

Distributed by Universal Uclick
www.facebook.com/garfield
© 2014 PAWS, INC. All Rights Reserved.
WHEN DID WE GET NEW CURTAINS?
JIM DAVIS 11-1

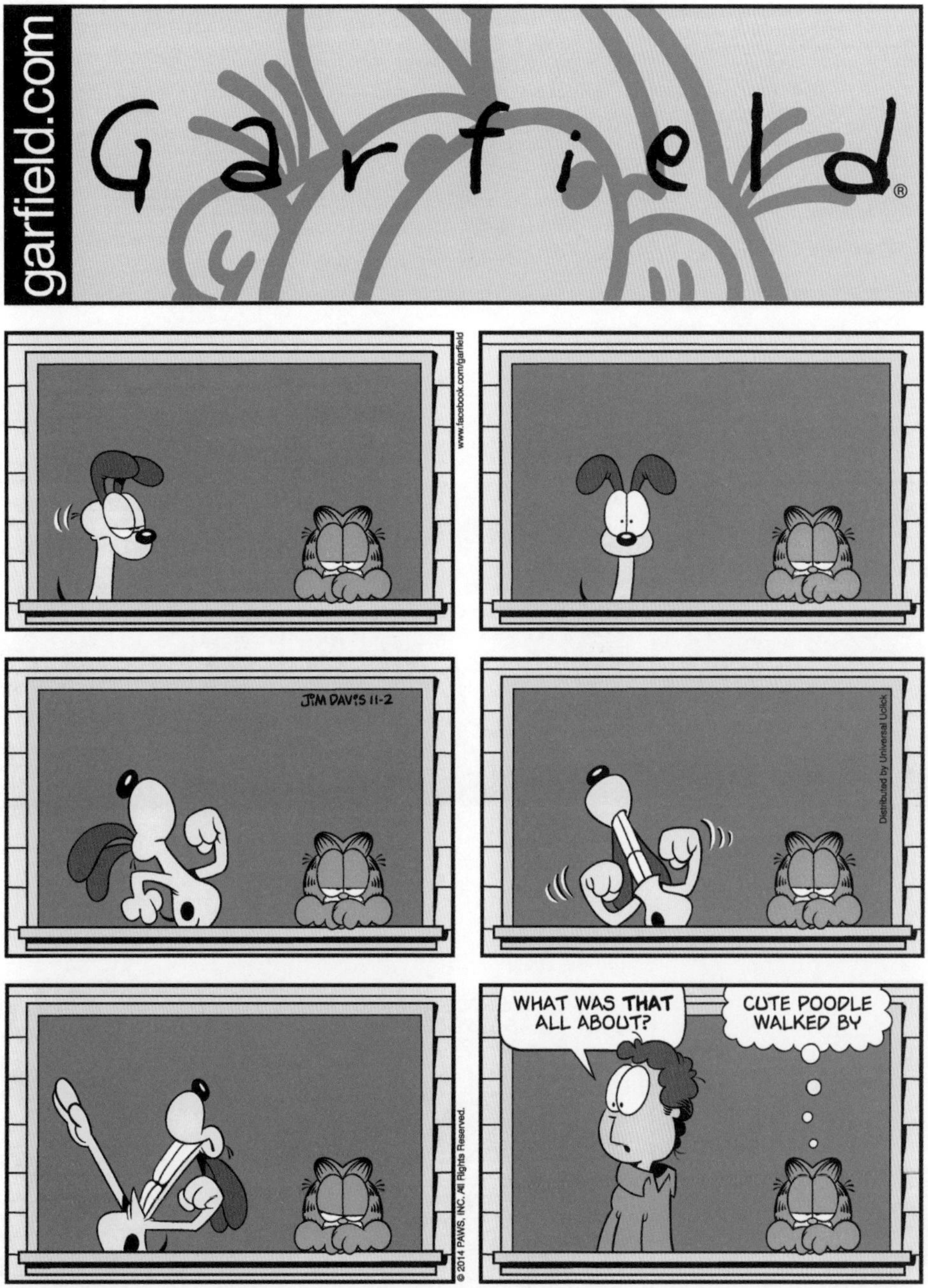
garfield.com
Garfield®
www.facebook.com/garfield
JIM DAVIS 11-2
Distributed by Universal Uclick
© 2014 PAWS, INC. All Rights Reserved.
WHAT WAS **THAT** ALL ABOUT?
CUTE POODLE WALKED BY

TIME TO GET UP!
SO?
JIM DAVIS 11-3
www.facebook.com/garfield
Distributed by Universal Uclick
"TIME TO GET UP"...THAT REALLY FROSTS ME! LIKE I HAVE A JOB! I'M A CAT! WHY WOULD I HAVE TO...
© 2014 PAWS, INC. All Rights Reserved.
PANCAKES
ZIP

GOOD EVENING, AND WELCOME TO...
www.facebook.com/garfield
Distributed by Universal Uclick
JIM DAVIS 11-4
© 2014 PAWS, INC. All Rights Reserved.
PREGNANT PAUSE THEATER
READY... AIM...

ODIE
JIM DAVIS 11-5
www.facebook.com/garfield
Distributed by Universal Uclick
YES. DOG FOOD IS **SUPPOSED** TO LOOK DISGUSTING
ODIE
© 2014 PAWS, INC. All Rights Reserved.
SLURP
GULP
CHOMP!
NARF!
ODIE

I'VE BEEN THINKING...
WOW! AND THEY SAID IT COULDN'T BE DONE!
www.facebook.com/garfield
Distributed by Universal Uclick
© 2014 PAWS, INC. All Rights Reserved.
JIM DAVIS 11-6
AND...
THERE'S MORE?!

WOW, GARFIELD, HAVE YOU LOST WEIGHT?
www.facebook.com/garfield
Distributed by Universal Uclick
YOU LOOK LIKE YOU'VE PACKED ON A FEW POUNDS THERE
© 2014 PAWS, INC. All Rights Reserved.
AWWW...BACK ALREADY?
I LIKE LIARS
JIM DAVIS 11-7

WHAT DO YOU THINK OF MY OUTFIT?
www.facebook.com/garfield
Distributed by Universal Uclick
© 2014 PAWS, INC. All Rights Reserved.
WELL?
HANG ON. I'M WORKING UP A HAIRBALL
JIM DAVIS 11-8

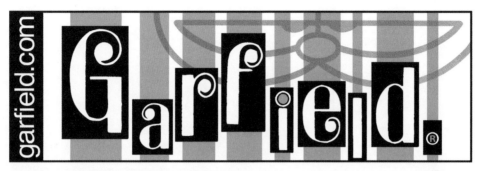

garfield.com
Garfield®
JPM DAVIS 11-9
www.facebook.com/garfield
Distributed by Universal Uclick
PATTA PATTA PATTA PATTA PATTA PATTA PATTA
RUNNA RUNNA RUNNA RUNNA RUNNA RUNNA RUNNA
BOING!
BOING!
© 2014 PAWS, INC. All Rights Reserved.

IS THAT ALL YOU'RE DOING TODAY?
I MADE AN APPEARANCE
JIM DAVIS 11-10
Distributed by Universal Uclick www.facebook.com/garfield
© 2014 PAWS, INC. All Rights Reserved.

GARFIELD, YOU HAVE A BAD HABIT
YOU LEAVE THE REFRIGERATOR DOOR OPEN
I'M TRYING TO SAVE ENERGY!
SO AM I!
JIM DAVIS 11-11
Distributed by Universal Uclick www.facebook.com/garfield
© 2014 PAWS, INC. All Rights Reserved.

"DEAR ASK A DOG"...
YIP! YIP! YIP! YIP! YIP! YIP!
THAT WASN'T THE QUESTION
JIM DAVIS 11-12
Distributed by Universal Uclick www.facebook.com/garfield
© 2014 PAWS, INC. All Rights Reserved.

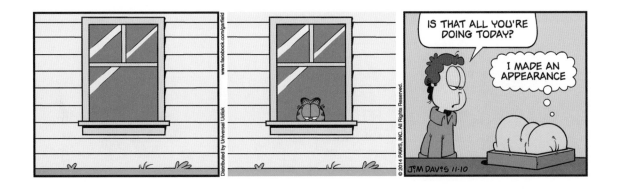

www.facebook.com/garfield
Distributed by Universal Uclick
ZOO
DO NOT FEED THE ANIMALS
© 2014 PAWS, INC. All Rights Reserved.
JIM DAVIS 11-13
NO POINT GOING IN THERE

HI, LIZ! HELLO! GREETINGS! HOLA! HOWDY-DOO! ALOHA! WHAT'S SHAKIN'? HOW'S IT GOIN'?!
www.facebook.com/garfield
Distributed by Universal Uclick
NOW IF YOU'LL EXCUSE US, WE'RE GOING TO RUN UP AND DOWN THE BASEMENT STAIRS 500 TIMES!
© 2014 PAWS, INC. All Rights Reserved.
CLOMP! CLOMP! CLOMP! CLOMP! CLOMP! CLOMP! CLOMP! CLOMP! CLOMP! CLOMP!
TRIPLE-SHOT LATTE MOUSTACHES
JIM DAVIS 11-14

www.facebook.com/garfield
Distributed by Universal Uclick
© 2014 PAWS, INC. All Rights Reserved.
SALAD CAN'T BE TRUSTED
JIM DAVIS 11-15

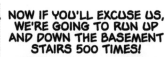

garfield.com
Garfield®
PHONE, FIND LOCAL FITNESS CENTERS
JUST A MOMENT
www.facebook.com/garfield
I HAVE LOCATED THREE. WHAT WOULD YOU LIKE TO DO?
I'D LIKE TO JOIN ONE
YOU?!
Distributed by Universal Uclick
YES, ME! I'M VERY HEALTH CONSCIOUS!
OH, REALLY?
YOU HAVE TWENTY-SEVEN PIZZA PARLORS ON SPEED DIAL
© 2014 PAWS, INC. All Rights Reserved.
MY SMARTPHONE IS SMARTER THAN I AM
HOW TOUGH IS THAT?
JIM DAVIS 11-16

THE CAT IS A FINK
JIM DAVIS 11-17
I WANT WHOEVER DID THIS CAUGHT!
RIGHT AWAY, SIRE
Distributed by Universal Uclick www.facebook.com/garfield
© 2014 PAWS, INC. All Rights Reserved.

PEST CONTROL? THERE'S A RAT IN MY BASEMENT
YES, YOU'RE ABSOLUTELY RIGHT
I SHOULD GET A CAT
CATS SHED
JIM DAVIS 11-18
Distributed by Universal Uclick www.facebook.com/garfield
© 2014 PAWS, INC. All Rights Reserved.

MAYBE THE RAT IN THE BASEMENT WILL JUST LEAVE
IT'S HANGING PICTURES
JIM DAVIS 11-19
Distributed by Universal Uclick www.facebook.com/garfield
© 2014 PAWS, INC. All Rights Reserved.

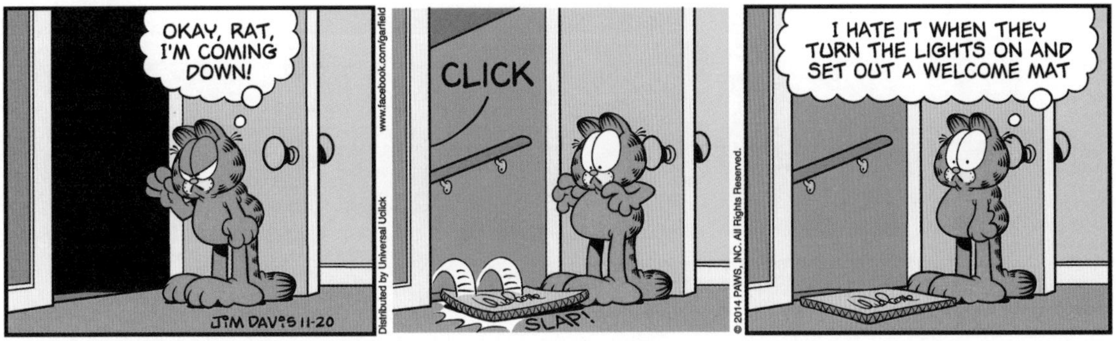
OKAY, RAT, I'M COMING DOWN!
JIM DAVIS 11-20
Distributed by Universal Uclick
www.facebook.com/garfield
CLICK
SLAP!
© 2014 PAWS, INC. All Rights Reserved.
I HATE IT WHEN THEY TURN THE LIGHTS ON AND SET OUT A WELCOME MAT

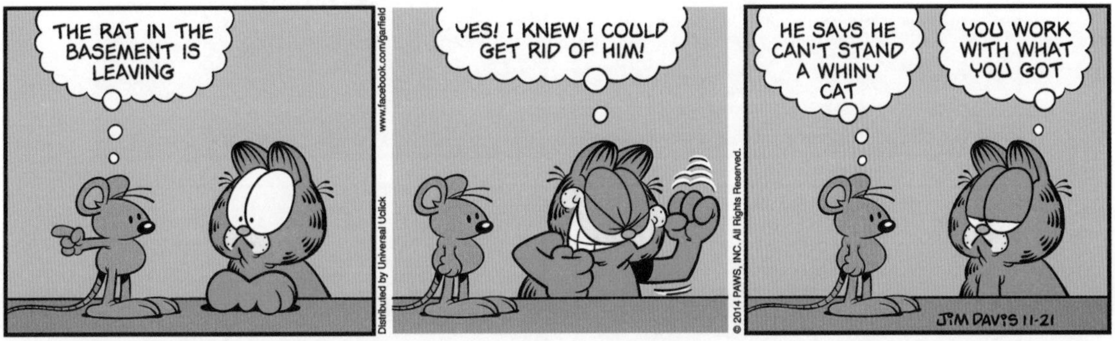
THE RAT IN THE BASEMENT IS LEAVING
Distributed by Universal Uclick
www.facebook.com/garfield
YES! I KNEW I COULD GET RID OF HIM!
© 2014 PAWS, INC. All Rights Reserved.
HE SAYS HE CAN'T STAND A WHINY CAT
YOU WORK WITH WHAT YOU GOT
JIM DAVIS 11-21

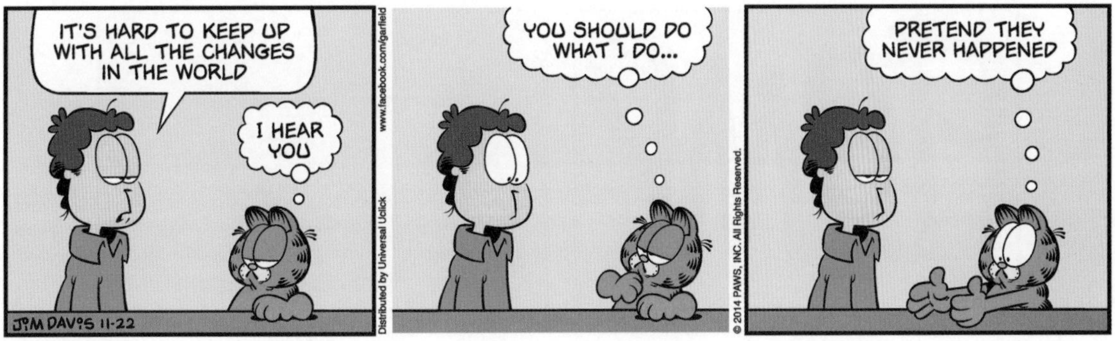
IT'S HARD TO KEEP UP WITH ALL THE CHANGES IN THE WORLD
I HEAR YOU
JIM DAVIS 11-22
Distributed by Universal Uclick
www.facebook.com/garfield
YOU SHOULD DO WHAT I DO...
© 2014 PAWS, INC. All Rights Reserved.
PRETEND THEY NEVER HAPPENED

garfield.com
Garfield®
www.facebook.com/garfield
LOOK, GARFIELD! A FALLING STAR!
IF YOU MAKE A WISH ON A FALLING STAR, IT WILL COME TRUE
DID YOU MAKE A WISH?!
Distributed by Universal Uclick
FLOMP
JIM DAVIS 11-23
© 2014 PAWS, INC. All Rights Reserved.
YES

I'M AWAKE!
AND THEY SAID IT COULDN'T BE DONE!
Distributed by Universal Uclick www.facebook.com/garfield
© 2014 PAWS, INC. All Rights Reserved.
JIM DAVIS 11-24

HELLO?...NO, THERE'S NO PEGGY HERE
NO, THERE NEVER WAS A PEGGY HERE
NO, I WILL **NOT** PRETEND TO BE PEGGY!
I LOVE WRONG NUMBERS
Distributed by Universal Uclick www.facebook.com/garfield
© 2014 PAWS, INC. All Rights Reserved.
JIM DAVIS 11-25

GARFIELD
WELL, NOTHING'S MOVING
GARFIELD
I HAVE HIGH STANDARDS WHEN IT COMES TO CAT FOOD
GARFIELD
Distributed by Universal Uclick www.facebook.com/garfield
© 2014 PAWS, INC. All Rights Reserved.
JIM DAVIS 11-26

I'M MAKING GRANDMA'S SPECIAL SOUP, GARFIELD
www.facebook.com/garfield
Distributed by Universal Uclick
I'M TRYING TO FOLLOW HER RECIPE
© 2014 PAWS, INC. All Rights Reserved.
WHERE DO I GET A COYOTE?
WE CAN SUBSTITUTE WITH CHOCOLATE CAKE
JIM DAVIS 11-27

DIET TIME, GARFIELD
www.facebook.com/garfield
Distributed by Universal Uclick
© 2014 PAWS, INC. All Rights Reserved.
JIM DAVIS 11-28
AND JUST AS I REACH MY TARGET WEIGHT!

CAT TREATS ARE A GREATER INVENTION THAN THE WHEEL
www.facebook.com/garfield
Distributed by Universal Uclick
KITTY Treetz
WHOA!...
© 2014 PAWS, INC. All Rights Reserved.
A WHEEL MADE FROM CAT TREATS!
JIM DAVIS 11-29

garfield.com
Garfield®
www.facebook.com/garfield
SNIFF SNIFF SNIFF SNIFF SNIFF SNIFF SNIFF SNIFF
SNORK!
CHOO!
SPLAT!
JIM DAVIS 11-30
Distributed by Universal Uclick
© 2014 PAWS, INC. All Rights Reserved.
WHAP WHAP WHAP WHAP WHAP WHAP WHAP
YAAAAAHH
THIS HAPPENS ALL THE TIME

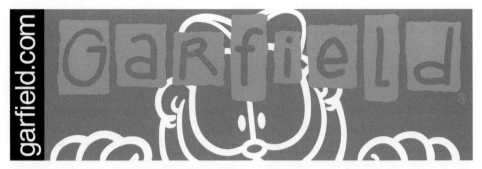

SOMETIMES WINTER CAN SEEM GRAY, DULL, LIFELESS, COLD AND UNFORGIVING
JIM DAVIS 12-1
www.facebook.com/garfield
Distributed by Universal Uclick
BUT THEN ALONG COMES CHRISTMAS
© 2014 PAWS, INC. All Rights Reserved.
AND ALONG COMES JON
A LITTLE HELP...

SO THIS IS YOUR SHOPPING LIST?
www.facebook.com/garfield
Distributed by Universal Uclick
NO
© 2014 PAWS, INC. All Rights Reserved.
THAT'S THE INDEX
JIM DAVIS 12-2

WHAT WOULD YOU LIKE FOR CHRISTMAS, ODIE? A CHEWY BONE, OR A SQUEAKY BONE?
JIM DAVIS 12-3
www.facebook.com/garfield
Distributed by Universal Uclick
© 2014 PAWS, INC. All Rights Reserved.
ODIE?
I THINK HE LOCKED UP

SANTA WILL BE HERE SOON
www.facebook.com/garfield
Distributed by Universal Uclick
WITH PRESENTS FOR EVERYBODY WHO'S BEEN GOOD
© 2014 PAWS, INC. All Rights Reserved.
AND YOU
AND ME!
JIM DAVIS 12-4

WHAT'S THIS?
I'M SENDING SANTA A PICTURE OF ME
www.facebook.com/garfield
Distributed by Universal Uclick
© 2014 PAWS, INC. All Rights Reserved.
NOT A VERY GOOD LIKENESS
OKAY, I ADDED THE HALO
JIM DAVIS 12-5

NOTHING LASTS FOREVER
www.facebook.com/garfield
Distributed by Universal Uclick
WRONG!
© 2014 PAWS, INC. All Rights Reserved.
FRUITCAKE DOESN'T COUNT!
JIM DAVIS 12-6

garfield.com
Garfield®
www.facebook.com/garfield
Dear Santa,
I have been good all year. Please see attached photos.
PAT PAT
X
Distributed by Universal Uclick
THIS IS FRAUD, YOU KNOW...
SHUT UP AND SMILE
JIM DAVIS 12-7

SANTA CLAUS KNOWS WHETHER YOU'VE BEEN GOOD OR BAD
HE'S A FAT GUY WHO DOES NOTHING 364 DAYS OUT OF THE YEAR
YOU HAVEN'T BEEN VERY GOOD
WHO IS **HE** TO JUDGE **ME**?!
Distributed by Universal Uclick www.facebook.com/garfield
© 2014 PAWS, INC. All Rights Reserved.
JIM DAVIS 12-8

I'VE HEARD THAT CHRISTMAS CALORIES "DON'T COUNT"
I SAY THAT SHOULD ALSO APPLY TO THE DAYS OF THE WEEK
HOW CAN YOU EAT SO MUCH?
TUESDAY CALORIES DON'T COUNT
Distributed by Universal Uclick www.facebook.com/garfield
© 2014 PAWS, INC. All Rights Reserved.
JIM DAVIS 12-9

LOOK, GARFIELD, A BANANA SLICER! THINK LIZ WOULD LIKE THAT FOR CHRISTMAS?
WHY DO YOU LOOK AT ME LIKE THAT?
WOULD YOU RATHER I ROLLED MY EYES?
Distributed by Universal Uclick www.facebook.com/garfield
© 2014 PAWS, INC. All Rights Reserved.
JIM DAVIS 12-10

GARFIELD, HOW ABOUT THIS FOR LIZ?...
A WRINKLE CREAM HOLIDAY GIFT SET!
YOU'RE GOING TO BE A LONELY, LONELY OLD MAN
JIM DAVIS 12-11
Distributed by Universal Uclick www.facebook.com/garfield
© 2014 PAWS, INC. All Rights Reserved.

SIGH...I NEVER KNOW WHAT TO GET LIZ FOR CHRISTMAS, GARFIELD
LOOK, YOU BE HER, AND I'LL TRY SOME GIFT IDEAS OUT ON YOU
FINE
TEETH WHITENING STRIPS!
I THINK WE SHOULD SEE OTHER PEOPLE
JIM DAVIS 12-12
Distributed by Universal Uclick www.facebook.com/garfield
© 2014 PAWS, INC. All Rights Reserved.

HO! HO! HO! I BET SPIDER CLAUS KNOWS WHAT **YOU** WANT FOR CHRISTMAS!
SCH WOP
ANGER MANAGEMENT CLASSES!
JIM DAVIS 12-13
Distributed by Universal Uclick www.facebook.com/garfield
© 2014 PAWS, INC. All Rights Reserved.

garfield.com
To: you
From: Garfield®
www.facebook.com/garfield
DING!
ZIP
SMOOOOOOOCH
Distributed by Universal Uclick
© 2014 PAWS, INC. All Rights Reserved.
CHRISTMAS COOKIE OVEN TIMER
JIM DAVIS 12-14

WHAT'S THIS?
MY CHRISTMAS LIST
www.facebook.com/garfield
Distributed by Universal Uclick
© 2014 PAWS, INC. All Rights Reserved.
NOBODY MAKES A CHEESE DANISH THAT BIG
THEN IT'S TIME SOMEBODY STARTED!
JIM DAVIS 12-15

ARBUCKLE HOLIDAY TRADITION NUMBER ONE...
www.facebook.com/garfield
Distributed by Universal Uclick
AAAAGGHHH!
© 2014 PAWS, INC. All Rights Reserved.
EEEEEVERY YEAR
JIM DAVIS 12-16

ARBUCKLE HOLIDAY TRADITION NUMBER TWO...
SLAM!
www.facebook.com/garfield
Distributed by Universal Uclick
© 2014 PAWS, INC. All Rights Reserved.
CAROLING
JIM DAVIS 12-17

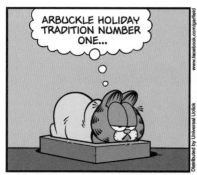

WE NOW RETURN TO "DICK, THE CAT WHO DIDN'T SAVE CHRISTMAS"
DICK, STOP CLAWING THE WATERBED!
OH, NO! THE PRESENTS ARE ALL SOAKED!
ALL RIGHT, DICK! NOW GO SWAT THE ORNAMENTS OFF THE TREE!

LIZ, I JUST DON'T KNOW WHAT TO GET YOU FOR CHRISTMAS!
OH, JON, **YOU'RE** ALL I NEED FOR CHRISTMAS
MAYBE SHE COULD EXCHANGE YOU FOR SOMETHING GOOD

THE HOLIDAYS ARE A TIME FOR PEACE AND LOVE...
SO HOW'S ABOUT A HUG, TUBBO?
HOW'S THAT HUGGING THING WORKIN' FOR YOU, LARRY?
BLOW IT OUT YOUR JINGLE BELL, CARL

garfield.com
garfield
TREE DECORATED... CHECK
www.facebook.com/garfield
HOUSE LIGHTS UP...CHECK
PRESENTS WRAPPED... CHECK
Distributed by Universal Uclick
STOCKINGS HUNG FROM CHIMNEY... CHECK
TOING
© 2014 PAWS, INC. All Rights Reserved.
SANTA TRAP TESTED... CHECK
JIM DAVIS 12-21

GARFIELD!
HEY, THEY NEEDED AN ALTO
JIM DAVIS 12-22
www.facebook.com/garfield
Distributed by Universal Uclick
© 2014 PAWS, INC. All Rights Reserved.

HELLO, SANTA'S PIZZA? I'D LIKE TO ORDER A LARGE PEPPERONI
WHY IS IT CALLED SANTA'S PIZZA?
WHUMP!
AH
JIM DAVIS 12-23
www.facebook.com/garfield
Distributed by Universal Uclick
© 2014 PAWS, INC. All Rights Reserved.

PRESENTS... COOKIES... EGGNOG...
IS THERE ANYTHING ABOUT CHRISTMAS I DON'T LIKE?
SMOOOO
OOOOOOOOCH
JIM DAVIS 12-24
www.facebook.com/garfield
Distributed by Universal Uclick
© 2014 PAWS, INC. All Rights Reserved.

IT'S CHRISTMAS!
THE ONE DAY OUT OF THE WHOLE YEAR...
WHEN SHREDDING IS NOT FROWNED UPON
Garfield
www.facebook.com/garfield
Distributed by Universal Uclick
© 2014 PAWS, INC. All Rights Reserved.
JIM DAVIS 12-25

I ATE SO MUCH I CAN'T MOVE
ME TOO
BEST CHRISTMAS EVER
EVER
www.facebook.com/garfield
Distributed by Universal Uclick
© 2014 PAWS, INC. All Rights Reserved.
JIM DAVIS 12-26

HI! I'M YOUR HOLIDAY OVEREATING NIGHTMARE!
MUAH-HA! HA! HA! HAAAAAH!
BUT WHAT **ARE** YOU?
THE LAST BELT NOTCH
www.facebook.com/garfield
Distributed by Universal Uclick
© 2014 PAWS, INC. All Rights Reserved.
JIM DAVIS 12-27

garfield.com
GARFIELD®
WHAT DO YOU WANT TO DO FOR NEW YEAR'S EVE, LIZ? HOW ABOUT DINNER AND DANCING?
www.facebook.com/garfield
I THINK I'D BE HAPPY JUST ORDERING PIZZA AND STAYING HOME WITH YOU, GARFIELD, AND ODIE
ARE YOU SURE?! BECAUSE I COULD GET A PET SITTER, AND
WHOP!
Distributed by Universal Uclick
© 2014 PAWS, INC. All Rights Reserved.
WAS I SAYING SOMETHING?
YEAH, BUT IT WASN'T IMPORTANT
JIM DAVIS 12-28

I GOT MY WIFE A TREADMILL FOR CHRISTMAS
THAT'S NICE
WHY ARE YOU STANDING OUT HERE IN THE SNOW?
I GOT MY WIFE A TREADMILL FOR CHRISTMAS
JIM DAVIS 12-29
www.facebook.com/garfield
Distributed by Universal Uclick
© 2014 PAWS, INC. All Rights Reserved.

2009 HAS SURE BEEN A LONG YEAR
DECEMBER
WE GOTTA GET A NEW CALENDAR
JIM DAVIS 12-30
www.facebook.com/garfield
Distributed by Universal Uclick
© 2014 PAWS, INC. All Rights Reserved.

MINE IS TO NOT BE SO CLUMSY
THUD
RESOLUTIONS ARE SO HARD TO KEEP
JIM DAVIS 12-31
www.facebook.com/garfield
Distributed by Universal Uclick
© 2014 PAWS, INC. All Rights Reserved.

MY RESOLUTION IS TO BE MORE SENSITIVE TO THE FEELINGS OF OTHERS
www.facebook.com/garfield
Distributed by Universal Uclick
SMACK
© 2015 PAWS, INC. All Rights Reserved.
THAT HURT!
I FEEL YOUR PAIN
JIM DAVIS 1-1

THIS YEAR I RESOLVE TO ABANDON MY SCAVENGING, VERMIN WAYS
JIM DAVIS 1-2
www.facebook.com/garfield
Distributed by Universal Uclick
© 2015 PAWS, INC. All Rights Reserved.
ARE YOU GONNA FINISH THAT?

MY NEW YEAR'S RESOLUTION IS TO LOSE WEIGHT
www.facebook.com/garfield
Distributed by Universal Uclick
YOU? LOSE WEIGHT?!
YEAH...
© 2015 PAWS, INC. All Rights Reserved.
I'M GETTIN' A REAL FLY GUT
JIM DAVIS 1-3

garfield.com
GARFIELD
HEY GUYS, CHECK IT OUT...
www.facebook.com/garfield
BURRP!
BUUURRRP!
BUUUUUUUUUUUU
Distributed by Universal Uclick
JIM DAVIS 1-4
UUUUUUUUURRRRRRR
© 2015 PAWS, INC. All Rights Reserved.
RRRRRRRP
HE'S THE MASTER, ALL RIGHT
URF

www.facebook.com/garfield
Distributed by Universal Uclick
© 2015 PAWS, INC. All Rights Reserved.
JIM DAVIS 1-5
AH, WINTER IS HERE

YOU KNOW WHAT THE WORLD NEEDS MORE OF?
www.facebook.com/garfield
Distributed by Universal Uclick
ME!
© 2015 PAWS, INC. All Rights Reserved.
LOVE!
THE WORLD LOVING ME!
JIM DAVIS 1-6

YOU NEVER KNOW WHAT MIGHT BE AROUND THE NEXT CORNER
www.facebook.com/garfield
Distributed by Universal Uclick
© 2015 PAWS, INC. All Rights Reserved.
YOU GO AHEAD. I'LL WAIT HERE
JIM DAVIS 1-7

DO YOU BELIEVE IN TIME TRAVEL?
www.facebook.com/garfield
Distributed by Universal Uclick
OBSERVE...
© 2015 PAWS, INC. All Rights Reserved.
JIM DAVIS 1-8
WHEN I GET UP, IT WILL BE FRIDAY

I DREAMED ABOUT YOU LAST NIGHT, LIZ
HOW SWEET
www.facebook.com/garfield
Distributed by Universal Uclick
I ALSO DREAMED ABOUT GODZILLA
DIFFERENT DREAM, I HOPE
© 2015 PAWS, INC. All Rights Reserved.
THEN LET'S SAY IT WAS
I'LL BE LEAVING THE ROOM NOW
JIM DAVIS 1-9

FIRST SNOWFLAKE OF THE YEAR. I WONDER WHAT KIND OF SEASON IT'LL BE
JIM DAVIS 1-10
www.facebook.com/garfield
Distributed by Universal Uclick
BLOOEY!
© 2015 PAWS, INC. All Rights Reserved.
PROBABLY A BAD ONE

garfield.com
Garfield®
www.facebook.com/garfield
UNGH!
FLUMP
ARRRGH!
Distributed by Universal Uclick
© 2015 PAWS, INC. All Rights Reserved.
JIM DAVIS 1-11

...AND THEN I FELL ASLEEP
HAVE YOU NOTICED HOW ALL MY STORIES END THAT WAY?
Z
JIM DAVIS 1-12
www.facebook.com/garfield
Distributed by Universal Uclick
© 2015 PAWS, INC. All Rights Reserved.

I'M THE BEST!
YOU'RE THE WORST
MY TURN
I'M THE BEST!
JIM DAVIS 1-13
www.facebook.com/garfield
Distributed by Universal Uclick
© 2015 PAWS, INC. All Rights Reserved.

IT'S SNOWING! LET'S MAKE A SNOWMAN!
BUT THE SNOW'S TOO POWDERY TO ROLL INTO A BALL
JIM DAVIS 1-14
www.facebook.com/garfield
Distributed by Universal Uclick
© 2015 PAWS, INC. All Rights Reserved.

MY FATHER IS A BOWLING BALL
REALLY?
UH-HUH
HE THINKS I'M SOFT
BA-DA-CHING!
JIM DAVIS 1-15
Distributed by Universal Uclick www.facebook.com/garfield
© 2015 PAWS, INC. All Rights Reserved.

I CAN'T FIND MY PANTS
WHERE COULD THEY BE?
THEY'RE PROBABLY HIDING
JIM DAVIS 1-16
Distributed by Universal Uclick www.facebook.com/garfield
© 2015 PAWS, INC. All Rights Reserved.

OH, YOU'VE GOT IT TOUGH
I COULD USE A PILLOW
JIM DAVIS 1-17
Distributed by Universal Uclick www.facebook.com/garfield
© 2015 PAWS, INC. All Rights Reserved.

garfield.com
Garfield®
www.facebook.com/garfield
JON!
THERE YOU ARE!
RIGHT THERE
INSTEAD OF SOMEPLACE ELSE
Distributed by Universal Uclick
LIKE OVER THERE
MAN! IT'S HARD TO CREATE EXCITEMENT AROUND HERE!
© 2015 PAWS, INC. All Rights Reserved.
JIM DAVIS 1-18

JIM DAVIS 1-19
www.facebook.com/garfield
Distributed by Universal Uclick
GARFIELD
© 2015 PAWS, INC. All Rights Reserved.
GOOD TIMES
BOOYAH

WANNA CHASE ME?
JIM DAVIS 1-20
www.facebook.com/garfield
Distributed by Universal Uclick
NO?
© 2015 PAWS, INC. All Rights Reserved.
WOULDN'T DO IT
SURE! MAKE THE CAT DO ALL THE WORK!

JUST LOOK AT THAT...
BEWARE OF LOG
www.facebook.com/garfield
Distributed by Universal Uclick
HOW SAD IS IT WHEN SOME-BODY CAN'T EVEN SPELL A SIMPLE WORD LIKE
© 2015 PAWS, INC. All Rights Reserved.
JIM DAVIS 1-21

I WAS VERY INVOLVED IN ATHLETICS, GARFIELD
I WAS A STUDENT MANAGER...
OF THE CHESS TEAM
HE WIPED THEIR BROWS

MUNCH MUNCH MUNCH
MUNCH MUNCH MUNCH MUNCH
ARE YOU GOING TO SHARE THAT POPCORN WITH ME?
PERHAPS IT'S TIME WE BREAK UP

REMEMBER THE TIME YESTERDAY...
WHEN I **ALMOST** ATE A DONUT?!
BY ANY CHANCE WAS THAT AROUND THE TIME THAT I **DID** EAT A DONUT?

garfield.com
garfield
www.facebook.com/garfield
BREAD
SQUASH
Distributed by Universal Uclick
SQUASH
SQUISH
SQUISH
SQUISH
SQUISH
SQUASH
© 2015 PAWS, INC. All Rights Reserved.
GAH!
JON'S BUTTER EXPIRES AT MIDNIGHT!
BUTTER
KACHUNK
JIM DAVIS 1-25

OKAY...
THERE'S A REASON FOR EVERYTHING...
WHY DID I WAKE UP?
JIM DAVIS 1-26
Distributed by Universal Uclick www.facebook.com/garfield
© 2015 PAWS, INC. All Rights Reserved.

I HAVE ROLLER SKATES!
I HAVE CLAWS!
JIM DAVIS 1-27
Distributed by Universal Uclick www.facebook.com/garfield
© 2015 PAWS, INC. All Rights Reserved.

OKAY, ODIE. WE'LL MAKE A SNOWMAN
JIM DAVIS 1-28
HMM...BUT THERE'S NOT MUCH SNOW...
Distributed by Universal Uclick www.facebook.com/garfield
© 2015 PAWS, INC. All Rights Reserved.

MY UNCLE ROSCOE WAS VERY WISE
HE'D SAY, "YOU HAVE TO ACCEPT PEOPLE, WARTS AND ALL"
HE HAD THIS GIGANTIC
STOP RIGHT THERE!
GARFIELD
JIM DAVIS 1-29
Distributed by Universal Uclick www.facebook.com/garfield
© 2015 PAWS, INC. All Rights Reserved.

CAT MANIA!
CATCH IT!
JIM DAVIS 1-30
Distributed by Universal Uclick www.facebook.com/garfield
© 2015 PAWS, INC. All Rights Reserved.

LIZ, I'M SICK
COULD YOU RUB MY SHOULDERS AND SAY "POOR BABY"?
WAS THAT A CHORTLE?!
LAUGHTER **IS** THE BEST MEDICINE
JIM DAVIS 1-31
Distributed by Universal Uclick www.facebook.com/garfield
© 2015 PAWS, INC. All Rights Reserved.

garfield.com
GARFIELD
FWEE
SIGH
PANT PANT
FWEE
SIGH
PANT PANT
FWEE
SIGH
PANT PANT
FWEE
SIGH
PANT PANT
ENOUGH WITH THE SIGHING AND PANTING!!
AT LEAST OUR NOSES DON'T WHISTLE!!
BARK!!
THE CABIN FEVER IS TURNING UGLY
PANT PANT
FWEE
JIM DAVIS 2-1
www.facebook.com/garfield
Distributed by Universal Uclick
© 2015 PAWS, INC. All Rights Reserved.

CHEER UP, GARFIELD
THAT'S BETTER!
NOW WHAT?
JIM DAVIS 2-2
www.facebook.com/garfield
Distributed by Universal Uclick
© 2015 PAWS, INC. All Rights Reserved.

I'M TAKING A TEST, GARFIELD
"WHAT IS YOUR MATURITY LEVEL?"
WHERE ARE MY CRAYONS?
THAT'S AN AUTOMATIC TEN-POINT DEDUCTION
JIM DAVIS 2-3
www.facebook.com/garfield
Distributed by Universal Uclick
© 2015 PAWS, INC. All Rights Reserved.

NEXT!
JIM DAVIS 2-4
BARK!
THIS EXPRESS LINE IS A TIME-SAVER
www.facebook.com/garfield
Distributed by Universal Uclick
© 2015 PAWS, INC. All Rights Reserved.

YOU KNOW, JON, GARFIELD IS ALMOST LIKE YOUR CHILD
FEED ME, DADDY!
I WISH YOU WOULDN'T GIVE HIM IDEAS
WAH!
JIM DAVIS 2-5
www.facebook.com/garfield
Distributed by Universal Uclick
© 2015 PAWS, INC. All Rights Reserved.

FOR MY FIRST TRICK...
I WILL DO THE IMPOSSIBLE
THIS CAT WILL FETCH THIS BALL
THAT'S A PUPPET!
JIM DAVIS 2-6
www.facebook.com/garfield
Distributed by Universal Uclick
© 2015 PAWS, INC. All Rights Reserved.

I'M DEPRESSED
ARE YOU TRYING TO MAKE ME WORSE?!
JIM DAVIS 2-7
www.facebook.com/garfield
Distributed by Universal Uclick
© 2015 PAWS, INC. All Rights Reserved.

garfield.com
Garfield®
www.facebook.com/garfield
JUST GREAT...I'VE BEEN SITTING HERE FOR SO LONG, I'M FROZEN TO THE FENCE
GARFIELD, WHAT ARE YOU DOING OUT HERE?
I'M FROZEN TO THE FENCE
YOU SHOULDN'T BE SITTING OUTSIDE IN THE COLD LIKE THIS
I'M FROZEN TO THE FENCE
WHY DON'T YOU COME INSIDE? I'M MAKING COCOA
I'M FROZEN TO THE...
Distributed by Universal Uclick
COCOA?
© 2015 PAWS, INC. All Rights Reserved.
JIM DAVIS 2-8

SOMETIMES DREAMS DO COME TRUE
JIM DAVIS 2-9
Distributed by Universal Uclick
www.facebook.com/garfield
© 2015 PAWS, INC. All Rights Reserved.
YOU DREAM ABOUT STUMBLING AIMLESSLY THROUGH A MEANINGLESS EXISTENCE?

SOMETIMES A MAN HAS TO MAKE TOUGH DECISIONS
Distributed by Universal Uclick
www.facebook.com/garfield
© 2015 PAWS, INC. All Rights Reserved.
I WONDER WHAT THAT'S LIKE
TO BE A MAN?
JIM DAVIS 2-10

Distributed by Universal Uclick
www.facebook.com/garfield
YOUR STARING AT ME DOESN'T BOTHER ME
© 2015 PAWS, INC. All Rights Reserved.
HOW ABOUT NOW?
OKAY, THAT'S A LITTLE CREEPY
JIM DAVIS 2-11

ODIE HAS NO IDEA WHAT'S GOING ON
WHAT IS GOING ON?
JIM DAVIS 2-12
www.facebook.com/garfield
Distributed by Universal Uclick
© 2015 PAWS, INC. All Rights Reserved.

WHAT PRETTY SNOW...IT LOOKS JUST LIKE POWDERED SUGAR FALLING ON FRENCH TOAST
DON'T WAIT UP
JIM DAVIS 2-13
www.facebook.com/garfield
Distributed by Universal Uclick
© 2015 PAWS, INC. All Rights Reserved.

I THINK I'LL GO POWDER MY NOSE
YOU'RE NOT GOING TO LEAVE, ARE YOU?
WHY WOULD I DO THAT?
MY DATE'S COMING BACK
MORE WATER, ROMEO?
JIM DAVIS 2-14
www.facebook.com/garfield
Distributed by Universal Uclick
© 2015 PAWS, INC. All Rights Reserved.

garfield.com
GARFIELD®
© 2015 PAWS, INC. All Rights Reserved
www.facebook.com/garfield
Distributed by Universal Uclick
JIM DAVIS 2-15
YAAAH!
THIS REALLY NEEDS TO STOP
YOU'RE STIFLING MY CREATIVITY!

YOU LOOK BORED
I'M NOT BORED...
I HAVE AN IMAGE TO MAINTAIN
JPM DAVPS 2-16
www.facebook.com/garfield
Distributed by Universal Uclick
© 2015 PAWS, INC. All Rights Reserved.

HOW'S IT GOIN' TONIGHT, FOLKS? FEELIN' GOOD?
JPM DAVPS 2-17
OH, THINGS COULD BE GOING BETTER
I HAVE THIS PAIN IN MY NECK
SO DO I!
NO KIDDING?
YEAH, CURLED UP UNDER THE SOFA ALL NIGHT
I HEAR YOU, GIRL. WHAT DO YOU DO FOR THAT?
OH, I JUST...
THAT WAS A RHETORICAL QUESTION!
GOOD STUFF!
YEAH, I LIKE IT!
ASK US ANOTHER ONE!
www.facebook.com/garfield
Distributed by Universal Uclick
© 2015 PAWS, INC. All Rights Reserved.

YAWN!
JPM DAVPS 2-18
YAWN!
NOTHING TO DO?
DID IT
www.facebook.com/garfield
Distributed by Universal Uclick
© 2015 PAWS, INC. All Rights Reserved.

I STRAINED A MUSCLE TODAY
www.facebook.com/garfield
Distributed by Universal Uclick
WOW!
© 2015 PAWS, INC. All Rights Reserved.
YOU HAVE A MUSCLE?!
JIM DAVIS 2-19

I THINK I'LL DO SOMETHING RUGGED AND MANLY
LIKE WHAT?
JIM DAVIS 2-20
www.facebook.com/garfield
Distributed by Universal Uclick
MOW THE LAWN WITH MY SHIRT OFF!
© 2015 PAWS, INC. All Rights Reserved.
I'M STUCK
NOW'S YOUR CHANCE TO MAKE A RUN FOR IT

I WONDER IF IT'S POSSIBLE FOR YOU TO BE EVEN LAZIER
www.facebook.com/garfield
Distributed by Universal Uclick
I COULD BE...
© 2015 PAWS, INC. All Rights Reserved.
BUT YOU'D HAVE TO DO IT FOR ME
JIM DAVIS 2-21

garfield.com
Garfield
MEOW
www.facebook.com/garfield
ROBOTS WILL NEVER REPLACE CATS
THEY COULD NEVER DO THE THINGS WE DO
Distributed by Universal Uclick
Z
JIM DAVIS 2-22
Z
© 2015 PAWS, INC. All Rights Reserved.
Z
THE TECHNOLOGY IS MORE ADVANCED THAN I THOUGHT!

KIDS...
DON'T LET THIS HAPPEN TO YOU
WAS THAT AN INSULT?
NO. THAT WAS A PUBLIC SERVICE ANNOUNCEMENT
JIM DAVIS 2-23
Distributed by Universal Uclick www.facebook.com/garfield
© 2015 PAWS, INC. All Rights Reserved.

I'M GOING TO GO ON A DIET
JIM DAVIS 2-24
A REALLY LOUSY ONE!
Distributed by Universal Uclick www.facebook.com/garfield
© 2015 PAWS, INC. All Rights Reserved.

CATS CAN TELL WHAT YOU'RE THINKING
ASSUMING YOU ARE
JIM DAVIS 2-25
Distributed by Universal Uclick www.facebook.com/garfield
© 2015 PAWS, INC. All Rights Reserved.

FRESH
FISH
Distributed by Universal Uclick
www.facebook.com/garfield
YOU SMELL LIKE YOU'VE BEEN ROLLING AROUND IN A DUMPSTER BEHIND A FISH STORE
JEALOUS...
© 2015 PAWS, INC. All Rights Reserved.
JIM DAVIS 2-26

WHEN I'M IN ONE OF MY CRAZY MOODS, **ANYTHING** CAN HAPPEN!
Distributed by Universal Uclick
www.facebook.com/garfield
OR NOT!
© 2015 PAWS, INC. All Rights Reserved.
JIM DAVIS 2-27

Z
Distributed by Universal Uclick
www.facebook.com/garfield
THE DAY IS HALF OVER!
AND SO IS MY NAP!
© 2015 PAWS, INC. All Rights Reserved.
JIM DAVIS 2-28

garfield.com
GARFIELD
www.facebook.com/garfield
CRUNCH CRUNCH CRUNCH
CRUNCH CRUNCH
CRUNCH CRUNCH
CRUNCH
CRUNCH
chips
CRUNCH CRUNCH
CRUNCH CRUNCH
CRUNCH CRUNCH
CRUNCH
CRUNCH
CRUNCH
CRUNCH
CRUNCHY
GOOSH!
Distributed by Universal Uclick
JIM DAVIS 3-1
© 2015 PAWS, INC. All Rights Reserved.
SQUISH SQUISH SQUISH
SQUISHY
SQUISH
SQUISH
SQUISH SQUISH
SQUISH
SQUISH

I WILL NOT BE BOTHERED BY TODAY, STARTING NOW
JIM DAVIS 3-2
OKAY, STARTING NOW
Distributed by Universal Uclick
www.facebook.com/garfield
© 2015 PAWS, INC. All Rights Reserved.

JIM DAVIS 3-3
BEWARE OF INVISIBLE DOG
WHO DO THEY THINK THEY'RE FOOLING WITH THAT...
BLAT!
Distributed by Universal Uclick
www.facebook.com/garfield
© 2015 PAWS, INC. All Rights Reserved.

CAT NEWS
WHOA...
CAT NEWS
THERE'S AN AWFUL LOT NOT GOING ON
CAT NEWS
JIM DAVIS 3-4
Distributed by Universal Uclick
www.facebook.com/garfield
© 2015 PAWS, INC. All Rights Reserved.

I LIKE TO THINK OF MYSELF AS SMART
www.facebook.com/garfield
Distributed by Universal Uclick
GOOD FOR YOU
© 2015 PAWS, INC. All Rights Reserved.
I LIKE TO THINK OF MYSELF AS SKINNY
JIM DAVIS 3-5

LET'S DO SOMETHING EXCITING!
www.facebook.com/garfield
Distributed by Universal Uclick
WE COULD TRY TO GIVE GARFIELD A BATH
© 2015 PAWS, INC. All Rights Reserved.
YOU COULD **TRY**
MAYBE NOT **THAT** EXCITING
JIM DAVIS 3-6

I'M NOT AFRAID OF THE CAT'S ROLLED-UP NEWSPAPER!
JIM DAVIS 3-7
www.facebook.com/garfield
Distributed by Universal Uclick
I SAY **ATTACK!**
© 2015 PAWS, INC. All Rights Reserved.
HE HAS A PHONE BOOK
I SAY **REGROUP!**

garfield.com
GARFIELD®
www.facebook.com/garfield
Distributed by Universal Uclick
© 2015 PAWS, INC. All Rights Reserved.
GAAAAH
JIM DAVIS 3-8

YAWN!
YAWN!
Distributed by Universal Uclick
www.facebook.com/garfield
© 2015 PAWS, INC. All Rights Reserved.
WHY MUST YOU OUTDO ME AT EVERYTHING?
BECAUSE I CAN
JIM DAVIS 3-9

I COULD CLIMB THIS TREE
Distributed by Universal Uclick
www.facebook.com/garfield
BUT THEN I'D JUST FALL OUT OF IT
© 2015 PAWS, INC. All Rights Reserved.
MIGHT AS WELL JUST SKIP TO THE END
JIM DAVIS 3-10

GO AWAY, ODIE. YOU BOTHER ME
Distributed by Universal Uclick
www.facebook.com/garfield
© 2015 PAWS, INC. All Rights Reserved.
I GUESS I ASKED FOR THAT...
JIM DAVIS 3-11

MOM, I HAVE TO GO NOW
JIM DAVIS 3-12
www.facebook.com/garfield
Distributed by Universal Uclick
I REALLY DO HAVE TO GO...
© 2015 PAWS, INC. All Rights Reserved.
OH, ALL RIGHT. I'LL TALK TO THE COW
JON, YOU KNOW HOW THE COW DRONES ON...

WHAT WOULD I DO IF LIZ EVER DUMPED ME?
www.facebook.com/garfield
Distributed by Universal Uclick
HMMM...
© 2015 PAWS, INC. All Rights Reserved.
YOU LOOK LIKE A CRIER
JIM DAVIS 3-13

WHAT COULD BE BETTER THAN BEING A CAT?
www.facebook.com/garfield
Distributed by Universal Uclick
© 2015 PAWS, INC. All Rights Reserved.
BEING A CAT WITH ICE CREAM!
JIM DAVIS 3-14

garfield.com
Garfield
I'M GONNA COOK DINNER FOR LIZ TONIGHT!
IS THIS YOUR WAY OF BREAKING UP WITH HER?
www.facebook.com/garfield
BAKING POWDER...THAT'S BASICALLY BAKING SODA, RIGHT?
GO FOR IT
HUH...THE BUTTER IS CRISPY. IS THAT NORMAL?
IN A COMIC STRIP, YES
I WONDER IF I SHOULD'VE ADDED THE EGGS BEFORE I PUT IT IN THE OVEN
DOES THE OVEN HAVE AN "UNDO" BUTTON?
Distributed by Universal Uclick
JIM DAVIS 3-15
OKAY, WHERE'S THE FIRE EXTINGUISHER?
RIGHT WHERE YOU LEFT IT THE LAST TIME YOU COOKED
© 2015 PAWS, INC. All Rights Reserved.
I AM SO, SO SORRY
JON'S SMART ENOUGH TO FEEL DISAPPOINTED IN HIMSELF, BUT TOO DENSE TO DO ANYTHING RIGHT

GOOD NIGHT, GARFIELD
GOOD NIGHT, JON
JIM DAVIS 3-16
www.facebook.com/garfield
Distributed by Universal Uclick
I'LL ATTEMPT TO, BUT FAIL TO, WAKE YOU IN THE MORNING
AND I'LL ATTEMPT TO, AND SUCCEED AT, SLEEPING IN
© 2015 PAWS, INC. All Rights Reserved.
I LOVE ROUTINE

DO NOT BEWARE OF DOG
JIM DAVIS 3-17
www.facebook.com/garfield
Distributed by Universal Uclick
LET'S BE FRIENDS
© 2015 PAWS, INC. All Rights Reserved.
RUB MY TUMMY

I'M GREAT. I'M GREAT. I'M GREAT
www.facebook.com/garfield
Distributed by Universal Uclick
I'M THE BEST, BEST, BEST, BEST, BEST
© 2015 PAWS, INC. All Rights Reserved.
MY THEME SONG
JIM DAVIS 3-18

GOOD DAY FOR...
JIM DAVIS 3-19
www.facebook.com/garfield
Distributed by Universal Uclick
© 2015 PAWS, INC. All Rights Reserved.
I'M GOING TO GO WITH "NOTHING"

JIM DAVIS 3-20
www.facebook.com/garfield
Distributed by Universal Uclick
AREN'T YOU GOING TO ASK ME ABOUT MY DAY?
© 2015 PAWS, INC. All Rights Reserved.
SO, HOW WAS YOUR DAY, AS IF I CARE?
TRY AGAIN

HOW ABOUT "SORRY"?
www.facebook.com/garfield
Distributed by Universal Uclick
OR "OOPS"?
© 2015 PAWS, INC. All Rights Reserved.
I'M TRYING TO THINK OF WORDS FOR JON TO LIVE BY
JIM DAVIS 3-21

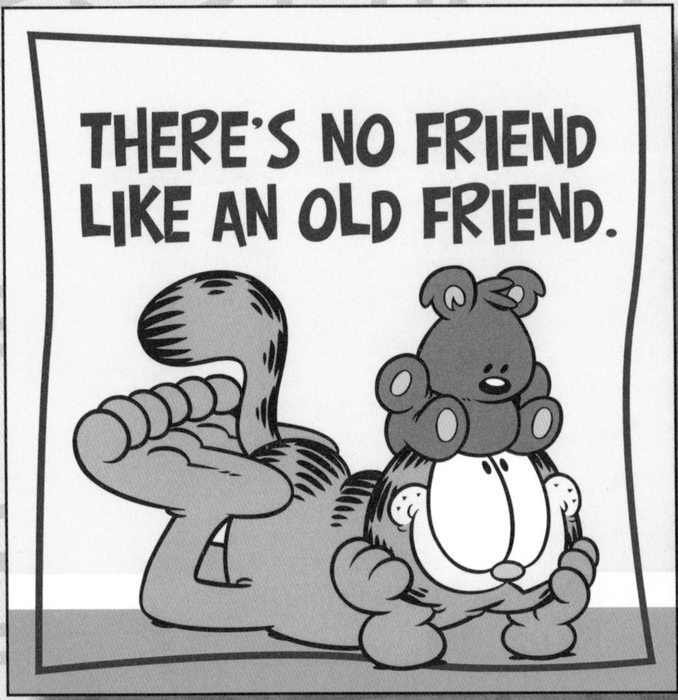
THERE'S NO FRIEND
LIKE AN OLD FRIEND.

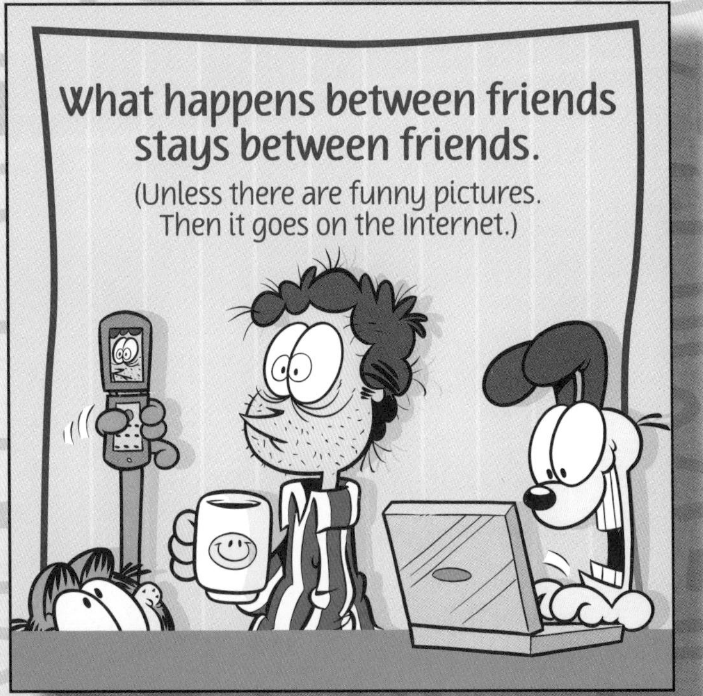
What happens between friends
stays between friends.
(Unless there are funny pictures.
Then it goes on the Internet.)

FRIENDSHIP

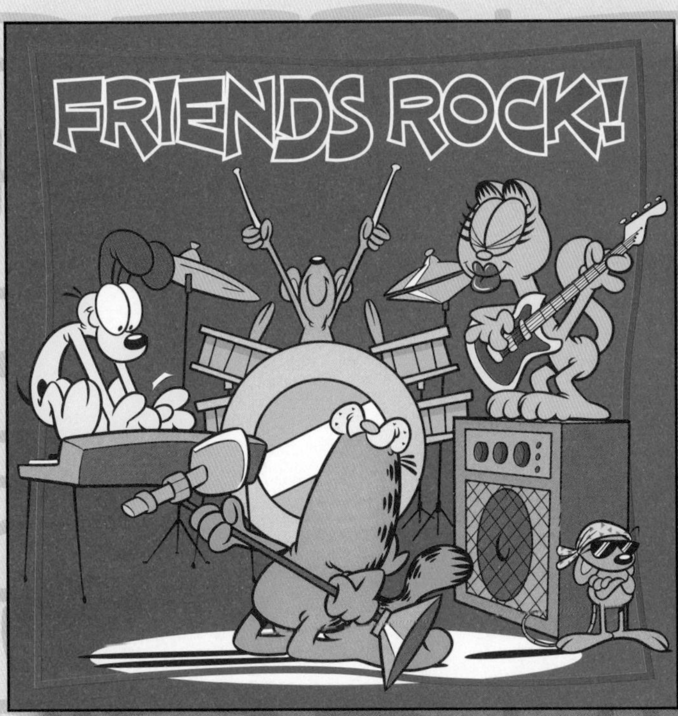
FRIENDS ROCK!

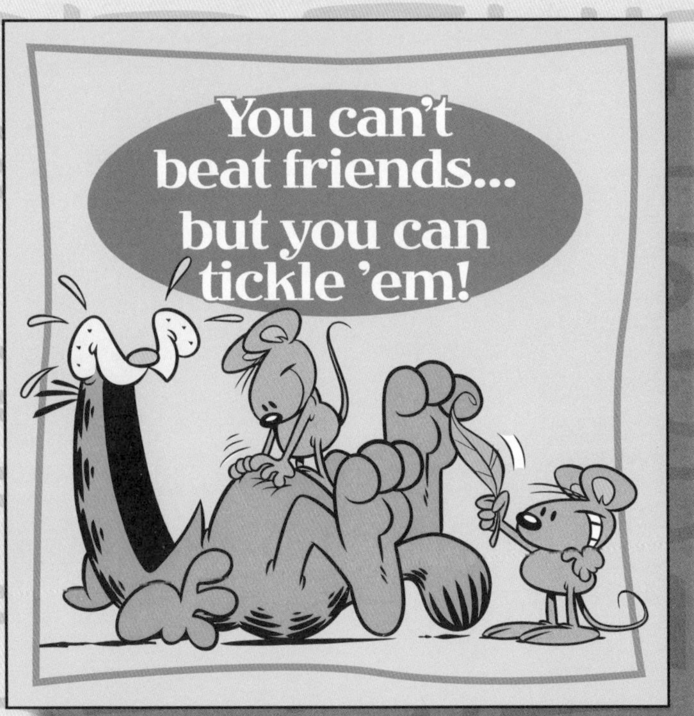
You can't
beat friends...
but you can
tickle 'em!

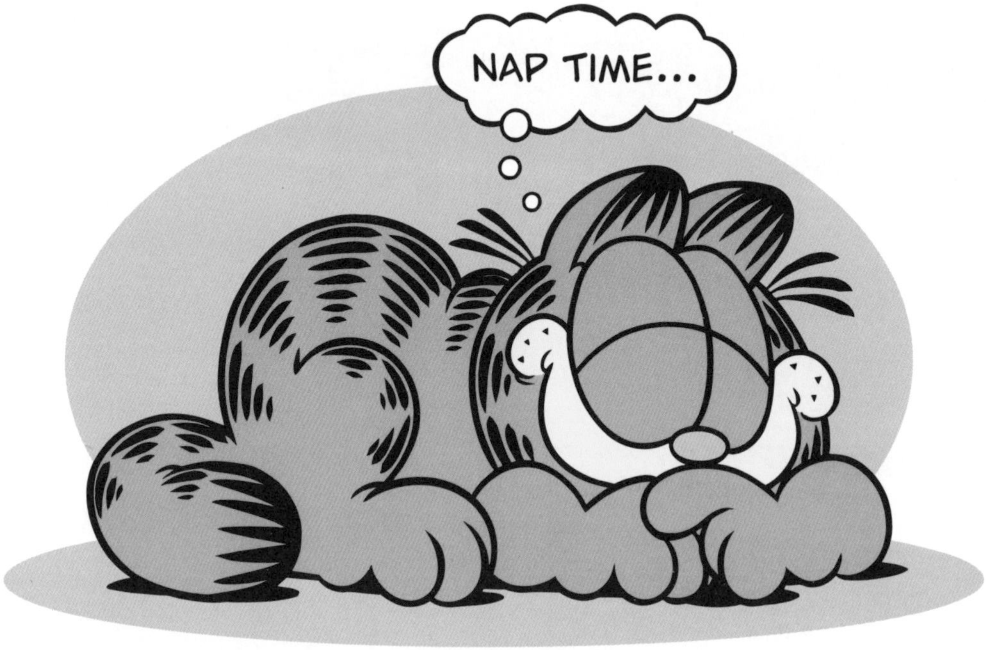
NAP TIME...